After the Baby Boomers

AFTER THE BABY BOOMERS

HOW TWENTY- AND
THIRTY-SOMETHINGS ARE SHAPING
THE FUTURE OF AMERICAN RELIGION

Robert Wuthnow

PRINCETON UNIVERSITY PRESS

PRINCETON AND OXFORD

LIBRARY OF CONGRESS CATALOGING-IN-PUBLICATION DATA
Wuthnow, Robert
After the baby boomers : how twenty- and thirty-somethings are shaping future
of American religion / Robert Wuthnow.
p.   cm.
Includes bibliographical references and index.
ISBN-13: 978-0-691-12765-1
ISBN-10: 0-691-12765-4
1. Young adults—Religious life—United States. 2. United States—Religion. I. Title.
BV4529.2.W88 2007
200.84′20973—dc22   2006028328

British Library Cataloging-in-Publication Data is available

This book has been composed in Janson

Printed on acid-free paper. ∞

press.princeton.edu

Printed in the United States of America

10   9   8   7   6   5   4   3   2

Contents

Figures and Tables

∞

FIGURES

TABLES

Preface

For the past century and a half, theologians and social scientists have found very little about which to agree. Theologians start from the premise that a supraempirical realm exists, or that the existence of such a reality or being is worth imagining. Social scientists' orienting premise is that the empirical is all that can be known. Accordingly, theologians generally stake their authority on the interpretation of texts, while social scientists stake theirs on the interpretation of data. Marx's assertion that consciousness does not shape events but is shaped by them, Weber's memorable analysis of modern life as an iron cage of rationality, and Durkheim's observation that men worshipped society when they thought themselves worshipping the gods are powerful reminders of the longstanding tensions between theology and social science.[1] Although there have been notable attempts to find middle ground (one thinks of Peter Berger's delineation of *methodological* "atheism," for instance, and Robert Bellah's emphasis on *symbolic realism*), social science as practiced has continued to diverge from theology both in practice and in presuppositions.[2] Indeed, the two are more often regarded as competing than as complementary modes of inquiry. Thus, it has been possible even in recent years for such a distinguished scholar as theologian John Milbank to caution against social science itself becoming a kind of all-encompassing naturalistic world view.[3]

There is, however, one point on which theologians and social scientists agree: from whatever source theological inspiration originates, it manifests itself in the concrete realities of human life. In theological language, this truth is expressed in the doctrine of the incarnation: the word made flesh. In social science, the same idea is captured from the ground up, so to speak, in arguments about the social construction of knowledge and belief. The individual person of faith is influenced by the social contexts in which he or she lives. Faith is thus not only a conviction about the unseen but also an expression of the opportunities a person has experienced to grow up in a particular culture, to be exposed to the values of one's parents, to mingle with like-minded and unlike-minded associates, to attend school, to work, to marry, and to reflect on life's decisions and mysteries. The flanks of our beliefs are always exposed.

So it is, too, with our organizations and institutions, including our churches and synagogues, mosques and temples. Because they require resources to exist, these places of worship exist only to the extent that they are able to adapt to their environments. They are the products of opportunity structures within those environments. The presence of a segregated racial minority provides opportunities for religious leaders to develop organizations located in those segregated communities. The eruption of a war and of civil violence in protest of that war creates space for religiously inclined groups to mobilize. A new generation shaped by new technologies or an uncertain job future opens a cultural location for new beliefs and practices to emerge. The point is not that theology is *only* a reflection of social circumstances. It is rather that religious beliefs and practices *articulate* with these circumstances. Theologians as different as Karl Barth and Paul Tillich, Reinhold Niebuhr and Jurgen Moltman all emphasize this point. For theology to be incarnate, it must be knowledgeable of the social circumstances to which it is addressed.

Sustained efforts to examine the relationships between religion and society with systematic, rigorous empirical evidence are relatively recent. While a few studies had been conducted earlier, most of the pioneering work was done in the 1950s and 1960s. Gordon Allport, Joseph Fichter, George Gallup, Charles Glock, Andrew Greeley, Gerhard Lenski, and a few others were among the first to engage in such research. Prior to these efforts, it was largely a matter of speculation as to whether church members, for instance, believed the same things about the Bible that church leaders taught, how the members of different denominations differed theologically, or whether church involvement influenced how people voted and treated their spouses.

The rapid growth of social scientific research about religion that began in the early 1970s was fueled with aspirations for hypothesis testing and theory building. Could evidence be found that Weber's arguments about the different economic views of Protestants and Catholics were still applicable? Did members of working class sects differ from members of middle class churches in the ways H. Richard Niebuhr had suggested? Were Marx's arguments about secularization valid? As evidence accumulated, though, the quest for scientific generalizations proved elusive. Quantitative research demonstrated, just as qualitative research did, that human behavior is highly variable and, for that matter, contingent. One of the most poignant examples of this realization was the conclusion from prejudice research that greater familiarity leads to greater understanding—unless it breeds contempt. Studies of religious behavior were true to form. While a few scholars continued to seek the holy grail of grand theoretical generalizations, the generalizations themselves failed to accumulate. Should historians of the social sciences during the last third of the twentieth century be interested enough to care, they would probably find it interesting, for instance, that the search for grand theories of religion moved from deprivation theory, to exchange theory, to arguments about religious economies, to rational choice theory, to arguments emphasizing monotheism—and all this in the writing of a single scholar.

Close consideration of the social sciences' contributions, though, demonstrates that theories serve more as *sensitizing concepts*, in Herbert Blumer's apt phrase, and that these concepts are as likely to have their origins in the wider society as in the scholarly community itself.[4] Research is less useful if it represents the hubris of one scholar seeking to impose his or her sensitizing concept on the field than if it genuinely illuminates the complexities of the world in which we live. Research about religion has in fact been oriented by three principal concerns in which the real world has taken precedence over the narrower interest of theory building for its own sake. The first of these is best described as *contemporary history*. Description and interpretation have pride of place in this research, just as they do in the best historical studies. The aim of such studies is to document and make sense of our times, using the tools of social science to collect the best evidence possible. Studies of recent religious movements, of the role of religion in recent presidential elections, or of changing patterns of religious involvement would all qualify as examples. The fact that so many studies have been possible has made the recent period especially rich for such documentation and interpretation. A second contribution is what might be termed *deep journalism*. Journalists write about what can conceivably be reported as news and for the most part news that can be gleaned within the space of a few days. Thus, a typical news story may cover the political candidate's speech to a religious group or the debate at a religious meeting about ordaining homosexuals. The deep journalism that social scientists are able to contribute probes more fully into the background of these events. It places them in context, often through research that takes years rather than days, and thus stands to correct errors, examine different perspectives, and illuminate the long view or social factors that cannot easily be reduced to a short news story. In these ways, the evidence social scientists collect becomes useful not only for future readers, but also for individuals and groups seeking to make sense of their times. Then a third contribution is *policy analysis*. Here the role of social science is to help decision makers by providing information that bears directly on the decisions they face. Just as economists and political scientists help decision makers by collecting information about unemployment rates or the possible effects of new tax laws, social scientists who study religion help decision makers by studying how religious organizations function, why they grow or decline, and how they may be affected by trends in the wider society.[5]

The relationship between generations or age cohorts and religious behavior has been of interest to social scientists for all three of these reasons. Religious developments in the past have often been carried by a new generation with needs and interests that differed from their parents'. Studies of baby boomer religion have contributed significantly to our understanding of the recent history of the United States. Baby boomer religion has also been of particular interest to journalists. What baby boomers believed and did could be reported as news. Sometimes inaccurately. And thus it was helpful to baby boomers themselves to know what other baby boomers were doing and what that might augur for the future. Policy analysis helped religious leaders think about how their organizations might need to adapt to meet the changing interests of baby boomers. Policy analysis also helped public officials determine how religion might affect elections or what its role was in setting political agendas.

The fact that baby boomers are rapidly moving into the ranks of the elderly means that it is essential to understand how the next wave of Americans are thinking and behaving. The current generation of young adults cannot be understood historically through connections to the civil rights movement or the Vietnam war the way baby boomers are. This generation has not had as clear an identity in the media, either. It was not framed by having been part of an upsurge in the birth rate, as the baby boomer generation was as a result of being born in the immediate aftermath of World War II. Younger adults, though, currently number in excess of 100 million and make up more than a third of the United States population. Younger adulthood is lengthening, too, extending from the early twenties to the mid-forties as a result of people living longer and taking longer to accomplish many of the developmental tasks of early adult life. Not only is young adulthood taking longer, it is also fraught with uncertainties—ranging from job security to national security—that may not be new but are nevertheless profound for young adults themselves. Add to these uncertainties the changes our society is experiencing as a result of information technology, immigration, and globalization, and one begins to see why it is important to understand how young adults are being affected.

Religion is sometimes described as an anchor of stability in the stormy sea of social change. For young adults, it sometimes remains a safe haven in a chaotic world. Yet even the most stable religious organizations are changing. And they are changing not simply because of the Internet or fears about terrorism or mood swings among teenagers. Religious organizations and the young adults who choose to participate—or not participate—in them are changing in ways that journalists seldom write about. The social trends and the responses of young adults to these trends have more to do with family dynamics than with whether a particular issue is in the news. Family and work, where one lives, whether one has children, and who one socializes with have powerful influences on religious behavior. There is no one sound bite to describe these influences. But there are several that recur: uncertainty, diversity, fluidity, searching, tinkering. The life worlds of young adults can be summarized in these words. And the life worlds of individuals also betoken larger developments in American religion and culture. The evidence from young adults points to a future in which some will be more committed than ever to rigid interpretations of faith traditions while others will not be involved in religion at all. The future that already exists among young adults is one of growing complexity, too, where it is possible not only for some people to be orthodox and others to be heterodox, but also for the same person to be both. Increasingly, young adults are taking their religious cues from a wide variety of sources, among which religious organizations continue to be important, but with input from science, philosophy, other religions, and the arts. Young adults are a divided generation, just as baby boomers were. They have yet to resolve differences over such hot-button issues as abortion and homosexuality. In many ways, they are even more divided than young adults were a generation ago. Above all, the religion and spirituality of young adults is a cultural bricolage, constructed improvisationally from the increasingly diverse materials at hand.

Religion is such a matter of speculation that it is seldom easy to get the facts straight—or to get them at all. Pundits who have mostly written about politics and public policy become overnight experts about religion. The authorities who appear on talk shows typically appear because they take predictable positions on hot-button issues, not because they have conducted research. As a social scientist, I have tried to muster as much hard evidence as I could for my conclusions. To do that, I drew from several dozen national surveys that have been conducted over the past thirty-five years. I read the reports, but I also obtained the data and did all of my own analysis. This was necessary in order to isolate what was happening among young adults. It also makes possible comparisons among people with different lifestyles and who belong to different faith traditions. Those comparisons are seldom present in published reports, let alone more detailed statistical analysis.

I was able to begin this project during the 2003–04 academic year as a result of a Guggenheim Fellowship that gave me the opportunity to devote my time fully to research and writing. I made extensive use of data that had been collected through grants from the Lilly Endowment, The Pew Charitable Trusts, the Templeton Foundation, and the National Science Foundation, among others. These surveys and their particular sponsors are described in the appendix. I also benefited from research support provided by the Woodrow Wilson School and the University Center for Human Values at Princeton University. The Center for the Study of Religion and the Department of Sociology were my intellectual home while writing the book and provided stimulation from colleagues and students who are too numerous to mention by name. You know who you are. Being a member of the baby boomer generation, I know how instructive it has been for my own self-understanding over the years to read about baby boomer lifestyles and religion. I hope this book will be helpful in a small way to my children and their generation.

After the Baby Boomers

∽ 1 ∽

American Religion

AN UNCERTAIN FUTURE

Observers of American religion have been keenly interested in baby boomers for a long time. Baby boomers were the future of the church. When they were young, they were supposed to have radicalized it with new ideas about race, gender, and social justice. Soon, though, prognosticators started seeing baby boomers as a "drop out" generation. Their dropping out was leaving congregations with fewer members. Then observers decided that baby boomers were coming back—but on their own terms, less interested in helping and more intent on finding themselves.

Many of these predictions were accurate, although some became more evident in retrospect than at the time. For one thing, baby boomers were a large cohort. They influenced American religion in sheer volume. As children in the 1950s, they encouraged their parents to attend church in record numbers and to view congregations as extensions of their families. As teenagers in the 1960s, they did start leaving the churches in droves. They were alienated from the "establishment" and more interested in civil rights demonstrations or campus protests than going to Sunday school. Later on, they became more individualistic and conservative, starting their own families and working hard at their jobs. Some of them flocked to megachurches where they could worship without the stale trappings of their parents' religion. Others became interested in evangelical politics, while still others explored New Age spirituality and new styles of meditation. In many ways, they did leave American religion different from the way they found it. Religious leaders were right in thinking that baby boomers' influence was a significant phenomenon to be understood.[1]

But things have changed. Baby boomers are no longer the future of American religion. As they grow older, they are rapidly becoming its past. The future now rests with younger adults. Baby boomers are now moving past their mid-life crises, becoming empty nesters, and retiring. To be sure, their influence on American religion remains strong. With the graying of America, they will be the most numerous group in the typical congregation. They will have more time to serve on committees and more money to put in the collection plate. They will also be the members who lament that things are no longer as good as they were in the 1960s (or 1980s).

They will not be so sure that change is a good thing, especially if it is being advanced by someone considerably younger than they are. Baby boomers will also increasingly be high-maintenance members. Besides populating the pews, they will require sick-visits from the pastor. As they die, or move away to retirement communities and nursing homes, they will leave the leadership of American religion in other hands.

Those hands will necessarily be younger. The future of American religion is in the hands of adults now in their twenties and thirties. As a percentage of the population, this age group is smaller than the baby boomer generation was. It is also less distinctly defined. Some observers call it Generation X or Generation Y (or both). Some refer to its members as "millennials," noting that they differ from baby boomers in having come of age around the turn of the millennium. Still others refer to it simply as the "next wave." Whatever the rubric, one thing is clear: younger adults are not only the future of American religion; they are already a very significant part of it. They are at least a sizable minority of most congregations. They are the young families who look to congregations for guidance in raising their children. They are the low-income families trying to balance tight budgets, hectic work schedules, and parenting. They are the young singles with time and energy to do volunteer work and look for companionship. They are the "unchurched" friends and co-workers struggling with questions about whether to be religiously involved at all. And because they have been overshadowed by the baby boomers, this current generation of younger adults is not very well understood, either by religious leaders or by scholars. Their lifestyles have seldom been scrutinized, and little is known about their church going habits, their spiritual interests and needs, and how their faith affects their families, their politics, and their communities. The need for better information about young adults is thus urgent for the present as well as the future.[2]

In the absence of solid information, speculation about the religious needs and interests of the next wave runs rampant. Self-styled cultural experts have been arguing that young adults will be the leaders of a great spiritual revival. Now that we have attained the material comforts afforded by middle-class incomes, say these experts, people will inevitably turn to spiritual quests. Other forecasters are placing their bets on technology. Persuaded that religion is somehow a function of gadgets and electronics, they predict an Internet revolution in which congregations will be replaced by Web sites and chat rooms. Still others see in their crystal balls that young adults will flock to jeans-and-sweatshirt ministries where everything is warm and supportive—as if that were something new.

The truth is, these futuristic speculations make headlines, but seldom make sense. The reason is that they are the product of someone's imagination, rather than being grounded in any systematic research—or, for that matter, a very good understanding of young adulthood and social change. Pastors and interested lay readers can titillate themselves reading such speculation in religious magazines. But they need to realize how flimsy this sort of information is. If their mechanic knew as little about engines as this, their car would scarcely make it around the block. But then their mechanic probably would not be intent on making headlines, either.

How to Think About Younger Adults

We need to begin by thinking more carefully about the place of younger adults in our society and their role in social change. The emphasis on baby boomers over the past few decades has conditioned us to think in terms of generations and, beyond that, to understand generations in a rather distinct way. Until recently, a generation was defined the same way a genealogy was: by the succession backwards from parents to grandparents to great grandparents, or ahead from parents to children to grandchildren. Each unit in that succession is a generation. Conceived this way, generations help us keep track of our ancestors and descendants. The problem with this way of thinking about generations comes when we want to make broader generalizations about historical events and social change. My father may have been born in 1920, yours in 1925, and someone else's in 1930, making it hard to say anything of a general nature about how we were affected by the Great Depression or World War II.

The baby boomer concept of generations is different. It suggests that people are largely defined by some major event or attribute that they have in common, even though their exact birth dates are different.[3] This definition emphasizes the fact that people a few years apart in chronological age will have the same cultural outlook if they have been exposed at roughly the same formative time in their lives to something as major as a war or a significant technological innovation.[4] For instance, baby boomers are often defined as people born between 1946 and 1964 because there was a noticeable bulge in the annual birth rate during these years. It mattered less, according to this definition, that one person was born in the late 1940s and another in the early 1960s, or that one person's parents might have been born in the early 1920s and another's in the early 1940s than the fact that they were members of a large birth cohort. This, in turn, mattered because a large birth cohort affected many of the experiences these people would have throughout their lives. For example, they might attend over-crowded classrooms in grade school or go to newly built schools as children, they might have the same experience of over-crowding when they went to college, and they might find it harder to get a job when they graduated or find that retailers were pitching products to them because they were such a sizable share of the market. In addition, this way of thinking about generations proved attractive because baby boomers were shaped by distinct developments in the wider society. These included, for instance, the emergence of rock 'n roll in the late 1950s and the Vietnam war in the late 1960s and early 1970s as an event that threatened lives and polarized campuses.

Baby boomers are not the only generation that can be defined in this sociological way. Other generations in American history can also be identified by a conjuncture of when they were born and the historical events they experienced. It makes sense, for example, to speak of baby boomers' parents as the World War II generation or in some cases as the Great Depression generation (or some combination of the two). World War II was the defining event for Americans who were young adults at the time. Although its economic and emotional impact influenced all age groups, it especially affected the lives of younger Americans. They were the soldiers who risked their lives on the battlefield, the wives who stayed at home worrying about their husbands, and the couples who waited to marry or have children until the war was over. In discussions of generations, those who were young adults during World War II or the Great Depression have thus come to be referred to sometimes as "builders." The term not only provides an alliterative reference alongside "boomers," but points to the fact that people in this generation tended to save their money because of having lived during the Great Depression and became involved in their communities and churches because of the patriotism they learned during World War II.

This way of thinking about generations has proven attractive, too, for understanding earlier periods in American history. For instance, the so-called Jazz Age or Roaring Twenties can be understood as a period of cultural history that particularly influenced younger people. Doing so emphasizes the fact that young adults at the time were more likely to have been influenced by the music or the changes in fashion and sexual mores than older people were. In American religious history, generational analysis has proven useful in understanding developments during the 1830s and 1840s known as the "Great Revival" or "Second Great Awakening." The revival meetings that became popular in these years included people of all ages, but were especially effective at reaching younger adults on the expanding western frontier. These people had moved away from their parents on the Eastern seaboard or had immigrated from Europe. They were separated in these ways from the influences of family traditions and were interested in forming their own institutions. New denominations, new religious movements, and new political movements were the result.[5]

For all these reasons, it is understandable that current observers of younger adults have tried to describe them as a distinct generation with an identity shaped by the confluence of their coming of age and developments in the wider world. Generation X became a popular rubric for awhile because it described a birth cohort that apparently did not have a clear identity and was searching for one. Those who enjoyed the alliteration of "builders" and "boomers" coined the term "busters" to describe this next generation, taking their cue from the fact that this birth cohort was smaller than the previous one. The term "millennials" pointed to the fact that younger adults were coming of age around the year 2000. It also presumed that the widely anticipated Y2K crisis was actually a life-shaping event, and it emphasized other developments such as the spread of personal computers and the Internet or the September 11, 2001, terrorist attacks on New York and Washington.

However, there are two reasons to be skeptical about this way of describing younger adults. One is that there is simply no evidence that younger adults currently have been decisively shaped by a particular historical event in the same way that the baby boomers were by the Vietnam war or by their parents waiting until after World War II to marry and have children. Those events had major effects on family life and personal life which, in turn, shaped how people participated in religious organizations. In fact, it was these effects on family life and personal life that mattered most, not simply having been born during a certain period. Thus, baby boomers were actually quite diverse, differing from one another as much as from their parents. Some married young, settled down and raised children, and made friends in their neighborhoods and churches. Others married later or did not marry at all, had no children or fewer children, and led more transient lives. Their religious practices were deeply influenced by these differing lifestyles. As I will show, the same is true for younger adults today. Most of what shapes their religious behavior is what happens in their families and at work, and these influences vary dramatically even for people who came of age at the same time. The other reason for being skeptical of generational language is that popular usages of it strain to draw contrasts with baby boomers, but in doing so are misleading. For instance, one reads in the popular literature that the millennial generation is supposedly defined by an interest in small fellowship groups that meet for prayer and Bible study during the week at churches or in homes. But precisely the same argument was made about baby boomers and, in fact, research has shown that baby boomers did gravitate to these groups.[6] Thus, it is hard to see why millennials should be identified on these grounds as a distinct generation. Similar claims are sometimes made about the distinctive interest of younger adults in personal experience as opposed to creeds or in novel liturgical styles. The next wave is said to be more interested in first-hand experience than anything else. Yet that was also said about baby boomers. The popular literature also makes arguments about "emerging" congregations that are somehow the wave of the future because they follow a new paradigm or hark back to models from the first century of Christianity. These discussions are tantalizing. They suggest to church leaders that if they only follow some new pattern, their congregation will attract young adults and grow. But we need to be skeptical about these arguments. Usually they are drawn from the personal experience of a few people, rather than from respectable research. Moreover, they seem strained because they seek to define a new generation by identifying something distinctive about it, instead of recognizing both the variability among younger adults and the continuities between the present and the past.

For these reasons, I will use the phrase *younger adults* (or simply *young adults*) to characterize the population of interest here. If readers need a sound bite, they are free to use words like busters and millennials. But they need to understand clearly whom I am describing. In subsequent chapters, I will present evidence mostly about younger adults who were between the ages of 21 and 45 in the years from about 1998 to 2002 and sometimes in comparison with younger adults of the same age between 1972 and 1976. This, of course, is an inclusive definition of younger adulthood. It corresponds statistically with the first *half* of adulthood for most Americans— the half when they are indeed young adults. It also provides the comparisons we need to make among people who are single or married, childless or with children, unsettled in their work or settled, and so on. By the time they are 21, most adults are to some degree "on their own," so to speak, meaning that they are no longer in high school or college and are earning at least part of their own livings. Yet, as we shall see, the maturational tasks of marrying, becoming parents, and becoming established in a career are taking longer now than in the past. By the time they are 45, most Americans have accomplished these tasks, if they are ever going to accomplish them. But for many Americans, these tasks are happening in their thirties, rather than in their twenties.

Americans between the ages of 21 and 45 are not just a harbinger of the future. They *are already* a significant share of the population. The major life decisions they are making about spouses, children, work, and religion are ones they will make during these critical young adult years, not earlier, and not later. Of course these decisions are influenced by how people are raised and what they learned in high school. But it is a mistake to think that we can somehow understand the decisions and interests of young adults by studying teenagers.[7] It is also mistaken to focus on college students—which is a growing, but still small segment of the young adult population. As interesting as those studies are, they cannot tell us whether it matters religiously, for instance, if someone marries at the age of twenty-one, waits until age thirty, or does not marry at all. The same is true for decisions about parenting and careers. And just because a young person espouses certain political ideas in high school, that does not tell us very much about how a person will actually vote a decade later, or how that person's political opinions will be influenced in the interim by his or her religious beliefs when that person is thirty.

In practical terms, young adulthood presents very significant challenges, both to the men and women who are facing them and to religious and community leaders. Most high school students, for instance, say they value marriage and expect to be married when they become adults. Yet a growing number of young adults do not marry, marry later, or do not stay married. Those are the realities of life that pose worries during young adulthood, affect one's self-identity, and cause people to seek emotional support. Apart from the personal issues such realities raise, they also affect religious organizations and the wider society. Church planners need to take into consideration how many young adults there are in the society and whether they are as active in their congregations as young adults were a generation ago. This is not to say that religious leaders should ignore the needs and interests of older Americans. However, the needs and interests that face people in younger adulthood are sufficiently different to warrant careful consideration in their own right.

THE POPULATION OF YOUNG ADULTS

Younger adults make up a sizable proportion of the American population. We gain a sense of their numbers in figure 1.1. The figure shows the total population of the United States over roughly the past seven decades broken down by age group. The age groups reported by the U.S. Census are not exactly the same as those I will be using, but are close enough. Over the period shown, the total U.S. population grew from 121.8 million in 1929 to 288.6 million in 2002. If, for the time being, we consider a generation to have been approximately 30 years, then the total population was about 80 million larger in 2002 than it was a generation ago in 1972, an increase of nearly 40 percent. The significance of the baby boom generation is evident in the bulge that begins to appear in the under age five category around 1947 and that continues in this age group until around 1964. As the baby boomers grew up, their effect is evident in the widening of the band for five- to fifteen-year-olds between the late 1950s and early 1970s, and then for older age groups in subsequent years. The figure also demonstrates, though, that it is misleading to emphasize the baby boom generation's importance simply on the basis of numbers. For instance, there were about the same number of children under age five in 2002 as there were of that age at the high point of the baby boom in 1961. Indeed, the number of young children in the United States during the 1990s was about the same as it was in the 1960s. More to the point, younger adults were considerably more numerous in 2002 than they were in 1972. To be exact, there

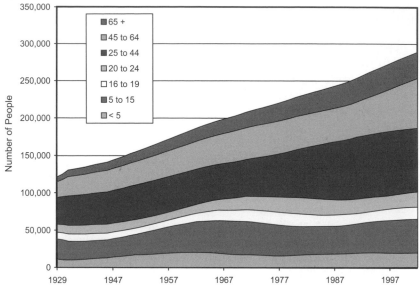

Figure 1.1. U.S. Population by Age Groups. Source: U.S. Census Bureau.

were 105.3 million Americans between the ages of 20 and 44 in 2002, compared with only 68.6 million in 1972. Or, if only 20- to 24-year-olds are considered, there were 20.3 million in that age group in 2002, compared with 18.1 million in 1972. Of course, another way to think about the significance of age groups is their *proportion* of the population. Absolute size notwithstanding, they may have more influence on the economy or on political decisions if their proportion is larger. By this indication, younger adults are also more important now than they were a generation ago. In 2002, Americans age 20 to 44 made up 36.5 percent of the total population, compared with 32.7 percent in 1972.[8]

There is another way of thinking about younger adults that is especially important when considering their role in American religion and the ministries of religious organizations to them. It is the *adult* population of the United States that supplies the potential pool of members, volunteers, and donors on which the vitality of American religion depends. Observers of American religion sometimes emphasize the increasing importance of older adults in making these arguments. Older adults may have more time and money, and, as longevity and health improve, there may be more older people to do the work and give the money on which religious organizations depend. That view, however, is shortsighted. The truth is that younger adults are just as important to the future of religious organizations, if not more so, than older adults. This potential can be seen from their share in the population. In 2002, adults age 20 to 44 made up 50.7 percent of the adult population of the United States. Not only was that a significant proportion; it was also approximately the same as it had been thirty years earlier (51.8 percent). In short, the so-called graying of the American population should not be emphasized at the expense of understanding the importance of younger adults. As a proportion of the adult population, younger adults are just as important now as they were a generation ago, and in absolute terms, they are a significantly larger group now than then.

Coming of Age at Forty

But is it legitimate to include people up to their mid-forties when talking about younger adults? When baby boomers were coming of age in the early 1970s, there was a popular saying that people over 30 were too old to be understood—or trusted. At that time, developmental psychologists argued that people pretty much established their adult identity during their late teens and were already fully formed adults by their twenty-first birthday. By the time they were in their thirties or early forties, they were probably going through a mid-life crisis, and soon after were thinking about retirement, declining health, and death. Religious organizations typically planned their programs with the same expectations about life cycle development. Confirmation took place around age twelve or thirteen on grounds that the person was sufficiently an adult to make an informed decision about joining the congregation. Confirmation classes were followed by a youth group or youth ministry of some kind that provided opportunities for peer interaction, instruction, and dating. For those who went off to college, campus ministries sometimes served a similar purpose. But for the adults in a typical congregation, the dividing point was usually between those in their twenties, who were single or married without children, and those in their late twenties or early thirties and beyond who were raising children. The younger adults were thus a small group, compared to the "real" adults, whose numbers included everyone from at least age thirty through retirement.

That was a view of the typical life cycle that made sense in the 1950s or 1960s, but it no longer makes sense today. One of the reasons it does not is that people are living longer now than they did a generation ago. Figure 1.2 shows how average life expectancy in the United States changed during the twentieth century. In 1900, life expectancy at birth was only 46.3 years for men and 48.3 years for women. Except for 1918, when life expectancy dropped dramatically because of the flu epidemic, average life expectancy has risen steadily, in large measure because of a reduction in childhood diseases and through the development of vaccines and antibiotics. By 1950, average life expectancy for men was 65.6 years and for women 71.1 years.

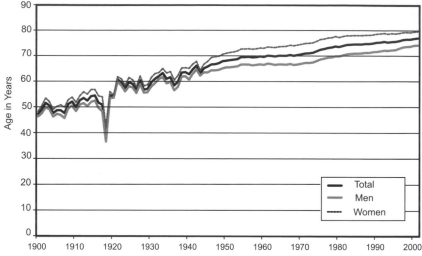

Figure 1.2. Life Expectancy at Birth. Source: U.S. National Center for Health Statistics, Vital Statistics of the United States.

In 1970, it was 67.1 years for men and 74.7 years for women. And in 2000, it was 74.3 years for men and 79.7 years for women. During the last half of the twentieth century, therefore, average life expectancy for American men and women increased by more than eight years.

The increase in life expectancy means that the *midpoint* of adult life for Americans age 21 and over is now reached at age 49. That figure is up from a midpoint of age 44 in 1950. Statistically, it means that younger adulthood could now be thought of as extending from age 21 through age 49, and older adulthood reaching from age 49 to age 77. Just as greater longevity has meant more time in later life to do things such as start a second career or travel, greater longevity also means more time in younger adulthood to do things that used to be compressed into a shorter number of years. Whereas it may have seemed urgent at one time to start a family at age 18 if one were to see one's children grow to maturity by the time one died, people can now wait longer to start families. They can also take longer to decide on a line of work and it may, in fact, take them longer to achieve financial independence.

Whether people actually postpone some of the developmental tasks they used to accomplish earlier is a question we shall consider in greater detail in the next chapter. To anticipate that discussion, though, let me say here that many younger adults *are postponing* some of these developmental tasks. According to the authors of a major collaborative project on early adulthood funded by the MacArthur Foundation, "it does indeed take much longer to make the transition to adulthood today than [it did a few] decades ago." Comparing statistics in 2000 with statistics in 1960, the researchers found, for instance, that completing all the major transitions (leaving home, finishing school, becoming financially independent, getting married, and having a child) was achieved by only 46 percent of women and 31 percent of men age 30 in 2000, compared with 77 percent of women and 65 percent of men of the same age in 1960.[9]

A twenty-seven-year-old man who works nights as a custodian and takes college classes during the day illustrates some of these processes. After high school, he went away to college, but spent the year partying and making bad grades because he had never been away from home before and had no idea what he wanted to do in life. He then worked for four years at a supermarket. Some of this time he still lived at home. He switched jobs several times and lived in several different states. For the past five years, he has been working his way through college, but not progressing as quickly as he would like. He gets depressed and wishes he had more self-discipline. Because he works at night and is on campus during the day, he seldom sees any of the people who live in his apartment complex. His friends are mostly buddies he worked with at the supermarket and who are now scattered or are people he has met in classes. On weekends, he gets together with a friend to shoot pool, goes fishing by himself, or visits his parents. He would get married if he met the right person, he says, but financially and emotionally, he isn't ready. Another man in his late twenties offered an interesting perspective: "In ten years, I'll be thirty-eight and that sounds really old to me," he said. "I would like to get married. Maybe have kids. But I don't know anymore. My life is so open right now. I just don't know."

As we will see in the next chapter, one of the most important changes among young adults is that they are indeed marrying later and having children later. These changes, together with the fact that many younger adults are taking longer to establish themselves in their careers and to settle into their communities, means that any religious activities that are influenced by these developmental tasks may also be happening later. Of course we must also take account of ways in which younger adults may be accomplishing developmental tasks earlier than in the past. For instance, more teenagers are probably sexually active than was true a generation ago, and some teenagers have had to become psychologically independent at an earlier age because of being raised by single parents. At the same time, the fact that *parents* are living longer may mean that younger adults remain psychologically dependent on their parents for longer periods than at a time when parents died younger.

The one thing that greater longevity overall and the extension of younger adulthood means for thinking about religion is that the future cannot safely be predicted simply by focusing on teenagers. In an earlier period, that might have been the case. If a teenager was part of an effective youth group, he or she could be expected to move rather quickly from that group at age eighteen to being a married parent a year or two later who participated in the same congregation. It is now more likely that a teenager may drop out of his or her congregation after confirmation at age thirteen and not feel the same urgency about participating again until he or she is a parent at age thirty-five. Meanwhile, the die may have been influenced by childhood upbringing or by the congregation's youth ministry, but most of the important decisions will have been made later. Decisions about marriage, friends, careers, and children will all have been made later. In this sense, more Americans are coming of age at forty than ever before.[10]

The Religious Significance of Young Adults

The relevance of these brief considerations about life cycle and development is that society has always felt it necessary to provide institutions for the support and socialization of its members who were not yet considered adults. Our elementary and secondary schools are the clearest example of such institutions. We invest resources in these institutions because we believe it is important to transmit knowledge to the coming generation. We also expect these institutions to keep pre-adults off the streets and out of the work force. Caretaker institutions of this kind now extend to preschoolers in the form of daycare centers and nursery schools. Increasingly, these institutions also exist for young adults after high school as well. For many younger adults, colleges, universities, and community colleges serve this purpose. For other younger adults, the military does, and for still others, prisons do. Religious congregations have followed suit. Sunday school programs for younger children, and high school or campus ministries for teenagers and young adults provide support and instill values.

The amazing thing about this pattern of support and socialization is that it all comes to a halt about the time a young person reaches the age of twenty-one or twenty-two. After providing significant institutional support for the developmental tasks that occurred before then, we provide *almost nothing* for the developmental tasks that are accomplished when people are in their twenties and thirties. And, since more of those tasks are happening later, this is a huge problem. It means that younger adults are having to invent their own ways of making decisions and seeking support for those decisions. Whereas dating and mate selection used to happen within the social milieu of the high school, congregation, or campus, it now occurs increasingly in bars, at parties, and through the Internet. Other major decisions, such as when to have children and how to raise them, or where to live and what kind of career to pursue, are also being made on an improvisational basis, largely without firm institutional grounding. It is little wonder that social critics write about the problems associated with *individualism*. In the absence of any institutional sources of support and stability, young adults are forced to be individualistic. They have no other resources but themselves.

Of course, we expect young adults to be independent enough to make their own decisions. I am not suggesting that we develop caretaker institutions for people in their thirties like the ones we have for teenagers. I *am* saying we should have a serious national conversation about the kinds of institutional support young adults do need. Instability in the work force means that young adults can seldom rely on their employers for this kind of support. The emotional and financial support young adults receive from their families is important, but much more available to the wealthy than to the majority. The need for supportive institutions is clearly suggested by the growing numbers of young adults who are overloaded with debt as a result of bad financial decisions. It is evident in continuing high rates of divorce and child abuse. And it is certainly evident in young adults' remarks about feeling uncertain and unsettled. As a thirty-year-old mother in Iowa told the MacArthur project researchers, "I don't know if I'm an adult yet. I . . . still don't feel quite grown up. Being an adult kind of sounds like having things, everything is kind of in a routine and on track, and [I] don't feel like [I'm] quite on track."[11]

Congregations *could* be a valuable source of support for young adults. They *could* be places where young adults gravitate to talk about the difficult decisions they are facing or to meet other people of the same age. Congregations *could* be guiding the career decisions of younger adults or helping them think about their budgets and their personal priorities. But, again to anticipate the evidence in subsequent chapters, this potential is often going unrealized. It will continue to go unrealized as long as congregations invest in youth programs for high school students and assume this is enough. It will also go unrealized if congregational leaders focus on their graying memberships and do not look more creatively to the future.

A Generation of Tinkerers

The single word that best describes young adults' approach to religion and spirituality—indeed life—is *tinkering*. A tinkerer puts together a life from whatever skills, ideas, and resources that are readily at hand. In a culture like ours, where higher education and professional training are valued, tinkering may have negative connotations. But it should not. Tinkerers are the most resourceful people in any era. If specialized skills are required, they have them. When they need help from experts, they seek it. But they do not rely on only one way of doing things. Their approach to life is practical. They get things done, and usually this happens by improvising, by piecing together an idea from here, a skill from there, and a contact from somewhere else.

The French anthropologist Claude Lévi-Strauss wrote of the importance of the *bricoleur* (the tinkerer) in the societies he studied.[12] The bricoleur in preindustrial societies is a handy person, a do-it-yourself craftsperson who uses the tools of his or her trade and the materials that happen to be at hand to fix things and keep them in good repair. The tools and materials that prove useful today may be different from the ones that were useful yesterday. The tasks of each day nevertheless reflect the past and the lessons one has learned. The objects the bricoleur produces are a *bricolage*—a construction improvised from multiple sources.

The key to understanding the life of the bricoleur or tinkerer is uncertainty. The tinkerer's life is sufficiently uncertain that it is impossible to solve problems through predefined solutions. A tinkerer does not go to the store and look for exactly the right part that will fix his plow. Instead, he muses about the problem, talks with the neighbors to see if they have ever faced the same difficulty, goes out to the junk pile and finds an old piece of angle-iron and a tin can to cut up, and uses his skills as a craftsman to piece together a makeshift solution.

Our world is filled with the kinds of uncertainty that make tinkering a necessity. Prepackaging and standardization notwithstanding, we constantly face situations that require us to improvise.[13] The path by which each individual seeks a life partner is different from the path anyone else has taken. Marriage counselors and online dating services may help, but the information processed and the decisions made will be unique. Within the same occupation or industry, no two career paths are alike. Making ends meet is less a matter of following some recipe for success and more one of juggling time and work demands, personal interests, and payments. Dealings with friends and family are also a matter of tinkering. Each person is shaped by the unique mix of people with whom he or she comes in contact and in turn makes an ongoing succession of choices about which people to associate with and how much to be influenced by them.

So it is with religion and spirituality. We piece together our thoughts about religion and our interests in spirituality from the materials at hand. Ordinary people are not religious professionals who approach spirituality the way an engineer might construct a building. They are amateurs who make do with what they can. Hardly anybody comes up with a truly innovative approach to life's enduring spiritual questions, but hardly anybody simply mimics the path someone else has taken either. Religion, we might suppose, is fundamentally a hedge against uncertainty. It offers meaning, as Clifford Geertz has observed, where there was no meaning.[14] Yet its meanings are seldom final. They depend on faith, and faith implies the possibility of new insights, surprises, and growth. A centuries-old creed may be a succinct statement of what a person of faith should believe. Making sense of the implications of that creed, though, is an act of tinkering.

The possibilities for tinkering increase with the expansion of available information and exposure to diverse cultures and networks. Like the farmer rummaging through the junk pile for makeshift parts, the spiritual tinkerer is able to sift through a veritable scrap heap of ideas and practices from childhood, from religious organizations, classes, conversations with friends, books, magazines, television programs, and Web sites. The tinkerer is free to engage in this kind of rummaging. Especially in young adulthood, the institutional constraints that might prevent it are absent. The directives given by one's parents are fewer. One's circle of friends is wider and one's knowledge of the world is greater. The structure provided by schooling, teachers, and the regimen of adolescent cliques is gone.

Bricolage is thus an apt description of the religion and spirituality of young adults. Bricolage implies the joining together of seemingly inconsistent, disparate components. The rusted angle-iron and tin can are from different sources, perhaps bound together only by an old strand of barbed wire. What at first seems like a straightforwardly orthodox belief, such as the view that the Bible is inerrant, turns out to be a jumble of orthodoxy and more relativistic assumptions about truth, salvation, and civility. Each person is a tinkerer. Each individual claims the authority—in fact, the duty—to make up his or her mind about what to believe. Slippage creeps in between the teachings of religious organizations and the practices of individuals. One teaches that premarital sex is always wrong; the other assumes this teaching does not apply to me.

To describe a generation of tinkerers implies, ironically, that a pastiche of metaphors is also required. Bricolage is an umbrella, handy because it is easy to carry wherever one goes. The way tinkerers put together their lives, though, involves a veritable plethora of activities that cannot be so easily classified. This is where the metaphors that observers have invented to describe American religion are both useful and misleading. Consider the idea of mosaic. American religion is sometimes described as a mosaic because it is composed of many different traditions.[15] Even a particular person's faith may be the product of parents and grandparents from different traditions. Mosaic is helpful in its connotation of diversity and the piecing together of this diversity. Yet it is too stable and coherent to capture the fluidity and uncertainty of contemporary life. Another metaphor is seeking.[16] Spiritual seekers are looking for answers. This is surely an important part of tinkering. Seeking implies uncertainty, for if a person already had answers, there would be no need to seek. Seeking, though, implies more unsettledness than may be present. Life may be a pastiche with which a person is content.

The economic metaphors that are sometimes used to describe contemporary spirituality are similarly helpful and misleading. To say that people participate in a religious economy or marketplace points to the fact that there is a world of suppliers competing to provide just the goods and services for which a tinkerer may be looking.[17] Today's tinkerers go to the supermarket as well as the scrap heap. Yet not all of their behavior takes place in the market. Young adults who "shop" for a new church are doing something very similar in intentionality and in dealing with competitors hawking goods to what shoppers do when purchasing a house or an automobile. Church hopping, though, is quite different from church shopping. Going to a church one week because of visiting one's parents in another city and a different church on another occasion with a friend is no more participating in a "market" than visiting one's parents or friends on other occasions is. The idea that spirituality can be understood as "rational-choice" behavior is similarly helpful, but limited.[18] Tinkerers undoubtedly make choices that are rational, if rationality means trying to get the job done and make the best use of the resources at one's disposal. It may be rational to choose a religion that promises eternal life in heaven, for instance, if one is convinced that the alternative is to spend eternity in hell. But the fact that many other people opt for different belief systems makes them no less rational. It rather begs the question of rationality to the point that rationality becomes meaningless apart from the cultural assumptions we make about it. Spirituality is sometimes the product of rational choices and sometimes the result of contingencies and influences that involve no choices at all.

The tinkering typical of young adults is hardly distinctive to this particular generation. To suppose so would be to overlook the extent to which baby boomers—and members of previous generations, for that matter—engaged in spiritual tinkering. The social environment in which contemporary tinkering takes place is nevertheless composed of distinctive features. The fact that young adulthood stretches over a longer period of time is one of these trends. When young adults at the start of the twentieth century waited longer to marry, their experience was different than it is now. Life expectancy, sexuality, gender roles, and relationships with parents are all different. The uncertainties young adults currently face at work, in relation to foreign competition, and financially are also distinctive, not because young adults in previous generations were free of economic worries, but because the particular shape of these concerns is now different. Religion and spirituality bear strong continuities with the past. Yet the life worlds of young adults today and their thinking about spirituality pose challenges for religious organizations that need to be understood, not historically, but in terms of the practical realities with which religious leaders are now faced.

An Uncertain Future

A central argument of this book is that unless religious leaders take younger adults more seriously, the future of American religion is in doubt. The reasons for this argument will become clear as we proceed. Younger adults are already less actively involved in their congregations than older adults are. Not only this, younger adults are currently less involved than younger adults were a generation ago. The demographics behind this declining involvement also do not bode well for the future. Religious involvement is influenced more by whether people are married, when they get married, whether they have children, and how many children they have than almost anything else. Religious involvement is also shaped by how committed people are to their careers and to their communities. All of these social factors have been changing. Religious leaders need to understand these changes. In addition, the *styles* of religious involvement that young adults prefer have also been changing—and not just in the ways that pundits suggest from having scoped out an interesting case here or there. How and how much people practice their faith has important consequences, both for their own lives and for our collective life as a nation.

It may seem overly pessimistic to suggest that the future of American religion is in doubt just because religious leaders are not doing more to enlist the energies of younger adults. Judging from annual statistics on church going produced by the Gallup Organization and other polls, American religion has not fared badly in the past three decades.[19] About the same proportion of the public claims to attend religious services in a given week now as in the early 1970s. To hear journalists tell it, whatever decline may have happened among mainline Protestants and Catholics has been more than made up for by huge growth in evangelical churches. Or, if native-born white Americans are not as active religiously as they once were, then at least new immigrants and African Americans will make up the difference.

We will want to consider these arguments more carefully in the chapters that follow. However, it is again useful to draw a lesson from what was said and what was learned about the future of American religion a generation ago from examining baby boomers. At first, the prospect of serious decline in organized religion seemed inevitable. Young baby boomers were dissatisfied with and uninvolved in organized religion. The more dismal of these forecasts were soon abandoned, however. It appeared that baby boomers were becoming involved again as soon as they married and had children. Even the trendier experiments baby boomers had once favored seemed to be less attractive as baby boomers aged. All this suggested that forecasts of religious decline were a false alarm. To be sure, observers did worry that boomers were perhaps lax in instilling religious values in their children, and that the piper would still have to be paid at some point in the future. Others, though, posed the reassuring possibility that the children of boomers might *rebel* against their parents by becoming even more religious than the previous generation. The long and the short of it, then, was that religious leaders could go about their business without worrying much about the future. Some analysts even went so far as to suggest that American religion, like American business, would have a rosy future simply because of free market dynamics. Somehow, competition among religious organizations would ensure a bright future.

But there was one undeniable indication of decline: the faltering membership and participation in mainline Protestant churches. These denominations lost between a quarter and a third of their memberships between the 1960s and the 1980s. Some argued that people wanted strict churches and these had become too lax.[20] The better evidence, though, showed that nearly all the decline in mainline denominations was attributable to demographics. Mainline members were better educated and more likely to be middle class or upper-middle class than the rest of the population. As such, mainline members married later, had children later, and had fewer of them. Memberships declined because there were simply fewer children being born into these denominations.[21] Evangelical Protestants, meanwhile, escaped these demographic problems. As long as they kept marrying young and having large families, their growth would make up for the mainline losses. There is just one problem: the same demographics that caused problems for mainline churches are now prevalent in the whole society. Already the growth in evangelicals denominations has diminished. The demographics are affecting how younger adults choose to be religious, and most of these factors will have adverse effects on religious organizations.

I do not mean to suggest that demographic factors are all that matter. American religion is only partly a matter of memberships and attendance. Religious leaders are right when they insist that people take seriously the idea of *faith communities*. Younger adults are no different from older adults in wanting to feel that they are part of a community—whether that is literally a congregation or small group, or a larger tradition such as the Catholic church, Christianity in general, or Judaism. What are the bonds that develop among younger adults? Are congregations a significant part of these social relationships? Are new styles of personal and public religious practice emerging?

Anecdotes are important in answering these questions. The vivid comment of a person during an interview about his or her faith can be especially revealing. So can be an example drawn from a congregation that has had particular success in ministering to younger adults. I will supply some anecdotes of this kind. It is equally important, though, to understand what is happening among younger adults in more systematic terms. We would not be content understanding what is happening in the economy from listening to an individual tell his or her story of success or failure. Nor should we be content to understand American religion that way. Foundations, religious organizations, and even government agencies have spent millions of dollars in recent years collecting information about religion from the population of the United States. None of this evidence is any harder to understand than the kind one might read in a major newspaper about the stock market or a political poll. It is, though, the kind of evidence that can be enormously helpful in understanding the lives of younger Americans and the role of religion in their lives.

The Changing Life Worlds of Young Adults

SEVEN KEY TRENDS

WHEN RESEARCHERS STUDY American religion, they often begin with polls about belief in God or attendance at religious services. They may then move to a consideration of which kind of congregations people attend and whether these congregations are growing or declining. Approaching religion this way is overly narrow. It reinforces the mistaken view that religion is self-contained—an autonomous religious market or religious economy in which religion is all that matters. I have never interviewed anybody for whom that was true. Their religious beliefs and practices are but one of the many activities and interests that make up their lives. The basic premise of social science research is that religion is embedded in a social environment and is thus influenced by this environment. What people do religiously depends on their opportunities to do it, and what they believe is shaped by their life situation.

The importance of considering the life worlds of younger adults is not just to make predictions about who will or will not attend religious services, though. Social scientists sometimes get caught up in making such predictions. They do so at the risk of forgetting that real people and real needs are at issue. A young adult whose life world is threatened by high job turnover has very different needs from an older adult with a secure job. A similar case can be made for knowing if young adults are mostly married and raising children, single and looking for companionship, or going to school, and so on.

I have selected seven key trends that religious leaders and scholars alike need to understand if they are to grasp the changing life worlds of today's younger adults. Several of these trends (we will see in later chapters) directly affect the religious practices of young adults. Several have only indirect effects, such as adding stress and uncertainty to young adults' lives. All of them demonstrate the extent to which our society is changing. Although the United States enjoyed relative peace and prosperity during the last third of the twentieth century, young adults live in a different world than young adults did a generation ago. The differences are not only that young adults then were more likely to wear long hair and beads or that young adults today use the Internet. There is no single explanation for the changes that have taken place. It is rather that the circumstances and attendant pressures of social life have changed, and the cultural norms about how to meet these pressures have evolved.

DELAYED MARRIAGE

Selecting a mate and marrying are among the most significant developmental tasks men and women face in their younger adult years. Although dating usually begins in high school (and thoughts about marriage presumably begin much earlier), most people do not select a mate and marry until they are in their twenties or thirties. Indeed, the process of dating, mating, and marrying is one that significantly defines younger adulthood as a segment of the population that includes people ranging from approximately age twenty-one through their late thirties or early forties. Figure 2.1 illustrates how marriage defines younger adulthood. Among men in their early twenties, only 12 percent are married, and among women in their early twenties, only 22 percent are married. By their late twenties, 38 percent of men and 48 percent of women are married. These proportions increase to 56 and 63 percent, respectively, among men and women in their early thirties. They increase again to 65 percent and 66 percent, respectively among men and women in their late thirties. At that point, the proportions have nearly reached their peak. They rise only to 67 percent and 68 percent, respectively among men and women in their early forties.[1] In short, younger adulthood is that span of societal time during which relatively few are married at the start and nearly all who will be are married by the end.

It is important to acknowledge that over the course of the twentieth century the trend was not as unfavorable toward marriage as some recent critics have suggested.[2] In 1900, for instance, 56 percent of the population age 15 and older were married, and in 2000, that proportion was again 56 percent. If the focus shifts to the second half of the twentieth century, though, a different picture emerges. In 1950, 68 percent of the 15 and over population were married, and that proportion peaked at 69 percent in 1960. Since then, the proportion married has declined steadily. Meanwhile, the proportion never married has risen, from 20 percent in 1960 to 27 percent in 2000. The proportion divorced has also risen, from about 2.5 percent in 1960 to almost 10 percent in 2000.

There are a number of reasons why the proportion of the U.S. population who were married increased between 1900 and 1960 and then decreased during the remainder of the century. For one thing, larger families early in the century meant more young people age 15 through 24 than later on and thus a larger number of people below the typical age at which people married. But the typical age at which people marry has also

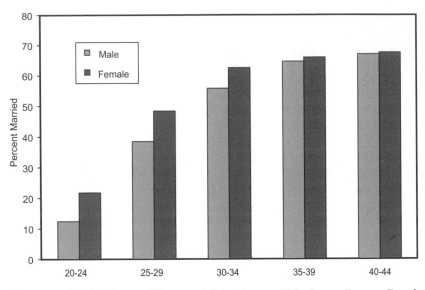

Figure 2.1. Marital Status of Younger Adults. Source: U.S. Census Bureau, Population Division, March 2002.

changed. This information is shown in figure 2.2. Here again, the major change took place during the second half of the twentieth century. In 1950, the median age at which people married (for the first time) was 22.8 years for men and 20.3 years for women. Median age at first marriage remained at roughly those levels until the mid 1960s. In 1965, for instance, it was 22.8 years for men and 20.6 years for women. Subsequently, median age at first marriage rose gradually. By 1980, it was 24.7 years for men and 22.0 years for women. In 1990, it was 26.1 years for men and 23.9 years for women. And in 2002, it was 26.9 years for men and 25.3 years for women. In the space of little more than a generation, then, men and women were marrying about four years later. For men, this change represented a return to the 1890s, when age at first marriage was about 26 years. For women, it was three years later than it had been in the 1890s.

For understanding the life worlds of younger adults, the fact that fewer people are married (instead of single, cohabiting, or divorced) and the fact that people are marrying later are both critical. The combined effect of these two developments is that far fewer younger adults, especially among those in their twenties, are married now than was true a generation ago when the baby boomers were young. Figure 2.3 shows these differences by comparing people of the same age and gender in 1970 and in 2000. Among men in their twenties in 1970, 59 percent were married; among men in

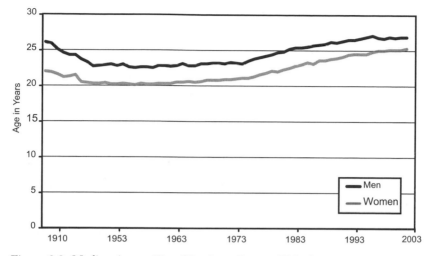

Figure 2.2. Median Age at First Marriage. Source: U.S. Census Bureau, Annual Demographic Supplement to the March 2002 Current Population Survey, Current Population Reports, Series P20–547, "Children's Living Arrangements and Characteristics: March 2002" and earlier reports.

their twenties in 2000, only 31 percent were married. In other words, the proportion married was about half what it had been three decades earlier. Among men in their thirties, the proportion married dropped from 83 percent to 59 percent, and among men in their early forties, from 84 percent to 66 percent. Women showed similar changes. Among women in their twenties, 69 percent had been married in 1970, but only 42 percent were in 2000. The proportion married among women in their thirties declined from 81 percent to 64 percent, and among women in their early forties, from 80 percent to 66 percent.

Few of the other trends that we will consider have been as pronounced as this one. It means, for instance, that married couples in their twenties were a majority—i.e., were typical—of their peers in the 1970s, but were atypical by 2000. For people in their twenties, it has become the norm to remain unmarried. And for people in their thirties and early forties, the change means that a much more sizable minority (a third) are now single or divorced, whereas that proportion had been no more than a fifth of their age group in 1970.[3] Because many other aspects of young adult life are affected by marital status—including children and the timing of children, housing needs, jobs and economic demands, and relationships with parents and friends—the importance of this shift in marital patterns can hardly be overstated.[4]

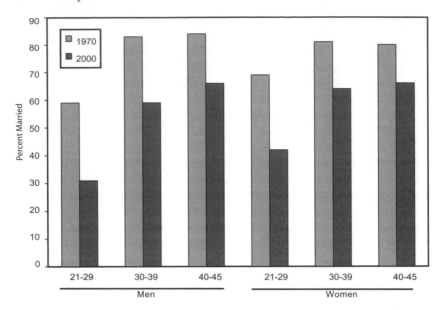

Figure 2.3. Percent Married by Sex, Age, and Year. Source: U.S. Census, Current Population Surveys.

Children—Fewer and Later

The second key trend that has taken place among young adults over the past few decades is having fewer children and having them later. According to the U.S. Census Bureau, the typical woman in the early 1900s gave birth to four children. That number declined significantly during the Great Depression, but rose again after World War II to an average of 3.7 children—thus comprising the "baby boom." By the mid-1970s, the average number of births per woman had fallen to about 2, and it has remained at roughly that level since then. The more specific effect of these changes among young adults can be seen in figure 2.4. In 1976, only 10 percent of women ended their childbearing years with no children. By 2000, that proportion had risen to 19 percent. Over the same period, the proportion with four or more children declined from 36 percent to 11 percent.[5]

That women are waiting longer to have children is evident from the information shown in figure 2.5. As recently as 1959, the median age at which mothers gave birth to their first child was 21.6 years. By 1999, that number had risen by about 3 years to 24.5 years. A similar trend occurred in the age at which mothers gave birth to their second child. In 1959, the median age of mothers giving birth to their second child was 24, while in 1999 it had risen to 27.5. Waiting longer to have children, like marrying

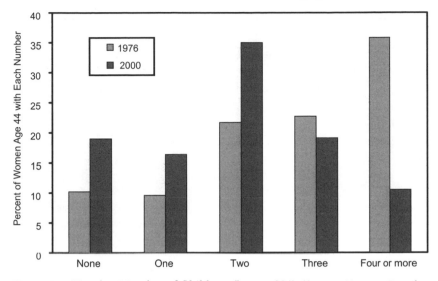

Figure 2.4. Trend in Number of Children. Source: U.S. Census, Current Population Surveys.

later, is also a way in which young adulthood has been extended. Both for women age 35 to 39 and for women age 40 to 44, the birth rate has risen since the late 1970s (from about 20 births per 1,000 women to approximately 40 among the former, and from about 4 to 8 among the latter). A century ago, women in these age groups might have been raising teenagers while giving birth to their fourth or fifth child. Currently, it is more likely that they are giving birth to their first or second child.

The net effect of people having fewer children and having them later, combined with other factors (such as women living longer after their child-bearing years), is evident in the so-called crude birth rate, figured as the number of births each year divided by the total population. The birth rate in the United States declined from about 30 births per 1,000 population in 1910 to between 18 and 19 during the Depression in the 1930s, and then climbed to 24 or 25 between 1946 and 1959, after which it declined to only 15 in 1973 and remained at that level through the end of the century (figure 2.6). The high birth rate during the decade and a half following World War II more than anything else defined the baby boomer generation. As a result of the high birth rate during those years, the baby boomer generation was large. It was also in many ways characterized at the start by an emphasis in the society at large on children and families.[6] Young adults of the early twenty-first century, in contrast, are not only a smaller cohort, relative to baby boomers, but also one that grew up in a time of differing

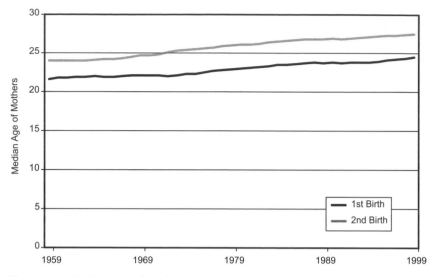

Figure 2.5. Median Age of Mothers at First and Second Births. Source: Vital Statistics of the United States, Median Age of Mother by Live-Birth Order.

social emphases. The young families that had children valued them, of course, but there were relatively fewer of these families.

A clearer sense of how changes in the number and timing of children have affected the life worlds of young adults is evident in whether or not young adults live in a household that includes children of their own. In 1970, 42 percent of men in their twenties reported living in a household that included at least one of their own children. By 2000, that proportion had fallen to 23 percent. Among men in their thirties, the percentage who lived in a household that included a child of theirs fell from 77 percent in 1970 to 53 percent in 2000. And among men in their early forties, the corresponding decline was from 76 percent to 60 percent. Among women, the changes were not as severe (probably reflecting the fact that more children were being reared by single mothers), but were in the same direction. Thus, 59 percent of women in their twenties had been living in a household that included a child of theirs in 1970, but only 42 percent were in 2000. Among women in their thirties, the decline was from 86 percent to 70 percent, and among women in their early forties, from 76 percent to 70 percent.

The fact that young adults are having fewer children and having them later has not, however, been accompanied by a shift in the number of children that young adults consider *ideal*. Two different national surveys have examined possible trends in these attitudes. In the General Social Surveys, adults age 21 through 29 who were surveyed between 1972 and 1976 said

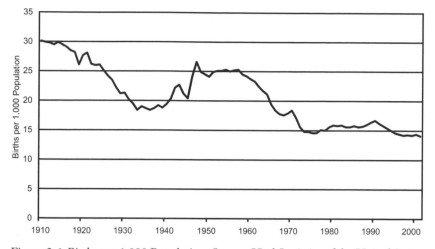

Figure 2.6. Births per 1,000 Population. Source: Vital Statistics of the United States.

on average that the ideal number of children was 2.7; among adults of the same age surveyed between 1998 and 2002, that average was still 2.7. The same lack of change was evident among respondents age 30 through 39, for whom the ideal number of children averaged 2.9 in both periods. Among respondents age 40 through 45, there was only a small decline (from 3.2 to 3.0).[7] National surveys conducted in the United States as part of the World Values Surveys in 1980 and in 2000 also failed to show any decline in the number of children young adults considered ideal. In fact, these surveys showed an increase among respondents in their twenties and thirties who thought large families were ideal. For instance, the proportion of respondents age 21 through 29 who wanted 3 or more children rose from 34 percent in 1980 to 44 percent in 2000, and among respondents age 30 through 39, from 33 percent to 41 percent. The World Values Surveys also suggested continuing high levels of *attitudinal* commitment among young adults to the value of being good parents. In 1980, 74 percent of respondents said parents' duty is doing what is best for their children, as opposed to leading their own life; in 2000, this proportion had risen to 91 percent. Among respondents in their thirties, there was a corresponding increase from 75 percent to 84 percent, and among those in their early forties, from 69 percent to 76 percent.[8]

Yet, if young adults still consider parenting important, the reality is that many will be disappointed. Compared with the 2 percent who say they want no children, for instance, as many as 20 percent probably will not have children. And compared with the 3 percent who want only one child, as many as 16 percent will have only one. Ideals are malleable, of course, and people frequently have to alter them to fit reality. Nevertheless, it is clear that one of the trends that has been taking place among young adults with regard to having children is a growing gap between ideals and reality.

Uncertainties of Work and Money

The third trend is most easily summarized as the rise of the dual-income family. It is more accurately described as heightened financial pressures and economic uncertainty. The dual-income family is how a growing number of younger adults have responded to these pressures and this uncertainty. Yet it is the broader climate of consumption, debt, work, stress, efforts to save, and increasing inequality that we must understand.

A useful place to begin is with the public's expectations about what must be accomplished to be considered a real adult—and when these tasks should be accomplished. When the public was asked about these expectations in the 2002 General Social Survey, nearly everyone agreed that becoming an adult involves being financially independent, not living with one's parents, being employed full-time, being able to support a family, getting married, and having children.[9] The average age at which younger adults think people should get married is about 26, and the average age at which they think people should start having children is about 27. The former is exactly the average age at which young adults actually do get married, and the latter is slightly older than the average age at which they have children. The more notable aspect of these expectations are the ones concerning work and money. The public, including younger adults themselves, believes younger adults should achieve financial independence between age 20 and 21, that they should stop living with their parents by age 21, and that they should also be employed full-time at age 21. The public also believes that younger adults should finish their formal schooling by the time they are 22 and be able to support a family before they are 25. In short, the major tasks involving work and money are all supposed to be accomplished within a five-year period, well before getting married and having children, and some of them even before completing formal schooling.

How well do younger adults measure up? Data on labor force participation suggest that younger adults are doing a reasonably good job of living up to expectations about being employed. In 2000, 72 percent of men age 21 through 29 were working full-time or part-time, and among those in their thirties, this figure rose to 81 percent, which was the same as among men in their early forties (figure 2.7). Among women in their twenties, 64 percent were working full-time or part-time, and the proportions increased to 68 percent and 72 percent, respectively, among women in their thirties and early forties. In comparison with 1970 figures, though, there were two notable differences. The first was that employment rates among men had

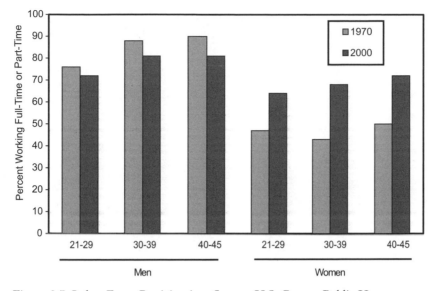

Figure 2.7. Labor Force Participation. Source: U.S. Census, Public Use Micro-samples.

declined—by 4 points for men in their twenties, 7 points for men in their thirties, and 9 points for men in their early forties. The second was the more familiar shift toward *increased* labor-force participation among women—an increase of 17 points, 25 points, and 22 points, respectively, among the three age groups.

These figures do not show whether young men and women were working full-time by the time they were 21, as the public thinks they should be, although they do indicate that the large majority of men and women in their twenties are gainfully employed. They also underscore the important shift that has taken place toward greater inclusion of women in the labor force. Women are not only more likely to be working outside the home than they were three decades ago; they are also more likely to be working full-time. Among those age 21 through 29, for instance, 45 percent were working at least 50 weeks a year in 2000, compared to only 26 percent in 1970; and among those in their thirties, 53 percent were, up from only 24 percent. This shift in employment patterns is in itself one of the major ways in which the life worlds of younger adults are different from those of their parents. To be a women in her twenties or thirties and not be in the labor force at present is to be a statistical anomaly, whereas in 1970 a woman in her twenties or thirties in the labor force would have been in the minority. What this means generationally is that the aspirations expressed by young women in the 1970s to be included in the labor force have been achieved

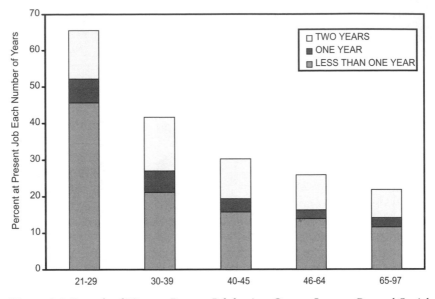

Figure 2.8. Length of Time at Present Job by Age Group. Source: General Social Survey, 2002.

to a much greater extent by their daughters than by themselves. The economy has also adapted, though, to the point that for many young families, two earners working full-time has become a necessity.[10]

Adults in their twenties and thirties may be employed, but employment rates alone do not reflect how new most young adults are to their jobs or the amount of turnover they experience. In one national survey, employed adults were asked how long they had worked in their present job for their current employer. Forty-six percent of those age 21 through 29 said less than a year, another 7 percent had been at their job only a year, and 13 percent, two years (figure 2.8). In short, two-thirds of workers in their twenties had been at their present job less than three years. Among workers in their thirties, these proportions were much lower; still about four in ten (42 percent) had been at their present jobs less than three years. Some of this turnover was undoubtedly the result of young people being promoted or assigned to new responsibilities within the same company. Yet, in another national survey, 29 percent of respondents age 21 through 29 said they had been with their current *employer* less than a year, and another 34 percent had been with their current employer only a year or two. In that study, a third of workers in their thirties and early forties had been with their current employer less than three years.[11]

The fluidity of the labor force for young adults is not only measured in how recently they have started at their present job or with their current employer. It is also indicated by declining expectations about the durability of jobs. In the 1950s, when William Whyte Jr. wrote his classic treatise *The Organization Man*, it was possible to imagine the organization man starting after high school at an assembly plant or after college as a chemist and continuing in that line of work until retirement.[12] Not everyone did, of course, but the point of Whyte's analysis was to show that working up the hierarchy by pursuing a single career in a single place of employment or industry had become the norm in the United States. That clearly is no longer the case. When asked in one national survey how many different *lines of work* they had been in as an adult, nearly half (48 percent) of respondents age 21 through 29 said 3 or more. And among those age 30 through 39, this proportion climbed to 58 percent.[13] The "organization kid" of today, columnist David Brooks has argued, may be as rigidly programmed as the organization man of the 1950s.[14] Yet the two are dramatically different in other respects. Even the highly programmed Ivy League student who majors in chemistry is unlikely to work at DuPont for a lifetime the way his or her father did. It is more likely that the chemistry major will hedge her bets by learning something about business and writing, work at Goldman Sachs to pay off her loans, pursue graduate work in a related field that appears more promising (say, genomics), and then switch to elementary teaching or journalism when the opportunities in this field dry up.

Another way of grasping the fluidity of the current labor market is through the standard job turnover indices produced by the U.S. Department of Labor. The government calculates total turnover in each of 10 industries—for instance, leisure and hospitality, finance, construction—as the sum of job separations and job openings over a 36-month period as a ratio of total employment in that industry. In all 10 industries, total turnover was more than 100 percent of total employment. In 6 of the 10, it was more than 200 percent of total employment.[15] The government data also reveal that job turnover is not restricted to traditionally blue-collar industries, such as construction and manufacturing. It is also quite high in the professions, business, and finance.[16]

From one perspective, high job turnover is good for young adults, especially in industries where job openings are more numerous than job separations (such as education and health). High turnover means opportunities for young adults entering the labor market for the first time or seeking new jobs with higher pay. Those opportunities vary from period to period, of course, and during the three years from 2001 to 2003, openings were fewer than separations in all but two of the ten industry categories. From a different perspective, high turnover also means greater difficulty for young adults seeking to make plans about marriage, children, health care, housing, and other major financial decisions. If a person is unlikely to be employed at his or her job for more than three years, it becomes very difficult to make long-range commitments.

As if job turnover alone was not a sufficient source of uncertainty, young adults in the twenty-first century have grown up during a time when a significantly larger number of businesses failed than during the period when baby boomers were young. Between 1955 and 1975 the business failure rate exceeded 60 per 10,000 establishments only once. After 1980, it was *below* 80 only once. In this respect, the last years of the twentieth century were like the last decades of the nineteenth and early years of the twentieth, when railroads, banking, land speculation, and the emerging automobile industry made fortunes for a few and bankrupted many. Microsoft, Oracle, Yahoo, and Google turned a few of the rising generation into overnight billionaires. But for more of their generation, business uncertainties affirmed the truth of the old saying: last hired, first fired.

Although young adults are working and—if women's participation in the labor force is considered—working harder than in the past, it is thus important to take account of the job uncertainties many in this age group face. That becomes all the more apparent when finances are considered. For the U.S. economy as a whole, the period from the time the baby boomers came of age until the recent past when the current generation of young adults came of age was one of unparalleled affluence. In inflation-adjusted dollars, gross domestic product per capita, personal income per capita, and consumption per capita all more than doubled between the early 1960s and the end of the twentieth century. But this was not all of the story.

Researchers at the University of Michigan have estimated the amount of financial support young adults age 18 through 34 receive from their parents—an interesting issue, given the public's view that young adults should be financially independent by the time they are 20 or 21. The study found that adults between the ages of 18 and 34 receive an average of $38,000 in cash and two years' worth of full-time, 40-hour-a-week labor from their parents. The cash alone was equal to 23 percent of what parents typically spend on children from the time they are born through age 17. In any given year, 34 percent of adults age 18 through 34 receive cash from their parents and 47 percent receive free labor. The researchers also found that the amount of financial help parents provide to young adults had increased by about 13 percent since 1970.[17]

Consumer Expenditure Survey data provide a more detailed picture of young adults' finances. These data are for households and thus do not include young adults who may still be living with their parents. Data are reported separately for households headed by persons under age 25, age 25 through 34, and 35 through 44. The largest category of household expenses for young adults is housing. As a percentage of all expenditures, housing amounts to 31 percent for adults under age 25 and rises to 34 percent for those age 25 through 34 and 35 through 44. Transportation is the second largest category, making up 21 percent, 21 percent, and 19 percent for the three age groups, respectively. Food comes next, accounting for 15 percent, 14 percent, and 13 percent of the total budget for the three age groups, respectively. Other categories include clothing (averaging about 5 percent), entertainment (also averaging about 5 percent), health care and health insurance (rising from 2 percent to 4 percent), and education (declining from 7 percent to 2 percent). Cash contributions (of which approximately half probably go to religious organizations) rise from 1.3 percent of total expenditures among those under age 25, to 1.8 percent among those age 25 through 34, to 2.6 percent among those age 35 through 44.[18]

Overall, Consumer Expenditure Survey data suggest that young adults are not experiencing acute financial pressures. In fact, among those age 25 through 34, after-tax incomes exceed expenditures by about 15 percent, and among those age 35 through 44, by about 20 percent. The proportion who own homes increases from 15 percent among those under age 25 to 49 percent among those age 25 through 34, and then to 68 percent among those age 35 through 44. The 5 percent or so of household expenditures that go for entertainment also suggest some flexibility in the budgets of young adults. Yet there are also indications of financial pressure. For instance, young adults under age 25 have expenditures that exceed after-tax incomes by about 20 percent annually. Debt, especially for housing, increases as the percentage of young adults with mortgages rises to 42 percent among those age 25 through 34 and to 56 percent among those age 35 through 44. Liabilities also increase, from approximately $2,000 for adults under age 25 to nearly $18,000 for adults age 35 through 44.

It is not the case that most young adults are deeply in debt or facing the imminent possibility of personal bankruptcy. Those proportions remain quite small. They did, however, rise significantly during the closing years of the twentieth century. Consumer credit is defined as short and intermediate-term credit extended to individuals, not including credit secured by real estate. It includes credit card debt, automobile loans, and student loans, but not home mortgages. In 1959, the total amount of consumer credit in the United States was slightly more than $56 billion. By 2002, that figure had risen to approximately $2 trillion. During the same period, though, consumer prices and incomes had also risen. To assess the actual trend in consumer credit, it is thus necessary to take these other changes into account. That can be done by dividing consumer credit by personal disposable income to create a "consumer credit index" (figure 2.9). Between 1959 and 1990, that index averaged .182, meaning that total consumer credit outstanding was approximately 18 percent of personal disposable income, and was never above .200. After 1995, it averaged .227 and was never below .200.

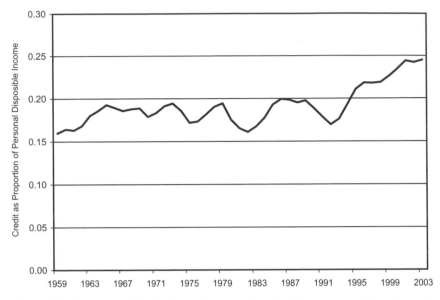

Figure 2.9. Consumer Credit Index. Source: Board of Governors of the Federal Reserve System; personal disposal income as base.

Personal bankruptcies also increased during the last years of the twentieth century and early years of the twenty-first. In only two years (1975 and 1976) between 1940 and 1979 were there more than 200,000 personal bankruptcies nationwide. During the 1980s that number gradually increased, reaching 616,000 by the end of the decade. The trend continued almost unabated during the 1990s and by 2003 reached 1,600,000—more than eight times what it had been 25 years earlier. Social scientists Teresa A. Sullivan, Deborah Thorne, and Elizabeth Warren examined the rise in personal bankruptcies between 1991 and 2001.[19] They found that bankruptcy filing rates per 1000 adults had risen for all age groups except for adults under age 25. In addition, they found that in both years the highest bankruptcy rates were among adults age 35 through 44, followed by adults age 25 through 34.[20]

The reasons young adults file for personal bankruptcy or become overextended on credit are complex. They include changes in bankruptcy laws and more aggressive marketing on the part of credit card and loan companies. Several other factors cannot be neglected, though. With two breadwinners required to sustain the standard of living desired by most young adults, the costs of transportation and day care, among other things, have risen. For instance, in 1960, approximately 80 percent of all households had no more than one automobile. By 2000, more than half of all households had at least two automobiles, and approximately 15 percent had three or more.[21] What was more, the average cost of operating each automobile also rose dramatically. According to the American Automobile Association, the average total cost per automobile per year (figured at 15,000 miles of driving) was only $2,154 in 1975, but increased to $7,533 by 2002.[22] The reasons for these increases included rising fuel prices (which more than tripled), maintenance costs (which rose four-fold), and costs of the vehicle itself and associated insurance (which increased five-fold).

The other aspect of family finances that must be considered is the number of young adults who live at or below the poverty line. Official poverty rates are at best an approximation of actual hardship. Many argue that incomes of twice the official poverty rate are still below the standard at which people can generally find decent housing and provide adequately for their children. What the official poverty rates do show, though, is that young adults are among those most likely to be poor. For the total population, approximately 15 percent of persons in their early twenties have incomes that put them below the poverty line. This proportion falls steadily, reaching a low of around 5 percent when people are in their late forties, and then rises again to around 10 percent among the elderly. For young Americans of color, the proportions are considerably higher. Approximately a quarter of African Americans in their early twenties fall below the poverty line, as do a fifth of Hispanics.[23] Poverty rates vary from year to year, but have generally remained within the 11 percent to 15 percent range for the population as a whole for the past several decades.[24] Where there has been greater evidence of long-term trends has been in income inequality. As recently as 1960, the richest 5 percent of the population took in only 15.9 percent of the nation's total income; by 2001, that proportion had risen by about a third to 21 percent. In the meantime, the poorest 40 percent of the population declined from 17 percent of the nation's total income to only 13.9 percent.[25] In a 1998 study, researchers at the Institute on Education and the Economy examined the effects of this rising inequality on the wages of young adults. They found that young adults who entered the labor market more recently were experiencing lower wage growth and greater inequality than young adults who entered the labor market a generation earlier had.[26]

How these trends in work, incomes, personal finances, and consumption may affect—or be affected by—religion among young adults is an open question. Religious beliefs and behavior in the past have sometimes been strongly influenced by economic factors, such as rising affluence or deepening divisions between social classes. However, recent research generally suggests that religion is influenced more by lifestyle and culture than by economic factors alone. What is certain is that religious organizations can ill afford to neglect the economic uncertainties that young adults of the twenty-first century typically experience. Those uncertainties are sources of stress in marriages. They are preoccupations even for the most spiritually minded. It is little wonder that adults in their twenties are often preoccupied with paying off loans, getting on their feet financially, and establishing themselves at their places of employment.

HIGHER EDUCATION (FOR SOME)

The fourth trend is more easily described than the previous one. It consists of rising levels of education. More young adults have graduated from college or attended college than ever before in our nation's history. Exposure to higher education influences how people think—or at least we hope so. It broadens their horizons, gives them a better sense of history, and communicates important vocational skills. It also sets young adults apart from their peers who have had fewer educational opportunities. Being in college creates social networks and shapes how people think about themselves. Having a college degree opens doors to graduate school and positions in the professions.

The baby boomer generation was very powerfully shaped by growth in higher education during the 1960s and 1970s. Being on campuses in that era exposed baby boomers to campus turmoil. The Vietnam War was a major source of this turmoil. Black nationalism, the feminist movement, and the counterculture were also prominent features of campus life. Baby boomers came away with new ideas about religion. A few embraced what would later be characterized as New Age spiritual practices—channeling, crystals, meditation, holistic healing. Others remained religiously uninvolved. Those who had been shaped by their campus experiences were quite different from those who had not been to college.[27]

The current generation of young adults differs from baby boomers in two important respects. One is that campuses have been quieter in recent years than they were in the 1960s and early 1970s. The other is that an even larger proportion of young adults has now taken advantage of opportunities to seek college degrees. This change is easily depicted. The percentages of young adults in 1970 and in 2000 who had finished four or more years of college are shown in figure 2.10. Within each age group and for men and women, the percentages are consistently higher in 2000 than they were in 1970. However, the increases among women have been significantly larger than among men. For men in their twenties, there was only a 1 point increase, and for men in their thirties the increase amounted to 6 points, and for men in their early forties, 8 points. In contrast, women in their twenties increased by 10 points; in their thirties, by 17 points; and in their early forties, by 18 points. Whereas men were significantly more likely than

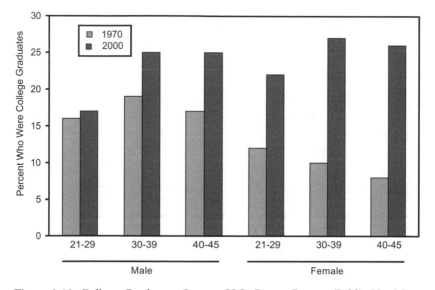

Figure 2.10. College Graduates. Source: U.S. Census Bureau, Public Use Micro-samples.

women to have four years or more of college in 1970, women were slightly more likely than men to have attained this much education in 2000.

It is important to note, though, that even among young adults the ones who have actually earned a college or graduate degree are still in a small minority. Only about a quarter have done so. This is an important fact to remember. Because research about young adults is often based on studies of college students—and produced by faculty in academic settings for readers with advanced education—it is easy to forget that the experiences and opportunities open to college graduates are not part of the typical young adult's life world. What is somewhat more typical is the experience of having at least taken some college courses. For instance, if all adults age 21 through 45 who have at least some college training are considered, then the proportion of men in 2000 who qualified rises to 52 percent, and of women, to 59 percent. Even with that larger number, though, young adults can hardly be characterized uniformly as having been influenced by going to college. It is more accurate to say that young adults are about evenly split between those with some college training and those with no college training.

LOOSENING RELATIONSHIPS

A fifth key trend is the changing nature of social relationships. Some observers argue that all Americans—especially young adults—simply have fewer social relationships than their parents and grandparents did. In political scientist Robert Putnam's colorful phrase, people are "bowling alone." Communities, he says, are breaking down. Instead of mingling with our neighbors, we sit at home and watch television. We especially distance ourselves from civic obligations. Compared to previous generations, we show up less often at the voting booth, join fraternal and other civic organizations less often, and seldom work together on community projects. Even our willingness to trust others, Putnam argues, has diminished.[28]

There is certainly some truth in Putnam's claims. However, a more balanced view suggests that social relationships have not so much declined as taken on new forms. The life worlds that young adults inhabit today are more porous than the ones people lived in a generation or two ago. We move around more—or at least stay psychologically mobile because we seldom know how long our jobs will last. At the same time, we more easily keep in touch with friends and family who live outside our immediate communities. We may not be life-long members of Kiwanis, but we volunteer for Habitat for Humanity. Habitat fits better with our complicated lives. We can show up to help hammer nails for an hour when we have the time, and then disappear when other obligations occupy our busy schedules.[29] Not all of these changes can be readily depicted with statistical data. But some of them, suggesting both decline of old forms and vitality of new ones, can.

Because it matters so much to the health of democracy in the United States, voting behavior is the form of civic engagement that is studied and discussed most frequently. And because it has so often been studied, voting behavior also provides one of the surest indications of how young adults' relationships have been changing. The news has not been good. In 1964, 51 percent of adults age 18 through 24 voted in the national election held that year, according to data collected by the U.S. Census Bureau (figure 2.11). In 2000, only 32 percent of that age group voted. This was a decline of 37 percent. Among adults age 25 through 44, the proportion who voted fell from 69 percent to 50 percent, meaning a decline of 28 percent. And the decline was not limited to young adults. Among those age 45 through 64, voting dropped from 76 percent to 64 percent, a decline of 16 percent. As critics argued, though, the declines had been greater among young people than among older people—suggesting that young people were somehow withdrawing into themselves or in other ways shirking their civic responsibilities.

We need to be cautious about accepting this argument simply at face value, though. Before 1972, the voting age was 21, rather than 18, meaning that the figures for 18- through 24-year-olds are not exactly comparable for the whole period. In fact, the proportions of this age group who voted between 1976 and 1992 were essentially the same. The up tick in 1992 further suggests the possibility that voter participation could increase

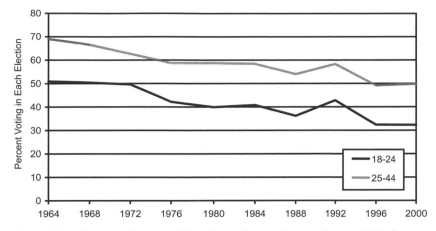

Figure 2.11. Voters as Percent of Population by Age Group. Source: U.S. Census, Current Population Report, November 2000. Note: Prior to 1972, data are for people 21 to 24 years of age with the exception of those aged 18 to 24 in Georgia and Kentucky, 19 to 24 in Alaska, and 20 to 24 in Hawaii.

again. Leaving aside these possibilities, it is nevertheless clear (especially among 25- through 44-year-olds) that there has been a significant decline in voter participation.

A second indication of declining civic involvement is evident in the DDB Needham Surveys from which Putnam drew extensively in his research. These surveys were conducted annually between 1975 and 1998, thus spanning the time when baby boomers were young adults to when their children were young adults. One limitation is that some of the surveys were conducted only among married people, making it necessary to exclude unmarried people in order to derive accurate trends. This limitation is actually an advantage, though. It means that whatever changes may have taken place because fewer young adults are now married have been eliminated. In short, the data provide a *conservative* estimate of change.[30] When young married adults were asked if they had worked on any community project during the past year, there was a small decline among those in their twenties (from 26 percent in 1975 to an average of about 20 percent between 1996 and 1998; figure 2.12). For those in their thirties, the decline was steeper (from about 50 percent to 28 percent).[31] (For those in their early forties, there was also a significant decline; from around 50 percent to approximately 35 percent).

If voting and community projects suggest that young adults are simply less involved in civic-minded relationships than they used to be, it is instructive to consider other evidence that paints a less gloomy picture of how social relationships have been changing. For instance, volunteering. In the DDB surveys, married respondents were asked if they had done any

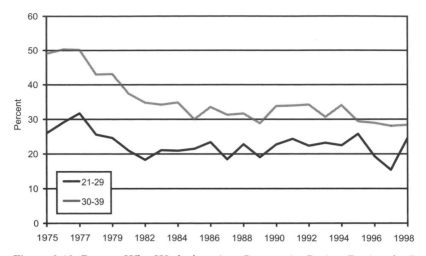

Figure 2.12. Percent Who Worked on Any Community Project During the Past Year. Source: DDB Needham Surveys, married respondents only.

volunteering during the past year. Among people in their twenties, the percentages *increased* from about 39 percent in the early years to around 46 percent in the more recent surveys (figure 2.13). Among those in their thirties, there was no significant change (nor was there any significant change among those in their early forties). The DDB data are thus consistent with results of other surveys suggesting that volunteering has either remained steady over the past few decades, or increased. Unlike community projects, volunteering connotes more diverse ways of helping others. A community project implies people coming together at the same times over a period of time to work on something of benefit to their immediate community. Beautifying the grounds around the local library would be an example. Newcomers to the community would be less likely to find such a project attractive than old-timers would. Busy people with odd work schedules would also be at a disadvantage. In contrast, volunteering can happen more sporadically, like at Habitat for Humanity. Or at one's church. It suggests greater flexibility, looser connections, and yet a continuing investment of one's time and energy in the well-being of others.

But Putnam is right in arguing that *some* kinds of social interaction— even informal ones—have become less common. For example, bowling emerged as a popular pastime among the leisured class at the end of the nineteenth century and became popular after World War II as an inexpensive activity for the middle class. Bowling leagues, as Putnam observes, became a way of meeting regularly with one's friends and neighbors. Dinner parties were popular in the same era. Instead of meeting at restaurants or socializing informally at work, people invited their friends and neighbors

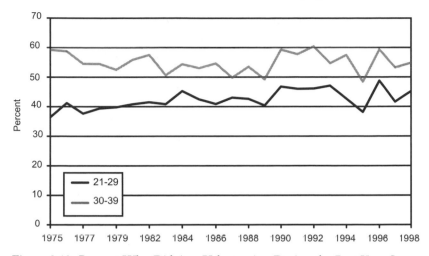

Figure 2.13. Percent Who Did Any Volunteering During the Past Year. Source: DDB Needham Surveys, married respondents only.

over for dinner. Usually the wife bore the brunt of the work involved. Picnics, too, were a common way of mingling. When few homes or churches had air conditioning, going to the beach or park was an attractive outing. All of these activities conjure up nostalgic memories of a by-gone era. And they are, in fact, less common among young adults, according to recent surveys, than they were among young adults a few decades ago. The percentage of young married adults in their twenties who go bowling at least once a year declined by 13 points between 1975–76 and 1997–98 (among those in their thirties, by 8 points). The percentage who have dinner parties declined between 12 and 16 points. And picnics, even more: 28 points among people in their twenties; 20 points among those in their thirties. Lest one think these activities are purely a thing of the past, though, I hasten to note that as many as two young adults in three still attend at least one dinner party and one picnic annually.

Other evidence also shows that certain kinds of social activities have declined among young adults. Among those age 21 through 45 in the General Social Surveys, for instance, 38 percent in the early 1970s said they spent social evenings with someone in their neighborhood several times a month, but only 34 percent said this in the 1998–2002 surveys. Conversely, the number who spent social evenings with neighbors only once a year or less climbed from 34 percent to 39 percent.[32]

The trouble with questions that were asked continuously since the early 1970s, of course, is that nobody thought in that period to ask about activities that would become more popular later. The *recent* DDB surveys, though, did ask about a wider range of activities. From these, we can see more clearly how young adults actually spend their time—and whether these suggest that people are "bowling alone." Some of them do. For instance, about two-thirds of young adults do exercises at home and a majority play home video games. Presumably, they do those alone. Yet, other activities are less solitary. Nearly everyone has gone out to lunch at least once during the past year. Maybe they ate alone. But it seems just as likely that going out to lunch has become an easier substitute for the traditional dinner party at home. Lunch involves business associates, informal socializing, and just meeting with friends. Going to the movies—something that four in five young adults do at least once a year—may be the same. Critics would say the socializing involved is minimal. Individuals sit in a dark room and stare at a screen. Yet at any theatre, few of these individuals are alone. They come with friends and family. We shall want to consider the Internet in Chapter 10. But it, too, is often a way of connecting with people, rather than a form of withdrawal from social life.

These newer ways of relating are usually quite selective and thus run the danger of insulating people among kindred spirits, rather than bridging the diversity of which our society is increasingly composed. A married woman in her early thirties says *Bowling Alone* definitely describes life in her middle-class suburb. "We get in our car and go to Wal-Mart or to work. We're so segmented. We don't see our neighbors. We don't even have a five minute meaningful conversation with folks." She stays in touch with a few friends by e-mail and has lunch with friends at work. But people unlike herself, let alone her neighbors, are harder to meet. "I didn't even realize our next-door neighbors went to our church," she says. "We'd been there almost three years before we met them."

The important point about social relationships among young adults is that they are changing. Young adults of today are no less social creatures than young adults were in the past. Fewer are married, so they may go out to lunch with their friends instead of joining the PTA. More women are in the labor force, so they may have less time to host dinner parties. But they may team up with a friend to go jogging every day. The potential implications for religion are profound. Congregations may be especially attractive as places to experience "community," when community is harder to find. Congregations that rely on dinner parties and picnics to attract newcomers, though, may realize to their embarrassment that times have changed.

GLOBALIZATION

Trend number six is the increasing exposure most young adults experience to the forces of globalization. These include the increasing ease and rapidity with which news from all parts of the world enters the typical American home on a daily basis. They include the fact that more young adults than ever before will work in jobs subject to competition from foreign workers. Or in jobs dependent on foreign markets. Globalization also includes the fact that middle-class Americans more often travel abroad than they did in the past, and, when they do, travel more often to distant parts of the world, rather than only to Canada, Mexico, or Western Europe. And the U.S. population itself is becoming more globalized as a result of foreign visitors and immigrants.[33]

A standard way of estimating the extent to which the United States is integrated into the global economy is comparing merchandise imports and exports with Gross Domestic Product (GDP). Between 1970 and 2000, total imports and exports in proportion to GDP more than doubled from 8 percent to 21 percent. Imports more than tripled from 4 percent to 13 percent, while exports rose from 4 percent to 8 percent. Adjusted for inflation, these increases were even larger.[34] Other measures also demonstrated increasing integration into world markets. For instance, merchandise exports increased from 15 percent of total *goods production* in 1970 to 43 percent in 2000.

The average person may be little affected by these aspects of globalization, even though jobs and consumer prices are ultimately influenced by them. International travel involves a smaller proportion of the population, but holds greater potential for shaping outlooks and experiences. Between 1975 and 2000, the total number of air passengers departing from the United States to foreign countries increased from approximately 12 million to more than 57 million. Of these, 5.9 million in 1975 were U.S. citizens, increasing to 27.4 million in 2000, and 6.1 million were foreign nationals, increasing to 30.1 million in 2000.[35]

In addition to the growing number of foreign nationals who visited the United States, the U.S. population itself became significantly more globalized as a result of immigration. During the 1970s, 4.5 million immigrants arrived, up from only 3.3 million during the 1960s. That number climbed to 7.3 million during the 1980s and to 9.1 million during the 1990s. Though smaller in proportion to the native-born population, these numbers were larger than during the great wave of immigration from Europe between 1900 and 1920.[36] In addition, an estimated 7 to 10 million undocumented immigrants came to the United States during these decades. As immigration increased, the proportion of foreign-born residents of the United States also increased. In 1970, only 5.8 percent of the population was foreign-born. That figure rose to 7.2 percent in 1980, 9.3 in 1990, and 12.3 in 2000.[37]

Because the recent immigration has included larger numbers of younger people than older people, its effects on the composition of the young adult population has been especially pronounced. I show in figure 2.14 the proportion of men and women in their twenties, thirties, and early forties in 1970 and in 2000 who were either noncitizens or naturalized citizens.

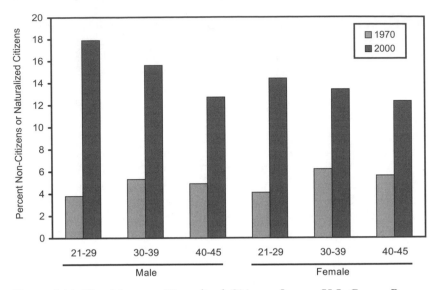

Figure 2.14. Noncitizens or Naturalized Citizens. Source: U.S. Census Bureau, Public Use Micro-samples.

Among men in their twenties, the proportion increased during this thirty year period from 3.8 percent to 17.9 percent. It grew from 5.3 percent to 15.6 percent for men in their thirties and from 4.9 percent to 12.7 percent for men in their early forties. Among women, the comparable increases were from 4.1 percent to 14.4 percent, from 6.2 percent to 13.4 percent, and from 5.6 percent to 12.3 percent.[38]

In subsequent chapters we will see how globalization influences the religious beliefs and behavior of young adults. Its relevance to religion stems from the fact that a significant part of the American population has long considered the United States a special people with a special relationship with God. America has also been an enclave in which the particular validity of the Christian (and Jewish) traditions and the value of participating in religious services could be taken for granted. Traveling abroad, working in jobs that require one to think about other parts of the world, being an immigrant, and having contact with immigrants are all developments that shake people loose of previously taken-for-granted beliefs and lifestyles.[39]

CULTURE—AN INFORMATION EXPLOSION

The seventh trend shaping the life worlds of younger adults is cultural. It is best described as an information explosion. Information has, of course, been expanding for as long as humans can remember. In recent decades, though, information has become far more accessible to the average person through the mass media and, most recently, the Internet. In addition, information has also become more diverse. Textual information, in the form of books and newspapers, has been supplemented increasingly by images. Network television, followed by cable television, and then followed by the Internet made visual imagery more abundant and easier to select in terms of individual tastes. Music also became more readily available. Not that singing or playing musical instruments were new. But radio programming expanded, the recording industry grew, and compact disks became more readily available. All of this meant that young adults at the start of the twenty-first century had easier access, not only to factual information, but also to the arts, than any previous generation had.[40]

More than anything else, the most recent generation of young adults has been defined by the computer and the Internet. When baby boomers were young, computer use was limited to the few who took special courses and willingly waited while a mainframe slowly cranked out computations. As recently as 1984, only 8 percent of households had home computers. By 1993, that number had risen to 23 percent. In the next seven years, it more than doubled to 51 percent. Internet access was even more recent. In 1997, 18 percent of households were linked to the Internet. Three years later, 42 percent were.

Computers and the Internet were easy enough to use—and were soon part of so many jobs—that their users were hardly limited to younger adults. Like other technological innovations, though, computers and the Internet were often learned sooner and more easily by the young than by the old. Young people had access to them in schools and were often encouraged by their teachers to use them. Whole careers in computer programming, software development, and broadband sales opened up to newcomers in the labor market. One of the clearest indications of the generational aspect of computers and the Internet was the response to a question in a 2002 survey asking people to rate themselves on Internet skills (figure 2.15). Men in their twenties rated themselves highest, 53 percent saying their skills were excellent. Men in their thirties and early forties came next, with about a third rating their skills as excellent. Only a quarter of men between their late forties and early sixties rated their skills as highly, as did only a fifth of men past 65. Women generally rated their skills lower than men did. But the same patterns prevailed. Those in their twenties rated their skills highest, and with each successive age group, the proportions who considered their skills excellent declined.

Other data also suggest that younger adults had become computer users earlier or that they used the Internet more often. For instance, in the same survey, more than half of adults in their twenties said they had used e-mail (52 percent) or the Internet (53 percent) before 1998; these figures were 8

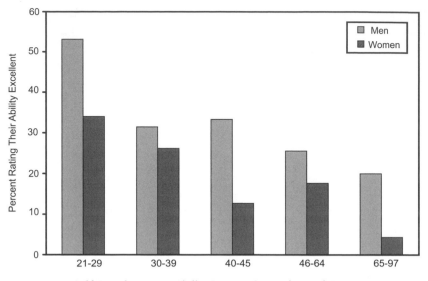

Figure 2.15. Self-Rated Internet Skills. Source: General Social Survey, 2002.

and 11 percentage points higher, respectively, than among adults between age 46 and 64. When the survey was conducted in 2002, adults in their twenties said they sent an average of 16 e-mails a day and received an average of 29. In comparison, adults ages 46 through 64 sent an average of 9 e-mails and received an average of 18.

The computer and Internet revolution has been similar for young adults at the start of the twenty-first century to the effects of television for young adults in the 1950s. But also different. In 1950, only 9 percent of households had television; by 1954, a majority (56 percent) did; and by 1960, 87 percent did.[41] The spread of television was thus as rapid, if not more so, than computers and the Internet. Yet television use was almost entirely restricted to the home, whereas computers and the Internet have had more pervasive uses in education and the workplace. Television opened doors for wider knowledge of news and entertainment. But it was not well-suited for connecting people the way e-mail has done.

The possibility that the Internet is becoming relatively more important to young adults than other sources of information is evident from data about television viewing. It is helpful to recall Putnam's argument that baby boomers were less civically involved because more of them spend more time sitting at home watching television. If that was the case (and critics questioned whether it was), it does not seem to be characteristic of younger adults. In fact, compared with young adults in the early 1970s, young adults at the start of the twenty-first century are *less likely* to spend long hours watching television. This is especially true among young adults in their twenties, where there has been a 12 point decrease in the percentage who watched four or more hours a day. Among this age group, the percentage who watched fewer than two hours a day increased by 7 points, and among young adults in their thirties, it increased by 9 points. Still, it is hardly the case that young adults have abandoned television entirely (only 6 percent watch no television).[42]

If television viewing has fallen off slightly, newspaper reading shows an even more dramatic decline. In the early 1970s, 49 percent of adults in their twenties read a newspaper every day; by the late 1990s, that number had dropped to 21 percent. Among adults in their thirties, the decline was from 70 percent to 29 percent. And among adults in their early forties, from 74 percent to 36 percent. Again, it was not that young adults had abandoned newspapers entirely. Only 9 percent claimed never to read them. But the overall decline was all the more notable in view of the fact that education levels among young adults had risen. Better educated people typically are more likely to read newspapers than people with lower levels of education. Within every level of education, though, there was a significant decline. For instance, among adults age 21 through 45 with only high school degrees, daily newspaper reading dropped from 64 percent to 24 percent. And among those with college degrees, it declined from 69 percent to 40 percent.[43]

We can only speculate about subtle shifts in perception or ways of knowing that may have accompanied the decline of newspaper reading and the rise of computers and Internet or the continuing prominence of television. These media are all filled with advertisements. Young adults are probably even more exposed than their parents were to advertising. There may be some validity to arguments about the impermanence of information on television or the Internet, compared with information in print. We are, in this respect, a throw-away society. We learn that ideas and opinions are not written in stone. As opportunities to switch channels and surf Web sites proliferate, we also gain the ability to follow our whims. All of these may be nearly imperceptible shifts in consciousness that also influence how young adults think about and experience their faith.[44]

The role of art and music is young adults' lives is sometimes regarded as little more than a form of entertainment. It is a very important part of their lives, though, and is one that we will see interacting with their faith as well. In only three decades, the number of Americans who earn their livings as artists has tripled, from about 700,000 to more than 2.1 million.[45] Americans spent more than $14 billion on music alone in 2000, up from only $6.6 billion in 1989.[46] Young adults are by no means the only market for art and music. But they are more likely than older adults to have taken art and music classes in school or to have received private lessons in ballet or creative writing. In qualitative interviews, young adults frequently point to art and music as sources of inspiration. When creeds and doctrines fail them, they turn to the more intuitive lessons of the arts.[47]

Apart from the *sources* of ideas and entertainment, culture shifts have also taken place in *attitudes*. The baby boom generation came of age during or immediately after the civil rights movement. Its leaders emphasized freedom of expression, civil liberties, and tolerance. Although racism and sexism often continued, it became unfashionable to be overtly bigoted.[48] These sentiments about rights, tolerance, and diversity became pervasive among young adults in that era, and they have, if anything, become even more common among the current generation of young adults. At least this is what standard questions in surveys suggest. For instance, when young adults are asked about allowing a book written by a homosexual to be in the local library or allowing someone who is antireligious to give a public speech, the vast majority (about four in five) of young adults say these activities are permissible. On statements like this, young adults at the start of the twenty-first century are also more likely to express tolerance than young adults were in the early 1970s. The differences range from only 2 percentage points to as many as 20 percentage points, depending on the activity at issue.[49] These questions are particularly interesting because they focus on *information*. They suggest that young adults are not only exposed to an increasing variety of information, but are also increasingly disposed to believe in the right of diverse groups to disperse that information.

The fact that young adults have retained—and broadened—baby boomers' support for civil liberties does not mean that young adults today are more liberal than they were a generation ago, though. When asked how they identify themselves in terms of political ideology, young adults are currently as divided as they were in the early 1970s. About four in ten plant themselves firmly in the middle of the road, but the remaining six in ten lean to the right or left. And more of the current generation than of their predecessors opt to the right. In the early 1970s, self-identified liberals out numbered self-identified conservatives by 35 percent to 27 percent. By the late 1990s, conservatives out numbered liberals by 32 percent to 30 percent.[50]

Religious views so often parallel political views, it seems, that these divisions in political ideology provide a hint of what we will see when we turn in subsequent chapters to religion. Young adults are generally quite tolerant. They have been reared in a culture that respects diversity, up to a point. But they are not ready to concede that anything goes. Many are guided by religious practices that encourage them to think conservatively about right and wrong. These practices, though, are in turn shaped by the social circumstances in which young adults live. Marriage and childrearing, work and money, education, relationships, globalization, and culture are among the factors defining their life worlds and their outlooks.

Summing Up

The key social trends I have described in this chapter are all ones that affect young adults personally. The typical young adult waits four or five years longer to get married than his or her parents did. That means expectations change. There is less pressure to find a mate in high school or even in college. It gives young adults more time to travel, establish themselves in a career, meet new friends, and develop an identity as an autonomous adult. It also means that friendships form where single adults gather, such as at work or after-hours gatherings, rather than in the contexts where married people might mingle. There may be rifts between young adults who remain single and their parents who wonder why "my son is thirty and not yet married." Delayed child rearing has similar effects on the life worlds of young adults. It means, for instance, that fewer young adults are focusing on the responsibilities of being parents and emphasizing the values they want their children to learn. Young women face new challenges that many of their mothers did not face. More are in the labor force, more have college degrees, and more are making tradeoffs between parenting and pursuing a career. Previous generations of young adults have experienced economic uncertainties. Yet the current generation is particularly susceptible to high rates of job turnover that are associated with broader trends in the economy, such as rapid technological change, greater use of outsourcing, and high rates of business failure. For many young people, the scramble to get on their feet financially shapes nearly every other aspect of their lives. Needing to stay mobile to please their employers, they sink shallow roots in their communities. Their social relationships depend more on long-distance travel and e-mail than on befriending their neighbors and helping with community improvement projects. They are part of the global economy. Their information comes from diverse sources. They have been taught to respect the rights of diverse groups and lifestyles. Yet they also want answers and have strong opinions about politics and ethics.

Life worlds are always local. Broad social trends never capture the particular characteristics of individuals or even of particular communities. Thus, a reader might consider the trends I have just described and conclude, well, none of this pertains to me: I live in a rural community where young adults still marry young. I am African American and know that education levels have not risen as much among people like me than among whites. I am an immigrant. Fair enough. We will look more closely at these variations in social patterns in subsequent chapters. For now, though, we need to bear in mind that broad social trends do define how people think about themselves—and how the society tells us to think about ourselves. When baby boomers were young, they by no means made up the majority of the

American population. Yet they became the focus of advertisers and they set the tone for tastes in music and debates in politics. The same is true of young adults today. Advertisers and employers know that young adults are marrying later and having children later. Online dating services have emerged in this context. Relocation specialists earn their livings helping young adults pull up stakes. Educational institutions seek students besides those who have just finished high school. Religious organizations are also affected by these changes. It is these religious implications to which we now turn.

Going to Church—Or Not

WHO PARTICIPATES IN CONGREGATONS?

AMERICAN RELIGION has always been a participatory faith. It was not enough simply to believe. Or even to belong, at least if belonging meant nothing more than having one's name on a membership roster. People of faith are expected to take part in their congregations. Taking part can mean a lot of things—serving on committees, helping at a soup kitchen, teaching Sunday school. At minimum, it means attending regularly scheduled worship services. And those who do attend regularly are dramatically more likely than those who attend less regularly to express interest and involvement in their faith by almost any measure of interest and involvement. They are, for instance, more likely to pray, to look to God for strength, to feel God's presence in their lives, to find comfort in their faith, and to have had life-changing religious experiences.[1]

A great debate has emerged around the topic of religious participation in recent years. Some observers believe it is declining. Others do not. Some argue that it is being replaced by more private expressions of faith—belief without belonging, as some writers describe it.[2] Still others question whether religious participation can be measured accurately at all. Perhaps people somehow want to be "religious" badly enough to lie to pollsters about how often they attend.[3]

Much of this debate is fairly easily resolved once we move from speculation to actual research. Overall, polls and surveys suggest that attendance at religious services among the full adult population of the United States has remained fairly constant for at least thirty years. Constant, but with perhaps some erosion in recent years.[4] The reason some observers think religious participation may have declined more than polls and surveys suggest is that research based on diaries suggests that it has. Diary studies ask people to record carefully what they do day by day and hour by hour. Thus, they require more thoughtful answers about what someone did, say, on a recent Sunday morning than is typically the case with a brief question in a survey. The trouble with these diary studies, though, is that they have not been conducted among very many people, and it is unclear whether the methods used over the past several decades provide comparable evidence. However, nobody claims that religious participation has been *rising* in recent decades.[5]

The debate about religious participation usually carries assumptions about what is happening among younger adults. These assumptions have not been examined very carefully, but they are especially important to our present interests. One assumption is that whatever decline may have happened in religious participation in the past was attributable to baby boomers and thus does not pertain to the current generation of younger adults. This assumption is consistent with evidence that religious participation was higher in the 1950s and early 1960s than it was by the middle 1970s. As baby boomers came of age, they apparently attended religious services less frequently than their elders. But the further implication of this argument is that this decline was a one-time phenomenon and has not been repeated among the more recent generation. There are two other ways of looking at the question, though. One is that the decline that occurred among baby boomers was a kind of slippery slope that would affect their children as well. For instance, baby boomers not only went to church less often than *their* parents, but also perhaps took it less seriously and thus did less well at encouraging their children to attend.[6] The other view is that the children of baby boomers grew up in a more conservative era, perceived something to be lacking in their parents' lives, and thus have actually become more religiously involved than their parents were.[7]

Attendance in Two Time Periods

The basic question that the debate about religious participation raises, then, is whether younger adults in recent years are attending religious services at the same rate, less often, or more often than younger adults did a generation ago. The data shown in figure 3.1 provide an answer to this question. These data are from the General Social Surveys and thus offer more detailed information about *frequency* of attendance than polls asking only about presence or absence at services during the previous week.[8] Like some of the results we considered in chapter 2, I have combined the answers from people age 21 through 45 who responded to surveys conducted in 1998, 2000, and 2002, and compared them with answers from people of the same age in surveys conducted between 1972 and 1976. Through these comparisons, we can see what kind of change, if any, has taken place in frequency of attendance at religious services among young adults.

The data in figure 3.1 show that there has been a decline in the percentage of younger adults who attend religious services regularly, and a corresponding increase in the percentage of younger adults who seldom or never attend religious services. Specifically, 6 percent of younger adults in the recent period claim that they attend religious services more than once a

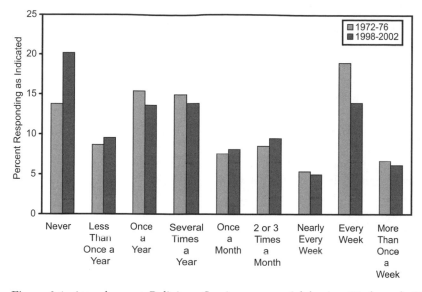

Figure 3.1. Attendance at Religious Services among Adults Age 21 through 45.
Source: General Social Surveys.

week, compared with 7 percent in the earlier period, and 14 percent in
the recent period claim they attend every week, down from 19 percent
previously. At the other extreme, 20 percent say they never attend, compared with only 14 percent earlier.

How should we think about these changes? On the one hand, it is important not to exaggerate their significance. In many ways, younger adults
at the start of the twenty-first century are like younger adults in the early
1970s. If we count as "regular" attenders, those who participate nearly every
week or more often, only a quarter (25 percent) of younger adults can be
considered regular attenders now, and fewer than a third (31 percent) were
in the early 1970s. The majority of younger adults either attend religious
services rarely or, if they attend more than that, are hardly regular enough
to be the core of any congregation. On the other hand, the fact that regular
attenders now characterize only 25 percent of younger adults, whereas this
proportion was 31 percent in the 1970s represents a decline that cannot
easily be dismissed. Had this decline not taken place, American congregations would have 6.3 million more regular attenders among younger adults
than they presently do.[9] If there are (as most observers believe) about
300,000 congregations in the United States, that means a loss of 21 younger
adults per congregation. I cannot think of a clergy person who would not
like to have 21 more younger adults in his or her congregation.

THE REASONS FOR DECLINING PARTICIPATION

Putting it in terms of what a clergy person would or would not like suggests that religious participation among younger adults has been declining because church leaders have done something wrong. That may be the case, especially when the failures of some congregations are compared with the successes of others. But there are larger changes taking place in the society, such as those we considered in chapter 2. These are changes that affect religious participation because they involve the life worlds in which younger adults live. There may be little that any particular church leader can do to alter these changes. Yet leaders of religious organizations need to understand how their organizations are being affected if they are to have any chance of making appropriate responses.

Marital Status

We saw in chapter 2 that changes in marriage patterns are one of the key social trends affecting the lives of younger adults. As more younger adults choose to marry later or not to marry at all, these changes are likely to have a significant impact on religious participation. There are several reasons for thinking this. One is that women generally are more interested in religion than men are, meaning that married men may participate in religion more often than single men because of their wives.[10] Perhaps a more important reason is that marriage is a significant form of settling down. It means making a commitment to another person, it may mean settling into a community and taking one's financial responsibilities more seriously, and for most couples it means at least starting to think about having children. All of these are what social scientists sometimes call traditional or conventional social roles. They imply conformity to mainstream social values. Religious participation is one of these traditional or conventional roles. An upstanding member of the community in times past was often a man or woman who participated actively in his or her congregation. The wedding itself is likely to have taken place in a congregation and may have required meeting with the clergy or attending church-sponsored classes. If children are planned, the prospective parents may also feel it important to start attending religious services in order to solidify their own faith and prepare for passing that faith along to their children. Beyond these reasons, married couples may simply feel more at home participating in congregations because congregations' programs are geared more to families than to single adults.[11]

The relationship between marital status and attendance at religious services among adults who were age 21 through 45 in 1972 through 1976 and

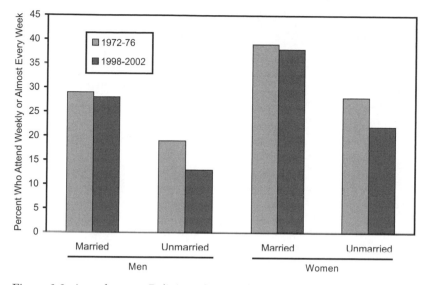

Figure 3.2. Attendance at Religious Services by Marital Status. Source: General Social Surveys, respondents age 21 through 45.

in 1998 through 2002 is shown in figure 3.2. The figure documents three very important patterns. The first is that married men and women in both time periods were more likely to attend religious services than never married men and women were.[12] The second is that married men and women were just as likely to attend religious services regularly in the recent period as they were in the earlier period. In short, there had been no decline in attendance among this group. The third is that never married men and women (and to some extent those who were divorced or separated) were less likely to attend religious services regularly in the recent period than they were in the earlier period. The overall conclusion, then, is that almost all of the decline in religious attendance that we saw a moment ago has taken place among those younger adults who have not married.[13]

This conclusion helps us to identify *where* the decline in religious attendance has occurred. It suggests, for instance, that single adults age 21 through 45 apparently do not feel as comfortable or interested in attending religious services as they did a generation ago. It also points to something even more important: married couples may be attending religious services at the same rate now as a generation ago, but there are significantly fewer of them. Specifically, in these General Social Surveys, 74 percent of those age 21 through 45 in the early 1970s were married, but by the 1998 to 2002 surveys, this proportion had fallen to only 45 percent. In contrast, the proportion of never married people rose from 16 percent to 35 percent, and the proportion of divorced or separated people rose from 10 percent to 18 percent.

The trend we saw in chapter 2 toward marrying later is part of what is happening in these results from the General Social Surveys. Among people in their twenties, for instance, there has been a very dramatic change in marital status: 62 percent in the 1970s were married, whereas only 28 percent in the recent surveys are; in contrast, only 30 percent were never married in the earlier surveys, but 63 percent were never married in the recent surveys. These changes are not limited to people in their twenties, though. Among those in their thirties, the proportion who were married dropped from 83 percent to 52 percent, and among those in their early forties, it dropped from 84 percent to 55 percent.

Religious attendance, therefore, has been adversely affected in two ways by the changing marital patterns among younger adults. Those who do not marry or who do not remain married are not only less likely to attend religious services regularly than those who are married, but they also are less likely to attend than their counterparts did a generation ago. In addition, the married group among whom attendance is highest has shrunk, while the unmarried group among whom attendance is lowest has increased in size. It is worth noting, too, that religious leaders have often expressed concern about the rising divorce rate, particularly because of its potentially negative consequences for children. Yet, in terms of what has affected participation in their own organizations, young adults remaining single has actually been more significant because this trend involves a substantially larger proportion of young adults than divorce does.

Children

Just as more younger adults are marrying later or remaining unmarried, so they are postponing having children (as we saw in chapter 2) and, when they do have children, have fewer of them. Having children and wanting to set a good example for them is one of the reasons adults go to church. As one young woman remarked, "I'm not sure about church for myself, but I want my children to have that exposure." For some people, passing on their religious values to their children is a matter of supreme urgency. They believe that only believers go to heaven when they die, so if they want to see their children some day in heaven, they figure it is important to take them to church where they will learn to be believers. For other people, exposing children to church is of less concern for its eternal consequences than for its effects on their lives in this world. Church is where children learn biblical stories that will give them strength, where they will make good friends, and where they will learn how to be caring and compassionate. Parents attend religious services, then, to make sure that their chil-

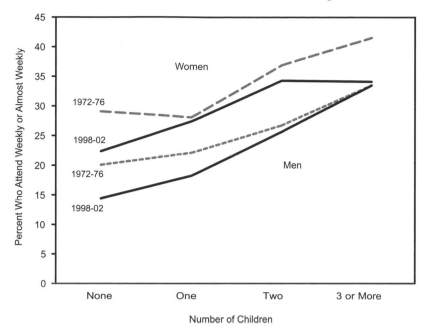

Figure 3.3. Attendance at Religious Services by Number of Children. Source: General Social Surveys, respondents age 21 through 45.

dren also attend. Even before children are old enough to attend, though, parents may attend religious services because they believe the congregation will strengthen their marriage and make them better parents.

The potential relationships between having children and attending religious services are complicated. A growing number of younger adults, for instance, have children out of wedlock or raise them as divorced parents, and these different patterns of parenting may be associated with different propensities to participate in religious congregations (more on this later in the chapter). It may make a difference if people have children later when they are more settled in their jobs and communities, and it may make a difference how old the children are. For now, though, it will suffice to examine how attendance varies among young men and women simply in terms of how many children they have.

As shown in figure 3.3, attendance varies considerably among young men and women depending on how many children they have. Those who have no children (with one exception) are least likely to attend religious services and those who have more than one child are more likely to attend than those who have only one child. These patterns were true in the 1970s and remain true in the more recent surveys. However, there have also been changes. Among men and women with no children, religious attendance is significantly less likely in the recent surveys than it was in the 1970s. Among those with children, the patterns for the two periods are more similar, although men with one child are less likely than they were in the 1970s to attend religious services, and women with two or more children are less likely to attend religious services in the recent period than in the earlier period.

Besides the patterns that can easily be seen in figure 3.3, there is also an underlying dynamic similar to the one we just considered for marital status. This is the fact that the proportion of younger adults who have no children has been increasing, while the proportion who have three or more children has been decreasing. For instance, in the General Social Surveys, 47 percent of those in their twenties in the earlier period had no children, but that figure rose to 60 percent in the more recent period. Among people in their thirties, the comparable increase was from 12 percent to 30 percent. And among those in their early forties, it rose from 7 percent to 23 percent. Meanwhile, the proportion with three or more children declined among those in their twenties from 10 percent to 9 percent; among those in their thirties, from 47 percent to 21 percent; and among those in their early forties, from 62 percent to 28 percent. In short, the group in which religious attendance was least common became larger, while the group in which it was most common became smaller.

I do not mean to suggest that younger adults have made decisions about child bearing (or marriage) entirely on grounds other than religion. It is quite possible that someone who attends church regularly, especially at certain churches, hears about the importance of marriage and having children, makes friends with couples who are having children, and thus is influenced by these experiences. We shall want to return to these considerations in later chapters.[14] However, the point here is that couples often make these decisions in terms of economic concerns or on the basis of the values to which they are exposed in the wider society, and the overall effect of trends in these decisions has not been favorable to religious participation.

Employment Patterns

The reason for considering trends in employment patterns is that, as we saw in chapter 2, younger women are much more likely to be employed full time in the paid labor force now than they were a generation ago. Scholars have speculated that full-time employment means less time for other things, such as doing volunteer work in the community, particularly because many women who work full-time are also mothers and because research shows that working women still do most of the housework. Religious participation may be decreasing, therefore, simply because more women are working full time and have less time to devote to religion.[15]

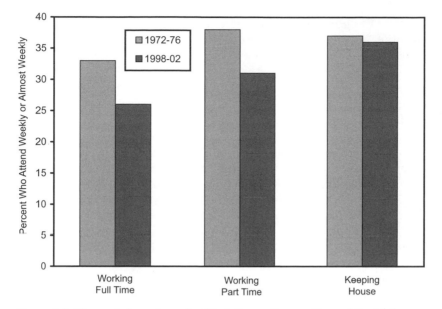

Figure 3.4. Women's Attendance by Work Status. Source: General Social Surveys, respondents age 21 through 45, women only.

The relationships between employment status and attendance at religious services are quite different for men and women. Among men, those who work full time are slightly more likely to attend religious services than those who work part time or are in school.[16] We should not put too much stock in these differences because they are largely a function of other factors, such as age, education, and marital status. However, it is important to note that fewer of the men who were working full time attended religious services regularly in the recent period than in the earlier period.[17] The more interesting comparisons are among women (shown in figure 3.4). The highest rates of religious attendance are among women keeping house, and these women were almost as likely to attend regularly in the recent period as in the earlier period.[18] But of course there were fewer of these women. In the surveys conducted in the 1970s, 49 percent of the women age 21 through 45 said they were keeping house, whereas in the more recent surveys this proportion was only 17 percent. The biggest changes took place among women who were working full time or part time. Among both groups, fewer attended religious services regularly in the recent period than in the earlier period. In both periods, the women who worked full time were less likely than those who worked part time to attend regularly.[19] The fact that women who worked full time had relatively low rates of religious participation also becomes more significant when the increasing size of this group is taken into account. In the surveys, for instance, 32 percent of those in the earlier period said they were working full time, and this proportion rose to 57 percent in the more recent period.

On the surface, these patterns seem to support the conclusion that women who work full time simply do not have enough hours in the week to attend religious services as faithfully as those who work part time or who keep house. However, that conclusion may be too simple. At least it does not appear that religious attendance among younger women is affected very much by the sheer number of hours they work in a typical week. For instance, among those surveyed in the recent period, 29 percent of those who worked fewer than 40 hours a week attended religious services regularly, 27 percent of those who worked 40 to 49 hours a week did so, and 27 percent of those who worked 50 or more hours a week did so.[20] Rather than the sheer number of hours mattering, it may be something else about working full time that matters more. I can only speculate, but it may be that having a full time job means that more of one's self-identity is invested in one's work than in avocational activities. Or it may mean that one's social relationships form more through the workplace than in other settings, such as one's congregation.

Education

For baby boomers, the fact that many of them had more education than their parents became a distinguishing feature of their generation. Going away to college, being on campuses crowded by the sheer size of their cohort, and attending college at a time when campuses were torn with social unrest all had implications for how they viewed the world. Yet studies of the relationships between levels of education and religious participation in the general public have usually shown that more education in itself does not dampen religious participation as much as might be imagined. It is true that people who have been to college are less likely to hold the kinds of religious beliefs that encourage some people to be regular participants at religious services (for instance, belief in a literal interpretation of the Bible).[21] But higher levels of education also appear to encourage people to be more active in their communities (perhaps like marriage does) and thus to be associated with *higher* levels of religious participation.

Data suggest that the relationships between education levels and religious attendance among younger adults are more complex than has often been supposed. Some of this complexity is attributable to the fact that younger adults whose highest degree was from a junior college do not follow any pattern that is consistent with those of other younger adults. In the 1970s, men with junior college educations had the lowest level of religious participation, while women with junior college educations had the highest. We can largely discount those figures, though, because hardly any men and women in those surveys fell into this category. The more important patterns are that among men (not counting those with junior college educations) religious attendance was consistently lower in the recent period at all levels of education than in the earlier period, and among women this was true for those with lower levels of education. It is also notable, though, that religious attendance is generally higher among men and women with higher levels of education than among those with lower levels. The exception to this pattern is that women in the recent period who earned graduate degrees were significantly *less* likely than those with bachelors degrees to attend religious services regularly (figure 3.5).

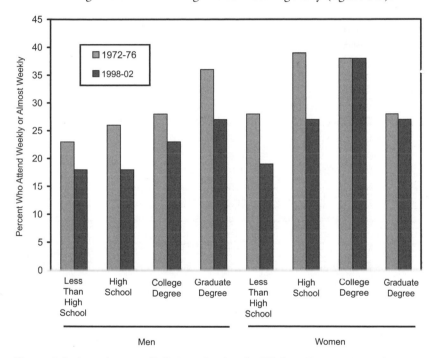

Figure 3.5. Attendance at Religious Services by Highest Degree Earned. Source: General Social Surveys, respondents age 21 through 45.

Although rising levels of education have certainly been an important force for change in American society, the implication of these results, then, is that their effect on religious participation among younger adults is mixed. As more men earn bachelors and graduate degrees, religious participation may rise. This increase may be modest, however, because in the surveys at least there was only a modest increase in the proportion of younger men who had earned bachelors or graduate degrees (from 22 percent to 25 percent). Higher educational attainment among women will perhaps reinforce religious participation, but not for women who earn graduate degrees. Here, though, the prospects for religious participation are likely to be influenced more by those with bachelors degrees (19 percent in the recent surveys) than by those with graduate degrees (5 percent in the recent surveys).

The Cumulative Impact

Do these changes in our society explain the decline in church attendance among young adults? Almost entirely. The statistics from which I draw this conclusion are included in the appendix (table A.3). They show that young adults in the late 1990s were significantly less likely to attend church regularly than young adults in the early 1970s were and that this decline is present even when such characteristics of the young adult population as age, gender, race, and education are taken into account. More to the point, they show that being married or unmarried has a stronger effect on church attendance than anything else, and that taking marriage rates into account significantly reduces the difference between church attendance in the late 1990s and in the early 1970s. Children also make some difference. With each additional child, attendance increases, net of marriage and other factors. And adjusting for the changing number of children among young adults further reduces the difference between attendance in the two periods. Working full time, in comparison, is not a significant predictor when these other factors are taken into account; however, when only women are considered, working full time does reduce the likelihood of attending regularly. Another factor—large doses of daily television viewing—also suppresses church attendance, much as Robert Putnam suggests it reduces community involvement in general. However, as we saw in chapter 2, television viewing has not increased among young adults and thus does not explain any of the decline in attendance over the past few decades. These conclusions are for adults age 21 through 45, but separate analyses of adults in their twenties, thirties, and early forties show that the same patterns pertain within each age group. This means that the postponement of marriage and children continues to suppress church attendance at least until adults are in their early forties.[22]

A Closer Look at Marriage and Children

The powerful effects on religious participation of getting married and having children are consistent with the conventional wisdom that younger adults return to church once they settle down and begin thinking about

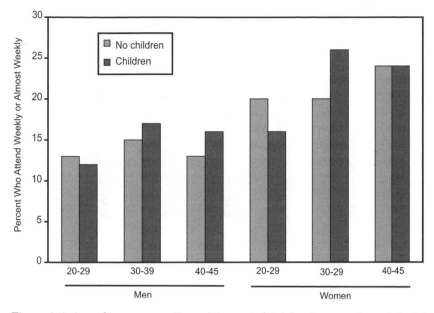

Figure 3.6. Attendance among Young Unmarried Adults. Source: General Social Surveys, 1998–2002.

raising a family. It is puzzling, though, that marriage seems to be a stronger influence than having children. The relationships among marriage, having children, and religious participation also bear closer examination because more younger adults are marrying but not having children, at least not until they are older, and at the same time more are having children without being married.

In figures 3.6 and 3.7 I compare the percentages of younger adult men and younger adult women in each age group who attend religious services nearly every week, looking separately at those who have no children and those who have one or more children. The results in figure 3.6 are for *unmarried* men and women and in figure 3.7, for *married* men and women. Looking first at unmarried men and women, the data show that in two of the three comparisons men with children are slightly more likely to attend religious services than men without children. Among unmarried women, those with children are more likely to attend religious services in only one of the three comparisons. Among both men and women who are in their twenties, being unmarried and having a child is associated with *lower* probabilities of attending religious services. There are at least two possible explanations for this pattern. One is that being an unwed mother or father runs counter to the norms of congregations and thus discourages people from attending. The other is that being a single mother or father imposes time

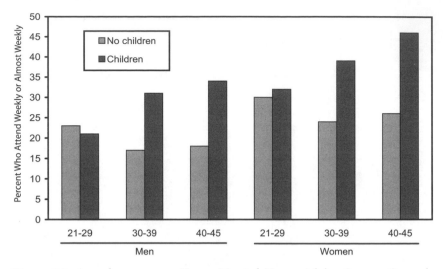

Figure 3.7. Attendance among Young Married Young Adults. Source: General Social Surveys, 1998–2002.

demands or puts one in a financial situation that makes it harder to attend religious services. The other thing these data demonstrate is that young men are significantly less likely to attend religious services regularly than young women, no matter what their family status is. For instance, among unmarried men in their twenties with no children, only 13 percent attend religious services nearly every week, whereas among unmarried women in their twenties with no children, 20 percent attend services nearly every week. It is also notable that among unmarried women, attendance is generally higher among those who are older than among those who are in their twenties, whereas among unmarried men there seems to be little indication of increasing attendance as they move out of their twenties.

In figure 3.7 similar comparisons are shown for married men and women. Among men in their twenties, those who have no children are slightly more likely to attend religious services nearly every week than those who have children. Among women in their twenties, those with children are slightly more likely than those without children to attend. However, men and women in their thirties and early forties are both more likely to attend services if they have children than if they do not. Although we cannot tell for sure from these data, the most likely explanation for the weaker effects among those in their twenties is that their children are *younger.* Having younger children may mean that it is harder to attend religious services because of needing to care for children. Or it may mean less interest in church than later when children are old enough to attend Sunday school. Here again, men are nearly always less likely to attend than women. It is also notable that among men and women who do not have children, attendance is lower for those in their thirties and early forties than for those in their twenties.

Overall, these results further demonstrate the close relationship between family patterns and religious attendance, but add some important nuances to the picture. First, there is considerable variation among younger adults in how likely or unlikely they are to attend religious services. At the extremes, only about an eighth of unmarried men in their twenties attend religious services regularly, whereas almost half of married women in their early forties with children do. No matter which age group they are in, or whether they have children or not, married men and women are more likely to attend religious services than unmarried men and women. This pattern again underscores the significance for religion of the fact that fewer people are marrying now than they did a generation ago and that those who do marry, marry later. Finally, the positive relationship between having children and attending religious services is by no means universal. It does not characterize the increasing number of younger adults who have children outside of marriage to the same extent that it characterizes those who are married when they have children.[23] And among those who are married, it does not characterize those in their twenties as much as those who are older.

COMMUNITIES

We saw in chapter 2 that Robert Putnam's arguments about the decline of community attachments is borne out among younger adults by some of the evidence, but not by other measures. One measure that has shown decline, as we saw, is the percentage of younger adults who spend social evenings visiting their neighbors. If younger adults are not as closely tied to their neighbors as they were in the past, we might suppose that this weakening of community attachments would also discourage them from attending church as regularly. However, this does not seem to be the case. Among younger adults surveyed between 1998 and 2002, exactly the same proportion of those who visited their neighbors frequently and of those who seldom visited their neighbors attended church regularly (25 percent in each case). This had also been the case among those surveyed in the early 1970s (when 28 percent in each case went to church regularly).

What these comparisons suggest is that church attendance may not be as deeply rooted in neighborhoods as it was during earlier periods in American history. For younger and older people alike, church is probably outside their immediate neighborhood, just as work, schools, and shopping are. In fact, data collected by the U.S. Department of Transportation show clearly that this is the case. In 2001, for instance, Americans made 6.7 billion trips in personal vehicles to religious activities, traveling a total of 45.3 billion miles—an average of 6.8 miles per trip. This number was comparable to the average distance traveled for work (6.1 miles), school (6.1 miles), and shopping (7.0 miles).[24]

The communities in which younger adults live have continued to change in another way that affects religious participation. This is the shift from living in small towns to living in suburbs, and, to a small extent, a similar shift toward suburbs as opposed to living in urban areas. Among people age 21 through 45 in the General Social Surveys conducted between 1972 and 1976, 54 percent lived in cities, 23 percent lived in suburbs, and 23 percent lived in small towns or rural areas. In the surveys conducted between 1998 and 2002, the proportion of younger adults living in cities had declined from 54 percent to 47 percent, the proportion living in suburbs had risen from 23 percent to 38 percent, and the proportion living in small towns or rural areas had dropped from 23 percent to 15 percent. These are not huge shifts, but they do continue patterns that began around the middle of the twentieth century as cities became crowded, as more people found jobs and housing in the suburbs, and as the agricultural base that had supported small towns shrank.

Traditionally, the strength of American religion has been in the country, rather than in the city. The churches that had been built in small towns and rural areas during the nineteenth and early twentieth centuries were numerous and continued over time to attract a large percentage of the population of these communities. As the population shifts toward suburbs, therefore, these changes have potentially negative consequences for religious participation. In the recent period, 31 percent of young adults living in small towns or rural areas attended religious services nearly every week, compared with 24 percent of those living in cities or suburbs. The same pattern was evident in the earlier period (when approximately 5 percent more in each location attended regularly). Further analysis of the data indicate that the shift in population from small towns to suburbs *does not* explain any of the overall decline in religious attendance between the early 1970s and the turn of the century. However, the shift in population does mean that religious organizations have had to respond—and will continue to respond—by relocating congregations.

Is the United States Becoming Like Europe?

The fact that more young adults in the United States are remaining single longer and having children later or less often, coupled with the fact that church attendance is being weakened by these changes, suggests the possi-

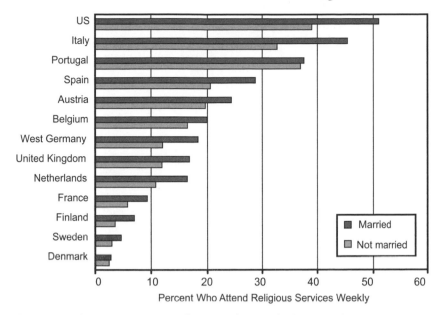

Figure 3.8. Persons 21 to 45 Who Attend in Each Country. Source: European Values Surveys, 1999–2000, U.S. World Values Survey, 2000.

bility that the United States is on the same trajectory as Western Europe. There, marriage and fertility rates have dropped so dramatically that demographers worry about the economic and political consequences.[25] For these and other historic reasons, Western Europe has also experienced low and declining rates of church attendance.

The data in figure 3.8, though, dispel the idea that the United States is likely to resemble church attendance in Western Europe anytime soon. While young adults who are married are more likely to attend religious services regularly than those who are unmarried in all of the thirteen countries shown, the United States is still by far the most religious. Only Italy and Portugal come close. Were we to examine a similar graph for young adults who do or do not have children, we would also see that having children and church attendance are positively associated in all these countries. Yet, young adults in the United States who do not have children are still more likely to attend religious services than young adults who *do* have children in every country except Italy.

Thus if one were to predict the future of church attendance from demographic factors alone, it would be worth noting that marriage and fertility rates are declining in the United States, just as they have been in Western Europe. It would also be worth considering that this convergence in demographic trends may also lead to some convergence in rates of religious participation. Still, the historic factors that have distinguished religion in Western Europe from religion in the United States—such as the presence of state religions and stronger working class political parties—seem likely to continue separating the two regions.

THE PROFILE OF REGULAR CHURCH GOERS

I have focused thus far on the proportions of young adults within various social categories (married, single, and so on) who attend religious services. A different way of considering the evidence is to paint a social profile of young adults who do attend services regularly. These are the young adults with whom pastors and other church leaders are most likely to have contact. For many such leaders, it may be less relevant to know that a lot of young adults do not attend services than to know the social characteristics of those who do attend.

The first observation is that church attenders age 21 through 45 are disproportionately female. Whereas infrequent attenders are about evenly divided between males and females, only a third of regular attenders are male, while two out of three are women. Second, young adults in their twenties are poorly represented among regular church attenders. Fewer than a quarter of those age 21 through 45 are in their twenties, whereas more than a third of the infrequent attenders are. Third, a majority of regular church attenders (60 percent) are married, whereas only 40 percent of infrequent attenders are married. A larger proportion of regular attenders also has children (73 percent) than among infrequent attenders (59 percent).

For the average congregation, these statistics mean that young women will outnumber young men by about two to one. About the same proportion of these young men and women (60 percent of each) will be married, but if the congregation were to function as a marriage market for the unmarried, single women would experience a notable dearth of single men. Were the congregation to gear its programs to the interests of the majority, it would logically have programs for married people and for young adults with children, rather than for unmarried adults. However, its planners might want to give more attention to the unmarried than they did in the past: the 40 percent of young adults who are unmarried represents an increase from only 18 percent a generation ago. The preponderance of women and the fact that fewer women than men are working full-time means that the congregation would probably still rely heavily on women to provide the volunteer labor to keep the church running. Leaders, though, would probably find it harder to solicit such volunteer labor or to schedule meetings than in the past: the 52 percent of young women who kept house in the early 1970s has fallen to only 21 percent now.

The current profile of regular church attenders also indicates that churches are increasingly attracting an *unrepresentative* cross-section of young adults. In the early 1970s, the vast majority of frequent and infrequent church attenders alike were married and had children. Currently, the typical church attender is married and has children, while the typical non-attender is single and does not have children. This does not mean that church goers have nothing in common with non-goers. It does, however, mean that the two groups of young adults differ in ways other than simply their religious behavior. Their life worlds—and thus their interests and needs—also differ.

RELIGIOUS ATTENDANCE IN PERSPECTIVE

There is no question that people attend religious services for religious reasons. Yet the likelihood of someone actually attending is undeniably conditioned by his or her circumstances. Statistical evidence identifies the broad contours of these circumstances. It matters especially for young adults if they are married or single, have children or do not have children, work outside the home or do not work, and so on. The precise reasons why these circumstances make the difference they do can be inferred from the patterns themselves. Married people, for instance, not only go to church more often than single people do, but have a more enduring relationship with a person of the opposite sex, have or anticipate having children to whom they must responsibly impart values, and have probably chosen a group of friends who lead lives similar to theirs.

The contrast between young single adults and young adults who are married and have children comes into sharp relief in the stories of particular individuals. For instance, a twenty-nine-year-old woman who is single and active in a Baptist church in her community says her biggest concern is "relationships," by which she means "finding a life partner who has the same values" as she does. Relationships, she says, are an issue with her because her "dating life is driving [her] crazy." And being involved in a church only makes things worse. "I am the only twenty something in this church, so sometimes it drives me more crazy. You are supposed to meet people doing the things you like to do, and I can't do that here at this church." The contrast is provided by a thirty-four-year-old woman who is married, has two children, and attends a United Church of Christ congregation. She grew up Presbyterian and was fairly active in church until she was sixteen. She lost interest in church during her last two years of high school and did not attend again until after college. When she got married, she and her husband decided to start attending church again. Sharing a common religious heritage was one of the things that drew them to each other and they wanted to pass that tradition along to their children. At first it was hard to feel at home where they attended because they were still unsettled as a result of uncertainties with her husband's job. After moving to a new community, though, they purchased a house, her husband's job seemed more secure, they started thinking about having children, and they joined their present congregation. She teaches a children's Sunday school class, is on the church council, and serves on another committee called "congregational wives." Although the church has only seventy-five members, about fifteen are young married adults with children. "This is the most involved I have been with church since I was a kid in my home church," she says. "I think it is a reflection of how comfortable I am here."

The fact that religious participation is influenced by the life worlds young adults have created for themselves forces us to rethink the assumptions we have inherited from discussions of baby boomers. Those discussions suggested that baby boomers' faith was shaped mostly by having been on college campuses during a period of acute unrest in our nation's history, by learning new values, and by having opportunities that had been unavailable to their parents. The truth, though, was that only a minority of baby boomers graduated from college, and by the 1980s it was clear that baby boomers were as different from one another as they were from their parents. In fact, their participation or lack of participation at houses of worship was very strongly shaped by the more intimate circumstances of their lives. The evidence we have considered in this chapter from the early 1970s shows that clearly. When baby boomers were young adults, they, too, participated in religion more often if they were married, had children, kept house, and lived in small towns or rural areas.

The current cohort of young adults is subject to the same influences. Only the influences that *reinforce* religious participation are weaker than they were a generation ago. The net result is fewer young adults contributing to the activities of local congregations or receiving support from these congregations. For many, the proverbial lessons of faith learned at their mother's knee may be powerful enough to sustain their interest in religion until the circumstances of their lives again make it convenient to participate. If religion is an institution that provides support and guidance during moments of major life transition, though, a large number of young adults will face these transitions without such support and guidance. They will seek it elsewhere, to be sure. Religious organizations will simply be less relevant for many than was true in the past.

The Major Faith Communities

THINKING BEYOND WINNERS AND LOSERS

OVER THE YEARS, writers have described American religion by distinguishing among several major faith communities or traditions. In the 1950s, Will Herberg argued that the nation's cultural identity was composed of three major traditions: Protestants, Catholics, and Jews. The argument was appealing. Although there were subdistinctions among different denominations and ethnic groups, each of the three was recognizable as a major tradition. Protestants and Catholics kept their distance from each other, right down to where they lived and who they allowed their children to date, and Christians and Jews parted company in similar ways.[1] A few years later than Herberg, the sociologist Gerhard Lenski wrote in *The Religious Factor* (based on a survey of Detroit) that African American churches should be added as a fourth major tradition. While most African Americans were Protestants, they generally belonged to denominations that were historically separate and to congregations set apart from the white community by segregation.[2] By the 1980s, it was becoming evident in thinking about American religion that the white Protestant category should be further divided. Evangelicalism had emerged as an umbrella label, complete with a national organization and several major television ministries, that gave members of theologically conservative denominations (such as Southern Baptists and Assemblies of God) with strict interpretations of the Bible a common identity. The historically mainline Protestant denominations that had mostly originated in Europe (Lutherans, Episcopalians, Presbyterians, Methodists, United Church of Christ, and American Baptists) meanwhile had embraced ecumenism and taken more progressive orientations toward biblical interpretation.[3]

Some writers question whether these are the best ways to distinguish religious patterns in the United States. It might be argued, for instance, that regular attendance at religious services is preferable, since all services in the United States have so much in common. The evidence we considered in the last chapter, in fact, shows the merit of examining patterns of attendance. It might also be argued that simple questions about belief, such as whether a person believes in God, could provide a less cumbersome way of describing American religion.[4] The five categories just mentioned—evangelical Protestants, mainline Protestants, black Protestants, Catholics, and Jews—have nevertheless become the standard in recent social science research (with a miscellaneous category for others, such as members of Orthodox, Muslim, or Buddhist groups, and a category for people unaffiliated with any tradition). Some studies do not ask detailed enough questions about the particular denominations or traditions with which people are affiliated to use this scheme, but the best studies do, making it practicable to examine religious traditions in this way. Among religious leaders and observers of American religion, there is also a great deal of interest in questions about the relative size of these various traditions and trends among them.[5]

Most of the writing about America's faith communities in recent years has argued that evangelical Protestantism is growing while mainline Protestantism is declining. Observers also argue that the number of Jews in the United States has declined, at least relative to growth in the overall population. Writing has focused less on black Protestant and Catholic churches, but competing arguments can be made about how they are holding their own or why they may be declining.[6] In considering the new wave of young adults, therefore, we must look closely at how these various traditions are faring, compared with their relative strength a generation ago, and what factors may be contributing to their growth, stability, or decline.

The Significance of Young Adults

The information in this chapter focuses on the size and social characteristics of the major faith traditions *among younger adults* in the United States. Before turning to that information, though, it will be helpful to look first at the *whole population* to see what proportion of each faith tradition is composed of young adults. This information is shown in figure 4.1. Each of the vertical bars in the chart shows the proportions of people in each religious tradition who are age 21 through 29, age 30 through 39, and age 40 through 45.

The chart reveals, first of all, how important younger adults are to all of the major faith traditions. Adults between the ages of 21 and 45 make up at least 40 percent of the adherents of every major faith tradition in the United States. This in itself is a notable piece of information. Secularist academics sometimes imagine that religion is just for old folks—and some clergy may draw the same conclusion when they look out at their congregations on Sunday mornings and see a sea of gray hair. But the truth is that younger adults still make up an important part of the constituencies of all the major faith traditions. And this means religious leaders risk the very future of their faith communities if they ignore the changes that are taking place among younger adults.

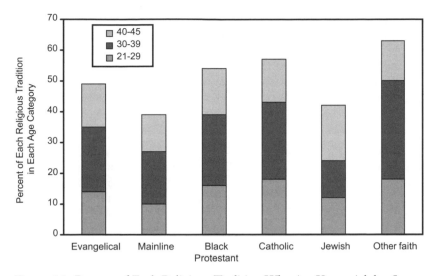

Figure 4.1. Percent of Each Religious Tradition Who Are Young Adults. Source: General Social Surveys, 1998–2002.

However, younger adults make up a *smaller* proportion of the adherents of several faith traditions now than they did a generation ago. Among white evangelical Protestants, there has been a 2 percentage point decline since the early 1970s in the proportion who are age 21 through 45; among mainline Protestants, a 5 point decline; and among Jews, a 6 point decline. And in all of the traditions, the proportion of affiliates who are in their twenties has declined: by 6 points among evangelicals, 7 points among mainline Protestants, 5 points among black Protestants, 6 points among Catholics, 11 points among Jews, and 11 points among those affiliated with other faiths. These percentage declines have occurred in part because the population as a whole has been aging. People live longer than they used to, and the large baby boomer cohort is now further expanding the proportion of Americans who are past the age of 45. For some religious leaders, this fact may suggest the importance of focusing greater attention on the needs of older adults than on the needs of younger adults. But if the future of American religion rests among younger adults, then religious leaders need to work harder to maintain the loyalties of this segment of the population as its numbers shrink. If they do not, their own memberships will shrink accordingly.

It is worth emphasizing that the major religious traditions are being affected differently by the overall aging of the population. Evangelical Protestants are often portrayed by the media as the most youthful branch of American religion—vitally reproducing itself with young families and providing avant garde programs that attract other young adults. But the facts do not entirely support this image. While it is true that evangelical denominations are composed of almost as large a proportion of adults age 45 or younger now as a generation ago (49 percent versus 51 percent), the proportion of evangelicals in their *twenties* has dropped dramatically. When one speaks of young adult evangelicals, one is thus speaking of adults in their thirties and early forties to a greater extent now than was true in the 1970s.[7]

Mainline Protestants show a similar pattern to that of evangelicals. But to an even greater degree, the proportion of mainline Protestants in their twenties has been shrinking. In the early 1970s, about one mainline Protestant in six was in his or her twenties, whereas now only one in ten is. Overall, the proportion of mainline Protestants between the ages of 21 and 45 has decreased from 44 percent to 40 percent. In comparison with evangelicals, mainline Protestants are, therefore, older on average. In fact, the mean age of adult mainline Protestants in the recent surveys was 52, a full four years older than the mean age of adult evangelicals.

In contrast to the two Protestant traditions that are composed largely of white Americans, the historically black Protestant denominations are now made up of a *larger* proportion of younger adults than they were a generation ago. In the early 1970s, 49 percent of their adherents were age 21 through 45, whereas that proportion has risen to 54 percent. Like the white Protestant denominations, though, the proportion of black Protestants in their twenties has declined (from 21 percent to 16 percent).

Roman Catholics show yet another pattern. Catholics have a higher proportion of younger adults than any of the Protestant traditions. In the early 1970s, 57 percent of adult Catholics were age 21 through 45, and this proportion has remained almost constant (56 percent). Yet, Catholics, too, have been declining in terms of the proportion who are in their twenties (18 percent now compared with 24 percent a generation ago). Thus, like Protestants, it makes more sense to think of younger adult Catholics as being people in their thirties and early forties now than was true in the 1970s.

This is also the case among Jews. In the early 1970s, 48 percent of adult Jews in the United States were age 21 through 45. That proportion has decreased to 42 percent. In the early 1970s, 23 percent of Jews were in their twenties, whereas only 12 percent were by the end of the twentieth century.

The miscellaneous category of people who adhere to other faiths is composed to a larger extent than any of the other religious traditions of younger adults. Over the past thirty years that proportion has risen from 60 percent to 62 percent. Again, though, the proportion who are in their twenties has decreased (from 29 percent to 18 percent).

It is worth noting, too, that the category of Americans who claim no religious affiliation is by far the one with the largest proportion of younger adults. In the 1970s, 74 percent of those who were nonaffiliated were age 21 through 45, and by the end of the twentieth century this figure had declined only to 69 percent. This category, though, also registered a declining proportion of adults in their twenties (from 44 percent to 27 percent).

We will consider in the rest of the chapter how these various religious traditions have been faring in terms of overall memberships among younger adults. For now, though, the main points to keep in mind are the following: the U.S. population has aged somewhat over the past thirty years, meaning that the average age of members of most faith traditions has also increased; that said, younger adults still make up approximately two-fifths of the members of the major faith traditions; but among these younger adults, a larger proportion are in their thirties and early forties and fewer are in their twenties than was true a generation ago. When the various traditions are compared, Catholics and black Protestants have the largest proportions of members between the ages of 21 and 45, mainline Protestants and Jews have the smallest proportions of younger adults, and evangelical Protestants fall in the middle.

THE MAJOR FAITH TRADITIONS

Figure 4.2 shows the proportion of Americans age 21 through 45 between 1972 and 1976 and again between 1998 and 2002 whose religious affiliations fell into each of the major faith traditions. In the 1970s, 22 percent of younger adults were affiliated with evangelical Protestant denominations, 26 were affiliated with mainline Protestant denominations, 9 percent were affiliated with historically black Protestant denominations, 28 percent were Roman Catholics, 2 percent were Jewish, 4 percent affiliated with some other faith, and 9 percent were nonaffiliated. By the end of the century, 20 percent were affiliated with evangelical denominations, 14 percent with mainline denominations, 8 percent with black Protestant denominations, 29 percent were Catholics, 2 percent were Jewish, 7 percent belonged to other faiths, and 20 percent were nonaffiliated.[8]

Several of these numbers are especially worth noting. It is common for journalists to write about the tremendous growth, vitality, and rising influence of American evangelicals. But, judging from these figures, those claims are highly exaggerated. Among younger adults, the proportion who identify as evangelicals has declined over the past three decades, not risen. Where journalists and popular accounts of American religion *are* correct is in emphasizing the decline of mainline Protestant denominations. While there has been some decline in these data among evangelicals, there has

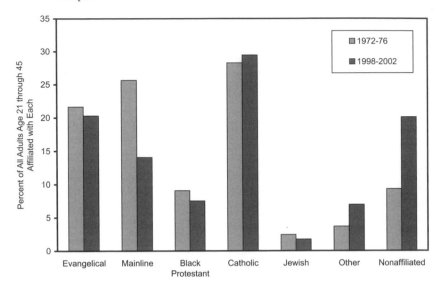

Figure 4.2. Affiliation with Major Religious Traditions. Source: General Social Surveys, respondents age 21 through 45.

been a dramatic decline in the proportion of younger adults who identify as mainline Protestants. We do need to qualify this observation in two ways. One is that the decline in mainline Protestant denominations occurred mostly during the 1970s and 1980s and by some indications mainline membership bottomed out in the early 1990s and remained nearly constant for the rest of that decade.[9] The other is that mainline denominations have benefited from the increasing number of *older adults* in the United States, such that overall decline is not as great as among younger adults. Still, the diminishing numbers of younger adults affiliated with mainline denominations is a significant aspect of American religion and one that does not bode well for the future of those denominations. In contrast to the numbers for evangelical and mainline Protestants, those for black Protestants, Catholics, and Jews have remained remarkably stable. This stability also runs counter to some popular perceptions, especially those focusing on the ill-effects of declining neighborhoods among African Americans, of church scandals on the loyalties of Catholics, and of intermarriage on the identities of Jews. In terms of affiliation, each of these traditions has actually done better than popular discussions would suggest. The rising proportion of younger adults affiliated with "other faiths" is less surprising. This category includes members of the Church of Jesus Christ of Latter-Day Saints, Muslims, Hindus, and Buddhists, among others, all of which have grown in recent years. The most notable of all these figures, though, is the large increase in the proportion of younger adults who are nonaffiliated. That proportion has risen in the space of a generation from one person in eleven to one person in five.

To understand better how the major faith traditions are faring among younger adults, we need to examine the sources of their decline, stability, or growth. It will also help us to know how these faith traditions are changing by examining such social characteristics of the people affiliated with them as their education levels, race or ethnicity, family patterns, and where they live. I begin by looking more closely at evangelicals.

EVANGELICALS AND MAINLINE PROTESTANTS

The fact that evangelicals make up a smaller proportion of younger adults now than a generation ago can be interpreted as disconfirmation of the popular perception of growth among evangelicals. But that perception is not entirely wrong. When evangelicals are compared with mainline denominations, the more theologically conservative of the two emerge in a more favorable light. Certainly, if one thinks about the balance within American Protestantism, then that balance has clearly shifted: from one in which mainline denominations held an edge among younger adults a generation ago by a margin of about 5 to 4, to one in which evangelicals now hold the edge by a margin of 3 to 2.

Evangelicals also emerge favorably in comparison with mainline Protestants when their ability to attract new recruits is considered. There has been a great deal of interest in recent years in the phenomenon known as religious "switching."[10] Evidence suggests that the proportion of Americans who switch from one denomination or religious tradition to another has risen over the past half century. This evidence has led some observers to speculate that evangelicals were doing well because they were attracting new recruits from other denominations—an idea that squares with evangelicals' theological emphasis on making converts. Nationally, 21 percent of younger adults were affiliated with a major faith tradition (as defined here) in the early 1970s that was different from the one they had been affiliated with at age 16, and this figure rose to 23 percent by the end of the century. As shown in figure 4.3, evangelicals did have better success in attracting new recruits than mainline denominations did. Moreover, evangelicals' success in doing this seems to have improved with time. Between 1972 and 1976, 21 percent of younger adults who were evangelicals had been something else at age 16, and by the 1998–2002 period, this proportion was 25 percent. Of course some of those who grow up evangelical switch to other traditions, which is why this ability to attract new recruits has not resulted in overall growth. In comparison, only 16 percent of the

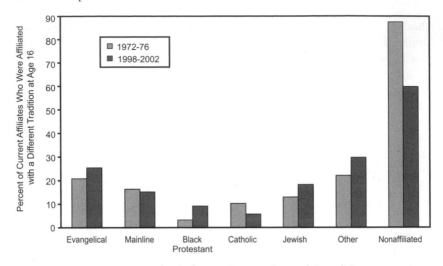

Figure 4.3. Converts to Each Tradition. Source: General Social Surveys, respondents age 21 through 45.

younger adults affiliated with mainline denominations in the earlier period had been something else at age 16, and this proportion declined slightly to 15 percent in the more recent period.

Judging from the other results in figure 4.3, evangelicals also do better at attracting new recruits than black Protestants, Catholics, or Jews, and nearly as well as the "other faiths" category. It is notable, though, that with the exception of Catholics, each of these other traditions was composed of a larger proportion of switchers in the recent period than a generation earlier. The pattern for the nonaffiliated category is another exception. In the earlier period, 87 percent of nonaffiliates had been something else at age 16, meaning that most nonaffiliates had been raised in a religious tradition. In the recent period, 60 percent of nonaffiliates had switched into that category since the age of 16, but 40 percent had been raised as nonaffiliates.

Stories of people switching to evangelicalism are not hard to find, and they illustrate this tradition's continuing appeal. A college senior, for instance, recalled the year he spent as a sophomore participating in a conservative Christian group on campus. Struggling with questions about truth and his own trajectory in life, he was drawn to the group. "There was this group of really hard-core fundamentalist superliteralist Christians," he recounts, "and they had it all figured out and it had to be exactly like how they said it. If you talked to them and you didn't agree with them, they'd kind of feel bad for you, like 'I hope you're not going to hell.' There was a lot of stuff that drove me crazy about them, but I could see that there was a genuine love in their hearts for God." He remembers saying, "Lord, the last thing I ever want to do is become one of these fundamentalist people." But in desperation he prayed, "If they have the truth, Lord, I'll do it." He adds: "I was scared praying that prayer, but I just wanted to be doing what was the truth." Two years later, he is no longer part of the group, but he understands why it was so attractive.

We might suppose, as some journalists do, that the reason evangelicals fare better among younger adults than mainline denominations have is that younger adults have increasingly been switching from mainline denominations *to* evangelical denominations. This supposition would be consistent with a popular impression that younger adults are religiously more conservative now than they were a generation ago, and it would be consistent with the idea that mainline denominations have become entrenched in old-style programs that appeal mostly to older people, whereas evangelical congregations have been more innovative. There may be truth in these ideas. But the rising proportion of evangelicals who are new recruits is not the result of more mainliners becoming evangelicals. In fact, that proportion has actually *decreased*. A generation ago, 12 percent of young adult evangelicals had been raised in mainline denominations, whereas in the more recent period, only 8 percent had. The main source of evangelical recruits is now former *Catholics*. That proportion has risen to 9 percent of evangelicals from only 4 percent a generation ago. Thus, in raw numbers, about 2 million young evangelicals are former Catholics, compared to only 600,000 a generation ago.

Why might evangelicals be doing better at attracting Catholics than they did in the 1970s? One reason may be the large number of Hispanic immigrants who have come to the United States in recent decades. The General Social Surveys, unfortunately, are not well-equipped to address this possibility. In the early 1970s, respondents were not even asked if they were Hispanic, and despite the large number of Spanish speakers now living in the United States, the General Social Surveys are still only conducted in English.[11] Despite these limitations, there is some indication even in the General Social Surveys of the increasing importance of Hispanics among young evangelicals. For instance, 4 percent of young evangelicals in the recent surveys who had grown up as evangelicals were Hispanic, but among those who had converted to evangelicalism from some other religious tradition, twice as many (8 percent) were Hispanic.[12]

These considerations about converts, former Catholics, and Hispanics all suggest that young evangelicals are a more diverse part of the population now than they were a generation ago. Being able to adapt to diversity is, in fact, one of the reasons that evangelicals have managed to do as well as they have numerically. For instance, the proportion of young evangelicals who are African American, while still quite small, has risen from 3 percent to 8 percent during the past generation. Geographically, young evangelicals are still more heavily concentrated in the South than anywhere else (about half live in the South), but that proportion has dropped while the proportions living in the Northeast and Midwest have risen.[13] The proportions of young evangelicals who live outside the South are also larger among those who converted to this tradition than among those who grew up as evangelicals.[14] Besides greater regional diversity, evangelicals have also shifted dramatically from being a religion of small towns and rural areas to a faith of the suburbs. Much of this shift occurred before the 1970s. But even in the past three decades, it has continued. Among young evangelicals, 35 percent still lived in small towns and rural areas in the 1970s, whereas only 21 percent did by the end of the century. In contrast, the proportion living in suburbs grew from 19 percent to 37 percent (the remainder lived in areas defined as cities). Once again, converts were less likely to live in small towns and more likely to live in suburbs than life-long evangelicals were.

The fact that evangelicals have become more geographically dispersed is not surprising. The largest evangelical denominations have worked aggressively to start new congregations outside of the South and in rapidly growing suburban areas. What attracts people to these churches, moreover, is not simply that they are close, but that they welcome newcomers to the community and in many cases play down particular denominational traditions. When someone moves, it is thus easier to join one of these churches, even if it means switching from one religious tradition to another. In the General Social Survey data, for instance, 66 percent of converts to evangelicalism had moved from where they had been living when they were 16, compared with only 51 percent of life-long evangelicals.

The increasing diversity of young evangelicals, though, does not fully account for their success relative to mainline denominations. Younger adults affiliated with mainline denominations are also more diverse than they were a generation ago. More of them live in suburbs and fewer live in small towns, just as among evangelicals. They are more diverse regionally than evangelicals are, and they are less concentrated in the Midwest (their traditional area of strength) than they were in the past. They have not been as effective at drawing in African Americans and Hispanics as evangelicals have, but they are more diverse racially and ethnically than they were. And converts to mainline churches are even more likely to have moved in recent years (77 percent have) than are converts to evangelicalism.

In short, evangelicals and mainline Protestants have experienced many of the same social changes during the past three decades, and these changes have forced both traditions to adapt. Evangelicals have simply adapted better. They have drawn in more converts, they have been more successful in attracting former Catholics, and they have done better at launching churches that drew in recruits in parts of the country that were not their traditional bastions of strength. The deeper reasons for this success undoubtedly lie in beliefs and attitudes, which we will take up in subsequent chapters. There is another important factor, though, that we need to consider here.

That factor is retention. Religious traditions stay in business not only by making new recruits, but also by retaining their members. Evangelicals do a significantly better job of retaining the young adults who grow up in their tradition than mainline denominations do. In the two time periods, 84 percent and 82 percent, respectively, of young adults who had been evangelicals at age 16 were still evangelicals when they were surveyed during young adulthood. In contrast, 73 percent and 70 percent, respectively, of those who had been mainline Protestants at age 16 were still affiliated with that tradition. Thus, even if the two traditions had been equally successful at making converts, evangelicals would have experienced greater overall numeric success.

Retention is usually thought of by religious leaders as a matter of providing compelling teachings and sufficiently attractive programs to keep members from straying. But human nature is often driven more by inertia than by persuasive reasons. If people are shielded from jarring incidents and from alluring opportunities, they typically stay the course. That appears to be the decisive factor for most evangelicals—and for most mainliners, too, but for fewer of them. Consider geographic mobility. As long as a person lives in the same community in which he or she grew up, it may be hard for that person to switch to a different religion. Or, if not hard, just unthinkable. There is no reason to change. In the 1998 to 2002 surveys, 46 percent of those who had grown up as evangelicals still lived in the same community in which they had been raised. That was 3 percentage points more than had lived in the same community in the 1972 to 1976 surveys. In contrast, only 38 percent of those raised as mainline Protestants lived in the same community, down from 42 percent in the earlier surveys. This is not a large difference, but it does suggest that fewer life-long evangelicals may have been exposed to the kind of unsettledness that encouraged them to switch religions than mainliners were. More important, though, is the *timing* of this unsettledness. Among those from evangelical backgrounds, 52 percent in their twenties had not moved, whereas among those from mainline backgrounds, only 36 percent in their twenties had not moved. There was a similar difference among those in their thirties. So, at a time when other aspects of their lives, including religion, may have been unsettled, young adults who had been raised as mainliners were moving around to a significantly greater extent than evangelicals were.

Why might this have been the case? Probably because of moving to secure an education and then having to move again to secure the kind of job for which one had been trained. In the recent period, only 16 percent of those in their twenties from evangelical backgrounds had graduated from college, whereas 27 percent of those in their twenties from mainline backgrounds had. Among those in their thirties, the respective figures were 20 percent and 38 percent. Acquiring a college education not only involves moving geographically. It exposes one to new ideas, new opportunities, and new friends—all of which contribute to the likelihood of switching religions.

Add to this another factor: differences in the timing of marriage and having children. The likelihood of staying single longer or not marrying at all has been a trend among evangelicals and mainline Protestants, just as it has in the society at large. Among those raised in both traditions, significantly fewer young adults are married than was the case a generation ago.[15] The two traditions differ, though, in the timing of marriage. While 60 percent of those from both traditions are married in their thirties, 35 percent of those raised as evangelicals are married in their twenties, compared with only 25 percent of those raised as mainline Protestants. Similarly, more of those who were raised as evangelicals and are in their twenties have children than among those who were raised as mainline Protestants.[16] If marriage and childrearing constitutes settling down, then evangelicals accomplish these tasks earlier than mainline Protestants and thus have fewer years in which to entertain possibilities for religious switching.

The differences between evangelicals and mainline Protestants should not be exaggerated. The majority in both traditions have been raised in their respective traditions and remain loyal to their tradition. They share a similar religious heritage. Sociologically, nearly all of them are white, the majority will eventually marry and have children, and they are widely distributed regionally. Yet the two traditions are often enough on different sides of social and political issues that scholars have been interested in whether the social factors that characterize the two might suggest any signs of convergence or point to continuing divergence. For instance, some scholars have emphasized rising education levels among evangelicals as a trend that will make them more like mainline Protestants in the future, while others note this trend but question whether it holds potential for ideological convergence.

Figure 4.4 shows the changes that have taken place over the past three decades in education levels among young adults who identify with the various religious traditions. Education is especially important in shaping beliefs and lifestyles. It exposes people to new ideas, such as the world views expounded by scientists and in the humanities. It also gives people access to jobs, social networks, and even a sense of being part of the social mainstream that is denied to those with lower levels of education. These potential influences are particularly significant for the young. Young adults are the ones whose life chances and outlooks will be most affected by exposure

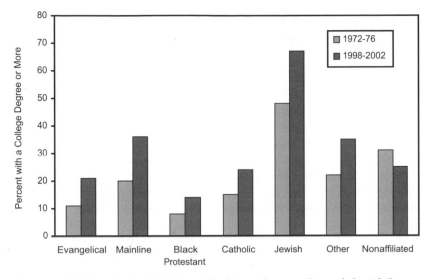

Figure 4.4. Education by Religious Tradition. Source: General Social Surveys, respondents age 21 through 45.

to higher education. Thus, the possibility that evangelicals were becoming better educated has been a matter of keen interest to social observers. What these data show, though, is that the education levels of young adult evangelicals still lag considerably behind those of nearly everyone else (except black Protestants). In the early 1970s, only 11 percent of young adult evangelicals had graduated from college, and that proportion rose to 21 percent by the late 1990s. However, during the same period the proportion of young adult mainline Protestants with college degrees rose from 20 percent to 36 percent. In short, young adult evangelicals at the end of the twentieth century were still thirty years behind their mainline counterparts in terms of attaining college degrees. They also lagged somewhat behind young adult Catholics and considerably behind young adult Jews and young adults affiliated with other faiths.

On other social characteristics, the present data also show very few signs of convergence between evangelical and mainline Protestants. Statistically, young adults who identify themselves as mainline Protestants are less likely than those who belong to evangelical churches to have children, and these differences are as strong, if not stronger, than they were a generation ago. The mainline Protestants are more likely than their evangelical counterparts to be white, and again those differences have not changed statistically. Mainliners are less likely than evangelicals to live in the South, just as they were a generation ago. In fact, about the only demographic factor of this kind on which there is discernible convergence is that mainliners used to be somewhat more likely to live in suburbs than evangelicals, whereas now that difference has disappeared.[17]

BLACK PROTESTANTS, CATHOLICS, JEWS

Between the early 1970s and the end of the twentieth century, the proportions of young adults who identified themselves with historically black Protestant denominations, as Catholics, or as Jews remained remarkably stable. In the earlier period, 9 percent said they were affiliated with black Protestant denominations and that proportion was 8 percent in the more recent period. The proportion who said they were Catholics increased from 28 percent to 29 percent. And the proportion who said they were Jewish remained almost constant at 2 percent (when rounded). In the case of black denominations, the reason for this stability is that American religion has remained overwhelmingly divided by race. Although there have been increases in the proportions of young adults who are African American in each of the religious traditions, these proportions remain small, ranging from 4 percent and 5 percent among Jews and mainline Protestants, respectively, to 6 percent among Catholics and 8 percent among evangelicals. Only among "other faiths" is there a larger proportion of African Americans—reflecting the growing number of black Muslims in the United States. In contrast, 98 percent of the members of black Protestant churches in this age group are African American, and this proportion is higher than it was in the early 1970s.

Among Jews and Catholics, the relative stability in proportions of younger adults affiliated with each is largely attributable to the fact that most Catholics are people who grew up as Catholics and most Jews are people who grew up as Jews. Despite increasing opportunities for religious switching, continuity characterizes most of the members of these traditions. Still, there is some switching (as we saw in figure 4.3) and both traditions have experienced demographic changes of other kinds.

Catholics are attracting fewer new recruits from other traditions among younger adults now than they did a generation ago. Then, nearly 6 percent of Catholics had been raised as mainline Protestants, whereas now only 2 percent have been. The proportion of Catholics who had been raised as evangelical Protestants remained more stable, but shifted from slightly above 2 percent to slightly below 2 percent. Hardly anyone in these surveys who was Catholic had been raised Jewish or black Protestant. If we turn the question around and ask where young adults who were raised Catholic have affiliated, the pattern is roughly the same. Fewer are now becoming mainline Protestants than was true a generation ago (2 percent instead of

4 percent), although (as we saw) more are becoming evangelical Protestants (5 percent instead of 2 percent).

Why might fewer people be switching into or out of the Catholic faith now than in the 1970s? The reasons are complex, but one of the main factors appears to be the relationship between faith and marriage. Not only are fewer young adults who were raised Catholic getting married (48 percent in the recent period compared with 71 percent in the earlier period), but the relationship between switching and marriage is also changing. Thus, in the 1970s, only 15 percent of those who had been raised Catholic and who were married had switched to another faith tradition, compared with 26 percent of those who were not married. By the end of the 1990s, the figure among the unmarried group was about the same (25 percent), while the figure for married Catholics had risen to 22 percent. In short, married Catholics were now more likely to switch out of the faith than they had been a generation earlier.

But if that is the case, it is surprising that Catholics have done as well as they have in the proportion of young adults who affiliate with this tradition. At an earlier time in American history, it might have been reasonable to suppose that this phenomenon was the result of a higher birth rate among Catholics than among Protestants. Research has shown, though, that Catholic and Protestant birth rates had already converged by the 1970s, and in the General Social Survey the proportion of young adults with children is actually lower among Catholics (75 percent) than among mainline Protestants (76 percent) or evangelical Protestants (81 percent) in the 1970s. The better explanation is that Catholic numbers have been bolstered by immigration. Thus, in the General Social Surveys conducted between 1998 and 2002 (despite no interviews being conducted in Spanish), 27 percent of Catholics identified themselves as Hispanic, compared with only 5 percent of evangelicals and 1 percent of mainline Protestants.

The situation among Jews is harder to determine with these data because of fewer respondents in the surveys. However, these data show clearly (as other studies have) that young adult Jews are considerably more dispersed geographically than they were in the early 1970s; for instance, the proportion of young adults who were raised as Jews living in the Northeast has dropped from 58 percent to 39 percent, while the proportions living in the South and West have increased from 7 percent to 17 percent and from 16 percent to 32 percent, respectively. An even more dramatic increase has taken place in the proportion of young adult Jews who report having moved since they were age 16. In the early 1970s, 58 percent said they were still living in the same city and other 12 percent were living in the same state, but in a different city, leaving only 30 percent who had moved to a different state. By the end of the 1990s, only 20 percent said they were still living in the same city and 19 percent reported living in a different city but the same state, while fully 61 percent claimed to be living in a different state. Another significant change is in the proportion of young adults among those who were raised as Jews who are married. That proportion has dropped from 68 percent to 43 percent, while the proportion divorced or separated has risen from 4 percent to 17 percent, and the proportion never married has increased from 38 percent to 39 percent. A corresponding increase in the proportion with no children has also taken place (from 44 percent to 54 percent). These ways of being unsettled do not all have adverse effects on the likelihood of young adults who were raised Jewish remaining Jewish. But some of them do. For instance, the rate of conversion away from Judaism is higher among young adults living in the West than among those living in the Northeast and it is significantly higher among those who are single or divorced than among those who are married and among those with no children.[18]

OTHER FAITHS AND THE NONAFFILIATED

The young adults classified as adhering to an "other faith" in these data are sufficiently diverse to the point that it is difficult to say much about who they are and how they may have changed over the past three decades. Three things, however, stand out. First, the proportion of young adults who fall into this category has increased (as noted previously, from 4 percent to 7 percent). Second, about a quarter of the people in this category are converts from another faith. Third, about half of these people can be identified with a major non-Western religious tradition, such as Islam, Hinduism, Buddhism, or Eastern Orthodoxy, and of those who have grown up in these traditions, the retention rates are very high (above 90 percent). While still a relatively small proportion of the U.S. population, these "other" traditions, therefore, seem likely to continue growing.

The nonaffiliated category is in many ways the most interesting, although we will have to postpone full consideration of what it means and why people choose it until a later chapter.[19] Being religiously nonaffiliated has become more common, but in the process its meaning has changed. In the early 1970s, only about one young adult in eleven was religiously nonaffiliated and, as I noted previously, the nonaffiliates had generally been raised in a religious tradition. To be nonaffiliated was thus to have made a decision to abandon one's religious identity. The nonaffiliated were in fact different from the religiously affiliated chiefly in having been in a context likely to have reinforced such a decision, namely, a college campus. By the end of the 1990s, religious nonaffiliation was less an act of nonconformity than it had been a generation earlier.[20] The proportion of young adults who were nonaffiliated had more than doubled. More had grown up nonaffiliated, meaning that fewer had made conscious decisions about being religiously unidentified. The nonaffiliated were now no more likely to have earned a college degree than young adults who remained religiously affiliated were. The link that had once associated being nonreligious with being better educated was now broken. Statistically at least, if not also culturally, it was possible to be religious *and* educated, rather than feeling as inclined to become nonreligious if one was educated.

BEYOND WINNERS AND LOSERS

One of the saddest developments in recent writing about American religion has been the tendency to view everything as if it were a competitive game, like sports or the business world. To be sure, competition exists among religious groups. I was forcefully reminded of this fact at a gathering of clergy at which I was discussing some of the information in this chapter. After I finished, one pastor held up his hand and said, "I'm not sure how to ask this so it doesn't sound crass, but can you tell us how to be the church in the community that steals members from other churches instead of losing members?" That kind of question stems from the fact that clergy salaries are usually better in large, growing churches than in small, declining ones. It is also reinforced, though, by the dominance of business in our society. Few countries in the world are so deeply wedded to the business mentality. "If you aren't growing, you're declining." "Don't let your competitors run you out of business." But thinking in terms of winners and losers is only part of the story in business, and is even less so in religion.

Evangelicals are winners to the extent that they have not lost membership among young adults, have retained their own youth fairly well, attracted converts, and adapted to a more diverse population. But they are not winners if winning connotes significant growth. By that standard, evangelicals have bogged down and become stagnant, compared with the growth they experienced a few decades ago and the growth they hoped for. Indeed, much of what interests pundits about evangelicals these days is not their numeric growth but their muscle-flexing in politics—which is all the more notable because they still represent only a minority of the public.

Thinking in terms of winning and losing is fundamentally wrong, though, for another reason. That is the fact that in religion, unlike in sports or politics, there is never a declared winner and, for that matter, the winner never takes all. Even if evangelicals doubled their membership, there is no sense in which they would have "won." American religion is pluralistic and will remain that way. It will because of its history and because of cultural inertia. People shop around and some switch traditions, but most do not. More importantly, there are symbiotic relationships among the various faith traditions. Mainline Protestantism is not "losing" to evangelicalism, except in a very limited sense of the word; it is instead strengthened by the presence of evangelicalism—strengthened sometimes by the competitive urge to stay in business, but more profoundly by being different, by providing a space in which theological diversity can flourish, by giving refuge to people who have become disillusioned with fundamentalism, and by upholding traditions of spirituality that have been neglected by evangelical churches. Mainline Protestantism also benefits, often unwittingly, by evangelicals raising their voices on behalf of Christian traditions and the rights of Christians more generally. The same is true of black Protestants, Catholics, and Jews. Unlike Coke and Pepsi, whose managers would be in legal trouble if they met to plot out common strategies, the leaders and rank-and-file members of the various traditions meet all the time to initiate community projects, hold joint services, and discuss common concerns. Beyond that, they also share a common culture and work among their own memberships to support such common values as caring, justice, and religious freedom.

The importance of considering the fate of the various religious traditions among young adults is thus not one of predicting winners and losers. It is rather that each tradition faces particular challenges and, collectively, these traditions shape the larger contours of American religion. The clearest way in which these contours are being shaped by the choices of young adults is in the divide that has emerged—and seems likely to continue emerging—between evangelicals and the nonaffiliated. By most indications, evangelicals are the most committed to their churches, while the nonaffiliated are the least interested in religion. The two appeal to rather different segments of the young adult population, which means (as we will see in later chapters) differences in how they think about other issues besides religion. As a force in the middle, the weakening position of mainline Protestantism is also noteworthy. Still, the fact that black Protestants, Catholics, and Jews are holding their own, and that the "other" category is growing, means that religious diversity will continue. The next wave of adult leaders will certainly not be radically different in terms of religious affiliation than the previous wave. In many ways, they are strikingly similar.

The Bible Tells Me So (I think)

RECENT TRENDS IN RELIGIOUS BELIEFS

IN 1967 THE GERMAN MAGAZINE *Der Spiegel* commissioned a national survey of religious beliefs in the Federal Republic of Germany. In that survey, 68 percent said they believed in God and 42 percent believed in Jesus as the Son of God. A generation later, in 1995, *Der Spiegel* conducted another study of the West German population. The percentage who believed in God had dropped to 56 percent, a decline of 12 points, and the proportion who believed in Jesus as the Son of God had dropped to 29 percent, a decline of 13 points. An even greater shift was evident in beliefs about the Bible. Earlier, two-thirds of the Germans surveyed regarded the Bible as the word of God; by 1995, only half did. Only one in ten believed the Bible was completely true. Not surprisingly, there was a significant age gap in the results. In 1995, younger Germans were about half as likely as older Germans to espouse traditional religious beliefs.[1]

Has the United States experienced a similar erosion in religious beliefs? In the eighteenth and nineteenth centuries, scholars provided good reasons to think that traditional religious beliefs would gradually wane. Scientific advances would discourage people from crediting God for events that could better be understood in terms of natural causes. After Darwin, we would be less likely to believe that God had created humans and that the world had come into existence in seven twenty-four-hour days. Higher criticism of the Bible would at least encourage believers to recognize its historical origins and its mythic dimensions. Over the long haul, superstition would diminish and people would depend more on reason and intellect.

In recent decades, scholars have been less sure about these arguments. The raw brutality of the twentieth century, fraught by totalitarianism and repeated wars and instances of genocide, was enough to cast doubt on arguments about the gradual triumph of reason. As the twentieth century ended, fundamentalist religions seemed to be on the rise, rather than diminishing.[2] Constant levels of church going in the United States were enough to convince some scholars that the whole line of argument about secularization that had been put forth by the most distinguished social theorists of the eighteenth and nineteenth centuries were wrong.[3] Other scholars speculated that the human brain was hard wired to believe in the supernatural. Some noted the continuing evidence of religious belief and concluded that it fit with some evolutionary pattern of cultural adaptation that had taken place over the past thirty million years.[4]

It is hard to avoid concluding that some observers *want* religious belief to be declining and others want it to not be declining. It is equally difficult, though, to avoid pointing out that the question cannot be resolved through theoretical speculation about changes presumed to be taking place over a five-hundred-year historical span, let alone a thirty-million-year span. If we come down to earth and ask what has actually been going on, then there are good reasons to think that young adults may be less convinced by traditional religious beliefs than they were a generation ago—but also good reasons to think otherwise. If religious belief is shaped by the beliefs and values of one's parents, then the young adults of today who were raised by the baby boomers of yesterday may hold less firmly to church doctrines and teachings than young adults did in the past. But it could be that whatever change has taken place already occurred among the baby boomer generation. Similarly, the rise in numbers of young adults who go to college, and the continuing emphasis our society places on science could mean that fewer young adults believe in certain literalist interpretations of the Bible than was true a few decades ago. Yet it could be, as some scholars argue, that beliefs of this kind are less influenced by education and more influenced by the sermons one hears, the friends one keeps, or the rhetoric of national leaders.

SOME POSSIBLE SCENARIOS

Is it possible, then, that religious orthodoxy has simply been declining the way some writers have suggested? Of course this is possible. It could be that young adults are less orthodox in their beliefs than young adults were a generation ago. And it could very well be the case that young adults nowadays hold to the traditional tenets of faith less firmly than older adults do who were raised in a different era. That is certainly one scenario, one way of thinking about change in American religion and one way of imagining what the future may hold. If this scenario is indeed the case, it suggests that orthodoxy is on a slippery slope.

But we need to use our social science imaginations to think a little more deeply about other possible scenarios. I can imagine at least seven interesting ways in which orthodox beliefs may be changing among young adults. We may not be able to test all of these possibilities as thoroughly as we would like. Yet, each one can be tested enough to give us some good hunches about what is actually going on. The first scenario is only a slight modification of the scenario about across-the-board decline in orthodox beliefs. It posits that orthodox beliefs have declined among young adults, but not in the American population as a whole. Statistically, this scenario is possible. Suppose belief in life after death is five percentage points lower among young adults now than among young adults in the 1970s. Suppose also that surveys of the whole population in the two time periods showed no change. What could account for this discrepancy is an increase of five percentage points among older adults. That would balance out the decline among young adults. In fact, an increase among older adults smaller than that could still make up the difference because increasing life expectancy has meant an increase in the size of the older adult population. This scenario is not only statistically possible, but also plausible. Young adults could be less likely to hold orthodox beliefs than in the past for several reasons: less fear of illness and death, less exposure to religious teachings as children, or greater preoccupation with careers and material success. Older adults could be *more* likely to believe in orthodox ways for other reasons: a longer time to contemplate illness and death, more emphasis in churches on the spiritual needs of the elderly, or disillusionment with material success. Thus, this is a scenario we need to consider.

A second scenario posits that the idea of "orthodox beliefs" is more fluid than discussions of them sometimes suggest. Specifically, people's beliefs are not so easily divided into two simple categories, one called orthodox and the other called heterodox (or disbelief). It may be that orthodox belief holds firm, for whatever reasons, but that change takes place in the kinds of beliefs that make up the residual category. The British sociologist Steve Bruce suggests this possibility in some of the insightful writing he has done about religious trends in the United Kingdom. Bruce points out that few people in the United Kingdom consider themselves orthodox believers, but few also regard themselves as atheists. A lot of people are what he calls "implicitly religious."[5] But being implicitly religious is nebulous enough that it can hide changes taking place among those who define themselves this way. When people were raised on orthodox beliefs, those beliefs might still inform their thinking, even if people disagreed with some of them. Later, people might question whether the beliefs themselves were relevant to their lives. In considering young adults in the United States, we need to take account of this possibility. For instance, in surveys that ask people their views of the Bible the most orthodox response usually says something about the Bible needing to be taken literally. Usually at least two less orthodox responses are also given, though. One says the Bible is divinely inspired, but need not be taken literally. The other questions whether the Bible is divinely inspired, suggesting instead that it is a collection of fables and other human writings. Clearly, it is statistically possible for a change to have taken place in the relative balance between the second and third views without any change necessarily having occurred with regard to the first. This, too, is a plausible scenario. Leaving aside older adults completely, imagine how a younger adult might think about the Bible. Some may hold to the orthodox view because they have been raised that way, heard that view articulated in church, or decided for themselves that the Bible should simply be taken on faith as the literal word of God and not subjected to second guessing. Those people might be as numerous now as in the past, especially if their thinking exempts the Bible from any of the criticisms that might be expressed in the wider culture. Among those opting for the less orthodox views, though, there could well be a shift from believing that the Bible is divinely inspired to thinking it is a book of human wisdom. Advocates of the view that the Bible should be taken literally sometimes argue, in fact, that a less orthodox view is necessarily a slippery slope. Start questioning which parts of the Bible to take literally and which ones to reject, they argue, and pretty soon the whole matter is up for grabs. What this example suggests is that we need to ask not only whether orthodoxy holds firm or has been declining, but also whether there may be a growing minority of young adults who opt for a purely secular interpretation of traditional religious teachings.

A third possibility is that orthodox beliefs have remained constant because of countervailing forces in the society. Let us consider the argument Peter Berger laid out some years ago in his widely read *Sacred Canopy*.[6] Berger argued that orthodox belief is more a matter of faith than of factual evidence or logic and is thus maintained mostly by being around other people who believe the same way. He called this a *plausibility structure*. Like-minded people go through life without questioning what they do or what they believe. If everyone drives on the right-hand side of the road and stops at red lights, it seems only natural that this is the appropriate way to behave. But put people in a more diverse context, Berger argued, and questions start flying. Why do we believe this way? Why do those people believe differently? Who is right? This argument is particularly relevant to the situation in the United States today. Through the various processes of globalization, more of the population is composed of Muslims, Buddhists, Hindus, people of other faiths, and secular humanists than ever before. American Christians are exposed to this diversity and to the wider diversity in the world that comes about through mass communications and travel. That would all suggest more questioning of orthodox Christian beliefs and thus an erosion in the number of young adults holding those beliefs. However, just the opposite argument has also been suggested. R. Stephen Warner has proposed what he calls a *new paradigm* that turns Berger's argument on its head.[7] Religious diversity, Warner contends, actually increases the likelihood that people will believe in the tenets of their own faith. The reason, Warner says, is that religion functions pretty much like the economy: a free market stimulates competition and thus causes all boats to rise.

Religious entrepreneurs work harder to spread their message and attract members. But it is possible that *both* Berger and Warner could be right. Perhaps diversity does weaken orthodoxy, as Berger suggests, but perhaps this weakening is counterbalanced by the competition that Warner posits. If so, we might find that religious orthodoxy remains relatively constant, even though it is influenced in some ways by increasing diversity.

A fourth scenario poses the possibility that people can be orthodox and heterodox at the same time. Religious beliefs at the popular level are never quite as systematic or consistent as they are in the minds of theologians. Suppose a person believes it is necessary to be a Christian in order to go to heaven. The logical implication of that belief is that people who are not Christians will not go to heaven. However, a person who holds the first of these beliefs may be unwilling to take the logical step required in acknowledging the second. He or she may believe, for instance, that God will find other ways to save non-Christians, or may argue that only God knows what will happen, thus denying that logic applies. This is what James Davison Hunter calls *cognitive bargaining*.[8] Religious beliefs nowadays, he argues, are negotiable. Nobody is burned at the stake for denying some particular creedal proposition. Everybody has the authority to make up their own minds. That is how we understand belief—something that is personal, idiosyncratic, and always somewhat tentative. In fact, Hunter argues that belief has come even more to be thought of in this way in recent decades. Thus, we might find that young adults are just as likely now as young adults were a generation ago to voice acceptance of orthodox teachings, and yet hedge their bets through cognitive bargaining.

The fifth possibility we need to consider is that young adults are not all the same. Even though they all live in the same society, they are not exposed to the same cultural influences. Consider the fact that somewhere around half of young adults currently spend at least some time on a college campus and the other half does not. That difference alone could affect how people think about traditional religious teachings. Religious beliefs are, to be sure, matters of faith, but they are also matters of the mind. One has to *know* about the teachings to believe in them. And educational settings are supposedly the major place in which we learn how to think. It is in these settings that we decide that science can answer some questions about life and not others, or that logic applies or does not apply to some kinds of decisions. Now, if a person's education stops with high school, it is unlikely that very much specifically will have been said in the classroom about religion—unless of course one goes to parochial school or has been home schooled. Public high schools leave religion out of the curriculum for the most part. This means a person with only a high school education could just as well hold to orthodox beliefs now as a person could who went to high school thirty or fifty years ago. Decisions about those beliefs would have been made in other contexts. The experience of someone who had gone to college might be very different. That person is likely to have taken some classes, say in philosophy or science, that specifically challenged his or her orthodox beliefs. If nothing else, going to college kept that person in an educational setting longer and thus increased the possibility of emphasizing rational, cognitive processes in matters of belief. Having said that, we also need to consider the possibility that college campuses are less favorable to religious orthodoxy than they were in the past. The historian George Marsden has amassed considerable evidence suggesting that this is the case. At least the long-term trend in the history of American higher education, Marsden argues, has been one of secularization. Fewer colleges are under the control of church boards than in the past, fewer require attendance at chapel services, more money is spent on science and research, and religion is more likely to be taught as a topic than as a conviction.[9] Marsden's argument may or may not apply to changes having taken place just within the last thirty years. But if it does, then we might imagine a scenario of declining orthodox belief among college educated young adults. By the same token, we might imagine one of no decline among young adults without college exposure. Or, because those with fewer privileges sometimes react against those with more opportunities, we might even posit that orthodox belief could have increased among those with lower levels of education while increasing among those with more education.

Having introduced the role of higher education, I want to suggest as a sixth scenario the possibility that the *relationship* between education and orthodox belief may be changing. This scenario may seem obscure at first, but it is an important one to consider. The unstated assumption in the previous scenario is that orthodox belief is somehow irrational and unscientific and thus conflicts with the more rational and more scientific world view espoused in American higher education. But suppose that assumption is wrong. Some would argue that orthodox religious belief is actually quite rational and scientific. That may be the case, but it is not my principal argument here. Instead, I want to suggest that higher education is often not as rational or scientific as we think. It tries to be. But research on the effects of higher education and on what actually happens when students are on campus points to other aspects as well. Higher education is, among other things, an avenue for becoming special. If you have a college degree and I do not, your degree sets you apart. It gives you prestige that I do not have. In the process of earning it, you also made friends with people like yourself and different from mine. You are part of what we used to call the "country club" set: you play golf for fun, dress differently, and get invited to dinner parties that the rest of us do not get invited to. I say we used to talk that way. That was when it really was distinctive to have been to college. It is no longer so special to have earned a college degree. The expansion in higher education over the past half century means at least that more people have been to college or junior college—quite a few more—and having a college degree is no longer a mark of being among the *elite* in most communities. What does this have to do with religion? At one time it was a mark of being *au courant* to have graduated from college *and* to be a religious freethinker. It was just in poor taste to be an educated intellectual *and* a believer at the same time. As the number of people who have been to college has grown, though, that segment of the population has also become more diverse. It includes more women and people of color, for one thing. It may also include more people who hold orthodox beliefs. In short, this scenario suggests that orthodoxy may hold steady, but change in terms of its social meaning. If it formerly ran counter to the social expectations of being an educated person, perhaps it no longer does.

Finally, we need to consider the possibility that orthodox beliefs are faring differently in different faith communities. Consider what we know thus far. Evangelical denominations, as we have seen, have pretty nearly held their own among young adults over the past generation, whereas mainline Protestant denominations have declined. Leaving aside black Protestants, Catholics, and Jews for the moment, the relative trajectories of the two Protestant traditions could hold an interesting story about orthodox beliefs. Is it possible that these beliefs have remained firm among evangelicals, possibly even having increased, but declined among mainline Protestants? The possibility that evangelical Protestants are still committed to orthodox beliefs is almost true by definition. The more interesting possibility is that these beliefs may be more common than in the past (or among young adults than among older adults). Some credence in this possibility comes from Christian Smith's research on American evangelicals. Smith found particular vitality among evangelicals in terms of beliefs, church practices, and child rearing. He also found that evangelicals felt themselves *embattled* in relation to the wider culture. Their beliefs were not only a matter of faith but also of distinguishing themselves from the wider culture.[10] By implication, it could be that young evangelicals are holding even more firmly to orthodox convictions than, say, older evangelicals because they feel themselves to be beleaguered by the wider culture. In contrast, mainline Protestants may be on the kind of slippery slope mentioned earlier. Their identity is, if anything, that of *not* being evangelical. It may be increasingly *de rigueur* to distance oneself from the orthodox beliefs that define people as evangelicals.

Some readers may now wonder if we can really distinguish among these scenarios and whether it matters. My answer on both counts is yes. We can determine with actual data which ones are better than the others. It also matters. As a social scientist, I find myself continually frustrated by questions from journalists about trends in American religion. For them, it always seems to be a matter of something going up or something going down, period. Social reality is more complicated than that. The same applies to students of social science who interpret arguments about secularization simply in terms of whether certain numbers are falling or remaining constant. There is a lot more to be understood about religious change than that. We cannot understand young adults' views about even the most standard orthodox beliefs unless we consider the complex ways in which these views can change.

Decline in Orthodox Beliefs?

Surveys conducted over the past half century by the Gallup Organization, Harris Poll, and other research organizations have periodically asked the public questions about such topics as whether they believe in God, an afterlife, heaven, hell, and the truth of the Bible. These questions are often not very good because they reduce topics about which there may be great uncertainty or theological disagreement to simple "yes" or "no" responses. Nevertheless, these are the questions about orthodox belief on which much of our sense of how "religious" the American public is are based. Despite their limitations, these questions have at least been asked the same way over the years and thus make it possible to assess trends.

There are plenty of reasons to think that the United States is becoming less religious in terms of these traditional beliefs. In the 1950s, when many of the polls were first conducted, the United States was experiencing a wave of religious fervor induced by anticommunism and the Cold War. Many people still lived on farms where their livelihoods were continuously affected by the "hand of God." A relatively small percentage of the population had been to college and thus been exposed to serious reading in philosophy or science of the kind that might have raised religious doubts. By the time the baby boomers came of age in the late 1960s and 1970s, all that was changing. Fewer people lived on farms and more went to college. In the eyes of some, religion was part of the "establishment" and for that reason to be regarded skeptically. Some religious leaders themselves were advocating the view that God was dead. The young adults of today are the offspring of those baby boomers. If their parents had become skeptics, they, too, would likely have been reared in an atmosphere of skepticism.

But the core religious beliefs that pollsters have studied have remained remarkably pervasive and stable. For instance, Gallup Polls that have asked variously about belief in God, a universal spirit, or higher power continue to elicit assent from between 90 and 95 percent of the public, just as they did in the 1950s. Other questions do not evoke that much belief, but suggest that a sizable majority of the public holds to some of the core tenets of religious faith. Between two-thirds and five-sixths of the public, for example, usually asserts belief in life after death, heaven, and hell.[11]

News releases provided by polling organizations rarely make it possible to determine if the trends reported for the whole population are the same among young adults. However, there are a couple of reasons for believing they are. One is that age breakdowns sometimes are reported for questions about religious beliefs, and these (unlike church going, which is generally lower among younger adults) usually show few differences between younger adults and older adults. For instance, a Gallup Poll conducted in 1994 found that 96 percent of the public believed in "God or a universal spirit," and the figures for respondents in various age categories ranged from 94 percent among persons 18 to 29 years old, to 97 percent among those 30 to 39 years old or 50 to 59 years old, 95 percent among those 40 to 49 years old, and 96 percent for those in their sixties or older.[12] The other reason is that some surveys actually do offer the opportunity to look in greater detail at younger adults, and these surveys show no evidence of declining beliefs. For instance, World Values Surveys conducted in the United States in 1980 and again in 2000 showed no significant decline in belief in God among young adults.[13]

The General Social Surveys included only one belief question in both the early 1970s and more recent surveys: a question asking people if they believe in life after death. The answers to this question suggest no decline in religious belief among young adults since the early 1970s. If anything, there has been an increase (see figure 5.1). For instance, among men in their twenties, the proportion who say they believe in life after death has risen from 74 percent to 79 percent; among men in their thirties, from 75 percent to 78 percent, and among men in their early forties, from 79 percent to 80 percent. Among women, comparable increases have taken place in each age group (5 percentage points for those in their twenties, 3 points for those in their thirties, and 5 points for those in their early forties).

Andrew Greeley and Michael Hout analyzed this question about belief in an afterlife for the whole population. They attribute the increase mainly to Catholics and Jews, and find that these increases appear to be the result of assimilation. That is, older cohorts who were more recent immigrants from other countries were *less* likely to believe in life after death, whereas Catholics and Jews who have lived longer in the United States are more likely to believe in life after death. Apparently, then, Catholics and Jews are influenced by the dominant Protestant culture, the longer they live in the United States, and that Protestant culture encourages belief in life after death.[14]

One wonders, of course, whether that argument is the reason *young adults* in the past thirty years have become more inclined to believe in life after death—and, if it is, whether the General Social Survey's lack of non-En-

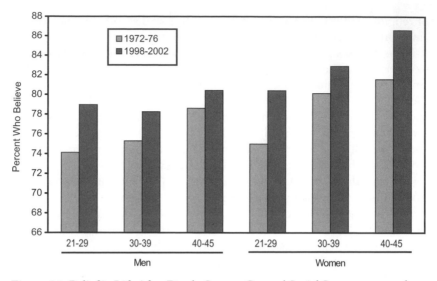

Figure 5.1. Belief in Life After Death. Source: General Social Surveys, respondents age 21 through 45.

glish-speaking respondents might bias the conclusion. The data for young people do show that Catholics and Jews are more likely to believe in life after death now than they did in the early 1970s. But the data also show that belief among black Protestants, mainline Protestants, and the religiously nonaffiliated has increased.[15]

Other questions about religious beliefs also suggest that these basic beliefs probably have not been changing very much—at least not enough to show up as differences when age groups are compared. In the Religion and Diversity Survey I conducted in 2003, for example, between a third and two-fifths of all age groups claimed to believe that the Bible is the actual word of God and should be taken literally. In the same survey, about two-thirds of young and old alike regarded Jesus as the divine son of God.[16]

ORTHODOXY, WITH RISING SECULARITY

The possibility that orthodox beliefs have held steady, but that those who reject these beliefs have become more secular is more difficult to test than the idea that orthodox beliefs have simply declined. The reason is that more nuanced questions are required, and these generally have not been asked with the same wordings over a long period of time or using a standard methodology. Some conclusions can be drawn, though, from the question about the Bible that we just considered. This question was developed for

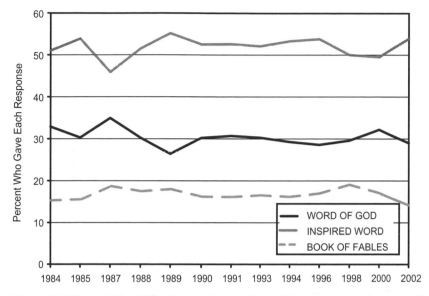

Figure 5.2. Views of the Bible. Source: General Social Surveys, respondents age 21 through 45.

use in the Gallup Poll and has been asked periodically since 1976. In that year, 38 percent of the public opted for the literalist view, 45 percent said the Bible was inspired but not to be taken literally, and 13 percent said it was a book of fables. In brief, these responses were quite similar to the ones from the Religion and Diversity Survey in 2003 (and the differences could be attributable to differences in research methodology). Other surveys in which the same question was asked also fail to suggest that there has been a significant shift in the general population from the view that the Bible is inspired to the view that it is a book of fables. For instance, a Gallup Poll in 1978 found that 11 percent regarded the Bible as a book of fables, while a 2004 survey conducted by the Pew Center for Research on People and the Press showed 13 percent.[17]

Over a shorter period, the General Social Surveys permit us to examine beliefs about the Bible among *young adults* and in surveys for which there have been no changes in methodology. As shown in figure 5.2, the proportions of adults age 21 through 45 who viewed the Bible as the word of God and to be taken literally varied from a high of 35 percent in 1987 to lows of 26 percent in 1989 and 29 percent in 1994, 1996, and 2002. Overall, though, the figures suggest only a very small decline over this 18 year period.[18] Similarly, the proportions who thought the Bible is inspired but not to be taken literally varied between 46 percent and 54 percent, but show no overall downward trend. And the proportions who regarded the Bible as a book of fables varied between 14 percent and 19 percent, also suggesting no overall decline.

This question about views of the Bible, I should note, has been utilized by scholars so frequently because, of all the ways one might think about orthodox beliefs, it seems to be the most telling single question available. And for good reason. The litmus test over which denominations have split has often been interpretations of the Bible.[19] Believers who held that the world had been created in seven twenty-four hour days argued that the Bible should be interpreted literally. Believers who insisted that the Bible was free of error and not to be judged by scientific or historical criteria argued for the same interpretation. Other believers who identified themselves as theological moderates or in some instances as "neo-orthodox" opted for the view that biblical inspiration could be divine without involving a literal interpretation. In contrast, those who held the Bible to be a book of fables generally denied that it had been divinely inspired. There is also reason from research itself to think that this survey question about the Bible does a good job of dividing the American public into those with orthodox beliefs on other items of faith and those with less orthodox views.[20] For instance, in the Religion and Diversity Survey there were seven other questions (including the one about Jesus) that dealt with such orthodox beliefs as Christianity being the only way to have a personal relationship with God and the Bible being the unique revelation of God's will and trustworthy for spiritual guidance. The responses to these questions were all highly correlated with responses to the question about views of the Bible. These correlations were also much higher, by the way, than that between the Bible question and the General Social Survey question about life after death. Thus, in most of the discussion that follows, I will focus on responses to the question about views of the Bible and occasionally on responses to other questions that correlated highly with it.[21]

It is significant that the conclusions from studies conducted at different times and those from comparing age groups within recent surveys are the same. In neither case, does it appear that young adults are less orthodox in their beliefs than they were in the past or than people are now who were young in the past. Nor is there evidence that people with nonorthodox beliefs have become more secular, at least in their views about the Bible. This also seems to be the case for beliefs about Jesus. Although we do not have time-trends for this question, the responses to the question mentioned previously about Jesus do not suggest that young adults and older adults differ very much in regarding Jesus as a human prophet like Muhammad or Buddha. Seventeen percent of those in their twenties said they believed this about Jesus, but so did 14 percent of those in their thirties and early forties, and 15 percent of those in their late forties through age 64. Only among those age 65 and older was the proportion significantly smaller (8 percent). If there has been a shift in these views, then, it probably took place awhile ago, rather than being distinctive to today's young adults.

Countervailing Effects of Diversity

The possibility that religious beliefs are being affected by increasing exposure to religious diversity is especially interesting in view of immigration patterns and the globalization of American culture. Since the events of September 11, 2001, Americans have become increasingly aware of tensions among the world's major religions and their implications for ordinary life. With Peter Berger, we might suppose that greater exposure to religious diversity would mean a weakening of conviction about the exclusive truth of Christianity. With Stephen Warner, though, we might imagine people feeling threatened by other religions and thus holding all the more firmly to their own beliefs.

Young adults are presumably on the front lines of these developments. Large numbers of immigrants are young and much of the immigration that has brought Muslims, Buddhists, and Hindus to the United States is fairly recent. Thus, young adults would have had more opportunities to mingle with people of other faiths in high school or in college than would have been the case for their parents or grandparents. However, the differences are most pronounced between people in their twenties and those in their thirties, and again between people in their late forties to early sixties and people age 65 or older. For instance, 32 percent of people in their twenties say they have had at least a fair amount of contact with Muslims, compared to about a quarter of those in their thirties through early sixties, and only 11 percent among those age 65 or older. Similarly, 20 percent of people in their twenties claim to have had contact with Buddhists, a proportion that drops to 13 percent among those in their thirties through early sixties, and the then drops to only 7 percent among those 65 or older. I point out these particular patterns because they suggest some important qualifications to the idea that exposure to religious diversity is simply increasing. It is, but the widest exposure to non-Western religions is limited to young adults in their twenties. This means that the effects of exposure to religious diversity on religious belief may be even more important in the future than in the recent past. Also, we need to recognize that contact between Christians and Jews is probably not increasing or at least is not limited to the young.

Does contact with people of other religions discourage religious orthodoxy or encourage it? It is pretty clear from the evidence in figure 5.3 that greater contact with diverse religious groups is associated with a *lower* likelihood of holding orthodox Christian beliefs, rather than with a higher likelihood of holding such beliefs. The comparisons shown in the figure

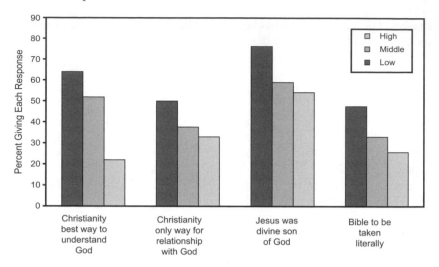

Figure 5.3. Religious Beliefs by Diverse Contacts. Source: Religion and Diversity Survey, respondents age 21 through 45.

are for three groups: those who said they had not had a fair amount of contact with any of the groups mentioned previously ("low"), those who had a fair amount of contact with at least one of the groups ("middle"), and those who had at least a fair amount of contact with two or more of the groups ("high").[22] Among adults age 21 through 45 with the most interreligious contact, only 26 percent thought the Bible should be taken literally, whereas 48 percent did among those with low interreligious contact. Similarly, 54 percent of those with high contact believed Jesus was the divine son of God, compared with 76 percent of those with low contact. The two questions about Christianity showed similar patterns.

We should not assume that interreligious contact is necessarily the *cause* of lower adherence to orthodox Christian beliefs. It could be the other way around: orthodox believers avoid contact, while less orthodox beliefs encourage such contact. We know, though, from other questions in the same survey that interreligious contact generally occurs in the workplace or through business dealings, rather than through deep personal friendships or in religious settings. Interreligious contact may thus be hard to avoid, and when it does occur, may encourage people to be less orthodox in their views. If that is the case, though, why have orthodox beliefs remained relatively unchanged in recent years? One reason is that most Americans still do not have extensive contacts with people from non-Western religions. The other reason is that Warner's argument about religious competition may have more validity than these results alone would suggest. My reason for suggesting this is that Berger and Warner, it seems to me, are actually talking about two different things. Berger's argument pertains mostly to people believing in the exclusive truth of their own tradition. That is the kind of belief that may erode when people become acquainted with adherents of other religions and realize that those people are good, reasonable people just like they are. Warner is not as concerned with belief per se, as with the energy people invest in promoting their beliefs. If they feel threatened by another religion, they may or may not entertain doubts, but they are more likely, Warner would argue, to feel it important to work hard on behalf of their own faith. Thus, it is interesting to consider a couple of other results from the same survey. I asked people the following question: "As you know, many Muslims, Hindus, and Buddhists from other countries have moved to the United States in recent years. As a result, do you think Christianity will become a lot weaker, a little weaker, a little stronger, or a lot stronger?" Among adults age 21 through 45, a majority (57 percent) thought Christianity would become stronger (23 percent said a lot stronger), while only 27 percent thought it would become weaker (and 16 percent thought it would remain unchanged or weren't sure). I also asked, "As a result of these new groups, do you feel your faith will be a lot stronger, a little stronger, a little weaker, or a lot weaker?" Sixty-six percent of adults age 21 through 45 said stronger (30 percent a lot stronger), while only 5 percent said weaker.

It is always wise to be cautious when interpreting questions about what people *think* will happen in the future. I find it interesting, though, that so many people believe their faith will remain strong, even though orthodoxy itself seems to be weaker among those with more exposure to religious diversity. Perhaps those who are the most orthodox will become more vigorous in defending their orthodoxy. Perhaps those who are less orthodox will also adhere even more strongly to their faith. However, these considerations also point to the possibility of another scenario.

ORTHODOXY MIXED WITH HETERODOXY

In this scenario orthodox religious beliefs do not tell the whole story. People may hold traditional views on some religious tenets, while adapting to the culture in other ways. An orthodox belief about the Bible can be so familiar that it serves as a kind of litmus test of being a devout, conservative Christian. We saw earlier that saying the Bible is literally true correlates well with other orthodox beliefs. In qualitative interviews people who are biblical literalists use such words as "inerrant" and "true" to emphasize their belief that the Bible can be trusted. Yet there is still room to interpret the Bible in ways that permit living comfortably with the complexities of contemporary life. For instance, the Bible may be literally true, but not the *only* way

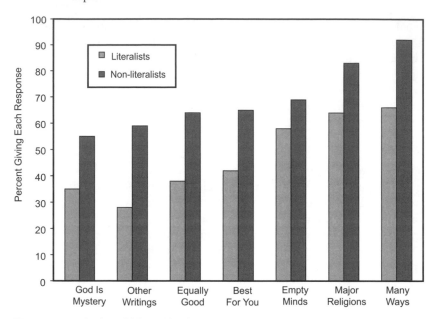

Figure 5.4. Beliefs Held by Biblical Literalists. Source: Religion and Diversity Survey, respondents age 21 through 45.

in which God's truths are revealed. Those truths may even be revealed in other writings, such as the sacred texts of other religions.[23] While insisting that the Bible should be taken literally, biblical literalists may not mean that in quite the way a theologian or philosopher would, either.

A woman in her early twenties provides a helpful illustration of biblical literalism in practice. She grew up in an evangelical church, was always taught that the Bible is divinely inspired and free of errors, and considers it important to regard the Bible as literal truth. Yet she learned about evolution in school and considers it possible to believe in both evolution and creation. Seeming contradictions like this bother her a little, but she thinks it is possible to reconcile the two. From day to day, though, her approach to biblical truth is more personal and practical. "When I read the Bible [which she does almost every day], I do it by myself with a notebook," she says. "I underline things that I think are pertinent to my life. Or things that are striking. Or things that I find to be really, 'Wow! I really find that true.' So I'll underline it and write it in my notebook and write about it." She says she picks out the things that she "sees as the truth."

The possibility of pick-and-choose orthodoxy makes it interesting to see how biblical literalists respond when asked questions that might evoke more relativistic or pluralistic responses. These are shown in figure 5.4. I have also included the responses of people who are not biblical literalists for purposes of comparison. The responses shown are for adults age 21 through 45. On every question, the nonliteralists are more likely to give the response shown than the literalists are—which simply confirms that these questions are tapping into nonorthodox views. But it is notable how many biblical literalists also give these responses. Thus, two-thirds of biblical literalists think "God's truth is revealed in many ways, such as history, nature, culture, and tradition," rather than "only in the Bible." Believing in these multiple sources of divine truth, of course, opens up possibilities for having to balance what one reads in the Bible against what one experiences in nature, learns from history, and so on. Almost as many biblical literalists (64 percent) agree that "all major religions contain some truth about God." Orthodox belief is thus compatible with religious pluralism at least to that extent. It does not require believers to reject all other religions as sources of falsehood. A majority of biblical literalists (58 percent) also hold the interesting view that "God can only be known as people empty their minds and look inside themselves." In short, whatever faith one has in the truth of the Bible is tempered by the view that one should not think very much about it—or anything else, apparently. The other responses shown in figure 5.4 are not held by a majority of biblical literalists, but suggest additional ways in which some biblical literalists soften the potential difficulties of holding too narrow a view of the Bible. For instance, about four in ten (42 percent) relativize their view that Christianity is the best way to understand God by saying it is best for them *personally* and not necessarily best for everyone. About a third (35 percent) assert that "God is a mystery and can never be understood by humans." This may be another way in which they can hedge if questions about how exactly to interpret the Bible become too thorny. More than a quarter of biblical literalists believe that "God's word is revealed in other writings besides the Bible."[24]

We can see even more clearly how young adults combine orthodox beliefs with other beliefs in figure 5.5. These responses are from the Arts and Religion Survey that I conducted in 1999. The items in the chart that elicited assent from the largest proportion of biblical literalists were "my religious beliefs are very personal and private" and "my spirituality does not depend on being involved in a religious organization." Other studies have shown how widespread these views are in the American public (not only among young adults). The interesting result here is that they are shared by about two-thirds of biblical literalists. Thus, a person might believe firmly in the Bible, but not talk about it very much or respect someone with a different interpretation because of regarding religious belief as a matter of private interpretation. Another notable aspect of biblical literalism that is evident here is the large proportion of biblical literalists who read the Bible at home less than once a week. To be sure, they read it more often than nonliteralists do; nevertheless, a majority (51 percent) of biblical

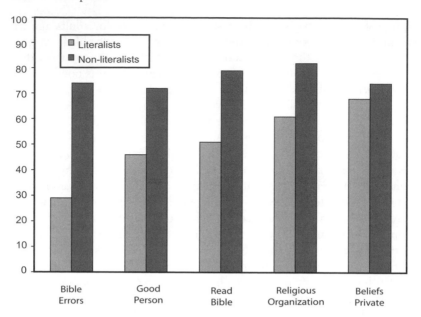

Figure 5.5. Beliefs and Practices of Biblical Literalists. Source: Arts and Religion Survey, respondents age 21 through 45.

literalists do not consult the Bible on their own even once a week. Believing in the Bible, again, appears to be an item of faith, more than something grounded in knowledge. In view of the frequency with which some religious leaders espouse the importance of biblical inerrancy, it is also noteworthy that about three in ten biblical literalists (29 percent) believe "the Bible may contain historical or scientific errors."

Writers who insist on arguing about religious belief simply in terms of whether it is declining or not declining miss the nuances of what we have just been considering. We know from research on other topics (such as political opinions) that people have a remarkable capacity to hold inconsistent beliefs and values. That is probably true with regard to religion as well. It is, though, not what I am suggesting here. My point is rather that orthodox beliefs are not quite as rigid or narrow as many people have supposed. I doubt if they ever were, but the present evidence suggests that they certainly are not currently. For those who favor the view that religion is withering on the vine, this may be the evidence they are looking for. However, it may also be the reason why orthodox beliefs are faring as well as they are. People do not reject them because they can so easily be hedged. Cognitive bargaining of this kind can take many forms. People can believe the Bible should be interpreted literally and yet regard it as one truth among many, as a private belief, and as one that a person should not even think about very much. None of this diminishes their sense that the Bible is true. It just gives them a way to negotiate their relationship with that truth.

DIFFERENT TRENDS AMONG EDUCATIONAL CATEGORIES

In this scenario I suggested that there may be *two cultures* among young adults in the United States today: one composed of those who have been to college and the other composed of those whose education stopped with high school. This is certainly an idea that economists have advanced. In their view, going to college puts young adults on a track for better and more stable jobs in the professions and higher incomes. Not going to college relegates young people to lower-paying jobs in construction and the service industry. I suggested further that these two cultures might tell us a lot about the fate of orthodox religious beliefs among young adults. Not going to college could leave a person unexposed to the kinds of criticism that might undermine some orthodox beliefs, such as belief that every word in the Bible should be taken literally. Going to college could expose a person to those kinds of criticism. Moreover, there are reasons to think the two cultures are more different from each other now than in the past. At least we have the testimony of some scholars that higher education is more thoroughly secular than ever before.

The best evidence we have to test this supposition is the question about views of the Bible in the General Social Surveys. As we saw previously, this question has been asked in surveys over a two-decade period using exactly the same methodology, and the responses among young adults overall suggest little change. Thus, if our hypothesis about cultural divergence is right, the reason for this lack of change would be that better educated young adults have become less orthodox in their beliefs while those without college educations have become more orthodox. The actual results are shown in figure 5.6. They show that just the opposite from what we predicted has been the case. Young adults with no college education have become *less* orthodox since the early 1980s, while young adults with some college education have become *more* orthodox. There has been some fluctuation in the two lines shown in the graph from year to year, but the two lines certainly have not diverged. When linear trend lines are computed, they show that there was about a 27 point spread between the two groups at the start of the period, but only a 15 point spread by the end.[25]

Since the actual data run counter to what the scholarly literature led us to predict, we obviously need to think differently about what has been taking place. Neither trend is dramatic and we do not have data over a long period, so we need to be careful not to draw too many conclusions from

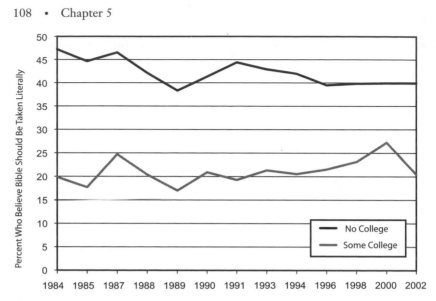

Figure 5.6. Biblical Literalism by Education. Source: General Social Surveys, respondents age 21 through 45 (percent who believe Bible should be taken literally).

this evidence. However, there is reason to think the trends evident here correspond to some of the realities in the wider culture. Young adults with college educations are more numerous now than they were a few decades ago. They are also more diverse racially, ethnically, and religiously, as well as being composed of larger numbers of women. Going to college still encourages people to reject orthodox beliefs, or at least the kind of person who rejects orthodox beliefs is more likely to go to college, judging from the gap separating the two lines in the graph. But a larger proportion of the college-trained population has retained its belief in an orthodox view of the Bible than in the past.[26] At the same time, those who go no further than high school are apparently exposed to secularizing forces more than in the past. One of these forces may be the public school system itself, which is sometimes accused of being hostile to religion because of adherence to increasingly strict interpretations of the separation of church and state. The other force may be television and other forms of mass media—also widely regarded as being alien to a religious world view, and perhaps especially influential to the thinking of people who have not been to college.

CHANGING RELATIONSHIPS WITH EDUCATION

As I mentioned earlier, another scenario is that the relationships between orthodox beliefs and levels of education have been changing. Specifically,

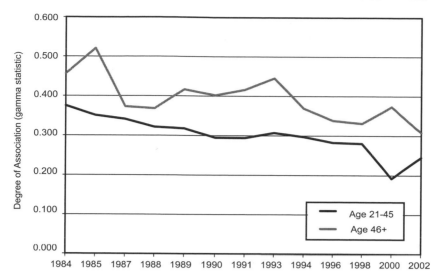

Figure 5.7. Relationships between Education and Views of the Bible. Source: General Social Surveys.

these relationships may be weakening as a larger share of the population goes to college and the college-educated population thus becomes less of an elite and more internally diverse. Statistically, this would almost have to be the case because the proportion of Americans with college training has been rising while, as we have seen, the proportion holding orthodox beliefs has remained constant. These changes are illustrated in figure 5.7. The chart shows the relationship between years of education and views of the Bible for each year in which a survey was conducted between 1984 and 2002. I have calculated these relationships separately for adults age 21 through 45 and for adults age 46 and older. Both lines slope downward and thus indicate weakening relationships between level of education and views of the Bible.

Substantively, this change indicates that more of the college-educated population takes a literalist stance toward the Bible than in the past or, viewed differently, that more biblical literalists are college trained than in the past. It could also mean several other things. One may be that campus cultures are not as hostile to biblical orthodoxy as they once were (or have been presumed to be) and this, in turn, could be related to the fact, as we saw, that young adults often hedge biblical literalism with other beliefs that render it more relativistic and personal. At least a biblical literalist would find more kindred spirits at college than formerly. If this interpretation is correct, it contradicts the inference that we might have drawn from Marsden and others about increasing secularization of colleges and universities.

It is more consistent with the argument advanced by historian Conrad Cherry and his coauthors about campuses formally being secular but informally providing many opportunities for believers to express themselves and maintain their convictions.[27] Yet another possible interpretation of these figures is that orthodox religious beliefs may not be as influenced by cognitive frameworks as they were in the past (or were assumed to be). The point could be made this way: if religious belief is presumed to have a strong rational basis, as some philosophers argue, then we would expect to see a close relationship between people's level of education and the kinds of religious beliefs they hold. But if religious belief is more about faith and experience than about rational arguments, and if education is as much about social status as it is about styles of thought, then we would expect a weaker relationship between religious belief and education. The trends evident in the data are not huge, so we should not make too much of them. However, it is valuable to consider the range of ways in which the changing relationships between belief and education can be interpreted.

Different Trends among Faith Communities

The final scenario I sketched out earlier suggests that orthodox beliefs may have fared differently in recent years in the different faith communities—specifically, that orthodox beliefs may have held steady or increased among evangelicals, but declined among mainline Protestants. To test this argument, we can again learn the most from the data about views of the Bible. Because we want to compare young adults affiliated with each of the major faith communities we discussed in the last chapter, we need to aggregate the results from some of the surveys in order to have enough people in each category. In figure 5.8 I have combined young adults in the three earliest years in which the Bible question was asked (1984, 1985, and 1987) and compared them with young adults in the 1998, 2000, and 2002 surveys. The main conclusion from this information is that the likelihood of holding literalist views of the Bible has changed very little during this period in any of the major faith communities (the number of Jews is too small to put much stock in those changes). The specific notion that orthodox beliefs may have increased among evangelicals but decreased among mainline Protestants is not supported.

There is one indirect way in which the differences among the major faith communities are relevant, though. As we saw in the last chapter, the relative size of those faith communities has changed, specifically with evangelicals remaining constant, mainline Protestants becoming fewer, and the nonaffiliated becoming more numerous. Thus, if we think about those different faith communities as places in which different beliefs are reinforced, we

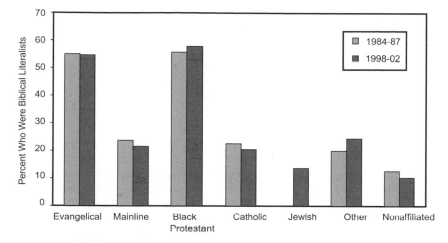

Figure 5.8. Biblical Literalism by Religious Tradition. Source: General Social Surveys, respondents age 21 through 45.

would have to conclude the following: evangelical churches are still reinforcing orthodox beliefs at about the same rate they were a decade or two ago, mainline Protestants are much less likely than evangelical Protestants to hold orthodox beliefs, and there are fewer of these mainline Protestants; nonaffiliation goes hand in hand with rejecting orthodox beliefs, and more young adults are nonaffiliated now than in the past. The overall likelihood of holding orthodox beliefs has not changed very much, therefore, but the location of nonorthodox views has shifted slightly from mainline churches to people who are nonaffiliated.

Spirituality and Spiritual Practices

THE ROLE OF FAITH IN PERSONAL LIFE

SPIRITUALITY IS ALWAYS about much more than going to church and agreeing or disagreeing with church doctrines. Spirituality is the shorthand term we use in our society to talk about a person's relationship with God. That relationship is always complex. For many people, how they think about it is certainly guided by what they see and do in their congregations. At a deeper level, it involves a person's self-identity—feeling loved by God, for example. These feelings wax and wane. Sometimes a person feels close to God, while at other times God seems distant, uncaring, or angry. Spirituality also manifests itself in what people do, especially those activities through which they attempt to relate to God or follow God. People who write about spirituality have come increasingly to emphasize this *doing* aspect of spirituality. A century ago, when William James wrote his famous treatise on the *Varieties of Religious Experience*, it made sense to scholars to think about religious experience as something that happened to people or that reflected some inward state or predisposition.[1] Today, it is more common to view the spiritual life in active, rather than passive, terms. Religious experiences happen because people seek them out, put themselves in harm's way, so to speak, where they can better feel God's presence or hear God speak. In other instances, religious experiences strike people unexpectedly, but then result in activity. People interpret what they have experienced, try to make it happen again, or make changes in their lives that reflect their experiences.[2]

The one thing that people who take an active interest in their spiritual life do is to make choices. They choose how much of their time and attention to devote to their relationship with God. They look for things to read, people to talk to, and other sources of guidance. Sometimes they seek answers to theological questions that are bothering them. Sometimes they search for ways of expressing some desire they may have to feel closer to God, to worship, or to serve. The choices they make may involve major decisions in life, such as who to marry and whether to marry someone of the same faith or a different faith. Other choices involve searching for a place to worship that fits one's interests and the needs of one's family. People also make choices about which religious services to attend, which teachings to accept or reject, and how to make sense of the messages about religion and spirituality with which they are constantly bombarded by the mass media.[3]

Some scholars believe these choices about religion and spirituality can be understood as rational choices and thus reduced to the same logic as economic decisions. My interest here is not to debate whether those economic analogies make sense or do not make sense. The more important point is simply that people do make choices—and choices usually involve some kind of seeking or search behavior. Moreover, the availability of choices and the need to engage in seeking have never been greater. We live in a free society, as our political leaders like to remind us. We are free to do as we please, at least within the constraints of law and human decency. Freedom in this ideal sense is also increasingly a reality of life for many Americans. The putative freedom a person has to buy consumer products of his or her choosing increases as people have more discretionary income to spend on such products. I may not have the wherewithal to purchase a fancy house, but I can choose among a range of inexpensive dwellings, and I can exercise great freedom in, say, purchasing groceries or deciding which television programs to watch. This kind of freedom is contingent on finances. The freedom to make choices about religion and spirituality is influenced to some extent by finances, too, but it is governed more by cultural norms and by religious organizations themselves. In one era, it may be unthinkable to choose the congregation one attends. That decision is made by where one lives or by one's extended family. In another era, it would be unthinkable not to make such choices.

A man in his late twenties says he has been making choices about spirituality ever since he graduated from high school. His parents were Christians and he went to church faithfully as long as he lived at home. At some point, though, it dawned on him, "I believe in Christianity, but that's all I've ever known, so how can I know it's the truth if I don't look around and see what else is out there?" His quest to develop a satisfactory faith of his own has involved piecing together ideas from any source that comes his way. A friend of a friend "knew this Muslim guy" who encouraged him to "check out the Qur'an." He read some of it and came away with new ideas about Jesus. About this time, *The Celestine Prophecy* was popular, so he read it. One day somebody left a copy of a book about Buddha where he was working, so he waded through it. His aunt was a "New Age-y type of person" who took him to a New Age bookstore and showed him some things to read. Through a cousin he got involved in a nonsectarian social justice group. The most memorable part of that experience, though, was witnessing a robbery and murder, which left him shaken and thinking harder than ever about God and the frailties of life. Since then, he has taken a college class in comparative religions, listened periodically to late-night religious radio stations, absorbed a lot of music, been deeply influenced by a friend who converted to Orthodox Judaism, and experienced little "revelations or epiphanies." He talks philosophy with one of his friends, looks at the stars and sunsets because "they are awesome," and buys fresh flowers every now and then to remind him of beauty as an aspect of spirituality. He considers himself a Christian mostly because Christianity emphasizes God's love. That has given him a sense of freedom to grow and explore. He summarizes, "I'm continuously messing up [but] I'm just learning more and more. . . . I'm going to learn for the rest of my life."

We cannot understand young adults' spirituality without paying special attention to the choices they make and the seeking in which they engage. Young adults are on the cutting edge as far as choice and seeking are concerned. Many have been reared by parents who encouraged them to think for themselves and to make such choices. The geographic mobility and general unsettledness of our society gives opportunities to make choices that are unprecedented. Seeking is also conditioned by living in a society that often does not supply a single best answer to our questions or needs. This is why seeking results in tinkering. It becomes not only possible but also necessary to cobble together one's faith from the options at hand. There may be many suitable congregations to attend. For many young adults, there are also options for combining teachings from different religions and for selecting innovative ways in which to express one's spiritual interests.

Our considerations in chapter 3 of who chooses to attend religious services and in chapter 4 of who remains in the religious tradition in which they were raised and who switches to a different tradition have already required us to think about the choices young adults make. Scholars have concentrated on these kinds of choices because information about them was readily available. But we now need to push deeper. There are myriad ways in which young adults behave as spiritual tinkerers. We need to understand the choices involved, why people make the choices they do, and how the necessity of choosing and tinkering becomes a distinctive style of spirituality.

Church Shopping and Hopping

I begin with two of the more common—or at least commonly discussed—kinds of spiritual tinkering: church shopping and church hopping. They sound so similar that they are sometimes confused. Church shopping involves tinkering with one's religious loyalties by looking for a congregation to attend, presumably one in which a person will settle and become a regular member. It usually involves a serious commitment to find a suitable place to worship, make friends, and pursue one's spiritual interests within a faith community. Church hopping involves going from one congregation to another, rather than settling into a single congregation. Surprisingly little research has been devoted to either phenomenon. Researchers who write about religious switching focus on shifts from one denomination or tradition to another, while neglecting the fact that people engage in shopping whenever they change congregations, even within the same denomination (except perhaps when they join a new congregation through a friend or family member). Church shopping is of great interest to clergy and to lay people themselves. Many churches have special programs for newcomers and some churches advertise themselves as being seeker friendly. Yet we know little about how many people may actually be in the market as church shoppers. Similarly, little is known about church hopping. Anecdotal evidence sometimes turns up individuals who say they go to more than one church regularly or who visit various congregations instead of settling into any particular congregation. Anecdotal evidence also suggests that this kind of hopping may be more common when people are young and unsettled than when they are older and settled. But research to date has not examined these suppositions.[4]

In a national survey I conducted in 1999, I was able to include a question that asked, "As an adult, have you ever shopped around for a church or synagogue?" Among adults age 21 through 45 who had attended religious services at least once a month while they were growing up, more than four out of ten (41 percent) said they had shopped for a place of worship as an adult.[5] The factors that increase the likelihood of having shopped for a place of worship include having lived at a number of different addresses. Among the majority of young adults who have lived at more than five addresses during their lifetime, 42 percent have shopped for a place of worship as an adult, whereas among those who have lived at three to five addresses, this proportion falls to 32 percent, and among those having lived at only one or two addresses, it falls further to 28 percent. The social class level of one's parents is another factor that affects the likelihood of shopping for a place of worship at least slightly: if one or both parents have a college degree, it is more likely that their offspring will have shopped for a church as an adult. The education level of the person has an even stronger relationship with the likelihood that he or she will shop for a place of worship. Forty-seven percent of young adults with college degrees say they have shopped for a church, compared with only 34 percent of those with high school degrees. These factors all point to the conclusion that people with more resources and greater opportunities are the ones most likely to engage in church shopping. Two other factors, though, also matter: being married and having children increase the likelihood of church shopping. The reason is probably that being married and having children are incentives to find a suitable place of worship. Church shopping is thus a reflection both of opportunity and desire.

Shopping for a place of worship presumably is like shopping for an automobile, a house, or even a spouse: one enters the market in order to make a selection, and once that selection is made, a person no longer stays in the market. What is popularly referred to as church hopping is different. Church hopping involves staying in the market, or, perhaps better, tinkering with several possible selections, rather than settling down with one. Among adults age 21 through 45, approximately four in five (81 percent) attend religious services at least once or twice a year and this number splits about evenly between those who always attend at the same place and those who do not. Thus, 42 percent of young adults say they sometimes attend at other places. And 16 percent say they do this frequently. Some of the factors that increase the likelihood of church shopping also increase the likelihood of church hopping, but some have just the opposite effect. Having lived at more addresses is associated with church hopping, just as it is with church shopping. Having parents with college degrees is, too, as is having been to college oneself. Unlike church shopping, though, church hopping is more common among single people than among married people. It is also more common among people without children than among people with children. Overall, then, church hopping is partly a function of opportunity and perhaps the kind of seeking mentality that comes with higher education, but church hopping is also a function of being unsettled. The fact that young adults move around as much as they do, marry later, and remain childless longer thus suggests that church hopping is a phenomenon more common now than in the past.

Church hopping is intentional for some young adults: they attend more than one place because they find variety appealing. It may also be a matter of expedience: perhaps they travel a lot, visit their parents, or see friends, and thus find themselves in different communities on weekends. They may simply go to one Baptist church some of the time and a different Baptist church on other occasions. There is a more dramatic form of church hopping, if it can be called that. This involves visiting places of worship quite different from one's own. The young person who goes with his or her Catholic youth group to visit a synagogue would be an example. So would the person traveling abroad who visits a mosque or Hindu temple. It is impossible to say how common this kind of visiting across religious lines was in the past, but chances are that it has become more common in recent years as travel has become easier and the United States has become more religiously diverse. Among adults age 21 through 45, 22 percent say they have attended services at least once at a synagogue, and an equal number have attended services at a Buddhist temple or center, 8 percent say they have attended services at a Muslim mosque, and 7 percent say this about a Hindu temple. In all, about one young adult in three (32 percent) has attended services at one or another of these places of worship. As with church shopping and church hopping, residential mobility appears to increase the chances of attending at diverse houses of worship: 37 percent of those who have lived at more than five addresses have done so, compared with only 26 percent of those having lived at only one or two addresses. Education, though, has an even stronger effect. Young adults with college educated parents are considerably more likely to have attended services at one of these non-Christian places of worship, as are those who themselves have graduated from college. Like church hopping, not having children is associated with this kind of religious activity (and so is being unmarried, although to a lesser degree). Finally, one of the most significant factors is travel: among those who have traveled (or lived) outside the United States, 42 percent have worshipped at a non-Christian place of worship, compared with only 18 percent of those who have not been outside the United States.

SOCIAL NETWORKS

Religious leaders have always recognized that it is one thing for people to come to church every Sunday morning and sit quietly by themselves among strangers, but quite another thing to feel that one is truly part of the congregation. In his classic study of religious behavior in Detroit in the 1950s, Gerhard Lenski emphasized this *communal* dimension of religious participation, as he called it.[6] The communal dimension is related to the issue of church shopping and church hopping because people who fail to settle into a congregation are also less likely to feel at home there. The communal dimension is also complicated. For some people, it may consist of nothing more than a sense of attachment, of feeling at home in a particular worship setting, whether or not one knows the other people there. For others, feeling truly attached to the congregation may require having many personal friends as fellow worshippers, while for still others one or two intimate friends in the congregation may be sufficient. Lenski, though, found that a good way of getting a general handle on communal attachment to the congregation was by asking people how many of their close personal friends belonged to the congregation. In more recent parlance, we would call this *social capital*. If one's close personal friends are in the congregation that means the congregation is important in a lot of ways. Our personal identity is reinforced by our friends. Our opinions and beliefs are, too. Peter Berger's idea of a plausibility structure referred to this relationship between beliefs and friendship networks.[7] Having trusted friends in the congregation who believe the same way we do reinforces our sense that these beliefs are good and true.

Unfortunately, the General Social Surveys from which we have been drawing information did not ask a question about congregational friend-

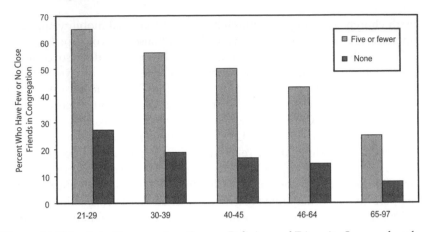

Figure 6.1. Friends in Congregation. Source: Religion and Diversity Survey, church members only.

ships in the 1970s and again more recently. Thus, we cannot make temporal comparisons to see if these kinds of friendships are similar or less common among young adults than they were a generation ago. We can, however, look at patterns among young adults in a recent survey and compare those with friendships among older adults in the same survey. These comparisons will not tell us whether things are changing, but they do provide a way of determining if young adults are as closely connected to their congregations as older adults are. We can also see if some of the same factors that influence church attendance also influence these friendship patterns.

Figure 6.1 shows the percentages of *church members* within various age categories who say they have 5 or fewer friends in their congregation or who have no friends in their congregation. The data are from the Religion and Diversity Survey. The key result is that young adults are much more likely than older adults to have few or no friends in their congregations. In fact, among those in their twenties 65 percent have 5 or fewer friends and 27 percent have no friends in their congregations. These proportions gradually diminish, but even among those in their early forties, more have few or no friends than among people in their late forties and older.

Why do so many young adults have so few friends in their congregations? It is not, as one pastor speculated, because lonely people gravitate to churches in hopes of finding friends. In fact, we know from other research that church goers tend to be more gregarious than people are who do not attend.[8] The social factors that encourage friendships are very similar to the ones that encourage attendance. The most important factor is being married. Among young adults in their twenties, those who are married are 10 percentage points more likely to have more than five friends in their congregation than those who are not married. Among those in their thirties, the difference is 8 percentage points, and the same is true among those in their early forties. Once marriage is taken into consideration, having children does not increase the likelihood of having friends in one's congregation. Perhaps surprisingly, the differences between men and women as far as having friends in their congregation are not statistically significant. What also matters, though, is being settled in one's community. In fact, the odds of having friends in one's congregation are reduced by about 20 percent for each time a person has moved since he or she was 18 years old.[9]

Some additional evidence on the religious practices of young adults comes from a national survey conducted for *Religion and Ethics Newsweekly* in 2004.[10] As in other studies, this survey found that regular attendance at religious services was quite low among young adults in their twenties. Only 29 percent said they attended services weekly. Attendance was higher among young adults in their thirties (32 percent said they attended weekly), but did not equal that of older adults until people were in their early forties (46 percent in that age group attended weekly). The study found that participation in other organized religious activities was also low among young adults. For instance, only 12 percent of young adults in their twenties participated weekly in an "informal religious or prayer group" (another 10 percent said their participated at least once a month), and the proportions in their thirties and early forties who participated weekly were not much higher (18 percent and 14 percent, respectively). Yet this lack of participation in organized religion did not mean that young adults were disinterested in religion.

The vast majority (more than four in five) said they talk about religion with their friends at least once or twice a year. And about half that many (two in five) talk about religion with their friends at least *once a week*. Moreover, unlike the pattern for church attendance, which increases with age, the proportion who talk about religion with their friends is *highest* among young adults in their twenties, next highest among young adults in their thirties, and lowest among young adults in their early forties.[11] I can only speculate about why this might be the case, but my guess is that young adults in their twenties talk more with their friends about everything—because they are not yet married and absorbed in their own families, and perhaps because they are still making up their minds about important life issues. In any case, the fact that young adults talk this much with their friends about religion flies in the face of arguments about religion having become a purely *private* matter. Most of us have probably been told that it is not polite to talk about religion or politics at dinner parties or other formal occasions. Yet, if these data are correct, it is perfectly acceptable to most people in young adulthood to discuss religion with their friends. Being "private" about one's faith means that it should be personal, a matter of opinion, and not dictated by the formal teachings of churches, but not that a person should be silent about it.

The importance of talking about religion with friends becomes clearer when information about young adults reading religious books, newspapers, or magazines is considered. The proportions are considerably smaller than the ones for talking about religion with friends. Instead of four-fifths saying they do this once or twice a year, about two-fifths do. And instead of two-fifths saying they do so once a week, about a quarter do. The other difference is that reading, like church attendance, is *lowest* among young adults in their twenties, and then gradually rises after that. For instance, only 24 percent of those in their twenties say they read religious materials once a week or more (as do the same proportion of those in their thirties), compared with 38 percent who do among those in their early forties. Again, I can only speculate about the reasons for this pattern, but assume that reading religious materials is encouraged by participating in religious organizations. It may also be stronger among people who are thinking about the religious training of their children.

The main inference from these two pieces of information is that religious ideas among young adults probably circulate more by word of mouth than through the books and magazines people read or even the sermons they hear. This means that young adults are probably influencing one another in forming opinions about religion much more than they are being shaped by the formal teachings of religious organizations. We are in this sense a culture besieged with information, and yet a society in which so much information has forced us to improvise, to rely on our friends and our personal experiences, and to view all information from published sources with a healthy dose of skepticism. From the perspective of religious leaders, one can look at this as a glass that is half full or half empty: it may mean that *some* young adults are particularly interested in church and religious teachings, and they become opinion leaders, spreading their ideas to other young adults through conversations with their friends; or, less favorably for religious organizations, it may mean that young adults are looking much more to their own opinions and those of their friends than to ideas grounded in religious teachings.

CIVILITY

If spirituality is a matter of improvising, it goes without saying that people have to get along with those who are improvising in different ways. We may talk to our friends about spirituality and appreciate their *opinions*, but we are unlikely to appreciate our friends telling us what to do, and we are probably reluctant to offer our own opinions too strongly. This is what

John Murray Cuddihy described as the culture of civility.[12] It becomes incumbent on each of us to hedge our religious convictions in a language of opinion and feeling.

A twenty-eight-year-old man who grew up in a Pentecostal church, still considers himself an evangelical Christian, and believes firmly that Christ is his Lord and Savior says: "My faith is inherently divisive. I'm one of the only Christians I know of among my friends and my views are harshly criticized a lot, either to my face or behind my back. I have friends in my circle who are atheists, gay, agnostic, Muslim, Jewish, you fill in the blank. I've had to ask myself and God, 'What shall I do with them?' Condemn them? Love them? And if I love them, what does that look like?" The answer he has come to is being a "waterer," a "beacon of light." But he adds: "I don't know how often I do that. That's a whole other conversation."

Evidence of how strongly social norms of civility influence the religious views of young adults is available from the *Religion and Ethics Newsweekly* Survey. Respondents in the survey were first asked if they agreed or disagreed that "It is important to spread my faith." About half of those in their twenties and thirties (53 percent and 54 percent, respectively) agreed, and then among those in their early forties 70 percent did (which was more, even, than among older people). Of course spreading one's faith can be done in various ways. To see what people had in mind, respondents were then asked if they agreed that "it is important to convert others." Framed this way, the statement drew agreement from considerably fewer respondents than the previous statement had. Thirty-six percent of those in their twenties and 37 percent of those in their thirties agreed, and then the proportion rose to 49 percent among those in their early forties. In contrast, when people were posed with a less obtrusive way of spreading their faith—"The best way I can spread my faith is by setting a good example for others to follow"—nearly everybody agreed. Eighty-seven percent of people in their twenties, 92 percent of people in their thirties, and 94 percent of people in their early forties agreed. In short, spreading one's faith means being a person who persuades by example.

Nancy Ammerman has called this kind of religious civility "Golden Rule Christianity."[13] Being a good Christian, according to this view, means following the Golden Rule. A person spreads his or her faith by treating people the way he or she would like to be treated. That applies especially to proselytization. You probably would not like it if someone from a different religion tried to convert you to that religion. So, following the Golden Rule, you would not try to convert them to yours, either.

But does this kind of civility hold among young evangelicals? After all, evangelicals are the ones who feel they have a mandate to tell others about Jesus. Their tradition teaches that only Christians will be saved and go to heaven. Judging from the same survey, young white evangelicals are indeed more inclined to believe this way than are young Americans in general. In fact, more than nine in ten agree that it is important to spread their faith (96 percent of those in their twenties, 93 percent of those in their thirties, and 93 percent among those in their early forties). With the exception of only a few people, they also agreed that the best way to spread their faith is by setting a good example for others to follow. Where there is less agreement is about the importance of making converts. About half say they strongly agree, a quarter to a third agree somewhat, and about one in six disagrees. This means, though, that evangelicals are much more inclined to believe in conversion than other young adults are. Indeed, evangelicals in their twenties are *more likely* to agree strongly that it is important to convert others than evangelicals in any other age group except those past the age of 65.[14]

Maybe young evangelicals *believe* they should convert others to their religion but do not actually put their beliefs into practice. Such would not be surprising. Many people give lip service to beliefs and values that make little difference to the way they live (for instance, telling researchers they hate materialism, despite having a $40,000 SUV in the garage). But, unless they are lying, young evangelicals also seem to be putting their convictions into action. Seventy-eight percent of evangelicals in their twenties say they have tried to convert others at some point in their lives, and 73 and 74 percent, respectively, of those in their thirties and early forties say the same. Again, these figures are about in the same range as those for older evangelicals (76 and 67 percent, respectively, for people age 46 to 64 and 65 and older). If young evangelicals are becoming timid about trying to convert others, it certainly is not evident in these figures.

The study also sheds light on *whom* evangelicals try to convert. Not surprisingly, evangelicals who have tried to convert anyone usually say they have tried to convert their friends (more than 90 percent say this). Almost as many say they have tried to convert family members (between 78 and 84 percent say this). But proselytization does not end there. Coworkers are fair game, too, it seems. Sixty-five percent of evangelicals in their twenties who have tried to convert anyone have tried to convert coworkers, as have 55 percent of those in their thirties or early forties. Evangelization also apparently takes place on airplanes and street corners. Sixty-one percent of evangelicals in their twenties who have tried to convert anyone say they have tried to convert strangers, and nearly as many of those in their thirties or early forties have (48 percent and 57 percent, respectively). In short, young evangelicals may be the exception to the rule when it comes to norms of civility, at least if civility means timidity in seeking to make converts.

Before we conclude too hastily that young evangelicals are out proselytizing people of other faiths, though, we need to consider what they say when asked specifically about talking to such people. In the Religion and

Diversity Survey, respondents who said they were Christians were asked, "In the past year, how many times have you talked specifically with anyone who was not a Christian to persuade them to become a Christian?" Among all Christians age 21 through 45, about half (48 percent) said they had done this at least once in the past year. The figure among *evangelical* Christians age 21 through 45 was 68 percent. Among these evangelicals who had tried to convert someone in the past year, though, only 11 percent claimed to have spoken about Christianity to a Muslim, even fewer had spoken to a Hindu (6 percent) or Buddhist (8 percent), and one in six (17 percent) had spoken to someone who was Jewish. Most of their evangelizing was thus with people who did not already belong to another religion. In fact, 55 percent said the person or persons they had spoken to were atheists, and 89 percent described them simply as "someone who did not go to church."

Are Converts Different?

The fact that so many young evangelicals have tried to convert others to born-again Christianity raises the interesting question of whether those who are *converts themselves* may be more aggressive about doing this than those who were raised as evangelicals. More than a half century ago, the writer Eric Hoffer popularized the idea in his book *The True Believer* that converts have a special stake in believing that their new-found faith is the one true path.[15] Hoffer was writing about converts to political ideologies, such as fascism and communism, rather than religion. But his ideas have often been entertained by scholars writing about religious conversion. Converts often describe their lives as before-and-after stories. Before they found Christ, they were angry and jealous, drank too much, and had bad family relationships; after they found Christ, they cleaned up their act and led victorious lives.[16] Associating their new life with being a Christian, they understandably want others to experience the same joy they have found. If this argument is valid, we would then expect that evangelicals in the data we have just been considering who did not grow up as evangelicals would be *more likely* than those who did grow up as evangelicals to say they have tried to convert others.

The *Religion and Ethics Newsweekly* data make it possible to test this idea because, even though the number of people in the study is not as large as in some other studies, 42 percent of white evangelicals between the ages of 21 and 45 in the survey said neither of their parents was a born-again Christian, while 58 percent said one or both of their parents was born-again. Thus, we can compare the two groups. The short answer is that converts to born-again Christianity, by this definition, are *less likely* than those who were raised in evangelical homes to say they have tried to covert others (by a margin of 70 percent to 77 percent). They are also less likely to say they strongly agree that it is important to convert others (45 percent versus 58 percent).

We need to be careful about making too much of these results. What they suggest, though, is that young evangelicals believe in making converts because they grow up in families and churches where that idea is taught, not because they have recently been born-again and need to validate their own decision. This is not to say, however, that psychological dynamics are absent from young evangelicals' efforts to convert others. As we will see in chapters 7 and 8, young evangelicals believe strongly that their own religious and moral convictions are right and that those of the mainstream society—"the world"—are wrong. Thus, it makes sense to them that people in "the world" should convert and become born-again Christians. If they did, the argument goes, then we would all be better for it.

SEEKING ANSWERS

Thus far, I have focused mostly on the choices young adults make in relation to faith communities. The evidence points to the willingness—even the necessity—of negotiating those relationships. Young adults are no longer born into faith communities that embrace them fully and command their allegiance over a lifetime. It becomes necessary to shop for a place of worship, rather than simply inheriting the congregation in which a person is raised. For some, this means participating in more than one congregation—congregational bigamy, rather than serial monogamy. In young adulthood, friendships are important to a person's religious identity, just as they are important sources of personal identity more generally. Yet these friendships are less likely to be concentrated in a single congregation and more likely to be composed of acquaintances from other spheres of life. For evangelical Christians, such diverse networks provide opportunities to share one's faith. However, norms of civility kick in to ease the potential abrasiveness of such encounters. Norms of civility mean that faith communities have blurred boundaries. Their members can pass back and forth across these boundaries more easily. The same is true of a different aspect of spiritual seeking.

This is the seeking people do when they are confronted with the intractable mysteries of life—with questions about God, heaven, how the universe came into existence, and what it all means. We saw in chapter 5 that a third or so of young adults believe the Bible is literally true. Presumably, the Bible supplies the answers they need to these questions about the mysteries of life. Yet we need to look more closely. Some might argue that biblical literalists, representing only a minority of young adults, fail to tell us the larger story about the seeking in which young adults are currently engaged. We saw some evidence in chapter 5 suggesting that even biblical literalists do not consult the Bible very frequently. We might wonder, too, if young adults are still interested in these intractable questions. So many distractions exist—sports, entertainment, work, families. Who now spends time thinking about questions that defy even the minds of philosophers and scientists?

One way to answer this question is to consider what people say when asked if they have ever spent time trying to imagine various things, such as the questions that religion, philosophy, and science sometimes address. These topic might include: what God is like, what angels are like, what heaven is like, how the universe came into existence, if there is life on other planets, and if there is a reality beyond the one we know.[17] What survey responses showed is that those of younger adults do not differ very much from those of older adults. Between 30 and 50 percent of people in all age categories have thought about these various questions a lot (most of the remainder have thought some about them). This pattern is notable because it disconfirms the idea, sometimes posited by secularists, that young adults are just too smart (or busy) to waste time considering the imponderables of life. There is a second observation, though, that partially qualifies the first. The responses to the particular questions do vary, and they vary in ways that make sense psychologically and culturally. The question that more people in all age categories have thought about than any of the others is the one about heaven. This is not surprising. Death is a constant. It is something that everyone faces, and thus the possibility of heaven and what it may be like is a relevant existential question for everyone. We saw in chapter 5, too, that as many people (if not more than a generation ago) believe in life after death now. The only surprising thing about the responses to the question about heaven is that interest in it does not increase with age (in fact, it is somewhat lower among people in their seventies and eighties). Had the question asked people if they had thought a lot *recently* about heaven (or death) the responses might have been different. The pattern of responses about what God is like is different than the one about heaven. Here, younger adults are less likely to say they have thought a lot about what God is like than older adults are. It may be that younger adults think they know what God is like. However, it is more likely that the nature of God is a theological or church-oriented question that simply does not interest young adults quite as much as older adults (though, about two in five younger adults think about it a lot). As we saw in chapter 5, many young adults believe God is simply a mystery that cannot be understood by humans, and many others believe that emptying one's mind is the only way to relate meaningfully to God. The question about angels shows few differences between younger and older people. This may be a function of the fact that books and other discussions about angels have been as popular as they have been in the wider culture. A person, young or old, hardly needs to be an active church goer to have been exposed to these discussions. The other questions—how the universe came into existence, life on other planets, and a reality beyond the one we know—are ones where religion and science intersect most clearly. And for that reason, they are probably of greater interest to young adults who are, or who have recently, faced them in high school or college or in conversations with their friends. In any case, younger adults are more likely than older adults to say they have thought a lot about these questions.[18]

The point of this information about the perennial questions of human existence is that young adults still think about them—at least as much as older adults do. This means that young adults are or have been engaged in a quest of some kind for answers to these questions. For some young adults, the quest is an intellectual one; it is a search for answers in the same way a person might look for answers to questions about the circumference of the earth or the population of the world. For many others, though, it is a search that involves dreams, fantasy, make-believe, symbols, and rituals. This is why the wording of the question asked people what they had tried to *imagine*.

When people seek answers to these kinds of spiritual questions, where do they look? Information does not exist that would tell us specifically where people go to find answers to questions about, say, God or life on other planets. However, we can say something about the range of influences that people credit with having shaped their thinking about *religion or spirituality* in general. Not surprisingly, Christian teachings and practices are the most commonly mentioned of these influences. Younger adults, however, are less likely to say that Christian teachings and practices have been an important influence on their thinking about religion or spirituality than older adults are. The second most commonly mentioned influence is music. And younger adults are *more* likely to say this has been important than older adults are. It is also possible of course that the *kind* of music that has been influential is different for younger adults and for older adults. (We will look more closely at music later in the chapter.) Studying or reading about science and studying or reading about philosophy are additional influences that younger adults mention more frequently than older adults. Finally, a larger proportion of young adults in their twenties has been influenced by Buddhism, Hinduism, or Islam than among adults in their thirties through fifties, with adults age 65 and older the least likely to have been influenced by these religions.

If we think of seeking, then, as behavior that crosses the traditional boundaries separating religion from other spheres of life, or Christianity from other religions, younger adults are seeking answers to religious and spiritual questions in ways that transcend these traditional boundaries. This is by no means a development limited to the current period. People who have had the resources and freedom to do so have long sought answers to the mysteries of life in art, music, philosophy, and science as well as through religion. And those opportunities are now available to a larger number of young adults than ever before. We might say, in fact, that *most* young adults nowadays shop for answers to deep spiritual questions in multiple venues. For instance, only 19 percent of young adults age 21 through 45 say their thinking about religion or spirituality has been influenced *only* by Christian teachings and practices, whereas 48 percent say they have been influenced by Christianity and at least one of the other influences I just mentioned, and 18 percent say they have been influenced by one of these other influences and not by Christianity (15 percent had not been influenced in any of these ways).[19] Moreover, the factors that reinforce seeking in venues beyond Christianity are largely the ones we saw earlier in considering church hopping: being single, not having children, having been to college, having a parent who went to college, and having traveled outside the United States.[20]

SPIRITUAL PRACTICES

In previous writing, I have stressed the importance of distinguishing between spiritual seeking and spiritual practice. Seeking often consists of casual shopping around, such as reading a magazine article about angels or chatting with a friend who happens to have been raised in a different religion. Seeking has its place. Especially in young adulthood, it is a way of exploring one's options, of moving beyond the received wisdom of one's religious upbringing and developing a deeper and more personal understanding of one's own. However, people who have sought casually in various venues usually report feeling at some point that they need to become more serious about their spiritual life if they are to grow in it and mature. Spirituality is in this respect like learning to play the piano. It requires practice.[21]

Within Christianity, it has always been customary to emphasize certain devotional practices as ways of deepening one's faith. Prayer and Bible reading are the two practices that have been emphasized the most. In addition, especially in recent decades, meditation has also come to be emphasized. Through these practices people become intentional about their relationship with God. Instead of waiting for the happenstance occasion when God speaks through a beautiful sunset or an illness, the person seeks to be in God's presence. Prayer involves talking to God and listening for God's leading. Bible reading may be the way in which God's leading is heard. Meditation quiets the mind and puts one in a prayerful attitude.

The question is whether young adults nowadays are cultivating these spiritual practices or not. On the one hand, interest in spirituality seems to be widespread. Judging from magazines and television, young adults are interested in all kinds of spiritual pursuits—from watching programs about angels and witches to attending movies and concerts in which religious themes are featured. In polls, 75 percent of adults age 21 through 45 say it is at least fairly important to them to grow in their spiritual life, and two in five (42 percent) say their interest in spirituality has been increasing (while only 8 percent say it is decreasing).[22] On the other hand, serious engagement in spiritual practices, like regular participation in congregations, may be something young adults do not make time for until they are older. If people in their twenties flock to *Lord of the Rings* and *Passion of the Christ*, it may not be until they are in their fifties that they start meditating and reading their Bibles.

This second possibility is the one best supported by evidence. Prayer is fairly common among the American public, perhaps because people count a quick "God help me" on the highway as prayer, but it is considerably less frequent among younger people than among older people. Fewer than half of Americans in their twenties (47 percent) pray nearly every day, while about three quarters (72 percent) of those in their late forties and older do. Bible reading follows a similar pattern, although far fewer Americans in any age group read the Bible than pray. About 20 percent of people in their twenties and thirties read the Bible nearly every day, whereas this proportion rises to nearly 50 percent among those in their late sixties or older. Although meditation has been promoted in recent years through alternative health organizations and in some businesses, as well as through religious organizations, it, too, is less common among young adults than among older adults. Only 8 percent of people in their twenties meditate nearly every day, compared to 31 percent of those age 65 and older. It could be that young adults are just too busy or have schedules that keep them from engaging in devotional activities every day. However, the evidence also suggests that large numbers of young adults are simply disinterested in these activities. For instance, among young adults in their twenties, about a quarter never pray, and a majority never read the Bible or meditate.

One other aspect of prayer deserves our attention, though. Prayer, as I mentioned, is usually thought of as talking to God and listening for God's leading. For this reason, discussions of prayer, whether in churches or among researchers, usually focus on the *content* of prayer. What do people talk about when they pray? Do they appropriately thank God for blessings received? Do they pray selfish prayers about finding parking places or winning the lottery? Do they ask for healing? And do they receive it? The information in figure 6.2 casts prayer in a rather different light. It shows what people *do* when they pray, not just what they talk about, and thus

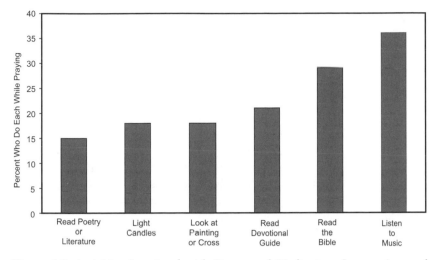

Figure 6.2. Activities Associated with Prayer and Meditation. Source: Arts and Religion Survey, respondents age 21 through 45 who ever pray or meditate.

emphasizes *context* rather than content. Among Americans age 21 through 45, a surprisingly large proportion (nearly two out of five) say they listen to music or sing when they pray or meditate (this is when they pray or meditate at home, not in church). That proportion is even larger than the proportion who read the Bible or a devotional guide when they pray. For a significant minority of young adults, looking at a cross or painting, lighting candles, or reading poetry or literature is part of their prayer life as well. In short, ambience is important. To be sure, psychologists can herd subjects into a laboratory and ask them to pray and study whether the prayers cause a dial to jump. But people who take prayer seriously know that how one prays and the context in which one prays are also important.

Music and Art

The role that music plays in the prayer lives of young adults and, as we saw earlier, its more general role as an influence on their thinking points to its importance as a broader consideration for understanding the changing nature of spirituality. It is not that music has been unimportant in the religious lives of older Americans. It is rather than younger Americans are more exposed to it and value it in a different way. This is especially true of music, but is also the case for the visual arts and some other kinds of artistic expression.

Other than simply listening to the radio, the most common form of exposure to music is through purchasing a tape or compact disc. More than four-fifths of adults in their twenties have done this within the past year, but this proportion gradually declines to about half that among people age 65 and older. Exposure to the visual arts is also quite common. About three-fifths of adults in their twenties have taken art classes while they were growing up; fewer than three in ten among those age 65 and older did so. The proportions who have attended a live concert or opera during the past year, who went dancing during the past year, or who played a musical instrument growing up are also much more common among the young than the old.[23]

This greater exposure to music and the arts among younger adults does not mean that they are more likely to find God through music and the arts than older adults are. It does mean that younger adults take a more inclusive attitude toward the relationship between the arts and spirituality. Whereas older adults worry about music and art sending the wrong signals, younger adults accept it. For older adults, spiritually uplifting music and art is more likely to be found in churches; for younger adults, it can be found anywhere.

Another distinction between younger adults and older adults is the kind of music they enjoy. Anecdotally, this generation gap is a source of frequent conflict between parents and teenagers. It sparks animated discussions in churches as well—both about what is appropriate to hear and what is preferred in worship services. We will consider the question about congregational worship in chapter 11. Here, though, I want to stress the importance of differences in musical preferences more generally. The most notable generation gap is in preference for contemporary pop/rock music. Nearly four-fifths of young adults in their twenties say they especially like it; fewer than one-fifth of adults age 65 and older do. Other kinds of music, such as classical and country, are generally favored more by older adults than by younger adults. This includes those who especially like Christian music and gospel music.

Evidence about music tastes flies in the face of two pieces of conventional wisdom. The first is that there is a huge market among young adults for Christian and gospel music—so huge that it drives sales, on the one hand, and encourages church leaders to emphasize it more in their services and ministries, on the other hand. This piece of wisdom comes from industry studies where it is the case that Christian and gospel music sells well to young adults, a fact that can be reconciled with the evidence at hand when we recall what we considered earlier about the high proportion of young adults who purchase tapes and compact discs. However, a relatively small fraction of young adults (fewer than a fifth of those in their twenties) say they especially like Christian and gospel music. This kind of music is actually preferred more widely among people in their forties and older. The other piece of conventional wisdom this evidence contradicts is the idea that young adults are musical omnivores—that is, they like everything. Omnivores are actually concentrated among middle aged and older people. For instance, only 12 percent of people in their twenties say they like four or more different kinds of music, compared with 24 percent of those in their early forties, 26 percent in their late forties to early sixties, and 20 percent age 65 and older.

It is hard to say whether young adults pick up cues about spirituality from music and art, whether they intentionally seek such cues, or whether they enjoy it strictly as a form of entertainment. Certainly the number of artists and musicians who believe themselves to be expressing spirituality in their work would suggest that spiritual interests might also be evident among their audiences.[24] We at least know that the boundaries that have sometimes kept religious people insulated from so-called secular art and music in the past are not strong for most young adults nowadays. For instance, among evangelicals in their twenties 81 percent say they especially like pop/rock music, about the same proportion as among mainline Protestants or Catholics of the same age. We also know that for a significant minority, if not a majority, of young adults, music and art are directly implicated in their quest for spirituality. For instance, 38 percent of adults age 21 through 45 say they have felt close to God singing or listening to religious music other than during a worship service; 21 percent have felt this way looking at a painting or sculpture; 34 percent say reading literature or poetry has been very or fairly important to their spiritual growth; 56 percent say music has been very or fairly important to their spiritual life; and 79 percent agree that art, music, and literature help us to experience the deeper meaning and purpose of life.

SPIRITUAL BUT NOT RELIGIOUS?

The final issue I want to address in this chapter is the perception that young adults are characterized by a growing separation between spirituality and religion. This is a curious and troubling perception. It is curious because throughout most of American history spirituality and religion were the same thing. Indeed, people seldom talked about spirituality because it was simply assumed that the spiritual life involved all the things one did at church or at home in conformity with church teachings. If young adults now consider spirituality something different from religion, that is troubling, at least to religious leaders.[25] Who, they wonder, will support the church in the future? Will people be guided by rock stars instead of clergy? Will massage therapists replace theologians?

We have already seen considerable evidence that suggests young adults are indeed seeking beyond the churches for answers to life's deepest questions and that many young adults are either disengaged from congregations and traditional devotional practices or finding new ways to practice their spirituality. Still, the phrase "I'm spiritual, but not religious" goes beyond these kinds of eclectic spiritual shopping. It suggests an explicit rejection of organized religion by people who are still interested somehow in spirituality. Journalists frequently mention hearing this phrase among people they interview. It was first reported in conversations with baby boomers and now is associated with their offspring. Church leaders also talk about conversations with people who claim to be spiritual, but without interest in religion. For church leaders, people like this are free riders. They want the benefits of believing that God loves them, or that they are protected by guardian angels, but are unwilling to invest their energies in religious organizations. They are harbingers of a future in which everyone has his or her own views about the sacred, with few paying much attention to what the clergy have to offer.

But these journalistic observations and clergy concerns have seldom been subjected to rigorous examination. Journalists typically have a hunch about some newsworthy story and look around until they find some anecdotal support for their story. Clergy talk mostly to the limited set of people who participate actively in their churches and form their opinions about the wider society from journalists. Thus, we need to consider the matter more carefully. Is the number of young adults who are spiritual but not religious large or small? Who are these people and how are they different from young adults who are actively involved in their churches? Does spirituality without religion signal a threat to organized religion, or does it pose opportunities?

One helpful way of approaching these questions is to consider the forces in our culture that encourage young adults to think it is possible to be spiritual but not religious. We saw in chapter 5 that about a third of young adults believe firmly that the Bible is the divine and literal word of God. Most of the remainder think the Bible is somehow divinely inspired, but not to be taken literally. That leaves open a great deal of room for personal interpretation about what the Bible says and about how divine inspiration enters into the human realm. We also saw that even biblical literalists are sometimes torn about how exactly to interpret the Bible. All of this fits well with the high value our culture places on individual freedom. We pride ourselves on being a free society, not only when we wage war in the Middle East, but also when we encourage our children to think for themselves, make up their own minds, and defend their own choices. We do that in religion, just as we do in the marketplace or at school. We are also a plural-

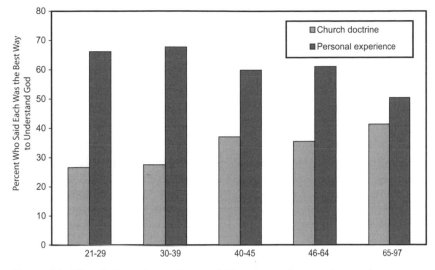

Figure 6.3. Church Doctrine or Personal Experience. Source: Arts and Religion Survey.

istic society, meaning that there are competing definitions of what is true and good from which to choose. In religion, church doctrines are a way of defining what is true and good. Church doctrines have been hammered out over the centuries by theologians and religious leaders. They carry the weight of history and tradition. But they also compete with one another. Catholic doctrines are not the same as Lutheran doctrines, which in turn are not the same as Presbyterian doctrines, and so on. It is thus difficult to take any of these doctrines as seriously as if there was more agreement among them. Put this together with our emphasis on individual authority, and it is not surprising that some people start to distinguish between the spirituality they know from personal experience and the church teachings they hear discussed by clergy and theologians.

Figure 6.3 shows how Americans respond when asked to choose between church doctrines and personal experience as the best way to understand God. Young adults overwhelmingly opt for personal experience over church doctrines, while adults in the oldest category are about equally likely to choose one or the other. Specifically, two-thirds of young adults in their twenties opt for personal experience, while only a quarter opt for church doctrines. The same is true among young adults in their thirties. People in their forties and fifties are a bit different, but still favor personal experience over church doctrine by a ratio of three to two. Then, among people age 65 and older, about half opt for personal experience and about four in ten opt for church doctrine.

A more direct answer to the question of how many young adults are spiritual but not religious can be derived from comparing adults age 21 through 45 who are religiously involved (attend religious services at least once a month) with young adults of the same age who are not religiously involved (attend religious services less than once a month, if at all). Not surprisingly, those who are religiously involved are more likely than those who are not religiously involved to indicate an interest in spirituality. In short, the dominant pattern among young adults is not spirituality *or* religion, but spirituality *and* religion. The people we are especially interested in, though, are the ones who are religiously uninvolved but who still indicate being interested in spirituality. Quite a few of them are. For instance, sixty percent of those who are religiously uninvolved say spiritual growth is at least fairly important to them, 30 percent say it is very or extremely important to them, 29 percent say they have devoted at least a fair amount of effort to their spiritual life in the past year, 25 percent say their interest in spirituality has been increasing, and 25 percent say they meditate once a week or more. We need to remember that about half (55 percent) of 21-through 45-year-olds are religiously uninvolved. Thus, a good answer to the question of how many young adults are spiritual but not religious would be somewhere between a sixth and a third, depending on which indication of spirituality is considered. Whether one regards that as a high proportion or a low proportion depends on one's perspective. Certainly it would be inaccurate to generalize and say that all or even most young adults are spiritual but not religious. Yet it is fair to acknowledge that a significant minority falls into this category.[26]

Young adults who are religiously uninvolved but who say their interest in spirituality is increasing tend to be in their thirties more than in their twenties, married rather than single, with children rather than without children, female rather than male, and better educated.[27] Their profile largely resembles that of young adults who become active in religious organizations. If maturing, marrying, and becoming parents encourage church involvement, these developments seem also to encourage interest in spirituality. This is mixed news as far as the future of churches is concerned. On the one hand, greater numbers of young adults who are unmarried and who wait longer to have children point to fewer being interested either in religion or spirituality. On the other hand, young adults who do marry and have children seem likely not only to become interested in spirituality, but also to express that interest by becoming more involved in churches.

The Nature of Spiritual Tinkering

The overall conclusion from the evidence we have considered in this chapter is that spiritual tinkering is quite common among young adults of today and probably will remain so among young adults of tomorrow. This is because spiritual tinkering was not just a form of restlessness that characterized baby boomers and then could easily be reversed among their offspring. Spiritual tinkering is a reflection of the pluralistic religious society in which we live, the freedom we permit ourselves in making choices about faith, and the necessity of making those choices in the face of the uprootedness and change that most young adults experience. It involves piecing together ideas about spirituality from many sources, especially through conversations with one's friends. We have seen that spiritual choices are not limited to the kinds of denominational switching that some scholars have been content to emphasize. Spiritual tinkering involves a large minority of young adults in church shopping and church hopping. It also takes the form of searching for answers to the perennial existential questions in venues that go beyond religious traditions and in expressing spiritual interests through music and art as well as through prayer and devotional reading.

Spiritual tinkering is only a tendency. It does not characterize all young adults and it is by no means limited to them. If a sizable minority of young adults seek in broad venues and make eclectic choices about their spirituality, another sizable minority settles into a congregation and follows a fairly scripted pattern of prayer and Bible reading in their devotional lives. They make choices too and in this way are spiritual bricoleurs. The challenge for religious leaders is knowing when to guide these choices and when to back off. It is sometimes argued that religious leaders who succeed in controlling the choices of their followers are likely to be most successful in building their congregations. Yet if all religious leaders followed that strategy, it would surely backfire. Choice is so much of our culture that many young adults value the freedom to make choices without the guiding hand of religious leaders.

∞ 7 ∞

Faith and Family

FACING THE DIFFICULT CHOICES

NOT LONG AGO, a faculty member in my department stopped me in the hallway and said, "I know you study religion, and I know lots of people are religious, but is there any evidence that religion *matters*?" For young adults, that is a very good question. Does it matter if I go to church or adhere to one religious tradition instead of another? Will it influence how I think about life? Will it make me a better wife, husband, mother, or father? These are the questions religious leaders ask, too. They may believe that faith is intrinsically important. But they also hope it makes some differences in people's lives.

Young adulthood is a time of difficult decisions. Most people choose—or at least try to choose—a marriage partner while they are in their twenties. Most make choices about birth control and the timing of children. They decide how many children they want and perhaps which gender they prefer. As young parents, they face decisions about how to raise their children. What values should they emphasize? Should both parents have jobs? And as they try to guide their children, countless other questions arise—questions about religion, relationships, neighborhoods, sexuality, the media, and where to find support.

Research is useful for thinking about these questions. Until recently, surprisingly little research had been done on the *relationships* between religion and family issues, even though specialists had studied each topic independent of the other. Fortunately, that has begun to change. Several valuable books on these relationships have now been published and other research is in progress.[1] This is not the place to describe what can easily be read elsewhere. However, I do want to consider several pieces of evidence that will help us understand more clearly how *young adults* relate their faith to decisions about family, and how these relationships have been changing.

CONSIDERING MARRIAGE

In a national survey conducted in 2004, 63 percent of the public said they were very worried or somewhat worried that the institution of marriage is under attack. Younger adults were less likely to express these worries than older adults were; for instance, among adults age 65 and older 70 percent said they were worried, while among adults in their twenties, only 54 percent did. Still, it was the perception of a majority in all age groups that something troubling has been happening to one of our most cherished institutions. Furthermore, the more someone went to church, the more likely that person was to be worried. Thus, among adults age 21 through 45 who attended religious services every week, 80 percent said they were worried that marriage was under attack. In comparison, only 39 percent of those who seldom attended religious services felt this way.[2]

One of our main conclusions in chapter 3 was that today's young adults are divided religiously on lines that correspond closely to their marital status. Young adults who are married go to church and often go to theologically conservative churches. Young adults who are not married are less likely to attend religious services; indeed, many are religiously unaffiliated. In that context, I argued that the growing number of young adults who remain single or marry later bodes ill for the future of participation in organized religion. We need to consider the possibility, though, that decisions about marriage are *influenced by* church attendance, rather than simply influencing it. Why might this be the case? Suppose a man or woman decides, for whatever reason, to be actively involved in a church. Chances are, that man or woman will be in a context where programs are geared toward families, where other young adults are married, and where there may even be sermons and classes about marriage. Any of these influences might encourage a person to think more seriously about getting married.

Church attendance does go hand in hand with valuing marriage, it appears. Our best evidence of this and of how it has changed over time comes from the World Values Surveys. In 1980, only 6 percent of adults age 21 through 45 in the United States who attended religious services weekly agreed that "marriage is an outdated institution," compared with 10 percent of those who attended religious services less often. By 2000, those who attended religious services weekly were still quite unlikely to say that marriage was outdated (only 5 percent agreed), while among those who attended services less often this proportion had grown to 17 percent. Of course these figures demonstrate that the vast majority of young adults *do not* believe that marriage is outdated. However, there has been a significant increase in the number of young adults who seem not to value marriage, and that increase has taken place entirely among young adults who are religiously uninvolved.

The fact that church attendance is associated with valuing marriage does not prove that church going actually reinforces this value. Further analysis of the data, though, reduces the possibility that the relationship between church going and valuing marriage is just an artifact of something else (such as married people being more likely to go to church *and* value marriage). When we statistically take into account the differences among married and unmarried young adults, those who are in their twenties and those who are in their thirties or early forties, women versus men, and the effect of having been surveyed in 1980 or 2000, the relationship between church going and valuing marriage is still statistically significant and strong.[3] Other measures of being religiously oriented, such as saying that God is important in one's life or that one derives comfort from religion, show similar results. However, these results are weaker than those for church attendance.[4] Thus, it seems likely that actually being part of a church has more of an effect on one's views about marriage than simply feeling positive about religion.[5]

HAVING SEX

For young adults who are not married, questions about having sex sometimes become a point of contention with the teachings of their churches. Baby boomers were often distinguished by having come of age after "the pill" and during the sexual revolution. Whether today's young adults are even more accepting of premarital sex, or whether they have become more cautious as a result of concerns about HIV/AIDS, sexually transmitted diseases, and discussions of out-of-wedlock pregnancies has been harder to gauge.[6]

In recent surveys, 22 percent of adults age 21 through 45 say that a man and woman having sex before marriage is always wrong and another 8 percent say this is almost always wrong. Twenty percent say it is only sometimes wrong and 50 percent say it is not wrong at all. Those figures are almost exactly the same as they were among young adults polled in 1977.[7] This overall lack of change, though, masks a very interesting phenomenon that has taken place when young people who are religiously active are compared with young people who are not religiously active. As shown in figure 7.1, high attenders (who go to church at least nearly every week) and low attenders (who go to church less often) are almost mirror opposites of each other in how they think about premarital sex. Among the higher attenders, more than half (54 percent) think premarital sex is always wrong; among low attenders, more than half (59 percent) think premarital sex is simply not wrong. The change between the earlier period and more recent period is also interesting. Low attenders became even more approving of premarital sex, whereas high attenders became more disapproving of it.

The information in figure 7.2 shows that young adults affiliated with the various faith traditions think quite differently about premarital sex. Evangelicals are the most likely to say it is always wrong, and they have

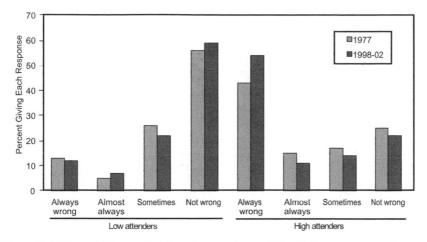

Figure 7.1. Views of Premarital Sex. Source: General Social Surveys, respondents age 21 through 45.

become more likely to say this over the past quarter century. In contrast, only a few mainline Protestants or Jews think premarital sex is always wrong. Black Protestants are more likely now than earlier to think premarital sex is always wrong, whereas Catholics are less likely to say so. Young adults in the "other faiths" category resemble evangelicals and black Protestants on this issue. The nonaffiliated are unlikely to say premarital sex is always wrong, and have shifted even further in this direction since 1977.

Judging from this information, young evangelical Protestants would be very unlikely to have sex before marriage. Indeed, only 30 percent think it is not wrong at all to have premarital sex. However, behavior does not always follow convictions. Fully 69 percent of unmarried evangelicals age 21 through 45 said they had had sex with at least one partner during the previous 12 months (figure 7.3). To be sure, this percentage was lower than the comparable figures for adherents of other religious traditions (which ranged from 78 percent among mainline Protestants to 95 percent among Jews). But it was not that much lower. And when all unmarried adults in this age range were compared, 63 percent of those who thought premarital sex was always wrong acknowledged having had sexual relations in the past year.

WEDDINGS

Systematic research on weddings and the role of religion in them is surprisingly sparse, given the fact that most people who marry do have weddings and that the majority of these presumably take place in houses of worship.

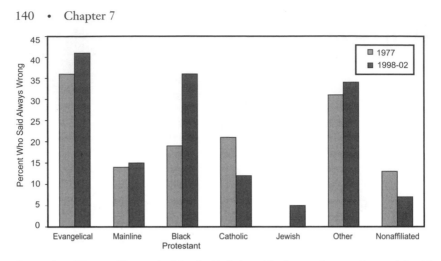

Figure 7.2. Views of Premarital Sex by Religious Tradition. Source: General Social Surveys, respondents age 21 through 45.

Apart from questions about ethnic and religious differences among marriage partners (which we will consider later in the chapter), weddings themselves are an interesting and important indicator of trends in social relationships. If people are bowling alone, as Robert Putnam alleges, then they may be having smaller weddings or inviting fewer friends because they simply do not have as many friends as people did in the past.[8] Thus far, we have seen little evidence to suggest this is actually the case. However, it is plausible to think that weddings may be diminishing in size compared to the days when people invited the whole town in which they lived or the whole congregation to which they and their extended families belonged. Friends and family are now likely to be scattered. The rising numbers of young adults who claim no religious preference or who seldom attend religious services also suggests that the large wedding to which church friends were invited may be a thing of the past.

In a national survey a few years ago, I asked everyone who was married to recall approximately how many people had attended his or her wedding. The results were surprising. Among those age 65 and older (whose weddings had presumably been longer ago), the average was 79 people. This number increased to 110 among people age 46 to 64 and then increased even further to 122 among people in their twenties.[9] Among all married adults age 21 through 45, 20 percent had weddings that might have been private or family-only, with fewer than 10 people. Another fifth had between 10 and 50 people, a fifth had between 50 and 100 people, a fifth had between 100 and 200 people, and a fifth had more than 200 people.

The effects of religion were also evident in the responses. Among married people age 21 through 45, Catholics had the largest weddings, averag-

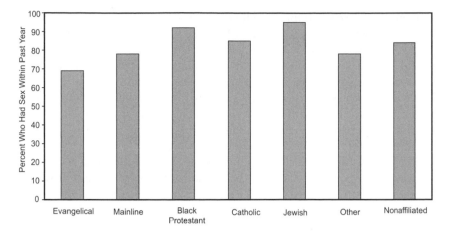

Figure 7.3. Sexual Activity among Unmarried Young Adults. Source: General Social Surveys, 1998–2002, never married respondents age 21 through 45.

ing 141 people in attendance. Jews follow with an average of 127 people. Those who belong to other faiths (such as Orthodox Christianity or the Church of Jesus Christ of Latter-Day Saints) average 105. Protestants average only 82. And those with no religious affiliation or preference have the smallest weddings, averaging only 72. Whether a person's congregation was theologically conservative, moderate, or liberal made relatively little difference, although moderate congregations averaged 126 people at weddings, followed by conservative congregations with 116, and liberal congregations with 103. Irrespective of religious tradition, wedding size varied considerably with frequency of attendance at religious services. Interestingly, those who attended almost every week had the largest weddings, averaging 142 people, followed by those who attended every week with an average of 117 people, and then declining to only 78 people among those who never attended religious services. Of course wedding size also reflects local customs and, increasingly, what families can afford. Thus, weddings averaged 114 people among young adults living in suburban areas, but only 95 among those living in central cities or small towns, and they ranged in size from 116 among people living in upper income neighborhoods to only 79 among people living in lower income communities.

Marital Happiness

Most married couples report happiness with their marriages. In General Social Surveys conducted between 1998 and 2002, for instance, the proportion among married couples of all ages who said they were "very happy" with their marriage was 63 percent. Because more couples are getting divorced than in the past, we might suppose that those who remain married would actually be more inclined to report marital happiness than was true a few decades ago. At least one of the arguments made sometimes about divorce is that it permits unhappy couples to escape being unhappy. Between the early 1970s and late 1990s, though, marital happiness declined by about 5 percentage points among married couples, with the sharpest decline (8 points) among couples in their twenties.

The reason for this decline among couples in their twenties is unclear. However, one possibility is that it has to do with the average age at which people marry. In the early 1970s, marrying in one's twenties was the norm. By the late 1990s, more people were remaining unmarried until their late twenties or early thirties. Thus, being married in one's twenties was less typical, meaning that there may have been greater disparities between one's lifestyle or expectations and those of one's friends and family. The General Social Survey data also show that marital happiness in the 1970s was lower among people in their early forties than among people in their twenties, suggesting that marital unhappiness may have been associated with couples staying married longer, rather than divorcing. By the late 1990s, even though marital happiness was lower, it was constant across age groups from those in their twenties to those in their early sixties.

Marital happiness is significantly more likely among those who participate regularly in religious services than among those who do not. Among married couples in their twenties, 73 percent of those who attend religious services weekly or almost every week say they are very happy with their marriages. This compares to 58 percent among married couples in their twenties who do not attend religious services that often. The comparable figures for married couples in their thirties are 67 percent and 61 percent, and for those in their early forties, 70 percent and 55 percent. Statistical analysis of the data show that these differences remain significant when age, gender, race, and education are controlled. Taking into account the differences between frequent and infrequent church attenders, married couples with religious affiliations are more likely to express marital happiness than married couples with no religious affiliations. Differences among the various religious traditions, however, are not significant.[10]

Parenting

In contrast to views about marriage (but like views about premarital sex), opinions about the desirability of having children have remained unchanged among young adults over the past generation (as we saw in chapter

2). Even though the birth rate has gone down, young adults still say the *ideal* number of children for a family to have is somewhere between 2.7 and three. Despite the fact that the number of young adults who actually have children has decreased, the proportion who think *never* having children is ideal also remains extremely small (around one percent). Just as it does for views about marriage, religious involvement influences how young adults feel about having children. For instance, young adults who attend religious services regularly (almost every week) say the ideal number of children to have is 3.1, whereas young adults who attend services less often put the number at 2.8. These numbers are exactly the same as they were in the early 1970s. What has changed, though, is the proportion of active church goers who want *large* families. In the early 1970s, 20 percent of young adults who attended church regularly said they wanted at least four children. In the more recent surveys, that figure has dropped to 12 percent. Religious tradition is also associated with thoughts about ideal family size, but not very strongly. Among evangelicals, the average number of children considered ideal is 2.9, among mainline Protestants it is 2.6; it is 3.0 for black Protestants, Catholics, and Jews; and 2.8 for people of other faiths and for the nonaffiliated. Again, there have been few changes in these numbers over the past three decades. The one exception is that the proportion of black Protestants who want large families (four or more children) has dropped from 41 percent to 24 percent.

Suppose adults who are now in their twenties or thirties live out their dreams and have as many children as they consider ideal. For every hundred evangelical couples, there would be 290 children and for every hundred mainline couples only 260. That would perpetuate the decline of mainline Protestants relative to evangelicals. But not by much. Thus, we need to exercise caution, as I have suggested earlier, in how we interpret the "demographic imperative" as a source of denominational growth or decline. Growth and decline are partly affected by how many children people want and have. Growth and decline are also influenced (perhaps even more) by the *timing* of those decisions. If a hundred couples gave birth to an average of 2.6 children and averaged age 30 when they had these children, in 60 years there would be 338 offspring. But if those hundred couples gave birth to an average of 2.6 children and averaged age 20 when they had them, there would be 439 children in 60 years or almost 30 percent more. In addition, waiting until age 30 means more discontinuity of the kind that often weakens ties with religious traditions (geographic mobility, travel, higher education). To the extent that religious organizations perpetuate themselves by encouraging families to have children, then, the most significant influence may not be the number of children (at least not at present), but *when* they have children, and, in this regard, encouraging young adults to marry sooner and to stay married may be the truly decisive factors.[11]

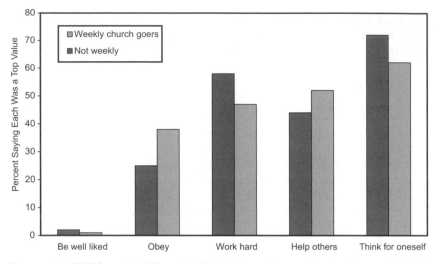

Figure 7.4. Childrearing Values by Church Attendance. Source: General Social Surveys, 1998–2002, respondents age 21 through 45.

In other ways, church involvement seems to reinforce family values among young adults—and does so as much as it did in the past. In the World Values Surveys, people were asked if they agreed or disagreed that "a child needs a home with both a father and a mother to grow up happily." In 1980, 56 percent of adults age 21 through 45 agreed and by 2000 the number had risen slightly to 61 percent. In the earlier period, weekly church goers were 14 percentage points more likely to agree than people who attended less often; in 2000, they were still 9 points more likely to agree. Another question in the World Values Surveys asked, "If a woman wants to have a child as a single parent but she doesn't want to have a stable relationship with a man, do you approve or disapprove?" Forty-two percent of adults age 21 through 45 in 1980 and 44 percent in 2000 approved. Weekly church goers were 26 percentage points less likely than irregular attenders to approve in 1980 and 24 points less likely to approve in 2000.

Besides encouraging people to value the traditional two-parent family, religious involvement also influences how they think children should be raised. Regular church goers are more likely than other young adults to think obedience and helping others are important values to instill in children. In contrast, less frequent attenders are more likely to stress thinking for oneself and working hard (see figure 7.4).[12] These questions have been included in the General Social Surveys only since 1986, but the patterns then were quite similar to those in the more recent surveys. The one significant difference is that regular church goers were significantly more likely to emphasize thinking for oneself in the more recent surveys. Jews, mainline Protestants, the nonaffiliated, and Catholics are the most likely to value thinking for oneself, while evangelical Protestants and black Protestants are significantly less likely to select this value. In contrast, evangelicals and black Protestants are *more likely* than any of the other groups to value obedience.[13]

These differences in childrearing values are important because they reinforce some of the differences among religious traditions that we have considered in previous chapters. Religiously conservative parents want their children to obey them; religiously liberal parents want their children to think for themselves. The former group is more likely to encourage conformity to the teachings of their tradition; the latter is more willing to let the chips fall where they may. The fact that regular church goers are more likely to encourage freethinking now than in the past, though, supports the main argument social scientists have been making about rising rates of spiritual shopping. Religious freethinking is a form of individualism that authorizes making choices, whether these are about which church to attend or which teachings to believe.

The most important change that has been influencing family life in recent years is the rising number of young families in which children are being reared by working mothers as well as by working fathers. More mothers in the labor market is a choice some families make because of training and opportunities for professional advancement. In other cases, it is a matter of economic necessity. Young adults are significantly more inclined to believe mothers can work without having adverse consequences for children than they were a generation ago. But they are still divided on this issue. In the surveys conducted between 1998 and 2002, 69 percent of adults age 21 through 45 agreed that a mother working doesn't hurt the children, up from 57 percent in 1977, while 31 percent disagreed, down from 43 percent. Religious involvement and religious tradition influence how young adults think about this issue. Regular church goers are 8 percentage points less likely than irregular attenders to think it doesn't harm children if their mother works. Evangelicals are the least likely to hold this view, while Jews, black Protestants, and the nonaffiliated are most likely to hold it. The relative rankings of the various traditions are the same as they were a generation ago, although within each tradition a larger share of young adults accepts the view that mothers working does not harm children.

RIGHT AND WRONG

Apart from raising children, young adults face difficult decisions in their own lives about what is right and what is wrong. Observers of our society worry that young adults have grown up fudging on exams, seeing their parents cheat on taxes, and learning relativistic values from public leaders and the entertainment industry. If these concerns are valid, then churches that teach an absolute standard of right and wrong may be an anchor in an impending cultural storm.

The World Values Surveys included a series of questions about behavior that people might or might not consider ethically or morally questionable and asked them to respond by selecting a number between one and ten, where one meant never justifiable and ten meant always justifiable. The questions asked about:

Claiming government benefits to which you are not entitled
Avoiding a fare on public transport
Cheating on taxes if you have a chance
Someone accepting a bribe in the course of their duties
Homosexuality
Prostitution
Abortion
Euthanasia—ending the life of the incurably sick

About three quarters of the respondents age 21 through 45 in 2000 said accepting a bribe was never justifiable, and these percentages had hardly changed over the twenty-year period. The other question that yielded stable results was the one about cheating on taxes. Three people in five in both of the surveys said this was never justifiable. All of the other questions showed significant changes. Young adults in 2000 were significantly more likely than young adults twenty years earlier to imagine that there might be circumstances under which falsely claiming benefits, avoiding a fare on public transit, homosexuality, prostitution, abortion, and euthanasia might be justifiable.[14] These shifts, incidentally, occurred during the Reagan administration and the heyday of the Christian right and at a time when colleges and businesses were focusing more attention on ethical issues than ever before. Yet the direction of change in the opinions of young adults was apparently toward a more relativistic stance than one defined by absolute rules.

As interesting as the shift itself in these responses is, the changing role of religion in them is even more interesting. The best way to illustrate this changing role is by considering the relationships between the responses to these questions and church attendance (figure 7.5). Church attendance is the one behavioral measure about which we have information in the World Values Surveys (the other questions about religion focus generally on beliefs and the importance of religion). Although people may not be completely truthful about how often they attend church, we would at least assume that church attendance should have some bearing on people's views about these kinds of presumed ethical and moral issues. And indeed it did

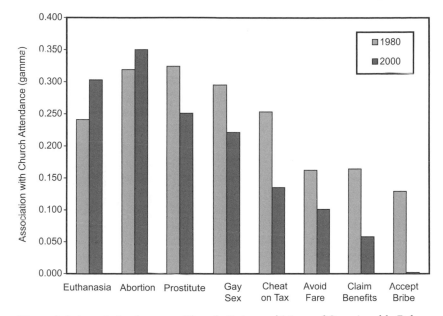

Figure 7.5. Association between Church Going and Views of Questionable Behavior. Source: World Values Surveys, 1980 and 2000, respondents age 21 through 45.

in 1980. The bars in the chart for 1980 are measures of association (gamma) which vary between plus-one and minus-one. In 1980, the relationships for all the questions were statistically significant and indicated that people who went to church more often were also more likely to say that each of these morally debatable activities was never justifiable. By 2000, that pattern had changed. Attitudes toward the four activities to the left in the chart were still significantly associated with church attendance; indeed, two of them were more strongly associated with church attendance than they had been in 1980. In contrast, attitudes toward the four activities to the right in the chart were all related with church attendance less strongly than in 1980 and two of them were not statistically related with church attendance at all.

The larger implication of these changing patterns becomes apparent when we look more closely at what separates the four activities on the left from the four on the right. The left-hand items refer to sexuality and life. The right-hand items refer to money and the ethics of social relationships in which money is involved. What people hear at church apparently still matters on questions about sexuality and life, but not on questions about money and relationships involving money. I am not suggesting that the shift away from absolutist rules on these issues is attributable to a decline in religious participation. We saw in chapter 3 that religious participation has declined, but not by that much. What I am suggesting is that church teachings seem to matter to a narrower sphere of activities than they used to. This is perhaps not surprising. Some churches, especially Roman Catholic and Protestant evangelical churches, have been particularly vocal about such issues as abortion and homosexuality. It is unfortunate, though, if churches no longer influence how people think concerning bribes and other matters of financial ethics.

One other point is suggested by these results. The reason church participation still bears a strong relationship with attitudes toward euthanasia, abortion, prostitution, and homosexuality may not be that people who attend change their attitudes as a result of attending. It may be that people who disagree with the churches on these issues have simply stopped attending. That, too, could account for the changing statistical relationships. If so, it nevertheless suggests that churches have a reputation for speaking out about some of these issues and not about others.

Empathy

Another aspect of parenting and family life that has received considerable emphasis in recent years is empathy. By empathy, I mean especially the ability to identify with people who are less fortunate than oneself—enough so to do something about it. Empathy is a value young children learn mostly from their parents. If they perceive their parents being moved by the plight of the poor and needy, they are more likely to grow up thinking it is important to care for others instead of pursuing only their own interests.[15] We would hope that empathy is reinforced by religious convictions. After all, even a minimal awareness of religious teachings should be enough to pick up such ideals as loving one's neighbor and helping the poor. But is this the case?

The Davis Empathy Scale was designed to assess how much or how little a person is inclined to express empathy. The scale consists of seven statements to which respondents are asked to respond on a five-point scale, where 1 means "doesn't describe me well" and 5 means "describes me well." The statements, four of which are positively worded and three of which are negatively worded, are:

I often have tender, concerned feelings for people less fortunate than me.

Sometimes I don't feel very sorry for other people when they are having problems.

When I see someone being taken advantage of, I feel kind of protective toward them.

Other people's misfortunes do not usually disturb me a great deal.

When I see someone treated unfairly, I sometimes don't feel very much pity for them.

I am often quite touched by things that I see happen.

I would describe myself as a pretty soft-hearted person.[16]

The scale itself is constructed by summing the responses to all the items (after reversing the negatively worded statements) and then, for present purposes, dividing the full scale such that approximately a third of respondents are classified as low, a third as medium, and a third as high (respectively, scores of 7 through 25, 26 through 30, and 31 through 35). The fact that approximately two-thirds of the respondents scored between 26 and 35 means that most people think of themselves as concerned or empathic.

Results from the General Social Survey indicate that the likelihood of scoring high on the empathy scale is greater among women than among men. Among both women and men, people in their twenties and thirties are between 5 and 10 percentage points less likely than older adults to score high on the scale.[17] Whether this difference stems from younger adults growing up more recently or the fact that they are still young cannot be determined from this evidence. It does, however, reinforce some popular perceptions that younger adults may not be as caring or may be more self-interested than older people.

Of greater relevance for our purposes here is the relationship between empathy and church attendance. The survey results suggest that empathy is greater among young adults who attend religious services frequently than among those who attend less frequently. This is true among both men and women. However, the relationship among men is weaker (only 5 percentage points, difference) than it is among women (11 points) and is not statistically significant. Although the survey was too small to make further analysis feasible, there is also some indication that the effects of church attendance may be more important for mothers than for fathers.[18] On the whole, though, it does appear that one of the positive ways in which religious involvement may affect family life is by encouraging empathy.

Threats to Today's Families

There is also a sense among many Americans that the family is under siege—not just by cultural patterns that discourage marriage or that inhibit good parenting, but by the mass media. According to this criticism, the media has mostly become a source for advertisers to tempt children and adolescents into materialistic, hedonistic lifestyles. The media may be a useful tool for keeping up on the news or seeking entertainment, in this view, but it is fundamentally a corrupt institution with little redeeming social value. It bombards children with tens of thousands of commercials. It penetrates the sanctity of the home and makes it harder for parents to teach children higher values.

Criticisms of the media have been voiced by teachers and other educators, by pediatricians, and by community watch-dog groups. Nothing seems to help. Media conglomerates argue that their first priority is to their stockholders, and thus can do no other than sell programming that caters to the most titillating tastes. If people continue to watch, at least some are worried, though, that the media is alien to their values. Religious involvement especially might be an alternative source of values. If so, the religiously inclined might at least perceive the tension between their values and those of the media.

Young adults depend on the mass media for information and entertainment, just as all Americans do. Young adults of the twenty-first century have grown up, like their parents, watching television. They have also grown up watching cable television programs, having money to purchase DVDs and go to the movies, and even at school have been exposed to advertising for soft drinks and fast food. Bombarded by a constant barrage of advertising and titillation, young people, we might suppose, have simply become whatever the media moguls tell them to be. Fortunately, young adults still sense that their spiritual and moral lives are not being fed by the media. Large numbers of young adults in all the major faith traditions believe the mass media are actually hostile to their moral and values. As shown in figure 7.6, these proportions range from 69 percent among white evangelicals to 58 percent among white mainline Protestants, 61 percent among black Protestants, 45 percent among Catholics, and 40 percent among Jews. Even among the religiously nonaffiliated more than a third (36 percent) regard the mass media as being hostile to their moral and spiritual values.

This is just one way in which religiously involved young adults perceive their families to be threatened by contemporary culture. They also worry about materialism, about the pressures children face to engage in such at-risk activities as drugs and crime, and problems with the schools, let alone tensions within marriages, the probability of divorce, and financial problems. Indeed, fear is probably one of the least understood dimensions of young adulthood. In our qualitative interviews, for instance, most young adults were worried that a parent, spouse, or child might die. Some worried about terrorism. Young parents were especially worried about how to protect their children from unhealthy influences in the culture. These influences ran the gamut, from bigotry and racism, on the one hand, to pornography and sexual abuse, on the other hand. With young families facing so

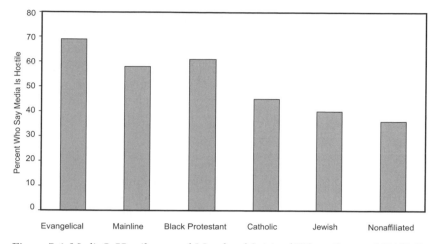

Figure 7.6. Media Is Hostile toward Moral and Spiritual Values. Source: 2004 Religion and Ethics Newsweekly Survey, respondents age 21 through 45.

many potentially destructive forces, another way in which faith communities could serve is by providing emotional and social support.

Seeking Support

Judging from how seldom they attend services, one might assume that congregations are completely irrelevant to a majority of young adults. However, congregations have always served as a form of social insurance, and that function is still important to how young adults think about congregations. By social insurance, I mean that congregations are places where people can seek help when they need it. Emotional support, marriage counseling, even a short-term loan. A clergy person or some committee is there when a sick child winds up in the hospital or a parent dies. In a 1998 survey, 54 percent of adults age 21 through 45 (among those who attended services at least once a year) said their congregation would help a great deal if they had a problem, and another 30 percent said their congregation would be of some help. Only 11 percent said their congregation would be of little help and 5 percent said it would provide no help. Because church going is low among people in their twenties and rises by the time people are in their early forties, it was also interesting in this survey that young adults in their twenties, thirties, and early forties were all about the same in terms of how much help they thought they could receive from their congregations.[19]

I have written elsewhere about the *ways* in which congregations provide support.[20] One of the most common ways is forming small, informal groups that offer emotional support and fellowship mixed with prayer and Bible study. In a 1991 study, I found that about 35 percent of young adults nationally were involved in a small group of this kind. In another national study, conducted in 1999, about the same proportion of young adults were involved. Not all of these groups are formally associated with congregations, but most of them are. The vast majority (more than three-quarters) regularly include prayer and Bible study. By their participants' own accounts, these groups *are* an important source of support. For instance, about two-thirds (63 percent) of the participants who were age 21 through 45 said their group had helped them through an emotional crisis. Almost as many (59 percent) said the group had helped them in making some difficult decision in their lives or helped them when someone was sick.[21]

A thirty-year-old woman who lives in Florida with her husband and two-year-old daughter illustrates the role support groups play for some young adults. Married shortly after college and having been reared going to church, she said "yes" when a friend invited her to join a small group that met regularly to discuss religious and spiritual issues. Had she been single and looking for a male partner, the group would likely have been less attractive. As it was, all the members were young married women like herself. "We became good friends," she recalls, "and we did a lot of prayer for each other because we had spouses who were trying to pass the bar, or trying to get a job once they were graduating, or struggling with exams, or getting started in their own jobs." A few years later and living in a different state, she again found support in a small group. This one was also composed of women her age but included some of the husbands. They met each week at the church, watched a Bible lesson on video, and then opened the meeting for discussion and prayer. Most of the support, she says, was "just keeping up with each other." Currently, she is in yet another group. They meet at a coffee shop where they can talk and pray. One of the women is expecting a baby and the others are "on that midnight phone call list" because she doesn't have family in town. "We're the surrogate sisters and aunts," she says.

Religious and Ethnic Diversity

Lastly, we need to consider the role of religion in relationship to young adults' views about religious and ethnic diversity. The growing diversity of our society comes home, so to speak, when young adults consider the possibility that a child of theirs might marry someone from a different religious or ethnic group. Less directly, diversity also comes home when people think about the composition of their neighborhoods. Religious convictions conceivably encourage people to be open-minded and accepting

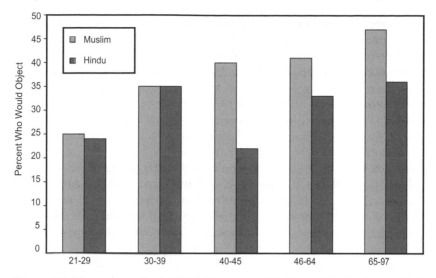

Figure 7.7. Views about One's Child Marrying a Muslim or Hindu. Source: Religion and Diversity Survey, half the respondents in the survey were asked about Muslims and half about Hindus.

of one's neighbors, even if those neighbors have different beliefs and lifestyles. However, religious convictions can also be a source of intolerance.

Younger adults, especially those in their twenties, are generally somewhat more accepting of the possibility that a son or daughter of theirs might marry someone of another faith than older adults are. This is evident in figure 7.7 which shows the percentages of each age group who would object (strongly or somewhat) if they had a child who wanted to marry a Muslim or Hindu who had a good education and came from a good family. The age differences are stronger for attitudes about intermarriage with Muslims than for the comparable attitudes about Hindus. Thus, among young adults in their twenties only 25 percent say they would object, whereas this proportion increases steadily to almost half of people age 65 and older. The attitudes about intermarriage with Hindus range only from a quarter who would object among people in their twenties to slightly more than a third among people age 65 and older.[22] A possible reason for the stronger age differences in attitudes toward Muslims may be that these attitudes were frequently discussed in schools, churches, and the media after the September 11, 2001 events as community leaders called on non-Muslims not to vent their anger about the attacks against Muslims in their communities. Younger adults may have been more exposed to and influenced by these messages than older adults. In contrast, little was said about Hindus, leaving these attitudes to be affected by other factors.

Even the attitudes about a child marrying a Muslim, though, show that an interesting social phenomenon is at work among young adults. Many attitudes are significantly influenced by levels of education. Especially attitudes that reflect propensities toward tolerance or intolerance are affected by levels of education. However, in this case levels of education do not seem to matter much. In fact, about the same proportion of adults age 21 through 45 who have college degrees say they would object to a child marrying a Muslim as among those who have only some college education or who have never been to college. Parents' education has little effect, either.[23] What does make a significant difference is whether young adults are married and have children. Among those who are married, 40 percent say they would object to a child marrying a Muslim, whereas only 26 percent of those who are not married say this. And among those who have children, 37 percent would object, compared with 27 percent of those who do not have children. The other factor that significantly influences these attitudes is religion. Among young adults who attend religious services almost every week, 51 percent would object to a child marrying a Muslim, whereas only 23 percent of those who attend less frequently would object. There are also huge differences by religious tradition. Fifty-six percent of young evangelicals say they would object, whereas only 29 percent of mainline Protestants, 26 percent of black Protestants, 29 percent of Catholics, and 33 percent of Jews would object. These same patterns were evident in attitudes toward a child marrying a Hindu.[24] In short, young adults may learn tolerance in school or through their general exposure to the culture, but when an issue strikes home, such as having a child marry someone of another religion, it is much harder to be tolerant if one actually has children or anticipates having them, and it is especially hard to be tolerant if one is a church-going evangelical Protestant.

One way to think about these attitudes toward interreligious marriage is that they represent ways of protecting the integrity and traditions of one's family. No matter how tolerant a parent may be in general, a parent always wants his or her children to be happy. When a son or daughter actually announces his or her intention of marrying someone from a different religion, parents are faced with the difficult choice of being accepting or expressing objections. But when the situation is hypothetical, a large minority of young adults say they would object, probably because they can imagine the hard compromises that would be required. Evangelical Protestantism provides additional reasons to resist interreligious marriage. To many evangelical Protestants, Muslims and Hindus are not really part of God's chosen few at all. It seems wrong to evangelicals to marry an unbeliever. But where exactly are these barriers that protect the family erected? Only around one's children? Or around one's neighborhood as well? If the thought of one's children marrying outside the faith is not welcome, perhaps strangers in the neighborhood are not welcome either.

Suppose a group of Muslims or Hindus announced their intentions of constructing a mosque or temple in one's community? This is the kind of issue that has in fact faced many communities in recent years. Some communities have embraced such plans while others have gone to great lengths to keep Muslims and Hindus out. The responses depend partly on whether there are property values to be protected, concerns about noise or traffic, and outspoken leaders to mobilize sentiment in one direction or another.[25] The responses, though, also depend on what ordinary people think. When asked what they do think, a substantial minority of the public says they would be bothered. Specifically, 42 percent say they would be bothered (18 percent "a lot") if "some Muslims wanted to build a large Muslim mosque in your community," and 35 percent respond similarly (18 percent "a lot") when asked about a Hindu temple. As with attitudes about intermarriage, young adults are less likely than older adults to register these concerns (indeed, about a quarter of young adults in their twenties say they would actually "welcome" a mosque or temple). The characteristics that reinforce objections to intermarriage also raise the likelihood of people being bothered by a mosque or temple in their community. Young adults who are married or who have children are more likely to be bothered than young adults who are not married or do not have children. Those who attend church regularly are not as happy about these new religious organizations moving into their communities as those who attend less regularly. Once again, evangelicals are much more likely to be bothered than are mainline Protestants, Catholics, or other groups. It also matters if people live in homogeneous communities or not and if they are stable residents or not. Thus, those who live in small towns or rural areas and in the South are more likely to be bothered than those who live elsewhere, and the more addresses one has had as an adult, the less likely one is to be bothered. Presumably, it is easier to contemplate change in one's community if one is a rolling stone. Unlike attitudes about intermarriage, though, these views do seem to be modified by levels of education. Parents' education makes some difference. But the largest differences are between young adults who have graduated from college and those who have not. Only 32 percent of college grads say they would be bothered by a new mosque in town, whereas 42 percent of young adults with only some college say this, and even more (46 percent) of those with no college do.[26]

FAITH MATTERS

The short answer to my colleague's question about whether it makes any difference that people are religious or not is yes, it does make a difference. Family life especially is so much a part of what congregations emphasize that young adults who actively participate in congregations differ in many ways from young adults who do not participate. Whether one is evangelical rather than affiliated with some other tradition often matters as well. Religious involvement encourages young adults to think more seriously about getting married and having children and, among other things, it influences their views about what is right and wrong to teach children, where to find support, and how much to accept close relationships with people of different faiths.

Skeptics can argue that these so-called influences are merely attitudes that may have little bearing on behavior. The fact that so many young adults who believe premarital sex is wrong engage in premarital sex is certainly evidence that behavior does not always conform to beliefs. Yet the more significant concern is that so few young adults are intensely involved in faith communities and that this number has been declining. A majority of young adults still consider religion relevant to their lives and believe they could depend on a congregation if the chips were down. Meanwhile, though, they are increasingly busy elsewhere and their behavior is thus less subject to the influences of any religious organizations.

❧ 8 ❧

The Divided Generation

RELIGION AND PUBLIC LIFE

RESEARCHERS WHO STUDIED baby boomer religion in the 1970s discovered early on that their subject matter was not monolithic. Some baby boomers were attracted to yoga, Zen Buddhism, Hare Krishna, and other groups with roots in Asian religions. Others dropped out of the Catholic, Protestant, or Jewish traditions in which they had been raised and turned toward political or academic pursuits. Still others got "saved from the sixties," in Steven Tipton's apt phrase, by embracing evangelical student ministries, joining communes, or adopting holistic health practices.[1] By the time researchers such as Wade Clark Roof and Dean Hoge studied them in the early 1980s, baby boomers were sorting themselves into broad categories marked by their involvement in various church traditions, their searching or shopping among several traditions, and their rejection of religion entirely.[2]

The young adults of today are no more monolithic than the baby boomers were. As we have seen, they pick and choose, exercising their freedom to adopt the particular religious practices and beliefs that suit them best. However, the marketplace metaphor goes only a small way in helping us understand the current patterns of religious belief and practice among young adults. It emphasizes the possibility of choice, but does not illuminate the social factors that influence those choices. As such, the marketplace imagery (and related ideas about "religious economies") portray a society composed only of free individuals maximizing their self-interests. It is like trying to understand Wal-Mart by looking only at the shoppers and paying no attention to the reasons Wal-Mart exists in the first place.

We need a more sophisticated view of society if we are going to understand why American religion is patterned as it is. That is especially so when we consider the relationships between religion and public life. If all we wanted to do was understand whether an individual prays, goes to church, and believes in God, the atomistic perspective of the marketplace might do. However, religion is also public. It influences how people vote, how they think about important social and political issues, and their likelihood of joining or supporting politically oriented social movements. This means, as Max Weber observed nearly a century ago, that religion is "this-worldly," engaged in the here and now and thus subject to being shaped by social forces, rather than withdrawing from society and isolating itself from society.[3]

I have argued in other work that the changing relationships between religion and social conditions can be understood better if we imagine a three-fold process consisting of *production, selection,* and *institutionalization.* Production sensitizes us to the fact that the opportunities to worship and to engage in religious practices are produced. They are produced by spiritual entrepreneurs who initiate new religious movements—leaders such as Martin Luther or Jonathan Edwards—and by lay leaders, missionaries, committees, and financial backers who put up the resources to start new congregations, service centers, and parachurch ministries. It is a truism, as the marketplace perspective emphasizes, that such initiatives can happen more readily in a free society than in one with a repressive religious or political monopoly. The more important consideration is that the conditions favoring such initiatives are more abundant at certain times and places than at others, even within a given market situation. Thus, there are times when the moral order that usually defines expectations about what is good and just becomes unsettled. Change of this sort amplifies both the opportunities and the perceived need for new ideas and new practices. The 1960s was an instance of such change. The 1830s, during which the so-called Second Great Awakening occurred, was another such time. The unsettledness that marks periods like this comes about as a result of major economic or technological change, but is sometimes amplified by war, political upheaval, migration, or generational conflict. The important fact is that the cultural and religious production that occurs results in a multiplicity of options. Many competing options usually emerge, at least at the start, rather than only one. Selection refers to the process of competition among those options and to the fact that some survive or flourish and others die out or decline. It helps to think of this process, not as a direct struggle between two competing groups or movements, but by envisioning an environment or field occupied by multiple groups and multiple niches. The groups adjust to one another as they strive to find an appropriate niche for themselves. For instance, one group may appeal to people who have few economic resources and thus need high walls to protect their resources; meanwhile, another group may attract a constituency composed of people with more economic resources or who have grown weary of the restrictions posed by the high walls of the other group. Finally, institutionalization sensitizes us to the fact that over time most groups, religious or otherwise, gain some autonomy from their environment. They do so by developing routines that become habits among their constituents, by forming schools or training centers to convey special knowledge to the next generation, by buying property and building buildings, and for that matter cultivating ties with people in power, such as political leaders.[4]

Production, selection, and institutionalization provide the conceptual tools to understand how American religion has adapted to its changing social environment in recent decades. The general unsettledness of the past half century and especially of the 1960s facilitated numerous initiatives, ranging from the ones I mentioned previously to others, such as campus ministries, faith-based pro-life and pro-choice movements, independent nondenominational churches, Pentecostal groups, and new immigrant congregations. These initiatives were facilitated not only by overt social unrest, but also by the affluence of our society, a cultural heritage that is generally favorable toward religion, and a spirit of entrepreneurialism. The social environment has "selected for" some of these initiatives and "selected against" others. For instance, most of the communes and religious cults that emerged in the 1970s died out within a decade. They did so partly because they were so strict, and demanded such full-blown commitment that few could participate in them for very long, let alone raise families, find jobs, and attract additional recruits.[5] The political climate increasingly shaped the field of religious organizations that survived as well. Divisions among baby boomers were evident from the start with regard to the Vietnam war, the so-called counterculture, and even tastes in music. By the 1980s, conservative religiopolitical movements such as Jerry Falwell's Moral Majority, had risen in political prominence. At the same time, more relativistic values were evident in higher education, the mass media, and among political liberals. The religious groups that increasingly became institutionalized in this climate gravitated toward the right or the left, often in stark opposition to one another.[6] What James Davison Hunter dubbed a "culture war" between groups advocating orthodoxy and groups advocating progressive ideas became a popular way of understanding the polarization that had emerged by the end of the 1980s.[7]

The culture wars imagery was never a particularly accurate way of thinking about American religion. It simply left out too much of what was happening in the middle, let alone the continuing and emerging divisions rooted in ethnic, racial, and even denominational traditions. Nevertheless, the idea of a culture war did capture the tensions that often existed when religious groups entered the political arena. Sitting quietly in their pews on Sunday mornings, many Americans may have felt comfortable as "moderates" who wished the extremists to their right or left would simply keep quiet. But the extremists did not keep quiet. Those on the right lobbied against abortion, while those on the left argued for choice. They used church basements to hold meetings and passed out political campaign leaflets in church parking lots. They encouraged church members to sign petitions or warned the religiously uninvolved that they needed to mobilize to combat the rise of "fundamentalism."[8] This was the legacy of the baby

boomers. It was hard to ignore because it divided denominations and congregations and captured the attention of politicians and pundits.

The question is where the current generation of young adults fits into
this legacy of religious and political conflict. Are they the products of their
parents' generation, poised to carry on the culture wars? Have they gravitated toward religious identities and lifestyles that put them clearly in one
ideological camp or the other? Or are there mitigating factors? Have they
decided to leave the culture wars to the older generation and move on?
Have they come to greater agreement about such hot-button issues as
abortion and homosexuality? Are they more united because of the threats
to our society from terrorists and the changing geopolitical climate in
which we now live?

The Split Between Conservatives and Liberals

Well before anyone wrote about culture wars, it was evident that Americans
were becoming increasingly divided along a conservative-to-liberal spectrum that included religious as well as political considerations. A 1984
poll conducted by the Gallup Organization showed that a fifth to a quarter
of the American public considered itself very conservative in religion and
about the same proportion considered itself very liberal. In the middle,
Americans were also split, leaning about equally to the right or the left. In
addition, these ideological identities corresponded closely to how people
responded when asked specific questions about their religious beliefs.
What was most disturbing was that religious conservatives mostly held
negative views of religious liberals, as did liberals of conservatives, and the
more contact each had with the other, the more these negative views were
reinforced.[9]

That study provides a baseline with which to compare the responses of
young adults in a more recent study—a survey conducted in 1999 that
drew on a similar sampling technique and asked the same question about
people's religious orientation. Figure 8.1 shows how adults age 21 through
45 responded in 1984 and in 1999 when asked to describe their religious
views along a 6-point scale where "1" meant very conservative and "6"
meant very liberal. In both periods, younger adults clustered in the middle
(as did older adults), rather than gravitating toward the extremes. However,
a significant amount of religious polarization also took place during this
fifteen year period. Simply put, more young Americans identified themselves as *very conservative* or as *very liberal* in 1999 than had done so in 1984.
Thus, the proportion who placed themselves at the most conservative point
on the scale increased by more than two-fold from 4 percent to 9 percent
and the proportion at the most liberal point almost doubled from 11 per-

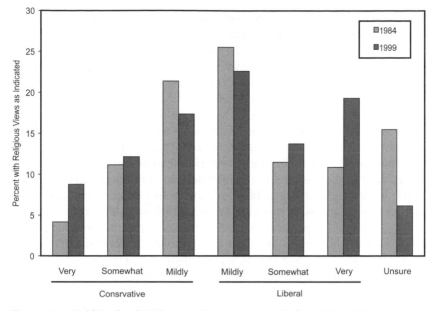

Figure 8.1. Self-Defined Religious Views. Source: Gallup Liberal-Conservative Survey, Arts and Religion Survey, respondents age 21 through 45.

cent to 19 percent. Overall, the two most conservative points and the two most liberal points on the scale drew over half the young adults (54 percent) in 1999, up from only 37 percent in 1984. Meanwhile, the proportion in the middle dropped from 47 percent to 40 percent and the proportion unwilling to identify their religious views in conservative-to-liberal terms declined from 15 percent to only 6 percent.[10]

This evidence suggests that young adults are more divided in their religious orientations now than they were in the early 1980s. The proportion who lean toward religious liberalism outweighs the proportion who lean toward conservatism (by 56 percent to 38 percent). But there is a large minority (about one person in five) who consider themselves staunch religious conservatives, while there is also a large minority (as many as one person in three) who are very liberal in their religious views. What also has to be considered is that the religious conservatives are much more active religiously than religious liberals are. For instance, among the religious conservatives in the 1999 study, 56 percent said they attended religious services nearly every week, whereas only 14 percent of the religious liberals did. To the extent that young adults are divided religiously, then, the division is along behavioral as well as ideological lines. On the one side are those who participate regularly in their congregations and hold conservative religious views; on the other side, are those who seldom participate in congregations and hold liberal religious views.

These self-descriptions also correspond closely to the various measures of religious belief we have considered in previous chapters. For instance, more than 90 percent of religious conservatives say the Bible is divinely inspired, while only two-thirds of religious liberals do. Half of the former say it should be interpreted literally, compared with a fifth of the latter. About three in five religious conservatives report having had a "born again" experience at some point in their lives, compared with about a quarter of religious liberals. More than half of religious conservatives claim they read the Bible at least once a week; about 10 percent of religious liberals do. No single survey question is capable of pigeon-holing people exactly, and this is especially true of something as complex as religion. Nevertheless, these are strong statistical patterns in these responses. They indicate that people who think of themselves as religious conservatives generally are in fact more conservative in their beliefs, while self-described religious liberals are less committed to traditional beliefs and practices.

Yet we need to be cautious in how we think about the religious divisions among young adults. The caveat that must always be considered when discussing polarization is that doing so runs the danger of neglecting the large number of moderates. Yet, closer inspection indicates that they, too, divide along familiar fault lines. For instance, among Protestants who say they hold moderate views, about one in five says he or she is an evangelical or fundamentalist, while the same number use the term "liberal" to describe themselves. Similarly, about a quarter of Catholics who say their views are moderate describe themselves as traditional Catholics, while another quarter describe themselves as liberal Catholics.

If ideology is reinforced by lifestyle, it is also worth noting the ways in which young adults who consider themselves religious conservatives differ from those who consider themselves religious liberals. Conservatives are more likely to be in their thirties and a large majority are either currently married or have been married, while liberals are more likely to be in their twenties and single. About three-quarters of religious conservatives are parents, while fewer than half of religious liberals are. Moreover, these differences in lifestyle are among the clearest ways in which religious conservatives and liberals differ. For instance, religious conservatives were more likely to have been reared going to church than religious liberals were, while religious liberals were more likely than conservatives to have grown up without any formal religious affiliation.[11] These differences, though, pale in comparison with the lifestyle differences separating the two groups.

What separates religious conservatives and religious liberals most clearly is how they view political and social issues. When asked about their *political* views, 70 percent of religious conservatives said they were also politically conservative (only 19 percent placed themselves left of center); in contrast, 77 percent of religious liberals said their political views were also liberal (while only 19 percent described their political views as conservative). Of course some of this apparent consistency is a function of people falling into certain response patterns when answering surveys. However, it also squares with what we know about the increasing role of religion in American politics. As more and more political leaders *and* religious leaders have combined religious and political themes in their public rhetoric, it is not surprising that many young adults now think of themselves religiously and politically in the same categories.

These categories also correspond with perceptions of how things are going in our society. Many young adults are quite concerned about social problems. For instance, almost half of young adults (48 percent) say the condition of the poor is an extremely serious problem in our society and almost that many (42 percent) say this about too much emphasis being placed on money. On these issues religious conservatives are slightly more likely to express concern than religious liberals, but the two groups do not differ dramatically. What sets the two apart is how they feel about moral corruption. Two thirds (67 percent) of religious conservatives feel this is an extremely serious problem, whereas fewer than half (46 percent) of religious liberals do. Half of religious conservatives also feel this way about people turning away from God, whereas only a quarter of religious liberals do.

It is little wonder, then, that young adults are divided when it comes to the various causes and issues promoted by special interest groups. If a conservative group decides it is time to clean up television, there is a ready constituency to put feet under the effort. And there is another constituency ready to be mobilized in opposition to this group. Even in matters of popular music and culture where, as we have seen, young adults are generally supportive of the latest tastes, such moral crusades and counter-crusades can be mobilized. For instance, fully 72 percent of young religious conservatives said they had heard a song in the past year that disgusted them, and 61 percent said this about some movie preview they had seen. Music and movies, though, are only some of the issues on which young adults are currently divided.

CIVIL RELIGION

Newspaper and television stories about religion often focus on specific issues, such as how religious groups feel about abortion or prayer in public schools. These are important, and they make for good news stories because some advocate on both sides of the issue can usually be found for a timely quote. Usually, though, the deep background is missed. That background has to do with how Americans understand the history of our country and the principles on which our nation was founded. In the 1960s, Robert Bellah borrowed Rousseau's term "civil religion" and applied it to the United States as a way of describing these deeper understandings.[12] Our civil religion is most simply described as the use of God language with reference to the nation. It includes a myth of origin in which the religious beliefs and practices of early settlers, explorers, colonists, and founding fathers and mothers are sometimes emphasized. It also includes assumptions about the religious values that make America strong and about what our nation should do to be good and to avoid evil.

Bellah suggests that civil religion in the United States is a pastiche of biblical ideals and what he calls civic republican traditions. The biblical ideas emphasize America's Christian (or sometimes "Judeo-Christian") roots, whereas the civic republican traditions focus on secular understandings of democracy, law, and justice. A careful understanding of American history emphasizes the contribution of both. However, in popular discourse it is easier to focus on one or the other. That, in fact, has been one of the underlying tensions in recent debates about religion and politics. Some leaders argue that America is fundamentally a Christian nation, or at least has been until now, and needs to do everything it can to preserve this heritage. Others are not so sure.

The public registers a striking level of agreement with statements that reflect the core tenets of American civil religion.[13] For instance, almost four people in five (79 percent) agree that the United States was founded on Christian principles, with 51 percent agreeing strongly, and only 18 percent disagreeing. Similarly, 80 percent agree that America has been strong because of its faith in God (54 percent agree strongly). However, younger adults are much less likely to hold these views than older adults are. Only 37 percent of adults age 21 through 29 agree strongly that the United States was founded on Christian principles, whereas 71 percent of adults age 65 and older agree strongly. On this statement, the percentages who agree strongly rise steadily as one proceeds from younger to older age groups. The same is true for other statements. Thus, 39 percent of adults age 21 through 29 agree strongly that America has been strong because of its faith in God, compared with 69 percent of those age 65 and older who say this. Even among younger adults, those in the youngest group are significantly less likely to agree with such statements than those in their early forties. For instance, only 15 percent of adults in their twenties agree strongly that our democratic form of government is based on Christianity, compared with 27 percent of those in their early forties. As a summary measure, I constructed a Civil Religion Index that gives people a point for each of four questions with which they strongly agreed.[14] Among adults in their twenties, 31 percent scored high (2, 3, or 4) on this index, and this proportion rose to 70 percent among those age 65 and older.

Why might young adults be disinclined to believe that the United States was founded on Christian principles and that its strength depends on its faith in God? We cannot look directly at trends because similarly worded questions were not asked in surveys thirty or fifty years ago. However, the striking differences between the responses of younger and older adults to these questions suggests that some change has probably taken place over time. This possibility seems especially likely in the present instance because the differences among age groups are so dramatic. We can also make some educated guesses about the sources of this possible trend. For instance, unlike questions about an afterlife or receiving comfort from God that might be expected to increase with age simply because older people are closer to death or faced with illnesses, there is no reason to think that rising belief in civil religion could be explained simply on the basis of such life cycle effects. A more plausible interpretation would focus on the possible effects of rising levels of education. A person with little formal education might believe that America was founded on Christian principles, for instance, whereas someone who had been to college and learned about the Enlightenment, deism, and the complex sources of America's founding principles would be less likely to emphasize the nation's Christian roots. Because younger adults are more likely to have finished high school and attended college than older adults are, this possibility might also account for how the different age groups respond to questions about civil religion. Further analysis of these data shows, in fact, that these responses are influenced by levels of education. People who have attained higher levels of education are less likely to score high on the Civil Religion Index. Among those who have been to college, those who majored in the social sciences and humanities are less likely to score high on the index than those who majored in other fields, such as the sciences, engineering, or business (where discussions of American history would have been less frequent). Those whose parents had graduated from college were also less likely to score high on the index.[15] *None* of these education factors, though, explains away (or even reduces) the differences between younger adults and older adults.[16]

The fact that the differences between younger and older adults remain even when levels of education are taken into account suggests to me that we are seeing evidence of a larger cultural shift. When people now in their sixties were growing up, it would have been easier to learn explicitly or to assume tacitly that the United States had been and still was a country based on Christian principles. Chances are, the religious convictions of the Puritans were emphasized in textbooks. In many schools, prayer in the classroom was still practiced. From reading the newspapers during the Cold War, a person could easily have gained the impression that America was a God-fearing nation pitted against godless communism. The Christian dominance in the culture might have been further reinforced by anti-Semitism or by expressions of intolerance toward atheists. Younger adults nowadays have grown up in a very different cultural environment. Whether a person goes on to college or not, that person is likely to have attended a grade school and high school in which very little was said about religion. Certainly prayer would not have been part of the public school room. More of one's cultural information would have come from television and even the best documentaries and news programs would not have emphasized Christianity. It would still have been common to hear public figures ask God's blessing on the nation, but without more extended commentary, those statements would have seemed perfunctory. In short, the cultural climate has changed. And one of the big results of that change—whether one believes it was a change for the better or worse—is that relatively few young adults currently believe strongly in the kind of integral connection between Christianity and the American nation that in earlier periods defined our civil religion.

Understanding how views about American civil religion have changed also goes a long way toward helping us make sense of the current culture wars about the place of religion in the public life of our nation. For instance, consider the recurring debates about whether it is appropriate to display the Ten Commandments in government buildings or teach them to children in public schools.[17] Young adults are less likely than older adults to favor these ways of bringing religion into the public square. For instance, only 37 percent of young adults in their twenties agreed strongly in the Religion and Diversity Survey that the public schools should teach children the Ten Commandments, compared with 58 percent among those age 65 and older. Even among young adults, though, there are clearly differences of opinion on this issue. And those differences can be understood largely in relation to how young adults feel about American civil religion. Thus, 69 percent of those who scored highest on the Civil Religion Index strongly agreed that public schools should teach the Ten Commandments, as did 68 percent of those who scored next highest; in comparison, only 19 percent of those who scored lowest on the index thought this.

Whether one favors teaching the Ten Commandments may have little bearing on the practical realities of American politics since the courts have generally taken the position that such teaching violates the Constitution. However, views about civil religion do matter in another important way: they significantly affect how people vote. Take the 2000 election, for instance, in which George W. Bush narrowly won over Vice President Al Gore. The left-hand map in figure 8.2 shows the states Bush won. The right-hand map shows the states in which at least 49 percent of the respondents in the Religion and Diversity Survey scored high on the Civil Reli-

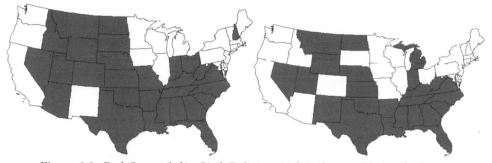

Figure 8.2. Red States (left), Civil Religion (right). Source: National Election Results, Religion and Diversity Survey.

gion Index. The two maps are strikingly similar.[18] If we look only at young adults, there were too few respondents in many of the states to do the same kind of analysis. There is, nevertheless, a strong relationship among those age 21 through 45 between how they scored on the Civil Religion Index and how they voted in 2000. For instance, 49 percent of those who scored low on the Index voted for Gore, while only 19 percent of those who scored high on the index did. Conversely, 32 percent of those who scored low voted for Bush, while 64 percent of those who scored high did.

The fact that civil religion is no longer as popular as it probably was in the past has one other important implication for young adults. It means that the main place in which this understanding of American history is reinforced is in religious contexts, not in the wider culture. Thus, young adults who attend church regularly (by a margin of 56 percent to 30 percent) are more likely to score high on the Civil Religion Index. And evangelicals are significantly more likely to score high than are mainline Protestants or Catholics (59 percent, 41 percent, and 33 percent, respectively). It is little wonder, then, that young adults who are active church-going evangelicals feel that they are in tension with the wider culture. Just as self-described religious conservatives feel divided from self-described religious liberals, evangelicals who believe strongly that America should be a Christian nation are divided from their contemporaries who do not feel this way.

Voting in Presidential Elections

The foregoing suggests that George W. Bush fared especially well in the 2000 election among young voters who held firm views about American civil religion and that those voters tended to be evangelical Protestants. How have religious convictions influenced other elections in recent years? In every presidential election since 1968 the Republican candidate has en-

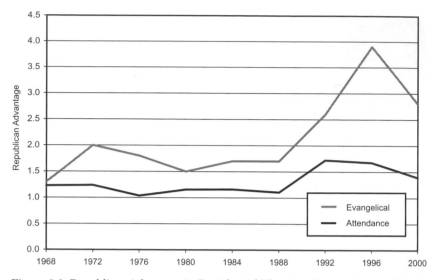

Figure 8.3. Republican Advantage in Presidential Elections. Source: General Social Surveys, respondents age 21 through 45.

joyed an advantage among evangelicals and, indeed, in every race except that of Jimmy Carter against Gerald Ford in 1976 the Republican candidate has also been favored by regular church attenders. I do not mean that a majority of church goers and evangelicals have always voted Republican. Their votes, like those of other Americans have been influenced by the economy and the popularity of the various candidates. However, when frequent church attenders are compared with less frequent church attenders, the former are usually more likely than the latter to vote Republican. Similarly, when evangelical Protestants are compared with the group of young adults who are least like them (and yet growing), namely, the religiously nonaffiliated, Republicans again enjoy an advantage among the former. Moreover, the gap between the churched and unchurched and between evangelicals and the nonaffiliated has been increasing.

The evidence is best illustrated by the numbers shown in figure 8.3. The lower line represents the percentage of church-going young adults age 21 through 45 (those who attended at least almost every week) who voted for the Republican candidate in each presidential election divided by the percentage of young adults who voted for the Republican candidate among those who attended religious services less frequently. The top line is a similar ratio computed by comparing the votes of young evangelical Protestants to the votes of religiously nonaffiliated young adults. The lower line shows that Republican candidates enjoyed an advantage of about 1.2 among frequent church goers from the late 1960s to the late 1980s. Then in the 1992,

1996, and 2000 elections that advantage was significantly larger. The upper line shows that young evangelicals were about 1.3 times as likely as nonaffiliated young adults to vote for Nixon in 1968. Then the Republican advantage ranged between 1.5 and 2.0 in the 1970s and 1980s. After this, it ranged between 2.6 and 3.9.

These figures are important because they belie two popular impressions about the relationship between religion and presidential elections in recent decades. The first is that George W. Bush won in 2000 because regular church goers voted for him by a landslide. The second is that the Republican advantage among evangelicals began in the late 1970s as a result of disillusionment with Jimmy Carter and solidified during the Reagan administration in the 1980s. Both are only half true, at least among younger adults. In the 2000 election, regular church going young adults did favor George W. Bush. Almost 60 percent voted for him, compared with about 43 percent among less frequent church goers. Yet the advantage George W. Bush earned in that election was actually less than Bob Dole's had been in the 1996 election or than Bush's father enjoyed in the 1992 campaign against Bill Clinton. As for young evangelicals, they had already given Richard Nixon the edge in 1972, and that edge was never as high during the Reagan or George H. W. Bush campaigns. Not until the 1990s did it exceed that of 1972.

Another stereotype that is disconfirmed by these voting patterns is that the so-called culture war between evangelicals and the rest of America was largely a split between evangelical Protestants and mainline Protestants. This was not the case among young adults. In all the elections between 1968 and 2000, young adults who were affiliated with mainline Protestant denominations voted for Republican candidates more consistently than any other young adults did, with the exception of evangelicals. Indeed, between 1968 and 1980, young mainline Protestants had been *more likely* than young evangelical Protestants to vote Republican. It was not until Reagan's second campaign that young evangelicals began to vote Republican in greater numbers than their mainline counterparts.[19]

Younger Catholics, Jews, and members of historically black denominations have consistently voted for Democratic candidates to a greater extent than evangelical or mainline Protestants. Black Protestants have overwhelmingly voted Democratic, Jews have generally voted Democratic but not with as large percentages, and Catholics have voted about the same way that young adults in general have voted. In the case of Catholics, though, it would be wrong to assume that the divisions evident among Protestants are absent. Catholics, too, are often divided theologically even though they remain in the same church. Traditional Catholics define themselves in terms of loyalty to church teachings and traditions, while liberal or progressive Catholics typically would like to see reforms. As shown in figure

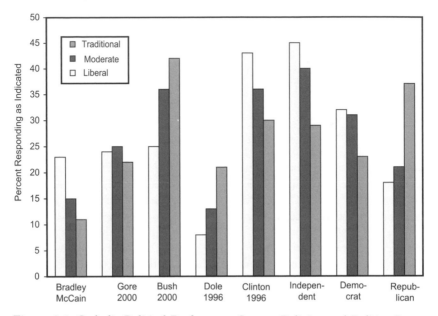

Figure 8.4. Catholic Political Preferences. Source: Religion and Politics Survey, respondents age 21 through 45.

8.4, these theological differences influence how Catholics think of themselves politically and how they vote. Specifically, among Catholics age 21 through 45 in 2000, about twice as many traditionalists identified themselves as Republicans (37 percent) as was true among liberals (18 percent). Conversely, moderates and liberals were more likely to identify themselves as Democrats or Independents than traditional Catholics were. Liberals were significantly more likely than traditionalists to have voted for Clinton in 1996, while traditionalists were almost three times as likely to have voted for Dole than liberals were. And during the 2000 campaign, traditionalists were significantly more likely than liberals to say they favored Bush, while the latter (instead of being more likely to favor Gore) were more likely to favor one of the other candidates (Bradley or McCain).[20]

The widening gap in voting patterns among young adults is thus largely understood in terms of the shift among young evangelicals toward Republican candidates and the growing number of religiously nonaffiliated young adults who have gradually given less and less support to Republican candidates over the years. It may also correspond to the differences in political preferences associated with theological differences among Catholics. Elections are never won or lost solely in terms of shifting loyalties among particular constituencies. Nevertheless, the differences that have emerged between young evangelicals and young adults who are religiously nonaffiliated are an important factor in understanding the current shape of electoral politics.

MIXING RELIGION AND POLITICS

Candidates from both parties have increasingly mixed religious rhetoric into their political discourse, although some have been more comfortable doing so than others. As the first Catholic president, John F. Kennedy went out of his way to deny that his religious convictions had any bearing on his conduct of public office. Lyndon Johnson also seldom made public reference to his religious beliefs. Richard Nixon seldom did, either, although he frequently invited evangelist Billy Graham to the White House. After the Watergate scandal and the brief presidency of Gerald Ford, the public was eager for a president who spoke openly about the importance of morality in public life, and in Jimmy Carter not only received that but also elected a born-again Christian to the highest office. Ronald Reagan was more comfortable speaking about God than George H. W. Bush was. Bill Clinton sometimes referred to God in public speeches and in the 2000 election both Al Gore and George W. Bush made references to God. Watchdog groups, such as Americans for Separation of Church and State, typically voice concern about candidates and public officials bringing religion too visibly into the public arena. Yet the American public is generally supportive both of political leaders talking about religion and of religious leaders talking about politics.

Younger adults, having grown up during a time when political candidates brought religion into their speeches, are slightly more likely to regard this mixing of religion and politics with favor than older adults are. About eight in ten Americans (79 percent) in their twenties, thirties, and forties believe it is okay for political candidates to talk about their religious views in public and for religious leaders to express their views on social and political issues, but this number slips slightly (to 77 percent) among people age 46 to 64 and then drops further (to 69 percent) among people age 65 and older. Considerably fewer young adults (about four in ten) think it is right for clergy to discuss political issues from the pulpit, but that number is also higher than it is for adults in their late forties to early sixties (34 percent), which in turn is higher than for adults age 65 and older (26 percent).[21]

Young adults affiliated with the various faith traditions do not differ from one another very much in how likely they are to consider mixing religion and politics in these ways acceptable. Evangelicals and black Protestants are somewhat more accepting than mainline Protestants and Catholics, but the differences are small.[22] Not surprisingly, young adults with no religious affiliations are less eager for religion and politics to become intertwined.

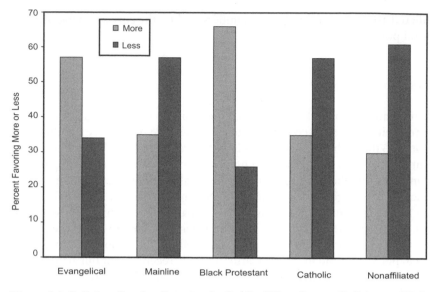

Figure 8.5. Religious Leaders Running for Public Office. Source: Religion and Politics Survey, respondents age 21 through 45.

Yet, even in this group about three-quarters think it is okay for political leaders to talk about religion and for religious leaders to talk about politics, and about four in ten say it is right for clergy to discuss social and political issues from the pulpit.

Other ways of bringing religion into the public arena also draw favorable responses from most young adults. For instance, approximately nine persons in ten would like to see religious groups take a more active role in promoting community responsibility and encouraging people to do volunteer work. Almost as many would like religious organizations to be more active in promoting racial equality and in emphasizing the needs of poor people in other countries. Equally large majorities would like religious congregations to work with government agencies to provide better services to the needy.

Where young adults from the various religious traditions part company is in how they think about religious leaders running for public office. Evangelicals have the example of television preacher Pat Robertson running for public office in 1988, and black Protestants have Jesse Jackson as a visible example of a clergyman running for office. In both traditions, clergy have also served as mayors, on school boards, and in other local capacities. In contrast, mainline Protestants and Catholics have been more circumspect about clergy occupying political offices. Attitudes among young adults affiliated with these traditions follow suit (figure 8.5). Fifty-seven percent of young evangelicals would like to see more religious leaders running for office, as would 66 percent of black Protestants. In contrast, only 35 percent of mainline Protestants and 35 percent of Catholics say the same. These percentages are only slightly higher than the 30 percent who respond similarly among young adults without religious affiliations.

Religious leaders running for public office is one of the more active ways in which religion can enter the public arena. Other activities that might also be regarded as an aggressive effort by religion to influence political life divide along similar lines. For instance, about half of evangelical and black Protestants age 21 through 45 would like to see more of religious leaders appearing on television talk shows, whereas only about a third of mainline Protestants and Catholics would, as would only a quarter of the religiously unaffiliated. In fact, a majority of mainline Protestants, Catholics, and religious unaffiliated young adults would like to see *less* of this. Young adults are also split in terms of how they feel about religious leaders forming political movements. Evangelicals and black Protestants would like to see more of this, mainline Protestants, Catholics, and the unaffiliated would like to see less of it.[23]

The curious aspect of these attitudes about mingling religion and politics is that they run counter, at least in part, with young adults' views about civil religion. Whereas young adults are less likely than older adults to think of America as a Christian nation, they are more likely than older adults to consider it acceptable for political leaders to talk about religion and for religious leaders to talk about politics. The two issues, though, are not the same. Civil religion implies a cultural *establishment* of religion, and especially of Christianity; in contrast, talking about religion and politics in the same venues can be interpreted as a *voluntaristic* form of free expression. The former can seem heavy-handed or inconsistent with historical reality, while the latter can be accepted as an opportunity for people of faith to speak about their various views. Still, the evidence also suggests that these two understandings of religion map similarly onto the current religious terrain. Young evangelicals tend to think not only that America was founded on Christian principles but also that clergy should run for office and initiate political movements. The religiously unaffiliated disagree on both counts. Nonevangelical Protestants and Catholics find themselves in the middle, thinking it is okay for political leaders to talk about religion, but worrying about more aggressive efforts to bring religion into the political realm.

HOT-BUTTON ISSUES: ABORTION

No single issue has done as much to polarize religious groups as questions about the legality and morality of abortion. Religious conservatives have waged a continuing struggle to criminalize abortion while religious liberals have generally argued that government should protect women's right to choose. Of the numerous studies that have been made of this issue, few have focused specifically on the attitudes of younger adults. Yet it is younger adults who are most directly affected. In considering the future of the abortion debate—which many observers argue has reached a kind of political and cultural stalemate—it is especially important to understand whether younger adults are becoming more or less accepting of abortion. Both possibilities are plausible. As more time has elapsed since the landmark *Roe v. Wade* decision in 1973 and as the culture has become more familiar with new medical procedures and reproductive technologies, the possibility that younger adults are becoming more tolerant of abortion is plausible. Observers also argue, though, that the pro-life movement has had considerable success in publicizing its arguments, meaning that young adults may have become more opposed to abortion than the previous generation of young adults was.

The truth of the matter is that young adults are more polarized in their attitudes toward abortion than their counterparts were a generation ago. The reason for this is not that some people have become more tolerant while others have become less tolerant. The overall trend among young adults has actually been a small increase in the percentages who oppose abortion. Young evangelicals, though, have become even more likely to oppose abortion than young adults who are not evangelicals. For instance, the proportion of young evangelicals who say abortion is wrong even in the case of preventing birth defects rose by 16 percentage points (from 17 percent to 33 percent) between the early 1970s and the late 1990s, whereas the proportion of nonevangelicals who said this rose by only 6 points (from 13 percent to 19 percent). On questions asking about abortion for other reasons, opposition among evangelicals also increased more dramatically than among nonevangelicals (figure 8.6). Whether it was abortion simply to prevent more children or because the mother was unmarried or abortion to protect the health of the mother or in instances of rape, young evangelicals at the end of the 1990s were decidedly more opposed to abortion than young evangelicals were in the early 1970s. And their opposition separated them more sharply from nonevangelicals, too.[24]

Hot-Button Issues: Homosexuality

The increasing resistance of young evangelicals to abortion would suggest that a similar trend may have been taking place in views about homosexuality. It, too, has become a hot-button issue. Denominations and local congregations have split over the question of whether homosexuals can be ordained. And on the national stage, questions about gay marriage have

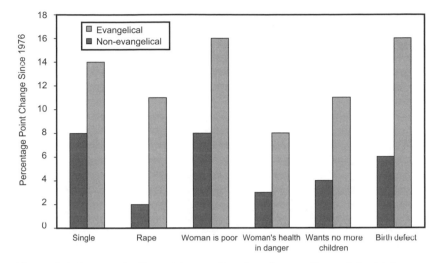

Figure 8.6. Increase in Opposition to Abortion. Source: General Social Surveys, respondents age 21 through 45.

become rallying cries for public leaders and political candidates. The empirical evidence, though, does not show that young evangelicals and nonevangelicals are becoming more polarized on this issue like they are on abortion. In fact, just the opposite is the case. Between the early 1970s and the late 1990s, young adults became markedly more tolerant of homosexuality, and young evangelicals shifted in this direction in larger numbers than nonevangelicals did. By the late 1990s, young evangelicals were still less tolerant of homosexuality than nonevangelicals were, but the gap had shrunk. For instance, the proportion of young evangelicals who said a homosexual should be allowed to make a public speech rose by 20 points (from 58 percent to 78 percent), while the comparable proportion among nonevangelicals rose by only 10 points (from 79 percent to 89 percent). The respective shifts in allowing a homosexual to teach were 30 points among evangelicals and 16 points among nonevangelicals. And on allowing a book by a homosexual to be in the library, 17 points and 10 points (figure 8.7). Thus, on each of these questions, evangelicals and nonevangelicals were more similar to each other in the late 1990s than they had been in the early 1970s.

There are two plausible explanations for this convergence in views about homosexuality. The first is statistical. Nonevangelicals were already largely supportive of these kinds of civil liberties for homosexuals in the 1970s, so there was less room for their percentages to increase than there was for evangelicals. The other is substantive. These questions are about civil liberties, unlike the questions about abortion, which were framed in terms of

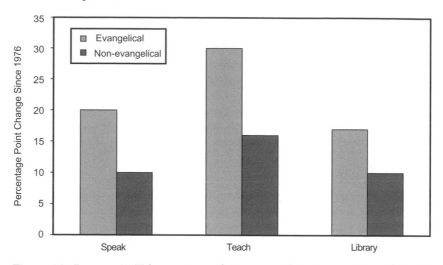

Figure 8.7. Increase in Tolerance toward Homosexuality. Source: General Social Surveys, respondents age 21 through 45.

morality (right and wrong). Evangelicals, like the rest of the public, draw distinctions between the two. They may believe, for example, that Islam is a false religion and thus morally wrong, and yet they respect the rights of Muslims to worship in the United States. The difficult question is when a moral argument becomes sufficiently compelling to warrant the curtailment of civil liberties. In the case of abortion, opponents have argued that abortion is the same thing as murdering babies and is thus so morally wrong that it should be outlawed, even if those laws infringe on the civil liberties of women. Among young evangelicals, that argument has apparently become increasingly persuasive. In contrast, evangelicals may believe that homosexuality is morally wrong, but are largely unpersuaded that it is so wrong as to warrant restricting the civil liberties of homosexuals.

Data from other surveys permit sorting out more closely how religion—especially evangelical identifies and beliefs—affect attitudes toward homosexuality. In the 2004 *Religion and Ethics Newsweekly* survey religious identity was a decisive factor in how people felt about gay marriage and civil unions for gays and lesbians (figure 8.8). Nearly two-thirds of white evangelicals (63 percent) voiced strong opposition to gay marriage (only 15 percent favored it). At the opposite extreme, only 18 percent of the religiously nonaffiliated strongly opposed gay marriage (54 percent favored it). Mainline Protestants, black Protestants, and Catholics fell in between. About a third of Catholics strongly opposed gay marriage, while slightly higher percentages of mainline Protestants and black Protestants did. Views of civil unions for gays and lesbians followed the same pattern, although oppo-

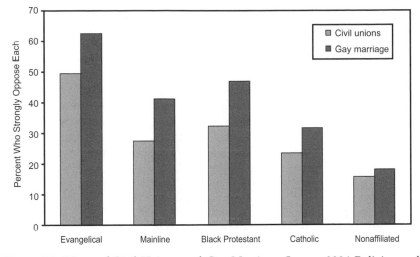

Figure 8.8. Views of Civil Unions and Gay Marriage. Source: 2004 Religion and Ethics Newsweekly Survey, respondents age 21 through 45.

sition was lower across the board. Half of evangelicals were strongly opposed to civil unions, compared with about a quarter of mainline Protestants, black Protestants, and Catholics, and only a sixth of nonaffiliated young adults.

This information shows clearly that young evangelicals remain overwhelmingly opposed to homosexuality, despite the trend toward greater respect for the civil liberties of gays and lesbians. Moreover, a significant minority of young evangelicals feel strongly enough about homosexuality that they would like help from the government in curbing it. For instance, among the 80 percent of evangelicals who said they oppose gay marriage, 41 percent would like to see the U.S. Constitution amended to outlaw gay marriage. About the same proportion (40 percent) said they would not vote for a political candidate who disagreed with their views about gay marriage.

The Religious Right

The phrase "religious right" came into popular usage in the early 1980s as a result of Jerry Falwell's Moral Majority movement and other organizations (such as the Religious Roundtable and later the Christian Coalition) that combined conservative politics and religion. Although the sharpest divisions among young adults are currently between evangelical Protestants and the religiously unaffiliated (as we have seen), the religious right divided evangelicals and mainline Protestants and more conservative Catholics

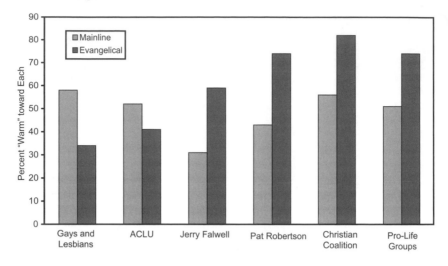

Figure 8.9. Feelings toward Selected Groups and Leaders. Source: 2004 Religion and Ethics Newsweekly Survey, all white evangelical and mainline Protestants

from more liberal Catholics as well. It did so, as some of the previous evidence has suggested, by emphasizing abortion as a litmus test of true belief and by encouraging religious leaders to run for public office. Further evidence of the split between evangelicals and mainline Protestants can be seen in figure 8.9. These results are also from the 2004 *Religion and Ethics Newsweekly* study. "Feeling thermometer" questions were asked in which respondents rated each of the target groups or individuals on a scale from 0 to 100, where 0 meant they felt cold and 100 meant they felt warm. For present purposes, I have counted scores of 50 or higher as "warm." I have also selected only those groups and individuals asked about in the survey who were identified by at least 80 percent of the evangelical and mainline respondents (excluding, for instance, James Dobson and Franklin Graham). For each of the groups or individuals shown, there is a significant difference between evangelicals and mainline Protestants. For instance, 74 percent of evangelicals feel warm toward pro-life, anti-abortion groups, whereas only 51 percent of mainline Protestants do. It is notable that evangelicals and mainline Protestants are as divided about gays and lesbians as they are about abortion groups. It is also notable that evangelicals and mainline Protestants are as polarized about particular individuals as they are toward groups. The largest of these differences, in fact, is toward television preacher Pat Robertson, where the spread between evangelicals and mainline Protestants is 31 percentage points. Catholics, black Protestants, and Jews, incidentally, are all more like mainline Protestants in their views toward these groups and individuals than they are like evangelicals.[25]

When the responses of evangelicals age 21 through 45 with the responses of evangelicals over age 45 to these groups and individuals are considered, younger evangelicals are just as likely as older ones to feel warm toward pro-life groups and the Christian Coalition. Feelings about Jerry Falwell and Pat Robertson also show few differences between younger and older evangelicals. The most notable differences, though, are in the responses toward groups that have been viewed negatively by the Religious Right. Younger evangelicals are significantly warmer than older evangelicals in their views toward gays and lesbians and toward the ACLU.

The fact that younger evangelicals are more favorable toward gays and lesbians and the ACLU may suggest some thawing in the culture wars that have pitted evangelicals against mainline Protestants and other religious groups. However, this possibility should not be overstated. A majority of younger evangelicals still regards gays and lesbians unfavorably. A majority of younger evangelicals also continues to favor the same conservative groups and leaders that older evangelicals favor.

WAR AND PEACE

For the baby boomer generation, the Vietnam War was the most divisive issue of all, not only separating them from older Americans, but also dividing them internally between those who supported the war and those who opposed it. The current generation of young adults also faces difficult questions about war and peace. The questions have not been as focused or as explosive as those concerning Vietnam. But young adults are having to make up their minds about how strong our military should be and whether it makes sense to invade countries that may appear to be a threat to our way of life or in need of democracy. On these questions, there appear to be few differences between younger adults (whether in their twenties, thirties, or early forties) and older adults. Among younger adults, mainline Protestants, black Protestants, and Catholics differ little from one another in how they respond to various questions about war and peace. Evangelicals and young adults who are religiously nonaffiliated are the outliers.

On each of the questions shown in figure 8.10, evangelicals are more likely than other Christians (mainline Protestants, black Protestants, and Catholics) to say that the action indicated should be an extremely important or a very important priority for American foreign policy. Evangelicals are more likely to say this about keeping America's military strong, controlling biological and nuclear weapons, fighting global terrorism, sending troops into other countries, and promoting democracy abroad. In contrast, the religiously nonaffiliated are least likely to say these actions

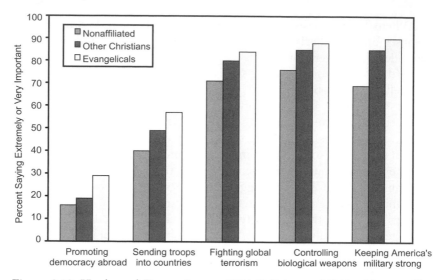

Figure 8.10. Hawks and Doves. Source: 2004 Religion and Ethics Newsweekly Survey, respondents age 21 through 45.

should be important priorities for American foreign policy. Thus, in comparison with evangelicals, the nonaffiliated are 21 points less likely to consider keeping America's military strong an important priority, and between 12 and 17 points less likely to say this about the other actions listed.

Why It Matters

In a valuable book about the transformation of American religion in general, but more about evangelicals than anyone else, Alan Wolfe argues that Americans who are not evangelical have nothing to fear from evangelicals.[26] The reason, he says, is that evangelicals seldom practice what they preach. They live as other people do, quietly focus on their own families, and (as we have seen) seldom go out of their way to proselytize others. Wolfe's point is well-taken. Yet his book concentrates on information collected by other researchers in ethnographic studies while neglecting to pay attention to data collected in surveys. What we have considered here points to a somewhat different conclusion. It does not suggest that evangelicals should be feared, at least not if that means fearing some violent attack on American cities or a breach of the U.S. Constitution. It does suggest, though, that religious convictions matter in public life. Young evangelicals care deeply about the future of America. They are worried about more than just their own families. Indeed, they want the nation to clean up its act morally and believe in politics as the way to achieve that aim. They would like to rid the society of abortion. Although they generally respect the civil liberties of gays and lesbians, a significant minority would also like to pass a constitutional amendment outlawing gay marriage. Wolfe may be correct if nothing to fear means that few evangelicals will march on Washington to have their way in these matters. But his argument should not be interpreted to mean that evangelicals are politically neutral or ineffective. Republican leaders are warranted in considering evangelicals their "base." Young evangelicals now are even more likely than they were a few decades ago to identify themselves as staunch religious conservatives and to vote for Republican candidates.

Political scientists point out that young adults *in general* may not be an important consideration in the political process because they fail to act on their political convictions. There is some truth to this claim. For instance, in one of the surveys we considered earlier only 16 percent of people in their twenties said they had contacted an elected official during the past year about an issue of concern—just half the proportion who had done so among people age 46 to 64. Even fewer of those in their twenties (6 percent) had given money to a political candidate or party. Yet, in other ways, younger adults were not so different from older adults. About the same proportion in all age groups had attended a political rally or meeting. And, probably because some of them were still working toward degrees, more in their twenties than in older groups had attended a class or lecture about social or political issues.[27] In this study, religious tradition was associated with neither higher or lower levels of political participation among younger adults. Evangelicals were the most likely to have contacted an elected official, mainline Protestants were the most likely to have given money to a political candidate or party, and black Protestants were the most likely to have attended a political rally or meeting and to have worked for a political campaign. In each instance, though, young adults affiliated with some religious tradition were more politically active than those affiliated with none. Those who attended religious services regularly were also more likely to have been politically involved than those who attended religious services less often.[28]

The other argument that is sometimes made against taking religion very seriously is that people in the middle are more than enough to counterbalance those at the extreme right (or left). This is the same argument that critics of the culture wars thesis have made. It correctly draws attention to the fact that many mainline Protestants and Catholics make political decisions on an issue-by-issue basis. It also correctly emphasizes that black Protestants usually vote differently from white evangelicals, despite sharing many of the same beliefs. Nevertheless, most of the evidence we have considered points to a widening gap between religious conservatives or evangelicals, on the one hand, and religious liberals or the unaffiliated, on the other hand. Whether mainline Protestants, Catholics, and other groups will be able to mediate between these extremes, or whether they, too, will be drawn toward the extremes, is one of the major questions that will shape American religion in the foreseeable future.

Emerging Trends

IMMIGRATION AND ETHNIC DIVERSITY

BETWEEN 1965 and the end of the twentieth century approximately 22 million immigrants came to the United States. An additional 7 to 10 million came as undocumented immigrants. The immigrant population included more young adults than the native born population did. There were also more children. No consideration of the future of American religion is thus complete without focusing on these new immigrants. The largest groups were from Spanish speaking countries, especially Mexico, and from East Asia, especially China and Korea. Case studies conducted by ethnographers in immigrant churches show that immigrants, now as in the past, frequently turn to religion as a source of identity. Some are even more religious than they were in their native countries.[1]

Congregation studies are limited because they focus only on the religiously involved. They miss the immigrants who seldom participate in congregations. To draw conclusions only from congregation studies is thus to risk overestimating the importance of religion among immigrants. Surveys do a better job of representing the whole immigrant population. The trouble with surveys is that the number of immigrants is often small. The typical Gallup or ABC poll from which news reports are generated, for instance, would likely include no more than a hundred or so immigrants, and other studies, such as the General Social Survey, miss people who cannot speak English. A few surveys, though, have been conducted among large enough samples and with non-English speakers. These surveys are the most useful sources for describing the religious involvement of immigrants and nondominant ethnic groups.

HISPANIC CATHOLICS

One of the best studies for comparing Hispanic Catholics with white Anglo Catholics is the Religion and Politics Survey. With a total of 5,603 interviews among persons who were interviewed either in English or in Spanish, it provides ample information with which to make these comparisons, even when focusing on young adults age 21 through 45. In this study, the majority of Hispanics age 21 through 45 (62 percent) indicated that their religious preference was Catholic. Only 12 percent identified themselves with evangelical Protestant denominations, 2 percent were affiliated with mainline denominations; 2 percent, with historically black denominations; 8 percent, with other faiths; and 14 percent were nonaffiliated.[2]

Hispanic and non-Hispanic Catholics differ on many demographic factors. For instance, the two are quite different in terms of regional location. Fifty-nine percent of Hispanic Catholics age 21 through 45 live in the West or South (including the Southwest), while only 35 percent of non-Hispanic Catholics of the same age do (they remain concentrated in the Northeast and upper Midwest). Half of young adult Hispanic Catholics live in cities; only 20 percent of young adult non-Hispanic Catholics do (most live in suburbs). More than four in ten (43 percent) of the young adult Hispanic Catholics preferred to be interviewed in Spanish (only 2 percent of other Catholics did)—revealing how much is missed about Hispanic Catholics in surveys conducted only in English. Information on socioeconomic status also shows how different young adult Hispanic Catholics are from their Anglo counterparts. Seventy percent of young adult Hispanic Catholics have no formal training beyond high school; only 36 percent of non-Hispanic Catholics have never been to college. Among the former, only 14 percent are employed in professional or managerial occupations and 21 percent are unemployed, whereas among the latter, 32 percent are in professional or managerial occupations, and only 8 percent are unemployed. Data from other research shows that young adult Hispanic Catholics also fall considerably below non-Hispanic Catholics in family incomes.[3]

The family patterns of young adult Hispanic and non-Hispanic Catholics are similar in one respect, but different in others. Overall, about the same proportion of 21- to 45-year-olds in each group are married (47 percent and 52 percent, respectively) and about the same proportion have never been married (39 percent and 37 percent respectively). However, these similarities mask the fact that Hispanic Catholics marry earlier than non-Hispanic Catholics do and also experience higher rates of separation or divorce in their thirties than non-Hispanic Catholics do. Hispanic Catholics also have larger families than non-Hispanic Catholics do.[4]

Religiously, Hispanic Catholics age 21 through 45 are somewhat more likely to attend services almost every week than non-Hispanic Catholics of the same age (42 percent versus 36 percent). However, they are less likely to consider themselves members at their place of worship (40 percent versus 67 percent). They are also substantially more likely to attend small parishes (38 percent are in parishes with fewer than 300 members, compared with 15 percent of non-Hispanic Catholics). They are slightly more likely to be in parishes that are growing—probably a reflection of being in parishes with an expanding immigrant population. And, despite

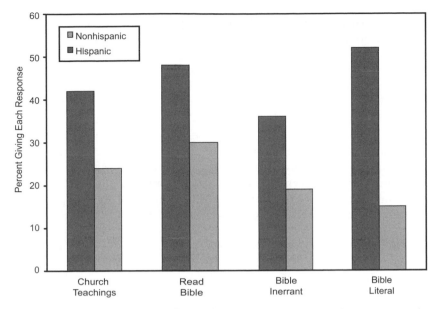

Figure 9.1. Religious Beliefs of Hispanic and Nonhispanic Catholics. Source: Religion and Politics Survey, Catholics age 21 through 45.

the fact that Hispanic and non-Hispanic Catholics are not as segregated from one another as white and black Protestants, there is also evidence of separation between the two. Specifically, 64 percent of Hispanic Catholics age 21 through 45 report that they attend parishes that are at least 50 percent Hispanic.

Like non-Hispanic Catholics, Hispanic Catholics between 21 and 45 hold diverse theological orientations. A larger proportion, though, hold conservative beliefs than among non-Hispanic Catholics. A majority (52 percent) of Hispanic Catholics in this age group believe the Bible should be taken literally. This compares with only 15 percent of non-Hispanic Catholics of the same age (figure 9.1). The former are more likely than the latter to believe that the Bible is free of any historical or scientific errors (36 percent versus 19 percent). They are more likely than the latter to read the Bible at least a few times a month (48 percent versus 30 percent). And they are more likely than the latter to agree that church teachings are the best way to know God (42 percent versus 24 percent).

This evidence is thus consistent with conclusions drawn in other research about the impact Hispanic immigration is having on theological divisions within the Catholic church: it is reinforcing those divisions. A sizable minority of young Hispanic Catholics are quite conservative in their beliefs and practices. Other young Hispanic Catholics, though, are more liberal in their religious views. They participate in services less regularly. Of those who were raised Catholic, a minority have also ceased identifying with any religion.

The growing presence of Hispanic Catholics is potentially important to the church and to their communities in two other ways. One is that they are highly interested in issues of social justice. Two-thirds say they are quite interested in social policies that would help the poor. An equally high proportion say this about overcoming discrimination against women. Almost as many say the same about their interest in racial and ethnic equality. In each instance, these proportions are higher among Hispanic Catholics age 21 through 45 than among non-Hispanic Catholics of the same age.

The other set of issues that are being reinforced by the growing presence of Hispanic Catholics are international. As immigrants or children of immigrants, Hispanic Catholics are more likely to have family members in other countries and, for this reason and other reasons, are more likely to think about the church in international terms and be interested in religious and other humanitarian efforts that address international needs. Thus, 64 percent of Hispanic Catholics age 21 through 45 say they are quite interested in policies to promote international peace, 60 percent say this about international human rights issues, and 43 percent do about relief and development programs. These proportions are significantly higher than among non-Hispanic Catholics of the same age.

A major challenge for church leaders and community officials, though, is mobilizing these and other concerns into political action. Young Hispanic Catholics are significantly less likely than young non-Hispanic Catholics to be registered to vote. They are also less likely to have participated in the political process in other ways, such as contacting an elected official about a matter of concern to them, attending a lecture about social or political issues, or attending a political rally. Very few have given money to a political candidate or political party, either. Of course these patterns reflect the fact that many Hispanic Catholics are recent immigrants who are not yet citizens.[5] Language barriers and lower socioeconomic status also work against political involvement.

Qualitative evidence shows that young Hispanics are as diverse in particular religious orientations and practices as they are in national origin, occupation, and educational levels. Many are interested in or have had exposure to charismatic or Pentecostal practices, such as praying for an "in dwelling" of the Holy Spirit and speaking in tongues.[6] Some practice a syncretic faith that combines Catholicism with voudoo or Santeria. There is also a growing Hispanic middle class for whom religion continues to be important, but who embrace a more personalized style of faith that seems compatible with assimilation into middle class occupations and more diverse neighborhoods.

A thirty-year-old Hispanic woman in California illustrates some of these developments. Her parents immigrated from Mexico a few years before she was born. She is the first person in her family to have graduated from college. She majored in Chicano studies and currently works at a community organization that helps Hispanic women and children who have been victims of abuse. She considers herself a devout Catholic. This means attending mass every week, praying every day, singing in her parish choir, and trying to put her faith into practice by helping others. Being a spiritual person, though, is more meaningful to her than following church teachings. For instance, she defines being a true Catholic simply as living God's word. She explains: "That is not necessarily just [following] the Bible, because not all of us even understand the Bible. I honestly don't even read the Bible anymore. What I do is I try to allow God to be in me and to show himself in me by the way I treat other people." Thus, when she prays, she "talks to God," but does not say structured prayers. Like the white Anglo evangelicals she has met, she believes God has "a plan for each of us," but she also believes God is "there for all of us," regardless of one's specific faith. Unlike her mother, she does not go to confession, and she says she has "issues" with the clergy. She hopes her children will grow up Catholic, but she herself married a Lutheran, and she would be happy if her children married outside the faith because "what's important for me is for someone to strengthen their relationship with God." If it sounds like her faith is an accommodation to middle-class culture, she insists that it is what makes her life meaningful. She works harder at her job than she would otherwise because she feels God called her to this particular job. She is convinced that what she does in this life will affect her in the life to come. Her greatest worry about American society is that everyone is chasing money, and her faith tells her that helping other people is a more worthwhile way to structure one's life.

A NOTE ON HISPANIC PROTESTANTS

Because Hispanic Protestants are an even smaller proportion of the American population than Hispanic Catholics are, it has been difficult to obtain systematic evidence about who they are and how they compare with other groups. But several striking differences between Hispanic Protestants and Hispanic Catholics emerged in the data collected by Robert Putnam, whose Social Capital Benchmark Survey was sufficiently large to render some comparisons possible. Whereas 57 percent of the Hispanic Catholics were interviewed in Spanish, only 33 percent of the Hispanic Protestants were. Similarly, 59 percent of Hispanic Catholics said they were not yet citizens, but only 30 percent of Hispanic Protestants did. Hispanic Protestants were significantly more likely to have family incomes of at least $30,000 (56 percent versus 41 percent) and to own their homes (51 percent versus 37 percent). They were also slightly more likely to have gone to college (33 percent versus 27 percent).[7]

There were also a number of indications that Hispanic Protestants were somewhat more likely to have become integrated or assimilated into the Anglo culture than Hispanic Catholics were. For instance, they were more likely to say they had a personal friend who was white (70 percent versus 59 percent). They were more likely to say they had a friend who was a community leader (32 percent versus 25 percent). And they were significantly more likely to say they would be "very much in favor" of a child of theirs marrying a white person (44 percent versus 25 percent). If trust is a measure of feeling integrated into the society, then Hispanic Protestants were also more assimilated than Hispanic Catholics in this way. By a margin of 37 percent to 22 percent, they said people (in general) can be trusted. They were more likely to trust people at their place of worship (69 percent versus 36 percent) and to trust white people (24 percent versus 15 percent). And they were more likely to say local government could be trusted most of the time (48 percent versus 37 percent).

Religiously, Hispanic Protestants different from Hispanic Catholics in the ways research generally has shown Protestants and Catholics to differ in other contexts. By a margin of 48 percent to 35 percent, Hispanic Protestants were more likely than Hispanic Catholics to say they were members of their church. They were also significantly more likely to attend services every week (50 percent versus 27 percent) and to participate in church activities other than attending services (46 percent versus 20 percent). They also were more likely to say they participated in some other organization affiliated with religion (24 percent versus 9 percent).

ASIAN AMERICANS

The religious beliefs and practices of Asian Americans are still a relatively understudied topic. While not as numerous as Hispanics, Asian Americans have been of interest to researchers and religious leaders because of their similar potential for altering the religious landscape. Ethnographers have conducted studies in congregations of Korean, Chinese, and Filipino Americans, noting that these congregations are typically populated by younger adults, many of whom are highly educated. The congregations are usually of recent origin and are growing. Members often report that they have become more religiously involved in the United States than they or their relatives were in Taiwan, Korea, and elsewhere. They feel it is the American way to be religious. Many members also identify with the broader evangelical tradition that they have become acquainted with in the United States.[8] For many second-generation Asian Americans, being religious is thus a way to retain a distinct identity but also to assimilate into the wider culture.

A woman in her mid-twenties whose parents came to the United States from Korea a few years before she was born illustrates how an ethnic church facilitates the process of assimilation. Her parents attended (and raised her in) a congregation composed of other first-generation Korean Americans. There was solace in their faith, especially for her mother, who found life in America difficult, but their daughter increasingly sensed tension between their faith and her father's insistence on being rational about everything, focusing on one's career, being successful, and encouraging her to do well in school. Her father prayed, went to church, and sent her to Catholic school because it was academically better than public school, but she felt he regarded religion as a bit too ethnic, old-fashioned, and superstitious. She, too, felt torn because she had been taught to believe in God, but refused to learn Korean, felt isolated in her parents' church, and "wanted to fit in" among her friends at school. The tension began to resolve itself when she was in college. She began attending a Korean American evangelical student organization. Its leaders showed her that it was possible to be rational *and* a person of faith. They took "such a scientific and intellectual approach" that faith became logical, she recalls. She came to view the Bible as a logical book with practical applications, whereas her father tended to see it only as a historical book. Since college, she has been attending a multiethnic evangelical church that includes both white and Asian Americans. In retrospect, she says the church of her childhood included people who went "because that's where all the Koreans meet," but who "gossiped too much" and was thus "detrimental," while her present church has given her a chance to "see people who . . . were intellectual and yet could still believe in Christ."

Because Asian American congregations are growing and include people who are well-educated and occupationally successful, some researchers and religious leaders regard these congregations as a bellwether for the future of American religion. The vitality of these congregations demonstrates that the religious market is functioning well. The religious market provides opportunities for new congregations to be planted. The growth of these congregations, these scholars argue, disproves the notion that America is gradually becoming more secular.[9] It certainly challenges more established churches to rethink their ministries and plan aggressively for a future in which the United States will be increasingly diverse.

The problem with conclusions like this is that they are drawn from where the action is, so to speak, rather than from a full consideration of where the action is not. Ethnographic studies provide rich descriptive de-

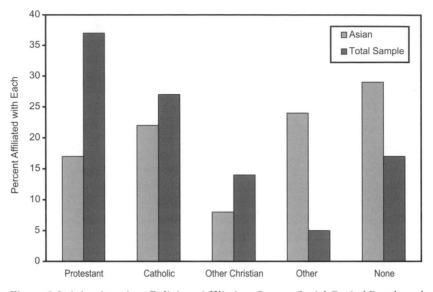

Figure 9.2. Asian American Religious Affiliation. Source: Social Capital Benchmark Survey, respondents age 21 through 45.

tail, but they are not well-suited for drawing broader generalizations. Indeed, they can be just as misleading as a journalistic story written by a reporter who finds an interesting new ministry and then announces that a major cultural trend is in the making. More systematic evidence is needed before making such generalizations.

Systematic evidence from representative surveys of Asian Americans has been difficult to obtain. The General Social Surveys, as I have noted, do a poor job of sampling recent immigrants who may not speak English well enough to be interviewed. The small number of Asians in the U.S. population also makes it difficult to study them through surveys that often include no more than a handful of Asian American respondents. Putnam's Social Capital Benchmark Survey is thus a major breakthrough in providing a source from which to draw information about Asian Americans, just as it has been useful for understanding Hispanic Protestants. With a total of more than 29,000 respondents, many selected from cities, it yielded 460 people age 21 through 45 of Asian ancestry. The two largest subcategories were Chinese Americans and Filipino Americans (making up 28 percent and 20 percent of these respondents). Japanese, Koreans, Vietnamese, Asian Indians, and others made up the remainder.

Figure 9.2 shows the religious affiliations of these young adults of Asian ancestry. For comparisons, I have also included the responses of all persons age 21 and 45 in Putnam's survey. Seventeen percent of the Asian Americans were Protestants, 22 percent were Catholics, 8 percent mentioned some other Christian affiliation, 24 percent selected a non-Christian option (such as Buddhism or Hinduism), and 29 percent said they had no religion. Of the Protestants, about a quarter were Baptists, a quarter were mainline Protestants (such as Methodists and Presbyterians), and a sixth were Pentecostal. Of the non-Christians, half were Hindu, a third were Buddhist, and a tenth were Muslim. It is especially important to note that the percentages of Asian Americans affiliated with Christian traditions are lower than for the whole sample, while the proportion of Asian Americans who have no religion is significantly higher. This does not mean Asian Americans are less religious than their relatives in their countries of origin. And it does not disconfirm the claim made by ethnographers that Asian Americans have become more religious as a result of exposure to American culture. However, it does cast doubt on the idea that Asian Americans are an especially "churched" segment of the American population. They are in fact much less churched than the general population of younger adults.

We can clear up some of the confusion about Asian Americans' religious commitments if we set aside those who are not religious at all. This in effect is what ethnographers and religious leaders do when they focus on Asian American congregations. They see vitality in those congregations because they are comparing them with other congregations, not because they have a sense of what other Asian Americans with no religious commitments at all are doing. Among Asian American *Christians* there is actually evidence to support the notion of special vitality. For instance, among Asian American Protestants age 21 through 45, 77 percent are actually a member of their local congregation—a higher proportion than among all Protestants in the same age group (63 percent). This is also true among Catholics, although the difference is much smaller (60 percent versus 58 percent). Attendance at religious services runs higher, too, among Asian Americans than in the nation at large for this age group. Forty-six percent of Asian American Protestants attend services every week, compared with 36 percent of 21- to 45-year-olds at large. Among Asian American Catholics, the difference is 12 percentage points (40 percent versus 28 percent). Thus, if one were a Protestant or Catholic leader, it would be justifiable to think that Asian American *members* were particularly involved.

A question in Putnam's survey about the perceived importance of religion in one's life leads to a similar conclusion. Overall, Asian Americans age 21 through 45 were less likely than others of the same age to agree strongly that religion is very important in their life (42 percent versus 55 percent) and more likely to disagree (30 percent versus 20 percent). Asian American *Protestants*, though, were 4 percentage points higher than other Protestants on this measure of commitment (72 percent versus 68 percent), and Asian American Catholics were 2 points higher (57 percent versus 55 percent).

Other questions also indicate higher-than-average levels of commitment at least among Asian American Protestants. For instance, they score higher than average in terms of participating in some specialized organization affiliated with religion (by 17 percentage points), participating in church activities other than attending services (17 points), and giving at least $100 a year to their church (13 points). However, one measure—doing volunteer work at their place of worship—indicates lower involvement (minus 11 points).

Students of ethnicity have often argued that religion is a means of assimilation for new immigrant groups. In the case of Asian Americans, it seems especially likely that Protestantism may function this way. Protestantism puts Asian Americans in contact with white members of the same churches or denominations. It may also reinforce certain values, such as individualism or service to the community. Asian Americans who are Buddhists or Hindus may experience assimilation in other ways (such as at work), but in their religious lives be more isolated from the wider culture. There is some evidence in the survey that supports this conjecture. Most Asian Americans in the survey said they had at least one friend who was white, for instance, but this proportion was significantly higher (88 percent) among Protestants (and among Catholics, 81 percent) than among Buddhists or Hindus (68 percent). Few of the respondents said they would be opposed to marrying a white person, but this proportion dropped to only 6 percent among Protestants (1 percent among Catholics) and rose to 18 percent among Buddhists or Hindus. Protestants and Catholics had also lived in their communities longer and were more likely to be citizens than Buddhists or Hindus were. In other ways, though, religious identities among Asian Americans have little bearing on measures of assimilation. The differences among Christians, non-Christians, and the nonreligious in views about whether people can be trusted are minimal. Non-Christians are actually somewhat more likely than Christians to think *white people* can be trusted. They are also more likely than Christians to think local government officials can be trusted most of the time.[10]

An important question, then, is whether the ideological divisions that exist among young adults in the general population are also evident among Asian Americans. Putnam's survey did not include questions about such hot-button issues as abortion and homosexuality. Given the fact that Asian American Protestants are highly religious and often involved in Baptist or Pentecostal churches, while another large segment of Asian Americans have no interest in religion, we would guess that these ideological divisions would be present. One clear indication is that Asian Americans with different religious identities respond quite differently when asked whether they

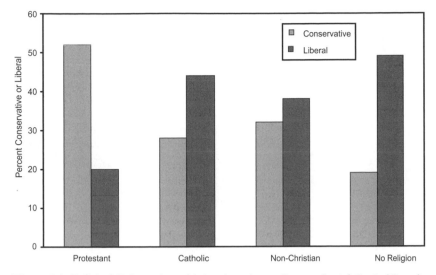

Figure 9.3. Political Orientation of Asian Americans. Source: Social Capital Benchmark Survey, Asian Americans age 21 through 45.

are political conservatives, moderates, or liberals (figure 9.3). By a ratio of five to two, Asian American Protestants say they are conservative rather than liberal. By a similar five-to-two ratio, nonreligious Asian Americans say they are liberal rather than conservative. Catholics and non-Christians fall in the middle and lean slightly more toward the left than the right.

HOSPITALITY OR HOSTILITY

Besides providing some evidence about Asian Americans and Hispanics themselves, recent research also permits some conclusions to be drawn about the *response* of the majority population to these minority ethnic groups. Young adults are presumably taught in school to be tolerant. They are likely to live in cities and suburbs where they are exposed to ethnic diversity and to work at jobs that include people with ethnic backgrounds different from theirs. Still, prejudice dies hard. Radio talk show hosts encourage listeners to believe that immigrants are stealing their jobs and that American culture will die if Hispanic children are not forced to speak English. Some of this prejudice is rooted in exclusivist religious orientations. As we saw in chapter 7, a sizable minority of young adults—especially among evangelical Protestants—is disturbed by the possibility that a son or daughter might marry a Muslim or Hindu. Religion can also

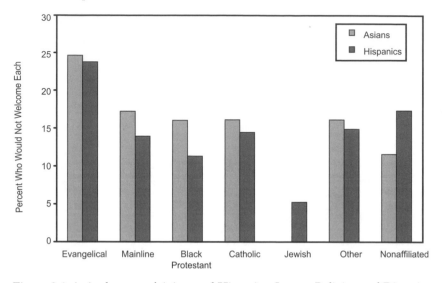

Figure 9.4. Attitudes toward Asians and Hispanics. Source: Religion and Diversity Survey, white and African Americans age 21 through 45.

reinforce prejudice, even toward Christians who happen to be of a different background.

Figure 9.4 shows the percentage of 21- through 45-year-olds in each major religious tradition who would *not welcome* Asians or Hispanics becoming a stronger presence in the United States (these responses exclude those of Asians and Hispanics themselves). Evangelicals are the least welcoming toward both; Jews are the most welcoming. The other groups fall in between and are fairly similar in their responses. The nonaffiliated are more welcoming toward Asians than they are toward Hispanics. Black Protestants are more welcoming toward Hispanics than toward Asians. Mainline Protestants, Catholics, and adherents of other faiths are quite similar to one another and in their views toward Asians and Hispanics.

Why are evangelicals the least welcoming toward Asians and Hispanics? We might expect otherwise. Evangelicals' Bible tells them to love their neighbors and show hospitality to strangers. Practically speaking, evangelicals might regard Asians and Hispanics as allies, since many belong to conservative Protestant churches and are politically conservative. Before considering the data, we need to think about some of the reasons evangelicals might not be favorably disposed toward Asians and Hispanics. One argument would suggest that it has nothing to do with religion itself, but is a function of the social characteristics that distinguish evangelicals from other young adults. The fact that evangelicals still fall behind other young adults in levels of education or in the education levels of their parents could be a factor. This is a plausible interpretation because higher levels of education generally go with greater amounts of tolerance—either because education teaches tolerance or because better-educated people have more money and better jobs and thus can afford to be tolerant. It might be that evangelicals live in small towns or in parts of the country that have fewer Asians and Hispanics and thus want to keep their communities the way they are. It might also be that evangelicals (as we have seen) are more likely than other young adults to be married and have children and thus are thinking about protecting their families from whatever social changes they fear will come with more ethnic diversity. An alternative line of reasoning would focus more on the religious and cultural characteristics of evangelicalism itself. It might be that evangelicals believe they have the biblical truth and thus are less tolerant of people different from themselves because these people may not have the truth. It could be that evangelicals spend so much of their time at their churches that they do not become acquainted with people different from themselves. Or it could be that evangelicals are unwelcoming toward Asians and Hispanics because of the politically conservative subculture in which they live.

The data from the Religion and Diversity Survey make it possible to tease out the validity of these various interpretations (appendix table A.4). When no other factors are taken into account, the odds of not welcoming Asians or Hispanics are almost twice as great among evangelicals as among nonevangelicals age 21 through 45. Taking account of a whole list of social factors reduces these odds a little, but not by much. The social factors that reduce the odds of being inhospitable the most are higher levels of education and being foreign born oneself. A few other factors make some difference. For instance, men are less hospitable toward Hispanics than women are, having children is associated with being less welcoming toward Asians, and living in a suburb or city is generally better than living in a small town or rural area as far as being welcoming toward Asians and Hispanics is concerned. Still, taking all these factors into account, the odds of being unwelcoming are about 1.7 times greater among evangelicals than among nonevangelicals.

The religious and cultural factors provide better explanations of the differences between evangelicals and nonevangelicals. Regular church attendance actually reduces the odds of being unwelcoming—an encouraging result for those who think going to church should reinforce teachings about loving one's neighbor. What people hear at evangelical churches, though, is not entirely favorable in this regard. Believing that Christianity is the only true way to have a personal relationship with God is associated with being less welcoming toward Asians and Hispanics. Believing that the Ten Commandments should be taught in public schools is associated slightly with being unwelcoming toward Asians. In addition, it may be the case that spending time in evangelical churches discourages welcoming attitudes simply by limiting people's contacts with others who are different from themselves. At least the data show that those who have more contact with Asians or Hispanics are also more welcoming toward them. The informal culture of evangelicals probably also makes a difference. For instance, evangelicals are less likely than many other Americans (especially Catholics and Jews) to have recent family members who came to the United States as immigrants and, perhaps for this reason, are less likely to say they value the legacy of immigrants' contributions. Political factors, too, may make a difference. At least those who voted for George W. Bush in 2000 are significantly less welcoming toward Asians than those who did not. When these factors are taken into account, much of the difference between evangelicals and nonevangelicals disappears. Not all of it, but at least half of it. In short, the religious and cultural factors provide an interpretation of *why* evangelicals are less welcoming toward Asians and Hispanics than nonevangelicals are.

It is worth underscoring that evangelicals are still less welcoming toward Asians and Hispanics than nonevangelicals are, even when all these other factors are statistically taken into account. However, the data do rule out the notion that these differences are simply because of extraneous social characteristics that happen to distinguish evangelicals from nonevangelicals. They point the finger at some of the evangelicals' cherished beliefs, especially their Christian exclusivism. It is not simply going to church that generates inhospitality toward strangers, though; nor (as other data in the survey show) is it simply believing that the Bible is true or feeling threatened (for instance, by terrorism). It is rather a mix of religious beliefs, combined with isolation from people different from oneself and a world view that diminishes the contributions of immigrants and believes the society would be better off if everyone practiced conservative Christian values.

This combination of beliefs characterizes some evangelicals (and, indeed, some nonevangelicals) and is enough to elevate their levels of concern about the growing presence of Asians and Hispanics in the United States. Overall, though, most young adults hold favorable views toward Asians and Hispanics. They may not like the idea of unrestricted immigration, let alone illegal immigration, especially in the aftermath of terrorist attacks and threats, but Asians and Hispanics are familiar enough that the growing presence of these populations is welcome to a majority of non-Asians and non-Hispanics. Still, the fact that a quarter of evangelicals are not welcoming means that evangelicals are a more likely source of mobilized resistance against newcomers than any other religious group is. It also demonstrates, contrary to what some believe, that religion matters. It influences how people think and the kinds of people with whom they associate.

A Closer Look at Church Involvement

From the evidence we have considered thus far, we are left with an interesting puzzle. Church going seems to encourage young adults to be more accepting of people from ethnic groups different from their own; yet evangelicals, who go to church more than anyone else, are less accepting. This evidence, though, poses a larger question about church involvement than one pertaining particularly to evangelicals. That larger question is this: as the United States becomes a more ethnically diverse society, will churches be a way in which young adults participate in this diversity, or will churches function, as they often have in the past, to shield young adults from diversity—insulating them, as it were, inside their own religioethnic enclaves?

Plausible arguments can be made on both sides of this question. On the one hand, church going is an important form of social capital. Young adults who participate actively in their churches meet other people, have opportunities to serve on committees, are drawn into volunteering for community organizations, and through these various face-to-face contacts develop ties with others. Even weak ties connect people beyond their own families, often through friends of friends. In the extreme case, we could compare an active church goer with a young adult who simply stayed home and watched television, surfed the Internet, or went on an occasional outing with close friends. The active church goer would meet a larger number of people on a more regular basis, and these people would not all be close friends who already had a great deal in common. Beyond that, church going might also build trust. Through church teachings, or through the experience of working together with others on projects, our prototypical young adult would presumably realize that people are not always conniving to fulfill their personal goals at the expense of others. People are good-hearted, altruistic, and willing to work for the benefit of others. At least that is the hope. In all these ways, then, an active church goer who was, say, white Anglo would have opportunities to develop contacts with and learn to trust others, including others from different ethnic or racial backgrounds. On the other hand, these expectations break down if churches are composed of homogeneous ethnic groups. Frequent church participation then merely focuses more of one's time among people like oneself. This, too, is a kind of social capital. It provides friends, opportunities to socialize, and reinforcement for one's values. However, it is what Robert Putnam has called a *bonding* form of social capital, rather than a bridging form of social capital. It consists of ties with people like oneself, but does not bridge between one's own ethnic group and people of other ethnic backgrounds.[11]

Most educators believe it is good to encourage young people to interact with ethnic groups other than their own. Segregated schools are considered bad, not only because the quality of education provided for African American students is often low, but also because they reinforce in-group ties and discourage interracial interaction. Colleges and universities take pride in being places where diversity of all kinds is encouraged. They try to admit students of color as well as white students, international students, and students from different parts of the country. The military and prisons are also increasingly composed of diverse racial and ethnic populations, as are amateur and professional athletic teams. The reality of actual friendships being made often falls short of the ideal, but the ideal is clear. In a world of different ethnic groups, it is better to find ways to promote interaction, trust, and understanding across ethnic lines than to keep ethnic groups apart.

The irony is that these formal institutional settings in which ethnic diversity is encouraged end for most young adults sometime in their early twenties. The hope is that by then they have learned how to interact with people unlike themselves. Yet there are strong pressures working against that hope. People make friends with people like themselves, marry people from similar backgrounds, and fall into a family pattern that increasingly focuses on their own spouse and raising their own children. This is where church involvement enters the picture. For a growing number of young adults in their twenties, church involvement along with marriage and child rearing is postponed. Their twenties is a time to play the field, as it were, dating widely, interacting with a diverse set of friends, sinking only shallow roots in their neighborhoods, and keeping open their opportunities for jobs and promotions. Only in their thirties do they begin to settle down, marrying, having children, purchasing a home, and becoming actively involved in a church. Their chances of interacting with ethnically diverse contacts are probably greater while their lives are still unsettled than once they have begun to assume family responsibilities. Church could further insulate them from ethnic diversity. Indeed, it probably would unless their church involvement became a way of pushing beyond their own family responsibility and keeping ties with the larger community.

Putnam's Social Capital Benchmark Survey is the best means available for examining these questions empirically. It was designed with questions about contact, trust, community participation, and bridging across racial and ethnic lines in mind. Because it included so many people, we can also use it to examine whether young adults who participate actively in their churches, and do so within particular traditions, are more likely or less likely to engage in this kind of bridging behavior. Most of the white people in Putnam's study claimed to have at least one friend who was African American, Hispanic, or Asian American (77 percent among respondents age 21 through 45). Still, the odds of having a friend of this kind were *higher* among regular church goers than among irregular attenders. This was true in eight of nine comparisons when young people were divided into evangelicals, mainline Protestants, and Catholics and then further divided by age. In most instances, the odds of having at least one interethnic friendship were about twice as high among regular church goers than among irregular attenders.[12]

Among these white respondents, church going was also positively associated with feeling that African Americans, Hispanics, and Asian Americans were trustworthy. In all but two of the comparisons, the odds of scoring high on a scale of interethnic trust were at least a third higher among regular attenders than among irregular attenders, and on average these odds were more than two-thirds higher.[13] The supposition that church involvement somehow isolates young adults from ethnic diversity or makes people less willing to trust others different from themselves is thus not supported by this evidence. There is more support for the conclusion that church going somehow reinforces interethnic contact and trust.

Why might it be the case that regular church goers have more ethnically diverse friends and are more trusting of ethnically diverse groups? One possible reason is that young adults who are actively involved in a church simply have more friends: the more friends a person has, the greater the chances of knowing diverse people (and trusting them). If this is the case, though, it is only very weakly evident in the data. For instance, active church goers in their twenties are 5 percent more likely than irregular attenders to say they have more than ten close friends; among people in their thirties, the difference is only 2 points, and among people in their early forties, 3 points. Another possible explanation is that church goers are more likely to be women or better educated than nonchurch goers. Statistically taking into account those differences, though, does not reduce the relationship between church going and having diverse friends or trusting diverse groups. A better explanation is probably that young adults who attend church regularly are also more involved in their communities in a variety of ways and thus meet and trust a more diverse set of people. For instance, regular church participants in their twenties are 19 percentage points more likely than irregular attenders of the same age to participate in at least three community organizations (not counting church); 19 points more likely in their thirties, and 14 points more likely in their early forties. Within each age group, the regular church participants were also more likely to have done volunteer work in their community than the irregular attenders were.[14]

This evidence does not mean, though, that today's young adults are participating in ethnically and racially diverse congregations. Some of course are. But most congregations remain relatively homogeneous. The link between church going and exposure to ethnic diversity is rather that church going puts a person in contact with a wider network of people. These are just as likely to be people one meets through a friend of a friend or from serving on a community board than at church itself. It is nevertheless a form of bridging, to use Putnam's word. Bridging can be stifled if congregations encourage members to spend *all* their evenings with other members of the same congregation. It is doubtful, though, that most congregations do that. Congregations are more like public spaces in which people gather for worship and study, and in so doing learn to trust others and discover opportunities to be involved in the wider life of their communities.

Congregations could certainly do more to encourage friendships and trust across racial and ethnic lines than they currently are. The criticism that Sunday mornings are one of the most segregated times of the week remains valid. However, that criticism is tempered by the fact that church going people are engaged in a broader process of building social networks. Mingling with others in their congregations builds trust and expands their networks. In an increasingly diverse society, these networks play an increasingly important role in holding the society together.

The Virtual Church

RELIGIOUS USES OF THE INTERNET

In CHAPTER 2 I reviewed some of the evidence on the growth of e-mail and Internet use. Among other things, we saw that younger adults are more likely than older adults to have computers or access to computers. In surveys conducted in 2000 and 2002 as part of the General Social Survey, for instance, 75 percent, 74 percent, and 73 percent, respectively of adults age 21 through 29, 30 through 39, and 40 through 45 said they personally "use a computer at home, at work, or at some other location," compared with 65 percent among 46- through 64-year-olds, and only 24 percent of those 65 and older. Thus, in considering younger adults uses of e-mail and the Internet for religious purposes, we can treat 21- through 45-year-olds as a single demographic group. Roughly three-quarters of this group make some use of computers and, of this three-quarters, nearly all (84 percent) said they sometimes use the Internet. In the General Social Survey, it was this group who were then asked a number of more specific questions about their uses of the Internet.[1]

Religion Web Sites

One way of assessing specific uses of the Internet among young adults is by asking them what kinds of sites they have visited in the past 30 days.[2] News, travel, work, and education sites are consulted by the highest proportion of adults age 21 through 45—each having been visited by a majority of young adults in the past 30 days (Figure 10.1). In comparison, religion sites rank near the bottom, having been consulted by only 20 percent of young adults in the past 30 days. Only 4 percent had visited religion sites more than 5 times during this period, another 4 percent had done so three to five times, and 12 percent only once or twice.[3]

The fifth of Internet users age 21 through 45 who visit religion Web sites is consistent with the results of a national survey conducted in 2001 in which a broader question found that 25 percent of all Internet users had "ever" looked for "religious or spiritual information or services online." The author of that study offered different comparisons that put virtual

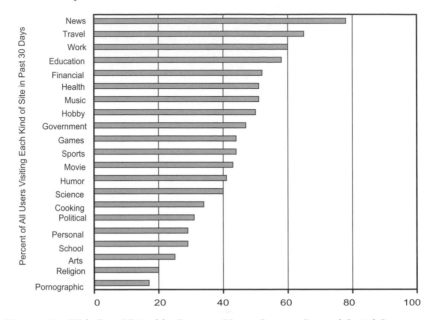

Figure 10.1 Web Sites Visited by Internet Users. Source: General Social Surveys, 2000–2002, respondents age 21 through 45.

religion in a stronger light. She concluded, for instance, that "religion surfers" were probably more common than people who gambled online, used Internet auction sites, traded stocks online, or did online banking.[4]

In the General Social Survey, young adults affiliated with evangelical churches were the most likely to have visited a religion Web site. Thirty-eight percent had done so in the past 30 days. In comparison, only 17 percent of young adults affiliated with mainline Protestant churches had visited a religion Web site during the same period. Black Protestants fell in between, with 26 percent having visited a religion Web site in the past 30 days. Catholics and Jews resembled mainline Protestants (17 percent and 19 percent respectively). Only 7 percent of the religiously nonaffiliated had visited a religion Web site in the past month. Among all respondents age 21 through 45, 43 percent of those who attended religious services at least nearly every week had visited a religion Web site, compared with only 12 percent among those who attended less frequently. Other demographic factors, such as gender, marital status, children, and level of education were unrelated to the likelihood of having visited a religion Web site in the past 30 days.[5]

Judging from this evidence, we probably need to exercise caution and conclude that by 2002 religion had not become a major aspect of Internet use among younger adults, at least not in comparison with other major uses of the Internet, such as news, travel information, and work. This is not to say it was unimportant. Certainly there were a few younger adults who frequently visited religion Web sites, and this number could only have been larger than a few years previously. Yet, these numbers were small. Nor does this evidence provide much support, either for the idea that virtual churches were replacing real churches or for the possibility that virtual churches were reaching people who had become disconnected from real churches. It was the churched, rather than the unchurched, who were visiting religion Web sites—probably as an add-on, rather than as a replacement for being involved in local congregations.

As for other kinds of Web sites, frequent church attenders, evangelicals, and black Protestants were less likely to have consulted most of these Web sites than mainline Protestants, Catholics, Jews, the religiously nonaffiliated, and infrequent attenders. However, these differences were generally small and probably due to differences in social status and location, more than religion itself. The one kind of Web use that undoubtedly did reflect religious differences was visiting pornographic sites. Whereas 20 percent of adults age 21 through 45 who used the Internet but attended religious services infrequently had visited a pornographic site in the past 30 days, only 5 percent of those who attended religious services nearly every week had done so. Among evangelicals, 12 percent had visited a pornographic site; 17 percent of mainline Protestants had; 9 percent of black Protestants had; 15 percent of Catholics had; and 26 percent of nonaffiliated persons had (there were too few Jews for reliable estimates).

Social Issues

If religiously involved young adults are not visiting religion Web sites in large numbers, they are nevertheless making use of the Internet in other ways that reflect their religious convictions. For instance, during the Democratic primaries in 2004, Howard Dean received considerable media coverage for having apparently found ways to solicit participation in his campaign among young adults through the Internet. According to the General Social Surveys, 44 percent of adults age 21 through 45 had already made use of the Internet during the twelve months prior to the 2000 and 2002 surveys to learn about political campaigns. There were few differences among people affiliated with the various religious traditions in responses to this question. However, when asked if they had used the Internet during the previous twelve months to learn about "morality/family issues," nearly half (49 percent) of young evangelical Web users said they had done so

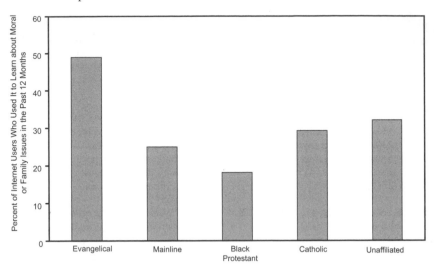

Figure 10.2. Internet Use for Moral Issues. Source: General Social Surveys, 2000 and 2002, Internet users age 21 through 45.

(figure 10.2). This was in comparison with only 25 percent of mainline Protestants, 18 percent of black Protestants, 29 percent of Catholics, and 32 percent of the nonaffiliated. Overall, 39 percent of frequent church attenders had used the Internet to learn about moral or family issues, compared with 30 percent of infrequent attenders.

Although fewer had used the Internet to learn about "abortion issues," the differences among young adults affiliated with the various religious traditions were also pronounced. Fourteen percent of Internet users age 21 through 45 who identified themselves as evangelicals said they had used the Internet in the past twelve months to learn about abortion issues. This was also true of the religiously nonaffiliated (14 percent), followed by Catholics (8 percent). In contrast, only 4 percent of mainline Protestants and none of black Protestants had done so. In short, the religious groups most likely to include people at either end of the spectrum about abortion— evangelicals and the nonaffiliated—were the ones with the highest percentages. Overall, 14 percent of frequent church attenders had used the Internet to learn about abortion issues, compared with 8 percent of infrequent attenders.

The fact that evangelicals and frequent church attenders more generally disproportionately used the Internet to learn about moral, family, and abortion issues is all the more notable when compared with their use of the Internet to learn about other social issues. For instance, 49 percent of Internet users age 21 through 45 overall had used the Internet to learn about foreign affairs in the past twelve months. Yet among frequent church attenders this proportion dropped to 38 percent, and among evangelicals, to 37 percent. From survey data alone, it is of course impossible to say exactly why evangelicals and frequent church attenders use the Internet to learn about moral issues, or what information they gain. It does appear, though, that the Internet holds potential for mobilizing or at least informing religious constituencies who are especially interested in moral issues.

An indication of this potential for mobilization comes from follow-up questions in the General Social Survey that asked Internet users to say if it was very true, somewhat true, or not true that they "visit political sites with points of view that you agree with," "visit sites that provide information without promoting a particular political point of view," and "visit sites that challenge your own opinions and provide different perspectives on political affairs." In addition, Internet users were asked if they had "ever taken any of the following actions because of something you learned about or discussed on the Web," including "signed a petition," "contacted a senator, congressman, or other elected official to express an opinion," and "attended a political meeting or demonstration."

Comparisons between Internet users who had learned about abortion issues from the Internet and those who had not indicate that people interested in abortion issues were especially likely to visit sites they agreed with or disagreed with, but only slightly more likely than people not interested in abortion issues to visit politically neutral sites. In addition, people interested in abortion were significantly more likely than the comparison group to say they had signed a petition, contacted an elected official, or attended a political meeting as a result of something they had learned on the Internet.

The differences between the small minority of young adult Internet users who visit sites about abortion and the rest of the young adult Internet-user population are probably more pronounced than would be the case for other comparisons. However, a question about using the Internet to learn about moral or family issues showed similar patterns. Those who had used the Internet for this purpose were 18 percentage points more likely than those who had not to visit sites they agree with, 21 percentage points more likely to have signed a petition, and 14 points more likely to have contacted an elected official. Evangelicals and the religiously nonaffiliated were the most likely to have visited sites they agreed with. Evangelicals, though, were no more likely than affiliates of the other religious traditions to have sent in a petition, contacted an official, or attended a meeting as a result of something they had learned from the Internet. Frequent church attenders also failed to exceed infrequent attenders in these activities. However, frequent church attenders were more likely than infrequent attenders to visit sites they agreed with, while being less likely to visit neutral sites or sites with which they disagreed.

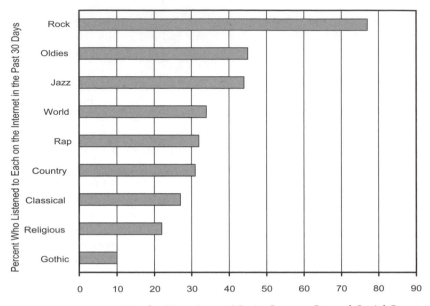

Figure 10.3. Internet Use for Listening to Music. Source: General Social Survey, 2000; Internet users age 21 through 45.

Care must be taken in interpreting these results. Yet they suggest that the Internet does hold potential as a way of mobilizing people around issues about which they care deeply. In the past, congregations have played a role in mobilizing young adults for a variety of issues—civil rights, anti-war protests, pro-life or pro-choice issues, and so on. In the future, congregation-based mobilization is likely to include an increasing role for Web sites, blogs, and e-mail lists.

THE INTERNET AND RELIGIOUS MUSIC

If the Internet holds potential for political mobilization, its role as a form of entertainment has already been demonstrated, especially as a source for listening to and downloading music. Data from the General Social Survey conducted in 2000 provide some information about the relative popularity of different kinds of music on the Internet. The survey asked respondents who had access to the Internet and who had actually used it to indicate how many times in the last month they had "used the Web to learn about or listen to the following kinds of music." The percentages of Internet users age 21 through 45 who said they had done this at least once for each kind of music are shown in figure 10.3. The results show, probably not surprisingly, that the largest percentage was for rock music. Seventy-seven percent of Internet users age 21 through 45 said they had learned about or listened to rock music on the Internet in the past month. Oldies and jazz (with 45 percent and 44 percent respectively) came in second and third. Religious music (with only 22 percent) was near the bottom of the list.

These data do not describe the particular kinds of religious music that Internet users may have been interested in. The data do suggest, though, that young adults who are interested in religious music on the Internet have eclectic tastes. For instance, 82 percent of those who had listened to religious music on the Internet had also listened to rock music on the Internet; 76 percent, to oldies; 59 percent, to country music; and 35 percent, to classical music.

More generally, the General Social Survey data suggest that religiously oriented young adults are quite likely to use the Internet to pursue their interests in music and the arts. Among Internet users age 21 through 45 who attend religious services at least nearly every week, for instance, 87 percent have used the Internet to order a book or poem, 80 percent have used the Internet to obtain information about music, 63 percent have listened to radio on the Internet, 57 percent have used the Internet to find information about artists, 54 percent have downloaded music from the Internet, 53 percent have visited a Web site associated with a particular author, and 42 percent have purchased a book after reading about a particular author on the Internet.

STAYING IN TOUCH BY E-MAIL

Figure 10.4 shows the average (mean) number of friends or relatives with whom respondents age 21 through 45 said they had been in contact at least once during the past year through various modes. Respondents were asked to think about friends and relatives, but not to include people at work or family at home. The modes of contact asked about included "seeing them socially, face-to-face"; "talking with them on the telephone"; "exchanging cards or letters through U.S. postal mail"; "seeing them at meetings or events related to church, clubs, or other groups"; and "communicating through electronic mail." The questions did not ask how often each mode of communication was used, only the number of friends or relatives involved. Nor does the information distinguish people who were contacted in several ways from those contacted only through one means or another. At best, then, the data provide a crude measure of the relative importance of the various modes of communication. Absent much else, though, it offers a glimpse at the role e-mail may be playing in helping people stay in touch. It helps specifically in answering the question of whether e-mail is helping

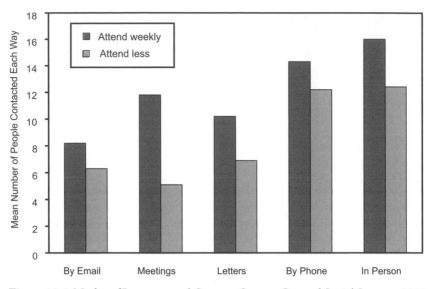

Figure 10.4. Modes of Interpersonal Contact. Source: General Social Surveys, 2000 and 2002, respondents age 21 through 45.

people stay in touch with a *wider* circle of friends and relatives than might be possible in person or through such personal contacts as at meetings. For our purposes, these data also make it possible to compare the ways in which frequent church goers stay in touch with friends and the ways in which infrequent church goers do this.

For both frequent and infrequent attenders, seeing friends and relatives face-to-face and talking to them by telephone remain the means by which they maintain the widest circle of contacts. Letters, meetings, and e-mail all involve relatively smaller numbers of friends or relatives. This result runs counter to much of the speculation suggesting that e-mail keeps people in touch with a wide circle of friends because of its ease and efficiency. In each comparison, though, frequent church attenders keep in contact with a larger number of people than infrequent attenders do. The results for "meetings" are especially notable, suggesting that frequent attenders do make contacts through their churches and other organizations. By a much smaller margin (8.2 versus 6.3), they also stay in contact with a larger number of persons by e-mail than infrequent attenders do.

Young adults affiliated with the various religious traditions resemble each other on these questions more than they differ. Evangelicals, mainline Protestants, and Catholics all keep in touch with an average of 7 or 8 friends or relatives by e-mail. Black Protestants keep in touch with only 3 or 4 friends or relatives this way (probably because of economic differences that make e-mail less available). The other notable difference is that evangelicals keep in touch with an average of 11 friends or relatives through meetings, while mainline Protestants do so with only 7, black Protestants with 8, and Catholics with 6.

A different way of describing the e-mailing practices of young adult church goers is to ask what proportion of e-mail users who attend church regularly send or receive e-mails from various categories of people, such as friends, family, coworkers, and church members. Among adults age 21 through 45 who use e-mail at all and who attend religious services weekly, about four in ten (39 percent) say they sometimes send or receive e-mails from church members. This proportion is almost as large as the percentage who send or receive e-mails from business contacts (46 percent) or from members of other groups or voluntary associations (47 percent). It is considerably smaller than the percentages who send or receive e-mails from friends or family members living at other locations (77 percent), but larger than the percentage who send or receive e-mail from family members who live at the same location (19 percent). In most of these comparisons, frequent church attenders were more likely than infrequent attenders to say they sent or received e-mails.

THE INTERNET AND SPIRITUAL SEEKING

Of the *religious* uses of the Internet, the most important use among young adults is seeking spiritual information—at least judging from survey responses. As a new form of information technology, the Internet permits people to seek information, including information about religious and spiritual practices or ideas. In the past, it would have been necessary to make a trip to the public library to find out about the history of one's religious tradition or another tradition. A person interested in astrology or witchcraft might have found it necessary to visit an astrologer or attend a meeting at a coven to gain information. Now it is possible to sit in one's dorm room or apartment and learn about esoteric traditions.

But what exactly do young adults look for when they visit religion Websites? In 2001, the Pew Internet and American Life Project conducted a follow-up survey among 500 people who had been identified in a national survey as having looked for information about religious or spiritual information or services online. Slightly more than half of these 500 respondents (280) were age 21 through 45. About a quarter (24 percent) of these young adults said they looked for religious or spiritual information online at least several times a week, 38 percent said they did so several times a month, and the remainder (38 percent) did so every few months or less often. Religiously, these young adults were quite committed to their faith. For instance, 81 percent described their religious commitment as "very strong," 85 percent said they were members at a house of worship in their community, 85 percent said they pray or meditate every day, and 75 percent attended worship services at least once a week.

Searching online for religious or spiritual information was clearly an add-on for these respondents, rather than at the core of their spiritual practice. When asked about the importance of various activities to their religious or spiritual life, only 13 percent said "going online to get religious or spiritual information" was important to their religious or spiritual life. In contrast, 85 percent said this about prayer or meditation and 69 percent said the same about group worship. Nearly half (48 percent) said small group study or prayer was important to their spiritual life and about the same indicated the importance of confession (46 percent) and talking to a minister, priest, or spiritual advisor (44 percent).[6]

If religious surfers are not using the Internet to replace more traditional practices, it is nevertheless notable that their religious practices are not fully contained by their congregations. Religious surfers are more likely to say that individual activities, such as solitary meditation or volunteering, are very important than they are to say that group study or prayer are. By a significant margin, they emphasize conversations with their friends (71 percent) rather than talking to a member of the clergy. Almost as many consider it very important to spend time in nature (41 percent) as to talk with a member of the clergy. In all these ways, then, they fit the profile of the spiritual tinkerer. Their religious life is grounded in the traditional practices of a congregation, and yet they are individualists who piece together spirituality on their own and in other ways.

This profile of religious surfers helps us understand how they make use of the Internet. Almost three quarters of religious surfers (72 percent) have used the Internet to look for information about their own faith. This high percentage again suggests that religious surfers are loyal to their particular religious traditions. However, half (51 percent) have used the Internet to look for information about other faiths—suggesting an interest in spiritual seeking or openness. In addition, the evidence points clearly toward practical uses of the Internet—seeking guidance (37 percent), getting ideas about ways of celebrating religious holidays (24 percent), and planning weddings (32 percent). In the past, these are the sorts of information a person would have gleaned from friends at church, the pastor, religious magazines, or a visit to the library. Now they can be found on the Internet. The results also show that hardly any religious surfers (only 2 percent) participate in online worship services. Thus, the Internet is not replacing participation in worship services at congregations, but simply adding ways of finding information beyond one's congregation.

Two specific questions in the religious surfer survey lend further support to the conclusion that the Internet is not replacing more traditional religious practices. One was a question that asked, "Overall, is using the Internet a major way you participate in your religious tradition or faith, or do you mostly participate in other ways?" Ninety-four percent said they mostly participate in other ways, only 2 percent said the Internet, 2 percent said both equally, and 1 percent were unsure. The other question asked, "In general, has using the Internet helped you feel more committed to your religious tradition or faith, less committed, or has it made no difference?" Eighty-four percent said it had made no difference, 15 percent said it had made them more committed, and only 1 percent said they were less committed.

Several other questions round out the picture of how religious surfers use the Internet. Music and prayer requests are the most commonly mentioned activities when religious surfers are asked about other uses of the Internet and e-mail (42 and 41 percent of religious surfers age 21 through 45, respectively, used the Internet or e-mail for these purposes). Almost as many used the Internet or e-mail to give religious or spiritual guidance (39 percent) or to download or listen to sermons or other religious instruction (36 percent). In comparison, relatively few used the Internet or e-mail to participate in religious dating services or to download religious computer games (4 percent for each).

Because these results pertain only to that subset of the population who have used the Internet to find religious or spiritual information there are relatively few differences between the responses of people in their twenties, thirties, or early forties—or for that matter, older. Nevertheless, there are a few differences, and these are worth noting because they do suggest some distinctive uses of the Internet among particular age groups. Religious surfers in their twenties are more likely than religious surfers of any other age group to have used the Internet to find information about their own faith *and* about other faiths. Perhaps for obvious reasons they are the most likely to have used the Internet to find information about religious ceremonies, such as weddings. They are the most likely to have used e-mail to plan religious activities and to have recommended a religious or spiritual Web site to a friend or relative. When asked if they would find it easier to seek educational or study materials online or offline, a majority of all age groups say online, but this proportion rises to 71 percent among religious surfers in their twenties. In contrast, only about 10 percent overall pick online when asked about the easier way to participate in spiritual discussions, but 17 percent of those in their twenties choose this option. They are also more likely than surfers in other age groups to say the Internet would be the easier way of finding people who share their religious beliefs.

Religious surfers in their thirties and early forties stand out only in a few respects. They are more likely than surfers younger or older to say religious material on the Internet encourages religious tolerance, but they are also the most likely to worry that material on the Internet more generally is often sacrilegious. They are the most likely to have sought and given religious or spiritual advice by e-mail. And, although only 6 percent have done so, they are the most likely to have used the Internet for matchmaking or dating services.

Among religious surfers between age 21 and 45, the differences between men and women generally outweigh any of the differences among specific age groups. Because religious surfers are a select subset of the population, both men and women are highly involved in their congregations and in their personal religious practices. But men are more likely to use the Internet for general purposes, such as seeking religious information, while women are more likely to use it for specific purposes, such as giving or receiving advice or planning events.

CONGREGATIONS AND THE INTERNET

None of this evidence suggests that the so-called virtual church is a major new phenomenon that is threatening traditional congregations. Narrowly defined, the virtual church is a Web site or chat room to which people come to worship. It sometimes includes video clips of real services, but often consists of little more than a printed sermon, a place to post prayers, and perhaps a way to make financial contributions. Hardly any religious surfers say they use these online worship sites. In a population of millions, even a few people can boost the number of "hits" at those sites. Yet their overall importance can only be regarded as minimal.

In comparison, the opportunities provided by the Internet for congregations, denominational offices, and other religious organizations to reach constituencies in new ways are profound. Even from the sparse evidence available from surveys, we can see that religiously committed young adults are using the Internet to seek information about faith traditions, to give and receive spiritual advice, to download religious music, to purchase religious books and other products, to plan events, to pray, and to stay in contact with like-minded believers.

The question for clergy and other religious leaders is whether the Internet will somehow diminish their own importance as sources of religious information. It is difficult to answer this question because we do not have evidence from enough people about which specific Web sites they visit. If these Web sites are mostly those of their particular congregations or denominations, then religious officials largely retain control over the kinds of information provided. If, however, the information comes from interest groups, such as Focus on the Family, from commercial sites, such as Beliefnet.com, or from booksellers and religious broadcasters, then religious officials may have more to worry about. Some of the evidence from the religious surfers study points to the former conclusion. For instance, 42 percent of religious surfers age 21 through 45 say they have one favorite Web site that they usually visit. Of these, more than eight in ten (82 percent) say this site has information about their own tradition. Half say the site is affiliated with a particular group or organization of which they are a member and, of these, 97 percent say they were already a member before they first visited this Web site. Other religious surfers, though, say they find their religious information usually by using a search engine and, when they do, search several sites to find the information they want.

In the final analysis, religious uses of the Internet are probably like the uses that were made of previous innovations in communication technology. Religious radio, religious television, religious publishing, and religious bookstores all provided new ways of communicating religious and spiritual information.[7] For its part, television was sometimes regarded as a defining feature of the baby boomer generation. Yet it was a universal medium that brought religious programming to people of particular age groups, just as it brought rock music or cartoons to others. The Internet seemed for a brief time to be a defining feature of the next wave of younger adults. They learned to use it first because of school or work. However, the Internet quickly spread to other age groups as well. It will continue to be a feature of the religious landscape. At the same time, all indications suggest that other developments are likely to define the religious practices of young adults in the foreseeable future to a greater extent that the Internet will. As we have seen, those are largely matters of family style, religious tradition, and orientations toward social and moral issues. Evangelicals and other religious conservatives will occupy one end of the spectrum, while young adults without deep religious convictions will occupy the other. How the middle ground will be defined will lie mostly in the hands of mainline Protestants, black Protestants, moderate Catholics, moderate Jews, and others interested in tackling the difficult tasks of being true to their convictions in ways that take full account of the complexities of the contemporary world.

Vital Congregations

YOUTHFUL AND DIVERSE

IF I WERE A RELIGIOUS leader, I would be troubled by the facts and figures currently describing the lives of young Americans, their involvement in congregations, and their spiritual practices. The conclusions that emerge from these facts and figures may not be entirely worrisome for religious leaders, but most of them should be. Young adults are less likely to participate in religious services than they were a generation ago. Those who do populate the pews are an increasingly skewed cross-section of young adults. They are the married minority, whereas the unmarried majority scarcely frequent congregations at all. The proportion of young adults who identify with mainline Protestant denominations is about half the size it was a generation ago. Evangelical Protestants have barely held their own. They are certainly not the numeric powerhouse they sometimes imagine themselves to be. The historically black Protestant denominations are not growing either, and the racial segregation that has long characterized American religion is still very much in evidence. Catholic numbers among young adults have been stabilized in the midst of church scandals largely by a rising proportion of young adult immigrants. Judaism may not be disappearing among young adults, but serious questions remain about its changing attractions. Meanwhile, a growing number of young adults is religiously unaffiliated and a rising proportion have been raised without religion.

A generation ago, observers argued that baby boomers were simply sowing their wild oats, reveling in the sexual revolution and campus turmoil, and would undoubtedly return to the fold and raise their children with proper, if somewhat more individualistic, religious training. To be sure, the evidence that baby boomers were dabbling with spiritual quick fixes was not reassuring. But there was hope in the sheer possibility that a free market might be as good for the soul as it was for capitalism. Whatever might happen, the next generation would find God in their own ways.

The next wave now makes up half of the U.S. adult population. It is numerically larger than the baby boom generation. Its hundred million members are making the crucial decisions that will affect the rest of their lives and the future of America. They are deciding who and when to marry, whether and when to have children, where to live and work, and what kinds of social relationships to establish. Their religious behavior is closely intertwined with these major life cycle decisions. No longer do they marry the girl or boy they dated in high school, settle in the same neighborhood as their parents, and work in the family business or farm. If they were a faithful Baptist or Catholic at age thirteen, they will likely have lived at least another thirteen years—and perhaps longer—before they settle down, marry, and have children. They will have had plenty of time to make decisions they could not have anticipated when they were thirteen. They are likely to have spent a full decade on their own, living away from their parents and their parents' congregation, mingling mostly with their own age group, and struggling to discover who they are while moving from place to place and from job to job.

Ours is not the kind of society that encourages continuity. The Baptist or Catholic at thirteen may comfortably remain one through high school, but nearly everything a young adult experiences in his or her twenties and thirties calls for consideration, choice, and change. A high school senior must decide on college, junior college, a job, or perhaps joining the military. By the time young adults are twenty-two, they are expected to be on their own financially and capable of figuring out the deepest questions about lifetime work and a lifetime partner. The culture dictates that people will not be overly dependent on their parents' guidance. Shopping malls, job fairs, dating services, guidance counselors, and advertising all encourage choices geared toward the future instead of the past.

Yet the fact that American culture discourages continuity does not diminish the need we all experience for personal coherence—including a connection between our present and our past. Thus, we do not see all Baptists becoming Jehovah's Witnesses or a majority of Catholics becoming Mormons. Instead, the typical pattern of religious behavior among young adults is, as I have suggested, *tinkering*. Tinkering is evident among the large number of young adults who believe in God, life after death, and the divinity of Jesus, for instance, but who seldom attend religious services. Their beliefs lend continuity with the past—with the Bible stories they probably learned as children—and their behavior lets them adapt to the demands of the present. Spending a weekend with friends, buying groceries and doing the laundry, or getting ready for a hectic week at work takes precedence over spending yet another Sunday morning at worship. Tinkering is equally evident in the quest to update one's beliefs about spirituality. The core holds steady, persuading one that the Bible is still a valuable source of moral insight, for example, but the core is amended almost continuously through conversations with friends, reflections about an especially meaningful experience on vacation or at work, or from a popular song.

Religious congregations face enormous challenges in providing mean-ingful venues for this kind of belief and practice. Young adults contemplat-ing marriage may feel compelled to consult a member of the clergy in order to secure a desirable spot on the congregation's calendar for their wedding; otherwise, it is simply more efficient to surf the Internet if they have a question about, say, Islam, mediation, or what their religious tradition teaches about premarital sex. Many congregations have gotten spoiled, thinking they can serve young adults by sponsoring a lively high school group and then catering to young married couples with children. That leaves out about three-quarters of their potential clientele. The faithful few come and make the clergy happy because they are there; the rest are out of sight and, if not out of mind, a mystery to religious leaders.

It is unfortunate, in my view, that religious congregations have not done a better job of figuring out what young adults want and need. I say this partly because evidence suggests that religion has more beneficial than harmful effects; for instance, in discouraging teenagers from using drugs, in helping parents to be better mothers and fathers, in keeping marriages intact, and so on. More to the point, though, the evidence suggests over-whelmingly that young adulthood is a time when other social institutions fail to be of much help. To repeat my central argument: We provide day care centers, schools, welfare programs, family counseling, colleges, job training programs, and even detention centers as a kind of institutional surround-sound until young adults reach age 21, and then we provide noth-ing. Schooling stops for the vast majority, parents provide some financial assistance and babysitting but largely keep their distance, and even the best congregation-based youth groups or campus ministries no longer apply. Yet nearly all the major decisions a person has to make about marriage, child rearing, and work happen after these support systems have ceased to function. This is not a good way to run a society. No wonder young adults experience stress and confusion, worry that they are not yet capable of behaving like adults, delay settling down, and often make bad decisions about jobs and money. This is not a criticism of young adults themselves. They do the best they can in the absence of much assistance or support.

Religious congregations could be a more important source of assistance and support for young adults than they presently are. Instead of investing so heavily in programs for children and the elderly, they could focus more intentionally on ministries to young adults. They could be less content to provide activities for married couples with children and work harder at programs for single adults with questions about marriage, work, and fi-nances, or with interests in serving their communities or building relation-ships. To meet these challenges, though, religious leaders would have to reflect seriously on what it is that might attract young adults.

What do young Americans want from congregations? Religious leaders might argue that this is the wrong way of asking the question. Should it not be: How can young Americans serve their congregations? What are their gifts? How are they willing to contribute? In this view, people should be givers with respect to their congregations, not takers. After all, congregations function largely on the time and money that people give voluntarily, not on the services that clergy provide.

But people have to get something out of the bargain, too. Everything social scientists have learned about volunteering, philanthropy, and joining organizations underscores this fact. There is no such thing as pure altruism. Human nature is self-interested. Not so much so that we never do things because they will benefit others. We willingly make sacrifices for our children. We write out checks to help soup kitchens and orphanages. Yet we also get something out of these activities. Maybe it is the good feeling that comes from helping others or a sense that we are making a small difference for good in the world.

The same is true about participating in congregations. People have to get something from their participation to make it worthwhile. Otherwise, there are too few hours in the week to do everything. A few more hours at work can make the difference between receiving or not receiving a promotion. Time taking one's children out to breakfast or to soccer practice may seem more valuable than sitting in church. Or, if someone truly wants to make a difference in the world, it may seem more effective to work at a soup kitchen than at a church, spend one's evenings working for a political candidate, or, for that matter, pour one's energies into being a soldier, doctor, foreign policy expert, or teacher.

Clergy can easily miss the significance of this point because their lives are devoted to the programs of their congregations. The congregation is very much their world. They come early and stay late. Indeed, statistics show that clergy work longer work weeks than people in nearly any other profession.[1] Spending so much of their time at the church and on church business means they have limited contact with people who never darken the door of a church. Even within their own congregations, the people they know best are the faithful members who serve actively on committees, teach Sunday school, and hold other leadership positions. They understandably would like more of their congregation to be this actively involved. It is easy for them to believe that God's work is better done through the congregation than in any other way.

The fact that a sizable minority of young adults attends religious services regularly means that some young people must be getting something from their congregations. As we have seen, young adults apparently feel there is something to be gained for their marriages and for their children if they attend religious services regularly. Research suggests that many congregations invest heavily in family ministries for this reason. They sponsor Sunday school classes and prayer groups that help young couples work through the rough spots in their marriages. They provide day care and Sunday school classes for the children. Research also suggests that people choose particular churches because they appreciate the preaching, the music, and other events. It may be, as some scholars have argued, that young adults participate in congregations as a way of hedging against the risks we all face as we go through life. The congregation reassures people that there is life beyond death. It provides more immediate resources, too. Most church goers (even those who go infrequently) believe their congregation would be there to help them if someone in their family became ill. And congregations do function in many ways as caring communities. Members provide emotional support to one another. Some members receive financial assistance. Others draw on church networks to make new friends or to find new jobs.

This all suggests that congregations may continue to attract a decent—though probably declining—number of young Americans simply by doing what congregations have always done. For all the talk about changing needs and new social conditions, there is a considerable amount of inertia at work in American religion. People sing the same hymns, participate in the same liturgies, and hear preaching about the same stories year in and year out. As long as the quality is not too bad, the very familiarity of the services makes them attractive. Sitting there in the same pew week after week, parishioners are vaguely reminded that this is how they worshipped as children, and how their parents and grandparents worshipped.

But religious practices also change—and need to change. When the American population began growing and moving westward during the nineteenth century, religious organizations responded by sending missionaries to start new churches on the frontier. Itinerant clergy who traveled among a circuit of churches became an innovation that helped staff these new churches in remote areas. At the end of the nineteenth century, new organizations such as the Salvation Army launched innovative ministries in cities to meet the needs of a greatly expanded working class and immigrant population.[2] More recently, immigrant congregations have once again emerged to meet the particular social and cultural needs of immigrants from Mexico, Korea, and elsewhere, and, as more of the population has moved to suburban areas and become used to long-distance commutes, megachurches have sprung up to provide services in different ways than the typical neighborhood church did in the past.[3]

What, then, are the characteristics of congregations that seem most effective at attracting young adults? What do these characteristics tell us about the needs and interests of young adults? Are there clues, either in these characteristics, or in what young adults say in surveys, that might

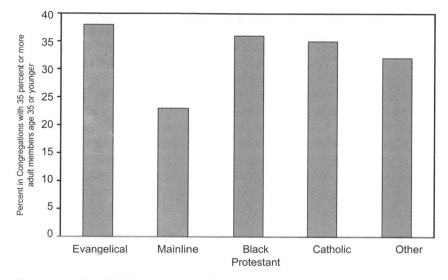

Figure 11.1. Youthful Congregations. Source: National Congregations Survey, unweighted results.

suggest opportunities for religious leaders as they think about the future of their organizations?

THE PROFILE OF YOUTHFUL CONGREGATIONS

A useful way of understanding what seems to be attractive to young adults is to examine congregations that have a higher-than-average proportion of young adults. For present purposes, I will define a *youthful* congregation as one in which at least 35 percent of its regularly attending adults are age 35 or younger. In short, youthful congregations are composed of a substantial number of people who are roughly between the ages of 18 and 35. This definition differs a little, of course, from our emphasis in previous chapters on young adults between the ages of 21 and 45. However, it was the way the data on congregations were collected, so we must be content with it. It does have the merit of sorting out youthful congregations from other congregations. Overall, about a third of Americans who participate in any congregation participate in a youthful congregation, by this definition.[4]

The percentages of U.S. church members within each major faith tradition who attend a youthful congregation are shown in figure 11.1. Thirty-eight percent of evangelicals attend a youthful congregation, 23 percent of mainline Protestants do, 36 percent of black Protestants do, and 35 percent of Roman Catholics do. These figures are consistent with what we observed in chapter 4 about the religious preferences of young adults. There, we saw that the religious preferences given by adults in the U.S. indicated that mainline Protestants tended to be older than members of the other traditions. Here, we see that the descriptions of their congregations given by clergy correspond to those patterns, thus giving us some confidence that clergy know what they are talking about when they estimate the age composition of their congregations. These figures also correspond to popular impressions and some statistics from denominations in which evangelical congregations appear to be younger than mainline congregations. Other than this difference, though, it is important to underscore that the percentages of young congregations among evangelicals, black Protestants, and Catholics are about the same. In short, evangelicals are not unique in creating congregations that attract large numbers of young adults.

Youthful congregations are young in another sense besides having a large minority of young adults. They were founded more recently. In fact, 30 percent of them were founded since 1970, compared with only 16 percent of the "old" or less youthful congregations. Thus, there is probably some truth in the anecdotal wisdom of church planners that says young people are more likely to be attracted to new congregations than to older ones. We need to be cautious about accepting all the implications of that adage at face value, though. The fact that newer congregations have more young adults does not mean, for example, that they have to be *brand new*. Nor does it mean they must adopt innovative worship styles to attract young adults.

Having a youthful membership does not necessarily mean that a congregation is vital or growing. However, there are several indications in these data suggesting that youthfulness is associated with vitality and growth. For instance, when asked what percent of their regular adult participants were new, clergy in youthful congregations gave an average of 16.4 percent, while clergy in less youthful congregations gave an average of 12.9 percent. This is not a large difference by any means (and we do not know if new members might have been offset by other members leaving), but it does suggest the possibility of a slight edge in growth. Despite having been founded, on average, more recently, youthful congregations are also more likely than less youthful congregations to be larger. Twenty-three percent have a thousand or more regular adult participants, compared with 18 percent of the less youthful congregations. Again, these differences are not large, but suggest that youthfulness and growth may go together.[5] Perhaps the most sought after indication of vitality in congregations is the number of children involved. For most of the past century (and sometimes longer), denominations kept careful records of baptisms and Sunday school attendance. They did this because their mission was, among other things, to train children. They also figured that larger numbers of children in one decade would mean large numbers of members in the next. Today, that expectation is less certain because of denominational switching and geographic mobility. Yet congregations still take pride in having children. And it is not surprising that congregations with more young adults also have more children. What is perhaps surprising is the *extent* of the differences. The pastors of youthful congregations report that an average of 414 children attend at least one of the Sunday school or other classes offered at the church in a typical week; in comparison, the figure for old congregations is only 271.[6]

Youthful congregations appeal to *populations* that have large numbers of young adults. It may seem banal to say this, but it is an important point. Youthful congregations are located in metropolitan areas where young adults live. They also are more racially and ethnically mixed. Fewer youthful congregations are overwhelmingly composed of white Anglos. More have at least a small minority of African Americans, Hispanics, and Asian Americans.[7]

In most other ways, the youthful and older congregations studied did not differ, except in some aspects of worship that could be attributed to the larger proportion of youthful congregations that were evangelical. Thus, nearly all services in both kinds of congregations included preaching and singing. About seven congregations in ten (among both youthful and older ones) had a choir and about half typically had a soloist. The vast majority (eight in ten) included silent prayer or meditation in the service and a time for people to greet one another and shake hands. Seventy-seven percent of the youthful congregations had a written order of service or program, although this was 9 percentage points less than among people who attended older congregations. Another difference was in the use of overhead projectors—used by 22 percent of the youthful congregations, but by only 13 percent of the older congregations. Ninety percent of both kinds used musical instruments, and pianos and organs were the instruments of choice for the majority of both. However, 35 percent of the youthful congregations that used any instruments also used drums and 40 percent used electric guitars (19 and 23 percent, respectively, in the older congregations).

MINICHURCH OR MEGACHURCH

The question of church size merits further consideration with additional data. Church prognosticators disagree about the merits of large and small congregations. The argument for large congregations is that they can provide more of what young adults are seeking—singles groups for people in their twenties, parenting classes for those in their thirties, and so on. Baby boomers allegedly started flocking to large congregations in the 1980s because they wanted multiple programs under one roof. It was easy to go one place and find everything they needed, like shopping at Wal-Mart. Recently, though, some observers have been arguing that young adults are rejecting that model. They want small congregations instead. Small congregations offer the chance to be informal, to exercise ownership of one's worship service, and above all to make more intimate friendships.

The truth is, young adults can be found in large congregations, small ones, and every size congregation in between. No single size predominates. Other than among Catholics, where parishes are traditionally large, only a small minority of young adults belong to congregations with 2,000 or more members—9 percent of evangelical Protestants, 6 percent of mainline Protestants, and 13 percent of black Protestants. Adding the ones that belong to congregations with at least 1,000 members boosts the figures only to 17 percent, 13 percent, and 16 percent, respectively. At the other extreme, only 21 percent of evangelicals, 9 percent of mainline Protestants, and 25 percent of black Protestants age 21 through 45 belong to congregations with fewer than 100 members.[8]

Further analysis of the data casts doubt on the notion that younger adults differ very much from older adults in belonging to large or small congregations. Nor is there any consistent indication that young adults opt for larger or smaller congregations on the basis of, say, being single or married, or having children or not having children. Size of congregation, not surprisingly, is still influenced by size of community more than by anything else. People who live in metropolitan areas, and especially in suburbs, are more likely to belong to large congregations than people who live in smaller towns or rural areas are. To the extent that church planners follow population projections, then, large congregations are likely to grow as the population living in suburbs continues to grow. Still, we need to be mindful of other population trends that function in different ways. For instance, we saw in chapter 9 that Hispanic Catholics attend smaller parishes than non-Hispanic Catholics—and the number of Hispanic Catholics is increasing.

If the size of congregations in which young adults participate varies, this variation is nevertheless associated with a different range of programs being available. For instance, 77 percent of evangelical congregations with more than a thousand members offer day care services, compared with only 33 percent of evangelical congregations with fewer than 200 members. Large mainline, black Protestant, and Catholic congregations are also more likely to offer day care than smaller congregations are. The same is true for social ministries, such as food pantries and homeless shelters. Large congregations are more likely to sponsor or help sponsor these ministries than small congregations are.[9] Thus, a young family who wanted day care or was interested in helping the needy would be more likely to find opportunities to become involved in these programs at a larger congregation.

Although it is hard to demonstrate with survey data, what makes a congregation, large or small, attractive to young adults is probably a sense of community. Young adults are not looking for salvation, Richard Flory and Donald Miller wrote after conducting field studies in a number of congregations in southern California, they are looking for love.[10] That may be especially true of single adults. Church is an unlikely place to find love if that means finding someone to marry. However, there can at least be companionship. A man who recently switched form a megachurch to a smaller church explained his decision this way: "I'd go to this [large] church and you're sitting next to a different person every time. I didn't have any connection there." At the new church, "I went there and I was like wow, you could just tell there was a sense of community."

The absence of community can be a compelling reason to stay away. The pastor of a church that has been successful in attracting young unmarried adults told me she finds it mildly amusing whenever someone mentions Putnam's idea of bowling alone. "What young people at my church dislike more than anything else is *sitting alone*," she said. Especially the women want to know if there will be someone their age with whom they can sit. At another church, the worship service itself was actually designed to break down the fear of sitting alone. Midway through, there was a fifteen-minute coffee break. It gave people a chance to get up, move around, greet someone new, and sit in a different place.

ALTERNATIVE STYLES OF WORSHIP

Perhaps the most generationally charged question for congregation leaders is whether to initiate so-called contemporary-style worship services. Stereotypically, young people want praise choruses and Christian rock; older people want Bach and Purcell. The different preferences cannot be reconciled easily because they involve *worship*. Worship is what social scientists call a public good. It affects everyone, unlike, say, a class or small group that can be geared toward one constituency without bothering another constituency. Moreover, worship is an official part of any congregational ministry, meaning that the content and style of worship is usually regarded as a biblical or theological issue. Sometimes the only compromise possible is to have two services, one for the young people and one for the old people. Short of that, young adults may wander away to a congregation that has the more relaxed worship style they desire.[11]

But journalists have begun to note that the stereotypic picture of generational preferences about worship may not be accurate. Some of the young people journalists interview say the innovative worship styles that appealed to baby boomers do not appeal to them. They think church services should

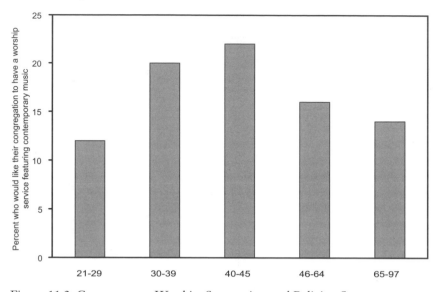

Figure 11.2. Contemporary Worship. Source: Arts and Religion Survey.

feel like church. They say the so-called seeker services that were geared toward people who disliked church are now passé. In the major research project I did a few years ago on the uses of music and the arts in congregations, I observed, too, that young adults were often as interested in preserving traditional worship as they were in changing it.

The responses in one of my surveys to a question about contemporary music in worship provide a good indicator of the popularity of contemporary-style worship among different age groups. Its greatest popularity appears to be among people in their early forties; in other words, among the tail-end of the baby boomers or oldest of the generation Xers, rather than among the emerging generation of young adults in their twenties and thirties (figure 11.2). Still, even among people in their early forties, fewer than a quarter (22 percent) say they would like to see their congregation have a worship service featuring contemporary music. And the lowest percentage of all (12 percent) is among people in their twenties.

This information will probably come as good news to church goers who think it is not quite the same going to church unless there is some Mozart or Handel. However, it does not mean that congregations can simply rest on their traditions. Depending on the denominational tradition, between a tenth and a quarter of young adults would like to see some experimentation with contemporary music. They would also welcome concerts, art festivals, poetry readings, and opportunities to discuss literature, music, and art. Because many of these activities do not involve corporate worship, they can also be initiated with fewer concerns from naysayers. If a quarter of the young adults in the congregation are interested in them, that is likely to be a core group capable of doing the work to make them happen.

MEETING THE CHANGING NEEDS OF FAMILIES

Congregations, as we have seen, are more likely to have young adults who are married and have children than they are to have young adults who are single. Congregations are for this reason likely to pour resources into programs that meet the needs of young families with children, more so than planning programs to attract other young adults. Some evidence to this effect is available from the National Congregations Survey. In that study, youthful congregations reported an average of 50 different classes that met at least once a month (compared with only 28 among nonyouthful congregations). Ten percent of youthful congregations also had special classes or groups specifically for parents and 13 percent had such groups oriented specifically toward families. In comparison, only 6 percent said they had special groups for single adults.

Large congregations can usually offer a mix of programs for children, parents, married couples without children, and single adults. For most congregations, though, some balance has to be struck between meeting the needs of members and starting programs in hopes of attracting people in the community who are not already members. This is where the emerging demographic divide in American religion becomes critical. Congregations that appeal to young married couples with children have a natural constituency, albeit a declining one, at least among people in their twenties. Congregations with conservative theological and social agendas may be especially appealing to young families with children. Such congregations offer certainty in an uncertain world. They give clear moral guidance and tell members they are doing the right thing in devoting themselves to their spouses and children. Yet the population of young adults also includes growing numbers of people who are not married, do not have children, and are not involved in congregations. For them, a congregation that champions childrearing and that offers simple answers to life's complex questions may be less appealing. It may be considerably less appealing if it offers few opportunities to meet and mingle with other single adults.

Even congregations that decide to focus their programs on families face new challenges because of the growing number of young mothers who work outside the home and the more complex schedules that result. A woman in her late twenties who pastors a Methodist church drove home this point. Asked what the main challenges facing her congregation were, she replied, "How can we help families who are being pulled in so many different ways. We're finding that programs we try to have here at the church, families don't attend. Either it's a weeknight or they don't want to come back on Sunday night. So [the difficulty is] figuring out what families need and what they want and how the church can be a support for them. There are so many things: soccer, baseball, scouts, whatever, which are all great things, but where does faith play in all of this? That's a big challenge. One of the things I'm going to start doing is visit families and talk with them one-on-one and see what they're thinking and see what they like about the church and what are we not doing that they would like to see."

The changing needs of families also include the special needs of gays and lesbians, single-parent families, and interreligious families—all representing departures from the traditional religiously endogamous nuclear family. It is harder for these nontraditional families to find congregations that welcome them and provide programs oriented to their needs. Yet there is a niche for congregations that try to do this. The question is only whether these congregations can be sufficiently vital to stand, as it were, in the middle between the traditional family-friendly congregation and that segment of the young adult population who are not involved in organized religion at all.

Interreligious Programs

Interreligious programs need to be distinguished carefully from ecumenical or interchurch programs. By interreligious programs I mean ones that include representatives of other faiths besides Christianity, such as Judaism, Islam, Hinduism, and Buddhism, not just Methodists and Baptists, or Protestants and Catholics. The need for greater understanding between Christians and people of other faiths is self-evident. It has been heightened in recent years by international conflicts between the United States and Muslim countries. It has also become more important because of the growing presence of Muslims, Hindus, and Buddhists who live in the United States. As we saw in chapter 4, a sizable number of young adults believe there is truth in all religions. That conviction, however, is often shallow. It rests on easy assumptions about cultural relativism, but seldom reflects much understanding of the teachings of the various religions.

In 1999, fewer than one young adult church member in five said he or she would like to see opportunities at his or her congregation to examine other world religions. At evangelical churches, this figure was 16 percent; at mainline Protestant churches, 19 percent; and at Catholic churches, 20 percent.[12] Perhaps the other young adults were thinking it would be better to learn about different religions someplace besides their congregation— maybe in night school or via television. After the September 11, 2001 attacks, the public became more interested in understanding other religions, at least in principle. Thus, in 2003, fully 84 percent of Americans age 21 through 45 agreed that people should learn more about religions other than their own (only 11 percent thought it was better to avoid learning about other religions). And these percentages were high among the adherents of all the major Christian traditions, ranging from 77 percent among evangelicals to 83 percent among black Protestants, to 87 percent among Catholics, and 88 percent among mainline Protestants.[13]

But practice does not always meet principle. Among the same young adults who overwhelmingly thought it was a good idea to learn about other religions, only a tenth had participated in a class in the past year that focused on the beliefs and practices of some other religion besides Christianity or Judaism (12 percent among evangelicals, 11 percent among mainline Protestants, 5 percent among black Protestants, and 7 percent among Catholics). And only a few more than that (13 percent) had participated in a worship service or other event at their congregation in which a non-Christian leader spoke (10 percent of evangelicals, 21 percent of mainline Protestants, 8 percent of black Protestants, and 10 percent of Catholics).

The gap between principle and practice on interreligious programs points to a large need that congregations could be working harder to fill. It is especially important that young adults gain understanding of other religions besides their own. They will be living in an increasingly diverse society and in an increasingly interconnected world. Bland assumptions about all religions being the same may work to prevent open hostility. But these assumptions serve poorly when reality demonstrates that religions are not all the same. At that point, the natural tendency is either to hunker down or throw up one's hands. Hunkering down pushes people into stronger assertions about the unique validity of their own religion. Throwing up one's hands is tantamount to saying that no religion matters very much. The result is greater polarization. Orthodoxy on one side. Irreligion on the other. The middle ground that mediates between these two extremes is missing. It shrinks because of too little attention to the hard work needed to make sense of one's own religion in the midst of other religions.

OPPORTUNITIES FOR INTERNATIONAL MINISTRY

If globalization increases the need for interreligious understanding, it also raises the stakes for religious organizations that want to be of value to the wider world. International ministries have been a part of religion in the United States from almost the beginning of our nation's history. Yet the nature of these ministries has needed to be refashioned from generation to generation. The question for the current generation of young adults is whether the increasingly globalized world in which they live will include religious programs or be guided only by commercial and political concerns.

A survey conducted for *Religion and Ethics Newsweekly* in 2004 found that 7 percent of white evangelical Protestants age 21 through 45 had gone on a religious mission trip to another country, 6 percent of white mainline Protestants had done this, 3 percent of black Protestants had, and 1 percent of Catholics had. These may seem like disappointingly low numbers and, in fact, they may be inflated because the study was biased toward better educated and more active church members. We also have no way of knowing if they are larger or smaller now than they may have been a generation ago. However, they do suggest that churches are having some success in initiating these kinds of mission experiences.[14] Another interesting result from this study is that 7 percent of Hispanics in the survey had gone on a mission trip of this kind. This finding suggests that one of the ways in which the growing ethnic diversity of the United States may be influencing American religion is by encouraging participation in international programs of this kind.

Besides sponsoring mission trips, congregations can host educational programs that raise young adults' awareness of needs and opportunities in other countries. Researchers have paid little attention thus far to these programs. However, it seems self-evident that such specialized organizations as World Vision, World Relief, and Save the Children can hardly function effectively if they do not have a strong base in local congregations.

OPPORTUNITIES FOR SERVICE

Apart from international programs, congregations will continue to be called on to provide social services in their communities. Whether congregations do this with government funding or on their own is not the issue. It is rather that congregations are locations in which people mingle with others, hear the value of caring for others reinforced, and experience opportunities for becoming involved in caregiving activities. There is widespread agreement across age groups about the *value* of helping the needy and serving the community through volunteering. In one national survey, 72 percent of the public said a person who helps the poor is someone they would admire a lot. In the same survey, 82 percent said doing volunteer work is important to being a good citizen (49 percent said it was very important) and 92 percent said this about helping the poor (67 percent said this was very important to being a good citizen). Among people in their twenties and thirties, these percentages were just as high as among people in their fifties or sixties.[15]

Valuing social service, though, does not always translate into concrete activities. In fact, young adults generally score lower than older adults do when asked if they have actually done any volunteer work to help the needy. But this is where religious participation comes in. Those who participate in religious congregations are also more likely to do volunteer work to help the needy than those who do not. For instance, respondents of all ages in Putnam's Social Capital Benchmark Survey were about ten percentage points more likely to have volunteered to help the poor or elderly in the past year if they were regular church goers than if they were not.

This positive relationship between church going and helping the poor or elderly could be a function of churches specifically encouraging that kind of helping behavior. Nevertheless, evidence also suggests that there is a more general relationship between church going and volunteering. Among adults age 21 through 45, those who attend church regularly are significantly more likely than those who do not attend regularly to engage in a wide variety of volunteer activities. For instance, the regular attendees are more likely than their counterparts to volunteer for youth activities, community development organizations, neighborhood associations, distributing food to the needy, and building houses for the poor. They are also more likely to volunteer for political campaigns, environmental projects, arts or cultural activities, and violence prevention efforts. These differences remain strong when other factors, such as age, gender, marital status, children, race, and education, are controlled. On average, the odds of frequent church attenders volunteering for these kinds of activities are about twice as large as the odds are for infrequent attenders volunteering.[16]

This positive relationship between church going and volunteering is one reason scholars who care nothing about the theological aspects of religion nevertheless regard it as a social asset. If fewer and fewer young adults participate regularly in religious congregations, volunteering of other kinds also seems likely to decline. Congregations are a resource for community leaders who wish to encourage volunteering. Being part of a congregation apparently exposes people to needs they might not think about otherwise and to opportunities to serve those needs. For young adults who say they value helping the poor and the needy, religious participation is an activity that puts them in harm's way of having to realize those values. The opportunity to serve, though, may also be a reason to continue participating in a congregation.

"I got involved in the congregation rather quickly," a twenty-nine-year-old man recalls, "because they asked me to help out with the youth program." At twenty-nine, he is still unmarried and, although he has a college degree, is working for a construction company while he decides for sure what career he wants to pursue. He went to a Catholic church every Sunday with his family while he was growing up, but quit attending after he finished confirmation classes at age thirteen. During his first two years of college, he was not involved in any religious organizations, but felt a desire (which he attributes to his religious upbringing) to find a purpose for his life. His nonreligious friends seemed to have more purpose than he did. Frustrated, he dropped out of college and spent a year working with Habitat for Humanity. During that year, he rubbed shoulders with people from a variety of faiths, lived with a Quaker family, and experienced a spiritual turning point in this life. After several years of moving around, going to school, and working, he returned to his home community and tried fitting into his boyhood church. He couldn't. "I never felt that it mattered one way or the other whether I was there or not to anyone in the community," he recalls. With his family's approval, he decided to try out other churches. He is a Presbyterian now. The church gave him an opportunity to serve. "My faith at this point is one of searching," he says. "I am trying to understand how to use my gifts and strength and talents to serve God."

A Future for Congregations

The question pastors ask me most often when I speak to clergy groups about trends in American religion is whether congregations have a future. Will they survive? By the time the current generation of young adults has retired, will local churches still look like they do now? Is declining attendance weakening congregations? Will the Internet replace them? Do church planners need to envision some entirely different form of cultivating the spiritual interests of the population? These are questions that stem from a genuine desire to read the signs of the times and adapt accordingly. They are driven, too, by sensationalist stories in the media about some supposed wave of the future that is replacing pulpits with LCD screens, pews with sofas, and sermons with chat rooms.

My view is that congregations *can* survive, but only if religious leaders roll up their sleeves and pay considerably more attention to young adults than they have been. It is true that cultures change slowly, meaning that we should not ignore the possibility that congregations will survive from sheer inertia. Despite our fascination with change, we want our children to share our values. We create institutions—schools, governments, businesses—that ensure continuity from one generation to the next. Religious organizations are even more indebted to the past than other institutions. A significant part of their mission is to remind people of the past. Their legitimacy comes from sacred texts written in the past and they frequently argue that they are maintaining the wisdom of ancient traditions. In the United States, religion is a massive institution that reflects the enormous investment of generations of clergy and lay participants. To be sure, congregations are not all of which American religion is composed. Religious and spiritual tastes are reflected in religious dieting programs, recording companies, conference speakers, retreat houses, publishing enterprises, and countless Web sites. However, the core of American religion continues to be its congregations. Houses of worship are a presence in most communities. These buildings represent sunk costs. Americans generally do not question why it seems more appropriate to worship God at a church than out in nature or at work. Beliefs are reinforced in the presence of others. Belonging is cherished. For all these reasons, it would be surprising if, say in fifty years, congregations had simply disappeared. But survival and vitality are two different things.

The question is not whether congregations have a future, but what the future of congregations will be. Young adults *are* currently less involved at houses of worship than young adults were a generation ago. Mainline Protestant churches have diminished in importance relative to other traditions. More of the potential clientele of congregations are single and childless and thus less attracted to churches that cater only to the married with children. Believers espouse traditional doctrines, sometimes adamantly, but also personalize and relativize their beliefs. Mobility and expanded opportunities to travel encourage spiritual shopping. Congregations are more diverse or at least composed of people whose social contacts are more diverse. For many, the arts and the Internet are ways of seeking spiritual insight. These are the realities to which congregations must adapt. Religious leaders will have to confront these challenges if they are to keep their congregations strong. They will have to invent evangelistic strategies capable of reaching busy adults who are no longer in high school or college. They will probably need to initiate programs less focused on the nuclear family and more appealing to single adults in their late twenties and thirties.

Scholars differ in their assessments of whether religion is good for our country. Some writers argue that religion encourages superstitious thinking that should be replaced by cold logic and science. Others worry that religion is a dangerous force with potential for bigotry and violence if it is not kept in check. The reality is that even for young adults—the busiest, best educated, and most cosmopolitan segment of our society—religion is potentially important. It engages as many as a quarter of them quite extensively in their congregations, and another half of the young adult population is at least somewhat inclined to participate in religion. For good or ill, that is the reality. The role of scholarship is to understand how this involvement in religion fits into our society—and thereby to encourage reflection about what its future should be.

The challenges that congregations now face as they become increasingly the domain of young adults are often questions about staffing, styles of worship, financing, recruitment, and membership. Those are perennial challenges, and they often consume the time and energy of planning committees. However, I have tried to suggest that there are larger questions for religious and other community leaders and policy makers to keep in mind. One of these is that young adults are increasingly a generation of bricoleurs who piece together their lives in highly diverse ways and from a multitude of sources. The temptation for some religious leaders will be to provide ready-made answers for the tinkerers who come their way. Even in those settings, though, the mixture of beliefs, lifestyles, and personal practices is seldom simple. The challenge is thus to encourage people to draw responsibly from the full range of resources at their disposal and to work at putting together their lives in ways that are collectively as well as personally beneficial.

A second challenge is to confront the polarization that continues and deepens between people who are actively and conservatively religious and those who are either less involved in religion or more open-ended in their approach to it. The culture wars between these two factions have not been healthy for the civic life of our nation. These wars are too easily exploited by interest groups and political candidates. Religious leaders and policy makers need not abandon their principles to work for the common good, but working for the common good must be emphasized more forcefully if the culture wars are to be transcended.

Finally, I want to reiterate what I said earlier about young adulthood lacking the institutional support it needs and deserves. We cannot hope to be a strong society if we invest resources in young people until they are eighteen or twenty and then turn them out to find their way entirely on their own. I am not talking about some system of public welfare or extended educational assistance. The bits and pieces of support are already there—in family networks, among groups of friends, at singles bars, in day care centers, and even in the work place. But we have not even begun to recognize the challenges that need to be met. We need a thorough-going discussion of the needs that young adults experience, just as we have had such discussions about the needs of children and those of the elderly. How young adults can more responsibly make complex decisions about careers, finances, marriage, and parenting must be an important part of these discussions. Religion is but one of the sectors that needs to be represented. Traditionally, religion has been an important resource for networking, for maintaining intergenerational ties, and for transmitting values to adults as well as to children. It can continue to be in the future, but only if it faces the changes currently taking place among young adults.

Appendix

෴

THE NATIONAL YOUNG ADULTS AND RELIGION STUDY

I initiated the National Young Adults and Religion Study (NYARS) in 2003. The purpose of the NYARS project was to generate a better understanding of the religious beliefs and practices of young adults in the United States and of the relationships between these beliefs and practices and social change in the wider society. The project was motivated by the fact, as I discovered from previous research and in conversations with religious leaders and foundation officials, that relatively little attention was being paid to the special needs and interests of young adults, either by researchers or religious organizations. The project was also motivated by the fact that considerable research had been conducted among baby boomers when they were young adults (and more recently), but that similar attention had not been devoted to understanding how the current generation of young adults might be similar to or different from that generation.

An initial review of the literature revealed that there were a number of trends in American society in which young adults were particularly implicated: changing patterns of marriage and child rearing, financial pressures, educational developments, and the Internet, among others. Yet few of these developments were being examined with an eye toward understanding how they might influence the religious beliefs and practices of young adults. Young adulthood itself appeared to be lengthening as the processes by which people became adults were taking longer. But studies of teenagers were not the best way to understand what challenges young adults might be facing in their twenties and thirties. The leaders of religious organizations needed to understand these challenges, at least if they hoped to remain relevant to the lives of young adults.

Unlike other research projects, the NYARS project did not require collecting new data by conducting a national survey or something similar. Because young adults are included in all surveys of U.S. adults, the relevant data were already there. The main task was to examine these data to see what they revealed about young adults and to do so paying particular attention to questions about religion and, where possible, changes having taken place in recent decades. Because so much attention has been devoted to baby boomers, it was especially desirable to examine similarities and differences between young adults in recent surveys and young adults in surveys conducted when baby boomers were young. Fortunately, a number of surveys were available. I describe the methodological strategy I used in analyzing these data and the particular surveys I used in the sections that follow.

Besides drawing on survey data, I commissioned approximately one hundred indepth, qualitative interviews. The purpose of these interviews was to hear in their own words from some clergy and from young adults themselves how they were thinking about religion and spirituality. These qualitative interviews were conducted with clergy, young adults engaged in various lay ministry roles, young adults who simply attended religious services, and young adults who no longer had any attachment to organized religion. I used a nonrandom network quota design to select interviewees. The design called for approximately equal numbers of men and women, approximately equal numbers of young adults who had graduated from college and who had not graduated from college, and as much diversity as possible with respect to race and ethnicity, region, and religious background. The nonclergy interviewees were all between the ages of 21 and 45. The interviews ranged in length from an hour to more than two hours and averaged about 90 minutes. All interviews were tape recorded and transcribed. Names and other identifying information (such as name and location of congregations) have been suppressed to honor the confidentiality of the interviews. Although the chapters focus mostly on reporting the quantitative data, I have included a few examples from the qualitative interviews and, more generally, used them in interpreting the quantitative data.

METHODOLOGY

The principal considerations in analyzing and presenting the quantitative data were: (1) focus on adults age 21 through 45; (2) compare the beliefs, practices, and lifestyles of people in their twenties, thirties, and early forties; (3) whenever possible, compare young adults in recent surveys with young adults in surveys a generation ago; and (4) otherwise, compare the responses of young adults with those of older adults. I briefly explain the decision to focus on 21- through 45-year-olds in chapter 1. There were also methodological considerations. Although nearly all surveys of "adults" since the early 1970s include respondents age 18 and older (because Americans age 18 and older can vote and thus are relevant to political opinion polls), very few surveys include a good method of sampling adults age 18 through 20. This age group includes a large numbe of people who are in college. Yet, residents of "institutions" are usually excluded from survey samples, meaning that a college student living in a dormitory would likely be excluded, whereas one living in an apartment would be included. Because the number of young adults attending college has changed over the past three decades, this is especially a problem when trying to assess trends. The problem is compounded by the fact that some surveys continue to use household sampling strategies, while others rely on random-digit dialing (RDD). Thus, a person living in an "institution" would probably be excluded from household samples, but might be included in an RDD if his or her college assigned phone numbers to individual rooms, but would be excluded or underrepresented if he or she lived in a dormitory with telephones only in each hallway. In addition, problems arise in knowing how to treat interviewees in this age group who live with their parents compared with those who live at their own residences. Substantively, though, my interest was less in college students, high school seniors, or those living with their parents, than in young adults in their twenties and thirties who were mostly on their own, facing such major life choices as marriage and having children, and yet largely without the kinds of institutional support found in schools, colleges, the military, prisons, families of origin, or religious organizations. As I explain in chapter 1, most of these life choices occur between the ages of 21 and 45. Including people up through age 45 permitted comparisons between those who were younger, unmarried, without children, and new to their jobs with adults who for the most part had accomplished these life tasks, but who had not yet moved into such later life tasks as becoming empty nesters, grandparents, or retirees. The decision to compare young adults age 21 through 29 with those age 30 through 39 and 40 through 45 was somewhat arbitrary. I opted for these categories partly for the ease of describing people in their "twenties," "thirties," and "early forties." Through exploratory data analysis, I also discovered that these divisions nicely captured the major differences among young adults: those in their twenties are less likely to be married or have children, those in their thirties are much more likely to have settled into these life patterns, and those in their early forties have pretty much peaked on these various life tasks. Readers will note that it was not always possible to use exactly the same age categories. For instance, the U.S. Census Bureau sometimes provides categories that make it possible to compare 20- through 44-year-olds, rather than 21- through 45-year-olds. I relied relatively little on published data, though. In nearly every case, I obtained the relevant data sets, did my own analysis, and thus was able to use the same age categories.

In analyzing the data sets, I always looked separately at respondents age 21 through 29, 30 through 39, and 40 through 45. Where there were important differences, I have reported these and depicted them graphically in the figures. Sometimes I was not able to make these comparisons, though, because there were too few cases in the survey or because other ways of dividing young adults (e.g., by gender or marital status) were more important.

I was able to make comparisons between young adults in recent surveys and young adults in earlier surveys by drawing on several data sets in which comparable data had been obtained for more than one time period. My strategy was to make comparisons about 25 to 30 years apart whenever this was possible. The most recent data at the time I did the quantitative analysis was from surveys conducted between 1998 and 2002 (and occasionally 2003 or 2004). The earlier data was mostly from 1970 through 1976. I chose these years as the relevant comparison point because they were the years when baby boomers were young adults. I recognize that there are various ways of defining baby boomers and that my definition of the relevant time period differs from some. However, very few surveys with relevant questions and replications in more recent surveys were done before the early 1970s. Thus, I tried to come as close as I could to comparing young adults at present with young adults of the previous generation. Because most children are born when their parents are between 25 and 30 years old, these comparisons actually provide a decent estimate of how one generation compares with another. From the census, on which I draw in chapter 2 for evidence about broad social changes, I analyzed data from 1970 and 2000. From the General Social Surveys, which provided the richest source for trends in religion variables, I aggregated the surveys conducted between 1972 and 1976 and compared the results with the aggregated surveys conducted between 1998 and 2002. I say more about this later, but, briefly, this strategy made it possible to do fairly detailed subcomparisons within each group (for instance, evangelical Protestants or families with 3 or more children). I also make some use of the World Values Surveys, conducted in 1980 and 2000, and the DDB Needham surveys, conducted between 1975 and 1998.

My analysis of the differences between young adults in earlier and more recent surveys differs from the strategy used by some researchers of emphasizing year-to-year time-series analysis or cohort analysis. I appreciate the statistical elegance of these methods. However, I found that they did not serve as well for my purposes as the ones I employed. Many of the survey questions in which I was interested were asked in an earlier survey and a more recent one, but not in enough of the intervening years to warrant time-series analysis. In other instances, the questions were asked of subsamples and thus included too few cases to describe year-to-year trends accurately. Nor was I as interested in examining trends among all conceivable cohorts as comparing two particular cohorts of young adults and examining in detail how they were similar or different.

The topics for which comparisons between recent surveys and surveys conducted in the early 1970s could be made were limited to fairly simple measures of religious commitment, such as church attendance, religious preference, belief in God, and views of the Bible. Researchers often focus on these measures because they are the only ones available. They are useful for painting with a very broad brush. But they do not go very far in telling us about the more subtle dimensions of religious belief and practice, spirituality, or the moral and lifestyle implications of religious commitment. Rather than simply leave out those important considerations because time comparisons were not available, I examined them using the richest recent surveys I could find and focusing on young adults. In these analyses, I compared young adults with older adults. Readers are cautioned not to consider the comparisons between young adults and older adults in the same way as the comparisons between young adults in recent surveys and young adults in surveys a quarter century ago. The differences between young adults and older adults are partly a function of the two having grown up in different periods, but also reflect differences in life tasks and maturity. Still, these comparisons are valuable for descriptive purposes. When young adults differ sharply from older adults (for instance, in how they perceive their computer and Internet skills), those differences may suggest a trend or at least a distinctive characteristic of young adults that needs to be emphasized. In other instances, though, I have tried to cast doubt on the idea that young adults are truly distinctive by showing that they differ little from older adults.

I opted for graphs rather than numeric tables for the simple reason that I am a visual learner and am usually able to grasp and remember material better when I see it than when it is presented mathematically or discursively. I suspect some of my readers are visual learners, too. In presenting this material to audiences of nonspecialists, I have found that the graphs help. Of course, graphs can distort information, so I have tried to standardize my use of graphs as much as possible and to supply discursive interpretations in the chapters and additional material in the notes. The choice of particular graph styles was dictated largely by how much information could reasonably be presented within the space of a single graph. I used 2-dimensional vertical graphs, for instance, for comparisons of the results of two time periods (as long as the number of categories being compared was small) because these graphs allow a good visual sense of how one period compared with the other. I used horizontal line graphs when there were too many categories to compare easily with 2-dimensional charts; for instance, when time trends were available or for comparing people in different age categories. The danger of using line graphs for both purposes is that age differences may be confused with time trends, so readers need to careful in recognizing these different uses. I relied on bar graphs mostly for showing the percentages responding to particular questions, especially when there were more than a half dozen or so of these comparisons to be made. In this appendix, I have included several supplementary tables of numbers. These were too complex to present in graphic form, but provide information that support the arguments at various points in the chapters.

Because I wanted this information to be accessible to nonspecialists, I have kept the discussion of statistical details themselves to a minimum. I assessed statistical significance through standard chi-square tests, using probabilities of .05 or less as a cut-off point. Because the national surveys from which I have drawn generally had sizable numbers, I seldom found it necessary to present results based on fewer than one hundred cases. In the several instances where zero-order measures of the strength of association were of interest, I relied on gammas. Most of the data considered involved ordinal-level measurement, making gamma a suitable statistic for this purpose. For this reason, I also relied mostly on binary logistic regression analysis whenever more than two variables were involved. In these analyses, I controlled for such factors as gender, age, and race, and indicated the results of particular models in notes. Whenever I refer to odds-ratios or adjusted odds-ratios, these are from logistic regression analysis. For readers unfamiliar with binary logistic regression analysis, dependent variables must have only two categories and odds-ratios greater than 1.0 mean positive relationships, while odds-ratios less than 1.0 indicate negative relationships. For instance, an odds-ratio of 1.6 might be interpreted as indicating that the odds of being x (say a regular church goer) were 1.6 greater (or 60 percent greater) among people in one category (say, women) than among people in another category (say, men).

Readers should be aware that the surveys from which I have drawn information differ in size (total number of people interviewed), method (in-person or telephone), and response rate. I describe each of the surveys in the next section. Because question wording influences responses, I avoided offering arguments about trends unless exactly the same wording had been used. I have provided the verbatim wording or questions insofar as it did not prove tedious to do so. Readers interested in exact wordings or in obtaining the data sets themselves for further anlaysis can find this information at the Web sites I have listed in conjunction with each of the surveys below.

The Surveys and Other data

The surveys described in this section are the ones from which I drew most extensively. I obtained each of these data sets and did my own analysis of the relevant questions. Additional data that were available only in tabular form are described in each chapter at the point where those data are discussed.

Arts and Religion Survey

The Arts and Religion Survey was designed by Robert Wuthnow and conducted by the Gallup Organization in Princeton, New Jersey. Respondents were asked questions about their creative and arts-related activities; their attitudes toward the arts; their religious activities, behaviors, beliefs, and affiliations; their spiritual (or "uplifting") experiences; their attitudes toward religion and spirituality; the role of the arts in religious contexts; the relationship between art and spirituality; and their involvement in charitable activities. In-person, in-home interviews were conducted with a random national sample of 1,530 noninstitutionalized U.S. adults ages 18 and over, living in the forty-eight contiguous states. The sample is a probability sample down to the block level, after which households and persons within households were selected through an enumeration process. Notably, the Arts and Religion Survey was one of the last surveys that the Gallup Organization did using in-home interviews. Each interview lasted approximately fifty minutes and included more than three hundred questions. The data were collected during the spring of 1999. Principal funding for the project was from the Lilly Endowment. The primary publication resulting from the study, which includes further details about the survey, was Robert Wuthnow, *All In Sync: How Music and Art Are Revitalizing American Religion*. The codebook and data set can be accessed and downloaded or analyzed interactively at the Web site of the Cultural Policy and the Arts National Data Archive (www.cpanda.org) or the American Religion Data Archive (www.thearda.com). Of the 1,530 respondents in the survey, 231 were age 21 through 29, 300 were age 30 through 39, and 210 were age 40 through 45.

Civic Involvement Survey

The Civic Involvement Survey was designed by Robert Wuthnow and conducted by the Gallup Organization in Princeton, New Jersey. Respondents were asked questions about their communities, satisfaction with their neighborhoods, memberships in various voluntary associations, volunteering, contacts made through volunteering, participation in political activities, attitudes about citizenship, trust, religious behavior, the characteristics of their congregations, and standard demographic information. In-person, in-home interviews were conducted with a random national sample of 1,528 noninstitutionalized U.S. adults ages 18 and over, living in the forty-eight contiguous states. The sample is a probability sample down to the block level, after which households and persons within households were selected through an enumeration process. Each interview lasted approximately thirty minutes and generated 271 variables. The data were collected during the spring of 1997. Funding for the survey was provided by the Lilly Endowment and The Pew Charitable Trusts. The primary publication resulting from the study, which includes further details about the survey, was Robert Wuthnow, *Loose Connections: Joining Together in America's Fragmented Communities*. The codebook and data set can be accessed and downloaded or analyzed interactively at the Web site of the American Religion Data Archive (www.thearda.com). Of the 1,528 respondents in the survey, 208 were age 21 through 29, 349 were age 30 through 39, and 192 were age 40 through 45.

DDB Needham Surveys

The DDB Needham Life Style Survey data used in this volume were collected by DDB Worldwide of Chicago, Illinois, a marketing research firm, between 1975 and 1998. Robert Putnam made extensive use of these data in *Bowling Alone* and subsequently negotiated their release to researchers for academic use. The data include 389 variables, the most relevant of which concern such activities as having dinner parties, meeting with friends, working late, volunteering, and participating in various community projects. The total unweighted sample size is 84,989. The data dictionary, tab-delimited data, and SPSS version of the data can be accessed and downloaded at www.bowlingalone.com. Of the total sample, 10,501 respondents were age 21 through 29, 16,487 were age 30 through 39, and 8,113 were age 40 through 45. Because the surveys in early years were conducted only among married people, it was necessary when examining trends to exclude all respondents in later surveys who were not currently married. Thus, among married respondents only, 4,423 were age 21 through 29, 8,301 were age 30 through 39, and 4,340 were age 40 through 45. Additional details about the data and a discussion of their validity are available in *Bowling Alone*.

Forgiveness Survey

The Forgiveness Survey was designed by Robert Wuthnow and conducted by the Gallup Organization in 1999 with a follow-up among a subsample of the initial respondents in 2001. The interviews were conducted by telephone using a proportionate stratified random digit sample drawn from telephone exchanges in the continental United States. The purpose of the study was to identify respondents currently involved in small faith-based groups and then determine how often these respondents reported having discussed forgiveness and other topics in their groups. The project thus provided a rare opportunity to examine the role of social support in small groups. It also served as an update to Robert Wuthnow's *Sharing the Journey: Support Groups and America's New Quest for Community*, which was based on national data collected in 1991. Respondents for the Forgiveness Survey were identified by a screening procedure in which all respondents age eighteen and over were asked, "Do you attend any prayer group meetings or Bible study groups" and "Are you involved in any other small groups, such as a self-help group, support group, men's or women's group, or Sunday school class?" Respondents answering "yes" to either of these questions were then asked approximately one hundred additional questions about the extent of their participation, the nature of their group, its membership, and its activities. Funding for the project was provided by the Templeton

Foundation. The total unweighted sample size was 1,379. Of these, 153 were age 21 through 29, 283 were age 30 through 39, and 214 were age 40 through 45.

General Social Surveys

The General Social Surveys (GSS) were conducted annually by the National Opinion Research Center (NORC) at the University of Chicago between 1971 and 1993 (except for 1979, 1981, and 1992) and biennially beginning in 1994. Questions about attendance at religious services and religious preference have been included in all the surveys as part of the "core" questions (along with standard demographic items), and special "modules" about religion have been included in some of the surveys. These questions have asked about views of the Bible, views of God, belief in life after death, prayer, attitudes toward prayer in public schools, attitudes toward atheists, spirituality, and the relationships between spirituality and the arts. Other relevant questions have asked about Internet use, views about the responsibilities of young adults, voting, and political party preference. The GSS is based on a national probability sample that currently follows a biennial, double sample design adopted in 1994 (this biennial, split-sample design was instituted, consisting of two parallel subsamples of approximately 1,500 cases each, with identical cores and different topical modules; in effect, the two samples can be viewed as representing the traditional GSS for two consecutive years, although they are fielded together). Full probability sampling is for all noninstitutionalized English-speaking persons 18 years of age or older, living in the United States. (As I have noted in the chapters, readers are cautioned that the GSS does not provide representative coverage of the increasingly large non-English-speaking population of the United States, especially the Spanish-speaking population.) The GSS interviews last approximately 90 minutes and are conducted in-person in respondents' homes. Through numerous callbacks, the GSS achieves a higher response rate than most other surveys. Principal funding for the GSS is from the National Science Foundation, with funding for special modules provided by other government agencies and numerous private foundations. GSS codebooks and data files can be accessed and downloaded or analyzed interactively at the GSS Web site (webapp .icpsr.umich.edu/gss). Copies of reports and an extensive bibliography are also available at this Web site. The 1998, 2000, and 2002 surveys can also be accessed at the American Religion Data Archive Web site (www.thearda .com). For comparisons of young adults in the earliest surveys and more recent surveys, I combined responses from the 1972, 1973, 1974, 1975, and 1976 surveys and from the 1998, 2000, and 2002 surveys (data from the 2004 survey were not available at the time I did most of the quantitative analysis). In the earlier years, each survey included approximately 1,500 respondents, while the later surveys included approximately 2,800 respondents. Thus, the total number of respondents for the 1972–76 combined surveys was 7,590 and for the 1998–2002 combined surveys, 8,414. In the 1972–76 surveys, respondents age 21 through 29 totaled 1,618, respondents age 30 through 39 totaled 1,421, and respondents age 40 through 45 totaled 725; in the 1998–2002 surveys, the respective numbers were 1,363, 1,887, and 1,112.

Liberal-Conservative Survey

The Liberal-Conservative Survey was designed by George Gallup Jr. and Robert Wuthnow and conducted by the Gallup Organization in Princeton, New Jersey. Respondents were asked questions about their their religious and political identities, their perceptions of religious liberals and religious conservatives, the extent and nature of their interaction with religious liberals and conservatives, their awareness of and participation in various religious and political organizations, their religious beliefs, and standard demographic information. In-person, in-home interviews were conducted with a random national sample of 1,522 noninstitutionalized U.S. adults ages 18 and over, living in the forty-eight contiguous states. The sample is a probability sample down to the block level, after which households and persons within households were selected through an enumeration process. Each interview lasted approximately thirty minutes and generated 248 variables. The data were collected during the spring of 1984. Funding for the survey was provided by Robert Schuller Ministries. The primary publication resulting from the study, which includes further details about the survey, was Robert Wuthnow, *The Restructuring of American Religion: Society and Faith Since World War II*. The codebook and data set can be accessed from the Roper Center for Public Opinion Research (www.ropercenter .uconn.edu). Of the 1,522 respondents in the survey, 272 were age 21 through 29, 366 were age 30 through 39, and 143 were age 40 through 45.

National Congregations Study

The National Congregations Study (NCS) was designed by Mark Chaves and conducted by the National Opinion Research Center (NORC) at the University of Chicago. The NCS data were collected in conjunction with the 1998 General Social Survey (GSS), a nationally representative sample of adults, using hypernetwork sampling. GSS respondents who attended religious services were asked to specify their congregation. Telephone and in-person interviews with one key informant (usually a clergy person or other staff member) were then conducted in each of the congregations identified. The total number of interviews conducted was 1,236. Weight variables control for multiple GSS respondents identifying the same congregation (WEIGHT1) and for larger congregations being more likely to be part of the sample (WEIGHT2). Funding for the study was provided by the Lilly Endowment, the Smith Foundation, the Louisville Institute, the Aspen Institute, and the Henry Luce Foundation. The primary publication from the project, which includes further details about the survey, is Mark Chaves, *Congregations in America*. The codebook and data set can be accessed and downloaded or analyzed interactively at the Web site of the American Religion Data Archive (www.thearda.com).

Pew Internet and American Life Religion Callback Survey

Respondents were identified through a national random-digit dialing sample of 2,247 American adults age 18 and over conducted by Princeton Survey Research Associates between August 13 and September 10, 2001. Of this number, 1,135 were Internet users. Among these, 500 respondents who said they had ever gone online for religious or spiritual information were reinterviewed by telephone. For results based on the total sample, one can say with 95 percent confidence that the error attributable to sample and other random effects is plus or minus 4 percentage points. Once the household was reached, interviewers asked to speak with the individual who had recently completed a telephone survey. Once the targeted person was on the phone, the person was asked several screening questions to make sure that he or she had gone online to look for religious or spiritual information. At least 10 attempts were made to complete an interview at every household in the sample. Of those initially interviewed, callbacks were completed with 66 percent. The callback questions asked about frequency of using the Internet in general and for religious or spiritual information, strength of religious commitment, congregation membership, attendance at religious services, prayer, involvement in small group studies or prayer meetings, specific uses of the Internet (such as for finding a new congregation or receiving faith-oriented guidance), perceived influences on one's faith of using the Internet, religious preference, and standard demographic information. The data can be accessed and downloaded at www.pewInternet.org. This Web site also includes a summary report of the study, Elena Larsen, *Cyberfaith: How Americans Pursue Religion Online*.

Public Use Microdata Samples

Public Use Microdata Sample (PUMS) files are avaible from the United States Census Bureau. These files contain all basic census information, such as age, sex, marital status, number of children, and other characteristics of the U.S. population. I used the 1 percent files for the 1970 and 2000 censuses and coded the age categories to match those for young adults in the rest of the analysis. In the 1970 data, there were 9,740 people age 21 through 29, 8,588 between age 30 and 39, and 5,472 between age 40 and 45. In the 2000 data, there were 7,824, 10,054, and 6,328 in the three categories, respectively. Technical documentation is available at www.census.gov/Press-Release/www/2003. The data can be downloaded from www.census.gov/census_2000/data sets/PUMS. Additional information is available at www.proximityone.com/cen2000.htm.

Religion and Diversity Survey

The Religion and Diversity Survey was designed by Robert Wuthnow and conducted by SRBI Associates in New York. A random-digit dialing (RDD) procedure was used to generate a nationally representative sample of adults. Random generation of the last two digits of telephone numbers selected on the basis of their area code, telephone exchange (the first three digits of a seven digit telephone number), and bank number (the fourth and fifth digits) ensured equal representation of all (listed and unlisted) residential households. The area code, telephone exchange, and bank number were selected proportionally by county and by telephone exchange within county. Up to 19 attempts were made to reach each sampled phone number (nonresidential numbers and nonprimary numbers, such as for fax machines or cell phones, were excluded) and the person age eighteen or over with the most recent birthday in each household was asked to participate in the interview. Each interview lasted approximately 35 minutes and yielded 255 variables. Questions asked about attitudes toward such religious groups as Muslims, Hindus, and Buddhists; contact with these groups; views about immigrants; various aspects of American civil religion; religious exclusivism or inclusivism, personal spirituality, religious participation, characteristics of congregations, and standard demographic information. The survey was conducted between September 2002 and March 2003. Funding was provided by the Lilly Endowment. The total unweighted sample size was 2,910. Of these, 479 were age 21 through 29, 592 were age 30 through 39, and 398 were age 40 through 45.

Religion and Ethics Newsweekly Survey

The Religion and Ethics Newsweekly Survey was designed and conducted by Greenberg Quinlan Rosner Research, Inc. Academic advisers to the project were John C. Green and Robert Wuthnow. The survey was conducted by telephone among 1,610 respondents age 18 years or older during March and April 2004. Telephone numbers were generated by a random digit dial process, thereby allowing access to all listed and unlisted phones.

The sample was stratified by state. Quotas were assigned to reflect the general population. The national representative sample of 900 was supplemented with oversamples of 401 White Evangelical respondents, 160 African American respondents, and 149 Hispanic respondents. The data were weighted by gender, age, race, region and religion to ensure an accurate reflection of the population. The sample size for the basic sample with these weights applied is 900. The survey included questions about religious preference, attendance at religious services, attitudes about homosexuality and gay marriage, proselytization, political parties, and involvement of religious groups in politics. There were 134 respondents age 21 through 29, 167 age 30 through 39, and 117 age 40 through 45. The questionnaire, methodological report, and summary of results can be viewed or downloaded at www.pbs.org/wnet/religionandethics/week733.

Religion and Politics Survey

The Religion and Politics Survey was designed by Robert Wuthnow and conducted by SRBI Associates in New York. A random-digit dialing (RDD) procedure was used to generate a nationally representative sample of adults. Random generation of the last two digits of telephone numbers selected on the basis of their area code, telephone exchange (the first three digits of a seven digit telephone number), and bank number (the fourth and fifth digits) ensured equal representation of all (listed and unlisted) residential households. The area code, telephone exchange, and bank number were selected proportionally by county and by telephone exchange within county. There were at least ten attempts to reach each sampled phone number and the person age eighteen or over with the most recent birthday in each household was asked to participate in the interview. A total of 5,603 interviews were conducted. Respondents were asked about their interest in various social and political issues, their political participation, their religious beliefs and activities, their views about religious involvement in politics, their congregation's activities, and standard demographic information. Each interview lasted approximately 20 minutes and generated 168 variables. The survey was conducted during the spring of 2000. Funding for the survey was provided by The Pew Charitable Trusts. The primary publication from the project was Robert Wuthnow and John H. Evans, eds., *The Quiet Hand of God: Faith-Based Activism and the Public Role of Mainline Protestantism*. The codebook and data set can be accessed and downloaded or analyzed interactively at the Web site of the American Religion Data Archive (www.thearda.com). Of the 5,603 respondents in the survey, 1,219 were age 21 through 29, 1,107 were age 30 through 39, and 778 were age 40 through 45.

Social Capital Community Benchmark Survey

The Social Capital Community Benchmark Survey (SCCBS) was done through the Civic Engagement in America Project at Harvard's John F. Kennedy School of Government under the direction of Robert Putnam. It was designed to examine how connected people are to family, friends, neighbors, and civil institutions for a random national sample and 40 community samples. The data were collected by telephone interviews by Taylor Nelson Sofres Intersearch in the summer and fall of 2000 and were used locally to help community foundations design social capital building strategies. The interviews lasted about 26 minutes and yielded information from approximately 200 questions. Religious preference and attendance at religious services were the main questions focusing on religion. Other relevant questions asked about participation in various voluntary associations, trust, volunteering, and socializing. Funding was provided by the Ford Foundation and local community foundations. The total number of respondents included in the surveys was 29,233 (3,003 of whom were from the national sample and the remainder from the community samples). There were 4,671 respondents age 21 through 29, 6,066 respondents age 30 through 39, and 3,680 respondents age 40 through 45. The codebook and data set can be accessed and downloaded or analyzed interactively at the American Religion Data Archive (www.thearda.com). Detailed results, reports, and further information about the survey methodology are available at the SCCBS Web site (www.cfsv.org/communitysurvey).

World Values Surveys

The World Values Surveys have been conducted in 65 countries in several waves since 1980. The first wave was conducted in 1980 and 1981, a second wave in 1990 and 1991, a third wave between 1995 and 1998, and a fourth wave in 1999 and 2000. Each national sample is representative of the adult population of the society and includes at least 1,000 respondents. Some of the surveys were conducted in-person in respondents' homes, but most have been conducted by telephone. I was able to make some use of these data for the United States by focusing on differences between the earliest and most recent surveys. Approximately 90 questions were asked in both the 1980 and 2000 surveys, including questions about religious preference, church attendance, belief in God, belief in life after death, belief in heaven, finding comfort in religion, the ethics of such questionable activities as cheating on taxes or accepting bribes, and standard demographic information. Some of the questions asked in both periods could not be used because of different response categories or coding. The survey conducted in the United States in 1980 included a total of 1,351 respondents, 322 of whom were age 21 through 29, 314 were age 30 through 39, and 111 were age 40 through 45. The 2000 survey in the United States was based on 1,134 respondents, including 208 age 21 through 29, 258 age 30 through 39, and 153 age 40 through 45. See also wvs.isr.umich.edu.

QUALITATIVE INTERVIEWS

In-depth interviews were conducted with clergy, lay members of religious organizations, and nonmembers between the ages of 21 and 45. The interviews were conducted by professional interviewers in 2004 and 2005, either in person or by telephone. As described previously, the interviewees were selected through a nonrandom quota design. Each interview lasted approximately 90 minutes and was tape recorded and transcribed. The clergy interviews were tailored to particular denominations and contexts. The lay interviews followed a prestructured format, although interviewers were free to ask additional probes in order to elicit complete answers, stories, and examples. The lay interview guide was as follows.

Lay Interview Guide

This is a study of the day-to-day activities that make up people's lives, and the kinds of activities people become involved with in their communities. There are no right or wrong answers. We are interested in your experiences and stories. I will be asking you to describe your experiences and tell your stories in your own words. Please answer in as much detail as you can. The questions will be divided into four sections: questions about your day-to-day life, questions about involvement in the community, some questions about religion or spirituality, and some questions about your plans for the future. With your permission, I will be tape recording the interview. Your identity will remain confidential.

For the tape, then, do I have your permission to record the interview?

Since your real name will not be identified, is there a pseudonym you would like to suggest?

1. Before we begin, I have a few background questions. First, in what year were you born?
2. So, you are currently how old?
3. And for the tape I will say that you are male/female.
4. What is the highest grade or degree you completed in school?
5. If any higher education: What was your major or area of specialization?

6. Are you currently employed, either full-time or part-time?
7. If yes: What is your occupation?
8. Are you married, single, separated, or divorced?
9. Do you have any children?
10. If yes: What are their ages?
11. In what religion, if any, were you raised?
12. What is your religious preference now?
13. And for the tape, let me say that you are in (name of town).

The first set of questions is about daily life. We are interested in what daily life is like for people these days. First . . .

1. During the week—that is, Mondays through Fridays—do you have a fairly standard routine, or are some days quite different from others?
2. As best you can, think about a typical week day—maybe a very recent one so you can remember what you did. Walk me through it. Start with what time you got up in the morning and give me a blow-by-blow description of what your day was like.
3. What else does a typical day involve? Anything else?
4. Tell me about a typical Saturday now. What would your routine on Saturdays be like?
5. Now, what about Sundays? For instance, tell me what you did last Sunday?
6. Outside of your usual routine, what are some things you especially like to do?
7. About how often do you do this?
8. And, when you are tired and just need to relax, what do you do?
9. What kinds of things usually wear you out?
10. And during a typical week, what do you look forward to the most?
11. Why do you look forward to that?
12. How are things for you financially?
13. What are some of your concerns or worries in terms of finances?
14. If working: How long have you been at your present job?
15. How are you thinking about your job—will you stay in it awhile or maybe switch to something else? Why will you (stay, or switch)?

The next set of questions concerns the community, social activities, and other social relationships.

1. First, give me a thumbnail sketch of where you live—your apartment or house, and what kind of neighborhood it is.
2. How long have you lived there?
3. How many *different* places have you lived in the past 5 years?
4. Is it easy or hard to meet people in your neighborhood?
5. What makes it easy or hard?

6. Thinking now about your friends, not just in your neighborhood, but anywhere, about how many people are really *close* friends?
7. How many of these would be people you could share intimate details of your personal life with?
8. For each of your closest friends, how do you know them? For instance, did you grow up with them, meet them in school, work with them, or what?
9. If you were in a new community and wanted to make some new friends, where would you look—or how would you go about doing this?
10. Do you currently belong to any groups or organizations that give you an opportunity to meet people?
11. If yes: What kind of group or organization is it? How often do you participate? What things do you do with the group?
12. Are you currently involved in any kind of volunteer activities?
13. If yes: What are you involved with? What do you do? How often do you do this?
14. If yes: What motivated you to get involved as a volunteer? Did anything else motivate you?
15. If yes: What do *you* get out of doing this volunteer work?
16. Remind me, did you say earlier that you are single, married, or something else?
17. If married: How did you meet your spouse?
18. If unmarried: Are you currently seeing someone?
19. If yes: How did you meet the person you are seeing?
20. Some people tell us that helping other people is one of the things they value most in life. Would that be true of you or not?
21. Why would this be true or you or not be true of you? Just put it in your own words.
22. What are the main ways that you try to help other people?
23. If you could, what things *would* you do more of to help other people?

The next set of questions is about religion or spirituality. We are interested in what people think or believe about religion, and whether or not spirituality is important to them.

1. To begin, I'd like you to take a few minutes and tell me the story of your spiritual journey. Start with your childhood and work your way up to the present.
2. What else has been important about your spiritual journey?
3. If you were to summarize, what would you say the biggest changes have been in how you think about spirituality?
4. Just so I'm clear, how would you define spirituality?

5. And what experiences or events or people would you say have had the greatest influence on your spirituality?
6. Why was this (experience, event, or person) especially influential?
7. People express their spirituality or pursue it in lots of different ways, such as reading, going to movies, attending religious services, getting out in nature, talking to friends. What are some of the things you do that connect with your thinking about spirituality?
8. How does (this) connect with your spirituality? [Ask for each thing mentioned.]
9. Are you currently involved with a religious congregation of any kind?
10. If yes: Tell me about it. What kind of congregation is it?
11. If yes: How often do you attend?
12. If yes: Why do you attend—that is, what motivates you?
13. If no: What are the main reasons you are not involved in a religious congregation?
14. Between the time you started high school and now, was there a time when you quit attending religious services completely, other than perhaps on holidays?
15. If yes: Tell me about that time. What happened and why did you quit attending?
16. At any time during or since high school, were you ever involved in a religious group for people you age, such as a youth group, campus ministry, or singles group?
17. If yes: What group was it and how long were you involved?
18. If yes: How did you get involved and what did you like best about it?
19. If yes: How did being in this group affect your religious views?
20. Give me a few sentences that would summarize your main religious beliefs at the present.
21. What are some questions you have or some things you don't understand about religion?
22. How, if at all, do your religious beliefs influence your thinking about politics?
23. And how, if at all, do your religious beliefs influence your views about family issues, such as sex, marriage, and raising children?
24. By the way, do you ever use the Internet for anything having to do with religion or spirituality? If yes: Can you give me an example?

The final set of questions concerns some of your thoughts about the future.

1. Looking ahead, what are some of the main things you hope to accomplish in the next 10 years?
2. Tell me why each of these is important to you.

3. When you worry about the future, what are some of the things you fear could happen to you or your family?
4. What helps you when you have these worries?
5. Can you imagine becoming more involved in a religious congregation or group in the next ten years?
6. If yes: What do you think might prompt you to become more involved?
7. What are some of the pressures you face that would nice to be free of ten years from now?
8. What would you need to do in order to reduce this pressure?
9. In what ways do you think the world will be a better place ten years from now?
10. How might the world be a worse place in ten years?
11. As you think about children being raised now, what are some of the biggest problems they face?
12. What do you think parents should do to help children face these problems?
13. Finally, did we touch on anything that you wanted to say more about?

SUPPLEMENTARY TABLES

TABLE A.1.
Adult Population by Age Group, 1940–2000 [Thousands of persons]

	20–24	25–44	Younger Adults	45–64	65 and over	Older Adults	Total
1940	11,690	39,868	51,558	26,249	9,031	35,280	86,838
1945	12,036	42,521	54,557	28,630	10,494	39,124	93,681
1950	11,680	45,672	57,352	30,849	12,397	43,246	100,598
1955	10,714	47,194	57,908	33,506	14,525	48,031	105,939
1960	11,134	47,140	58,274	36,203	16,675	52,878	111,152
1965	13,746	46,912	60,658	38,916	18,451	57,367	118,025
1970	17,202	48,473	65,675	41,999	20,107	62,106	127,781
1975	19,527	54,302	73,829	43,801	22,696	66,497	140,326
1980	21,590	63,470	85,060	44,504	25,707	70,211	155,271
1985	21,478	73,673	95,151	44,602	28,416	73,018	168,169
1990	19,323	81,291	100,614	46,316	31,247	77,563	178,177
1995	18,391	84,933	103,324	52,806	33,769	86,575	189,899
2000	19,204	85,138	104,342	62,494	35,080	97,574	201,916

Source: Department of Commerce, Bureau of the Census.

TABLE A.2
Household Expenditures by Age Group

	18–24	25–34	35–44
Number of consumer units (in thousands)	8,737	18,988	24,394
Income before taxes	$20,773	$49,133	$61,532
Income after taxes	20,206	46,875	58,457
Age of the reference person	21.3	29.8	39.7
Average number in consumer unit:			
Persons	1.9	2.9	3.2
Children under 18	0.4	1.1	1.3
Earners	1.3	1.5	1.7
Vehicles	1.1	1.8	2.2
Homeowner	15	49	68
With mortgage	8	42	56
Without mortgage	7	8	12
At least one vehicle owned or leased	71	89	92
Average annual expenditures	$24,229	$40,318	$48,330
Food	3,621	5,471	6,314
Food at home	1,926	3,093	3,601
Food away from home	1,696	2,378	2,712
Alcoholic beverages	394	395	367
Housing	7,436	13,727	16,350
Utilities, fuels, and public services	1,348	2,503	3,026
Household operations	198	895	1,010
Personal services	99	650	580
Other household expenses	99	245	430
Housekeeping supplies	226	389	589
Laundry and cleaning supplies	77	125	152
Other household products	95	173	295
Postage and stationery	54	92	142
Household furnishings and equipment	812	1,469	1,823
Apparel and services	1,365	1,989	2,101
Transportation	5,102	8,423	9,400
Health care	640	1,417	1,980
Entertainment	1,212	2,027	2,685
Personal care products and services	329	488	615
Education	1,664	571	738
Tobacco products and smoking supplies	286	315	376
Miscellaneous	422	678	841
Cash contributions	319	743	1,247
Personal insurance and pensions	1,382	3,972	5,183
Life and other personal insurance	51	230	409
Pensions and Social Security	1,331	3,742	4,774

Source: Consumer Expenditure Survey, 2002.

Table A.3
Logistic Regression Analysis of Attendance at Religious Services (Odds Ratios)

	Model 1		Model 2		Model 3		Model 4		Model 5	
YEAR	0.655	***	0.800	***	0.834	***	0.840	**	0.877	
AGE	1.387	***	1.282	***	1.177	***	1.181	***	1.127	*
MALE	0.609	***	0.614	***	0.638	***	0.654	***	0.685	***
BLACK	1.256	***	1.446	***	1.390	***	1.394	***	1.839	***
DEGREE	1.152	***	1.151	***	1.186	***	1.190	***	1.192	***
MARRIED			1.978	***	1.786	***	1.785	***	1.762	***
CHILDREN			—		1.167	***	1.164	***	1.154	**
WORK FT			—		—		0.934		0.908	
TV HRS			—		—		—		0.795	***
Constant	0.256	***	0.171	***	0.157	***	0.160	***	0.256	***
−2 log likelihood	9218.097		9075.525		9019.954		9018.532		3631.310	
d.f.	261.662		404.234		437.878		439.301		199.467	
Nagelkerke R sq.	0.046		0.071		0.077		0.077		0.085	

Note: * $p < .05$, ** $p < .01$, *** $p < .001$ (Wald statistic); General Social Surveys, respondents age 21 through 45.

TABLE A.4.
Adjusted Odds-Ratios of Attitudes toward Asians and Hispanics (logistic regression models)

	Would not welcome Asians			Would not welcome Hispanics		
Evangelical	1.903 ***	1.686 ***	1.380 <	1.836 ***	1.674 **	1.526 *
Male		1.296	1.401		1.317 <	1.443 *
Black		0.888	0.727		0.733	0.623 <
Urban		0.858	0.941		0.592 *	0.640 <
Suburban		0.671 *	0.777		0.760	0.837
South		1.044	0.860		1.176	1.006
West		0.946	0.939		1.376	1.412 <
Education		0.765 **	0.899		0.736 ***	0.848 <
Parents' education		0.955	0.943		0.758 <	0.757
Married		1.010	1.103		0.688 *	0.745
Any children		1.560 *	1.352		1.292	1.205
Foreign born		0.422 <	0.485 <		0.179 *	0.192 *
Church attendance			0.712 <			0.657 *
Asian/Hispanic contacts			0.788 **			0.690 *
Immigrant legacy			0.672 ***			0.687 ***
Ten Commandments			1.139 <			1.058
Christian exclusivism			1.224 **			1.209 *
Voted for Bush			1.433 *			1.080
Constant	0.172 ***	0.312 ***	0.411 ***	0.170 ***	0.475 *	0.658 ***
Chi-square	16.197	51.017	115.163	14.161	63.729	106.533
d.f.	1.000	12.000	18.000	1.000	12.000	18.000
−2 log likelihood	1108.824	1067.424	1003.278	1096.233	1038.405	995.602
Nagelkerke R square	0.022	0.069	0.151	0.019	0.086	0.141

Source: Religion and Diversity Survey, white and African American respondents age 21 through 45; *** p < .001,
** p < .01, * p < .05, ^ < .10 (Wald Statistic).

Notes

Preface

1. Marx and Engels, *German Ideology*; Weber, *Protestant Ethic and the Spirit of Capitalism*; Durkheim, *Elementary Forms of the Religious Life*.
2. Berger, *Sacred Canopy*; Bellah, *Beyond Belief*.
3. Milbank, *Theology and Social Theory Beyond Secular Reason*.
4. Blumer, *Symbolic Interactionism*.
5. See also Wuthnow, "Is There a Place for 'Scientific' Studies of Religion?" and "Studying Religion, Making It Sociological."

Chapter 1
American Religion: An Uncertain Future

1. The literature on baby boomer religion is extensive, but see especially Carroll and Roof, *Bridging Divided Worlds*, Cheung, *Baby-Boomers, Generation-X, and Social Cycles*, Hoge, Johnson, and Luidens, *Vanishing Boundaries*, Roof, *Generation of Seekers* and *Spiritual Marketplace*, and Waxman, *Jewish Baby Boomers*.
2. On "generation X," "busters," and "millennials," see Barna, *Invisible Generation*, *Baby Busters*, and *Generation Next*; Beaudoin, *Virtual Faith*, Craig, *After the Boom*, Flory and Miller, *Gen X Religion*, Howe and Strauss, *Millennials Rising*, Rosen, *Masks and Mirrors*, Sacks, *Generation X Goes to College*, Thau, *Generations Apart*, and Zullo, *God and Gen-X*.
3. In sociology, the class work on generations was done by Karl Mannheim, especially *Man and Society in an Age of Reconstruction*, *Ideology and Utopia*, *Essays on the Sociology of Culture*, and "Problem of Generations."
4. Wuthnow, "Recent Patterns of Secularization."
5. Cross, *Burned-Over District*, remains the classic study in which the generational aspects of the Second Great Awakening are emphasized.
6. Wuthnow, *Sharing the Journey*; the small groups movement grew as baby boomers matured but its membership included many of the older generation as well.
7. Readers interested in religion among teenagers should consult Barna, *Generation Next* and *Third Millennium Teens*, Smith, Denton, and Regnerus, "Mapping American Adolescent Subjective Religiosity," and Smith and Denton, *Soul Searching*.
8. See appendix table A.1 for further details.
9. Furstenberg, et al., "Between Adolescence and Adulthood"; and Settersten, Furstenberg, and Rumbaut (eds.), *On the Frontier of Adulthood*.
10. I recognize that researchers who study teenagers would probably be able to show that there is a significant statistical relationship between some behavior patterns at thirteen and those when the same people are thirty-five. I would guess

some of those relationships are weaker than they were a few decades ago. More to the point, I am simply stressing the importance of looking at the developmental tasks that take place when people are in their twenties and thirties, rather than assuming these tasks are all completed during the teen years. The papers in Settersten, et al., *On the Frontier of Adulthood*, are especially valuable in describing these changes. I would emphasize, though, that people in their twenties and thirties are already adults, not making a transition to adulthood. Put differently, we need to thinking of adulthood as a phase of life, not as a status that either has or has not been achieved.

11. Furstenberg, et al., "Between Adolescence and Adulthood," 2.

12. Claude Levi-Strauss, *The Savage Mind.*

13. Standardization has been emphasized much more in the sociological literature than the continuing (if not increasing) importance of improvisation; for instance, see Ritzer, *The McDonaldization of Society.*

14. Geertz, *Interpretation of Cultures.*

15. Hammond and Johnson, *American Mosaic.*

16. Roof, *Generation of Seekers.*

17. Warner, "Work in Progress Toward a New Paradigm."

18. Mostly advanced by economist Lawrence Iannaccone; e.g., "Religious Markets and the Economics of Religion." For critical appraisals of this approach, see Chaves, "On the Rational Choice Approach to Religion," and Bruce, *Choice and Religion.* My own dispute with the rational choice approach is that it purports to be a more rigorous theory than it is and, more importantly, fails to illuminate about 90 percent of what I find interesting about religion.

19. Gallup and Lindsay, *Surveying the Religious Landscape.*

20. Kelley, *Why Conservative Churches Are Growing.*

21. Hout, Greeley, and Wilde, "The Demographic Imperative."

CHAPTER 2
THE CHANGING LIFE WORLDS OF YOUNG ADULTS: SEVEN KEY TRENDS

1. These figures are from the Current Population Surveys conducted by the U.S. Census in 2002. The age categories shown are those used by the Census Bureau and thus do not correspond exactly to the age categories (21 through 29, 30 through 39, 40 through 45) that I will use throughout much of the volume. That marriage proportions plateau among people in their late thirties and early forties is further illustrated by the fact that 70 percent of men age 45 through 49 and 66 percent of women the same age were married (about the same proportions as among those age 35 through 39 and 40 through 44).

2. The so-called marriage movement has focused more on rising divorce rates than on increases in the never married population, but has garnered support from a wide range of social scientists and policy makers; see especially Popenoe and Elshtain, *Promises to Keep*; Waite and Bachrach, *The Ties That Bind*; and Waite and Gallagher, *The Case for Marriage.*

3. The fact that fewer young adults are married does not mean that the proportion who are *living alone* has increased in the same proportion; the number of cohab-

iting unmarried adult couples of the opposite sex, for instance, grew from .5 million to 4.1 million between 1970 and 2000; some young adults also lived in group quarters or with parents; Grimm, "Hitch Switch."

4. Reasons for the trend toward later marriage include; more young adults staying in school longer; difficulties in gaining financial independence; greater acceptance of cohabitation and sexuality before marriage; contraception; and knowledge that younger marriages are more likely to end in divorce.

5. U.S. Census Bureau, "Motherhood: The Fertility of American Women, 2000," *Population Profile of the United States: 2000* (Internet Release).

6. This point has been made especially by Halberstam, *The Fifties*, who emphasizes the extent to which neighborhoods, community gatherings, advertising, automobiles, and even housing floor plans were focused on children.

7. The General Social Surveys are described in the appendix.

8. See the appendix for a description of the U.S. component of the World Values Surveys.

9. These questions were included in the 2002 General Social Survey in conjunction with the MacArthur project on early adulthood that I mentioned in chapter 1 and are discussed at greater length in Settersten, *On the Frontier of Adulthood*.

10. This is one of the themes, for instance, in Warren and Tyagi, *The Two-Income Trap*.

11. These results are from my Arts and Religion Survey, conducted in 1999 (see appendix for further details). Among workers age 21 through 29, another 26 percent had been at their present place of employment 3 to 5 years; among those age 30 through 39, 14, 29, and 25 percent, respectively, had been at their present place of employment less than a year, 1 to 2 years, or 3 to 5 years. Among those 40 through 45, these figures were 14, 20, and 17.

12. Whyte, *Organization Man*.

13. Arts and Religion Survey conducted in 1999. Among those age 40 through 45, 35 percent said they had worked in 4 or more different lines of work.

14. Brooks, "The Organization Kid."

15. Since turnover includes both separations and openings, 200 percent means that there were as many new employees within a 36-month period as there were total employees.

16. Total turnover as a percentage of total employment for the 36 months including 2001, 2002, and 2003 was as follows: construction, 266 percent; manufacturing, 155 percent; trade and transportation, 202 percent; information, 161 percent; finance, 157 percent; professional and business, 246 percent; education, 217 percent; leisure and hospitality, 340 percent; other services, 201 percent; and government, 117 percent. Separations exceeded openings in every industry except finance and government.

17. Diane Swanbrow, "Much Money Flows from Parents to Young Adults," *University of Michigan Record Online* (November 3, 2003); Schoeni and Ross, "Material Assistance Received from Families during the Transition to Adulthood."

18. See appendix table A.2 for further details.

19. Sullivan, Thorne, and Warren, "Young, Old, and in Between: Who Files for Bankruptcy?"

20. Personal bankruptcy and debt are examined in greater detail in Sullivan, Warren, and Westbook, *The Fragile Middle Class*.

21. U.S. Census Bureau, "Tracking the American Dream—50 Years of Housing History," http://www.census.gov/hhes/www/housing.html.

22. American Automobile Association, *Your Driving Costs* (Heathrow, Fla.: AAA, 2003).

23. U.S. Census Bureau, Current Population Survey, March 2001.

24. Wuthnow, *Saving America?*, 178.

25. U.S. Census Bureau, Current Population Reports, P60–218, Money Income in the United States, 2001, http://www.census.gov/hhes/www/income.html.

26. Bernhardt, Morris, Handcock, and Scott, "Inequality and Mobility: Trends in Wage Growth for Young Adults."

27. My writing on these influences includes *The Consciousness Reformation, Experimentation in American Religion*, and *The Restructuring of American Religion*.

28. Putnam, *Bowling Alone*.

29. My arguments on this point are developed in Wuthnow, *Loose Connections*. Putnam, *Better Together*, presents a number of interesting qualitative studies that also suggest relationships are not so much declining but changing. See also Baggett, *Habitat for Humanity*.

30. I say "conservative" because married people are generally more involved in their communities and have a more stable set of friends than single people do; thus, eliminating the growing number of young adults who are single from consideration means being able to focus only on changes taking place among married people. Single respondents were included in more recent surveys, but not in the earlier surveys, making it necessary to exclude them in order to derive accurate trends. The DDB surveys and efforts to demonstrate their validity are discussed in some detail in Putnam, *Bowling Alone*.

31. My summary of these trends is drawn from an examination of linear trend line estimates from the points shown in the chart.

32. I mention this result for young adults in the General Social Surveys because Putnam also stresses the decline in socializing within neighborhoods. I hasten to note, though, that two other questions in the General Social Surveys did not show a decline. The percentage of adults age 21 through 45 who said they spent a social evening with relatives several times a month held steady at 56 percent in 1972–76 and 1998–2002, and the percent who spent time in bars this often also remained constant (at 22 percent).

33. Particularly useful discussions of globalization are Beck, Sznaider, and Winter, *Global America? The Cultural Consequences of Globalization*; Bordo, Taylor, and Williamson, *Globalization in Historical Perspective*; Eckes and Zeiler, *Globalization and the American Century*; and Kofman and Youngs, *Globalization: Theory and Practice*.

34. Chained (1996 dollars) figures are available from the Bureau of Economic Analysis only since 1987, when total merchandise trade was 12 percent of GDP, rising to 23 percent in 2000 (compared with an increase from 14 percent to 21 percent for unchained data), http://www.bea.doc.gov/bea/dn1.htm.

35. Following the attacks of September 11, 2001, total air passengers departing to foreign countries dropped in 2001 to 52.5 million. Seeing these figures, one person asked me if the increase since the early 1970s might be attributable to popu-

lation increase in the United States. No, population grew by 40 percent while U.S. citizens departing for foreign destinations grew by 360 percent.

36. Between 1901 and 1910, 8.8 million immigrants arrived, equaling 10.4 percent of the native-born population, and between 1911 and 1920, 5.7 million arrived, a rate of 5.7 percent compared to the native-born population. The comparable rates for the 1970s, 1980s, and 1990s, respectively, were 2.1, 3.1, and 3.4. U.S. Bureau of Citizenship and Immigration Services (http://uscis.gov); for a valuable comparison of the two waves of immigration, see Foner, *From Ellis Island to JFK*.

37. U.S. Census Bureau, *Historical Census Statistics on the Foreign-Born Population of the United States, 1850–1990*, Working Paper no. 29, February 1999; and Current Population Survey, 2000, http://www.census.gov/population/www.socdemo/foreign/databls.html.

38. On immigration, see especially Portes and Rumbaut, *Immigrant America*; Portes and Rumbaut, *Legacies*; and Alba and Nee, *Remaking the American Mainstream*, and "Rethinking Assimilation Theory."

39. The history of American religious pluralism is usefully described in Hutchison, *Religious Pluralism in America*, Marty, *The One and the Many*, and Eck, *New Religious America*.

40. For perspectives on the development of information and information technologies, see especially Beniger, *The Control Revolution*, Rheingold, *Virtual Community*, and Starr, *Creation of the Media*.

41. U.S. Federal Communications Commission http://www.fcc.gov.

42. These data are from General Social Surveys aggregated from 1972 to 1976 and from 1998 to 2002.

43. General Social Survey results. A similar decline in the proportion of Americans (young and old alike) who had read novels, short stories, poetry, or plays in the past year was noted in surveys conducted in 2002, 1992, and 1982; Bradshaw and Nichols, *Reading at Risk: A Survey of Literary Reading in America*.

44. I examine evidence about religious uses of the Internet in chapter 10; books that discuss the possible connections between Internet culture and faith include Beaudoin, *Virtual Faith*, and Brasher, *Give Me that Online Religion*.

45. U.S. Census Bureau http://www.cpanda.org.

46. Recording Industry Association of America, 2002 Consumer Profile, http://www.riaa.com.

47. Wuthnow, *All in Sync, Creative Spirituality*.

48. Skrentny, *The Minority Rights Revolution*, is one of the best overviews of these developments.

49. Among adults age 21 through 45 in 1998–2002 General Social Surveys and comparable 1972–6 General Social Surveys, the percentages responding as follows, respectively, were: allow antireligionist to speak, 80, 78; allow antireligionist to teach, 66, 56; allow antireligionist book in library, 76, 73; allow communist to speak, 73, 68; allow communist to teach, 67, 51; allow communist book in library, 73, 69; allow homosexual to speak, 87, 75; allow homosexual to teach, 84, 64; allow homosexual book in library, 79, 67.

50. I examine these divisions in relation to young adults' religious orientations in chapter 8; scholarship about these ideological divisions runs the gamut from viewing them as a culture war, to questioning whether a culture war exists because the divi-

sions have not become more acute than they were, to emphasizing common ground among those in the middle; see especially Hunter, *Culture Wars*, DiMaggio, Evans, and Bryson, "Have Americans' Social Attitudes Become More Polarized?," Evans, Bryson, and DiMaggio, "Opinion Polarization," and Wolfe, *One Nation After All*.

CHAPTER 3
GOING TO CHURCH—OR NOT: WHO PARTICIPATES IN CONGREGATONS?

1. Although church attendance is only one indication of how involved in religion a person is, church attendance is also a powerful predictor of other religious beliefs and practices. The 1998 General Social Survey included some additional questions about religion that were asked of part of the sample. The differences between regular church attendees and those who attend less regularly on these questions are dramatic. Specifically, the percentages who responded to each question as follows among persons who attend religious services nearly every week or more often and among persons who attend less often, respectively are: pray privately once a day or more (apart from at church), 81, 34; look to God for strength a great deal, 77, 23; strongly agree that God watches over them, 86, 47; strongly agree that they carry their religious beliefs into other dealings, 47, 15; feel God's presence every day, 68, 29; find comfort in religion every day, 72, 24; desire closeness to God every day, 71, 30; consider self very religious, 42, 8; consider self very spiritual, 43, 14; had a life-changing religious experience, 67, 31 (based on 201 regular church goers and 545 less frequent church goers).

2. See especially Westerhoff, *Will Our Children Have Faith?*

3. An excellent overview of the recent research is available in Chaves and Stephens, "Church Attendance in the United States," see also Chaves, "Abiding Faith."

4. Gallup and Lindsay, *Surveying the Religious Landscape*, Putnam, *Bowling Alone*.

5. Hadaway, Marler, and Chaves, "What the Polls Don't Show" is the source of much of the recent debate about the accuracy of survey data on church attendance; on diary evidence, see especially Presser, "Data Collection Mode and Social Desirability Bias in Self-Reported Religious Attendance"; other useful contributions to the debate include Hadaway, Marler, and Chaves, "Overreporting Church Attendance in America," Hout and Greeley, "The Center Doesn't Hold," Hout and Greeley, "What Church Officials' Reports Don't Show," Smith, "A Review of Church Attendance Measures," and Marcum, "Measuring Church Attendance."

6. The research literature suggests parental effects on their children's religious involvement sufficient to infer that if religious involvement declined among the baby boomer generation, it would decline further among the next wave of young adults; for instance, see Caplovitz and Sherrow, *The Religious Drop-Outs*, Hoge and Petrillo, "Determinants of Church Participation and Attitudes among High School Youth," Potvin and Sloane, "Parental Control, Age, and Religious Practice," Greeley, *The Denominational Society*, and Ploch and Hastings, "Effects of Parental Church Attendance, Current Family Status, and Religious Salience on Church Attendance."

7. Through in-depth qualitative interviews, I examined perceptions of these generational continuities and discontinuities in my book *Growing Up Religious*.

8. In this respect, the General Social Survey data are preferable either to Gallup polls that ask only whether a person did or did not attend religious services in the

past seven days; the GSS data are also based on better sampling methods and have higher response rates than the DDB Needham surveys. The exact wording of the GSS question is, "How often do you attend religious services?" (An interviewer instruction says, "Use categories as probes, if necessary," and supplies the following categories: "never, less than once a year, about once or twice a year, several times a year, about once a month, 2–3 times a month, nearly every week, every week, every week, several times a week." The GSS question was asked in exactly this form in all GSS surveys. The GSS question differs slightly from attendance questions used in telephone surveys by other research firms, in which the phrase "Aside from weddings and funerals" is added. I do not dispute critics who say the GSS data may overestimate the extent of church-going, drawn as it is from self-reports; however, I find no compelling evidence that bias of this kind has increased; the GSS questions were asked in exactly the same way in the surveys at issue here; by aggregating the data from the 1972 through 1976 surveys and from the 1998 through 2002 surveys, I also reduce the likelihood of random error that might be present because of timing and events surrounding a particular survey or the influence of other questions asked in a particular survey.

9. I base this estimate on the U.S. Census figures discussed in chapter 2. In 2002, there were 105.3 million adults between the ages of 20 and 44; 25 percent of that number is 26.3 million; 31 percent is 32.6 million, meaning a loss of 6.3 million regular attenders.

10. Two recent articles that include references to much of the literature on religion and gender are Miller and Stark, "Gender and Religiousness" and Stark, "Physiology and Faith"; the relationships between marriage and husbands' religious involvement are examined in Wilcox, *Soft Patriarchs, New Men*.

11. I am indebted to Penny Edgell for emphasizing this point; among other of her publications, see, for instance, Edgell, "Evangelical Identity and Gendered Family Life" and Becker and Hofmeister, "Work, Family, and Religious Involvement for Men and Women."

12. The question wording did not permit separate analysis of respondents who were cohabiting.

13. The main patterns of interest are those for married and never married people. For divorced men, there was no change between the early 1970s and late 1990s (15 percent in both periods attended religious services regularly). Among divorced women, there was only a slight change (from 26 percent to 23 percent). Among the relatively few separated men and women, the respective figures in the early and more recent periods were 10 and 17 and 22 and 20.

14. I consider the influences of religious involvement on various family activities and attitudes in chapter 7. I recognize that frequent church attendance is not only affected by marital status and children but may also influence the likelihood of being married and having children.

15. The literature on gender, household work, and civic involvement is quite large, but see especially Hook, "Reconsidering the Division of Household Labor," Karniol, Grosz, and Schorr, "Caring, Gender Role Orientation, and Volunteering," Ozorak, "Love of God and Neighbor," Wilson, "Volunteering," and Wilson and Musick, "Who Cares? Toward an Integrated Theory of Volunteer Work."

16. For instance, in the 1998–2002 surveys, 21, 19, and 17 percent, respectively, among men working full-time, part-time, or in school attended religious services weekly or almost weekly (the number of men who said they were "keeping house" was too small to make comparisons).

17. In the earlier surveys, the figure was 28 percent compared with 21 percent in the more recent surveys.

18. In the earlier period, the figure was 37 percent and in the more recent period 36 percent.

19. Among women working full time, the figure declined from 33 percent to 26 percent and among women working part time from 38 percent to 31 percent.

20. A more extensive analysis conducted by Hout, Fischer, and Latham ("Time Bind and God's Time") also concludes that attendance at religious services is "relatively inelastic to family time pressures."

21. See chapter 5.

22. The usual caveats about inferring causality from statistical models apply, but the conclusions drawn here are from straightforward and commonly accepted methods of analyzing the source of trends. The models presented in appendix table A.3 treat religious attendance as the dependent variable and year as the independent variable (thus estimating the decline in attendance between time 1 and time 2), control for several correlates of attendance (such as age, gender, and race), and then test whether the year effect can be explained away by introducing additional variables (such as marital status). Marital status does in fact reduce the year effect to insignificance. One caveat is that other variables not available in the data might also have had similar effects. Another caveat is that religious participation may be a cause of marital status rather than an effect. That possibility cannot be ruled out entirely, although there is a considerable literature on marital status suggesting otherwise.

23. In binary logistic regression analysis of the effects of selected independent variables on the likelihood of attending religious services nearly every week, the odds of attending services among married people are 1.559 greater among those who have children than among those who do not (significant at the .001 level), controlling for gender and age; in contrast, among unmarried people these odds are .894 (not significant at the .05 level).

24. U.S. Department of Transportation, *National Household Travel Survey, 2001*, nhts.ornl.gov.

25. For instance, the crude marriage rate (per 1,000 population) dropped in Germany from 9.5 in 1960 to 5.1 in 2000; in France from 7.0 to 5.1; in the United Kingdom, from 7.5 to 5.1; and in Sweden, from 6.7 to 4.5; Battaini-Dragoni, *Recent Demographic Developments, 2002*. The crude marriage rate for the United States (8.3) remained significantly higher than for any of these countries.

CHAPTER 4
THE MAJOR FAITH COMMUNITIES: THINKING BEYOND WINNERS AND LOSERS

1. Herberg, *Protestant-Catholic-Jew*; survey research conducted in the early 1960s by Charles Glock provided evidence of further denominational distinctions;

see Glock and Stark, *Religion and Society in Tension*. Niebuhr, *Social Sources of Denominationalism*, was one of the earliest efforts to classify American religious traditions.

2. Lenski, *The Religious Factor*.

3. For a more detailed discussion of these developments and their impact on efforts to classify religious preferences, see Wuthnow, "The Religious Factor Revisited."

4. Classifying respondents according to denominational preferences makes sense when examining the United States, but does not serve well, of course, for cross-national comparisons, and for that reason cross-national surveys (such as the World Values Surveys, from which I draw in chapter 5) generally use other questions, such as beliefs about God and the Bible or so-called subjective measures of religiosity (such as respondents' self-perception of the importance of religion in their lives). Denominational classifications do require detailed questions to be asked in order to distinguish among, say, different kinds of Baptists, Presbyterians, and Lutherans.

5. The classification scheme I use in this chapter is the one developed by Steensland, Park, Regnerus, Robinson, Wilcox, and Woodberry (2000) for use with the General Social Surveys and other surveys in which detailed questions about religious preference or affiliation are asked. The GSS question asks, "What is your religious preference? Is it Protestant, Catholic, Jewish, some other religion, or no religion?" and then follows with a question about denominational preference ("What specific denomination is that, if any?"). The detailed coding procedure and the denominations included in each category are described in Steensland, et al. (2000). This so-called reltrad variable has become widely used in social science research both for comparing religious traditions and as a control variable for religious tradition when other variables are being examined. It has proven useful in studies examining a wide range of correlates of religious affiliation and involvement, including volunteering, racial attitudes, religious identities, gender roles, obesity, mental health, participation in the arts, and political participation; see Perl and Wiggins, "Don't Call Me Ishmael," Hinojosa and Park, "Religion and the Paradox of Racial Inequality Attitudes," Myers, "Religion and Intergenerational Assistance," Brooks and Bolzendahl, "The Transformation of U.S. Gender Role Attitudes," Kim, "Conditional Morality?," Sutherland, Poloma, and Pendleton, "Religion, Spirituality, and Alternative Health Practices," Scheufele, Nisbet, and Brossard, "Pathways to Political Participation," Beyerlein and Chaves, "The Political Activities of Religious Congregations in the United States," Kim, Sobal, and Wethington, "Religion and Body Weight," Meyer and Lobao, "Economic Hardship, Religion, and Mental Health During the Midwestern Farm Crisis," Wuthnow, "Religious Involvement and Status Bridging Social Capital," Park and Reimer, "Revisiting the Social Sources of American Christianity," Evans, "Religion and Human Cloning," Evans, "Polarization in Abortion Attitudes," Brooks, "Religious Influence and the Politics of Family Decline Concern," Reimer and Park, "Tolerant Incivility," Ellison, Boardman, and Williams, "Religious Involvement, Stress, and Mental Health," Marsden, "Religious Americans and the Arts in the 1990s," and Becker and Dhingra, "Religious Involvement and Volunteering."

6. Social science research on the growth or decline of various religious traditions must be sharply distinguished from the so-called church growth literature written by church consultants to help congregations devise strategies for growth; some of the more important contributions to the social science literature on growth and decline include Hout, Greeley, and Wilde, "The Denominational Imperative," Hoge and Roozen, "Some Sociological Conclusions about Church Trends," Iannaccone, "Why Strict Churches Are Strong," Kelley, *Why Conservative Churches Are Growing*, Roof and McKinney, *American Mainline* Religion, and Mathisen, "Tell Me Again: *Why* Do Churches Grow?"

7. Journalistic accounts and stories about evangelicals in religious magazines are often difficult to assess because of lack of clarity about how evangelicals are defined. In the research literature, the following operational definitions are most commonly used: any person who identifies himself or herself as someone who is "an evangelical or born again," usually resulting in about 40 percent of the adult population being classified as evangelicals (and thus favored in media stories that tout the political importance of evangelicals); someone who is a church-going Protestant and self-identifies as an "evangelical," as opposed to being a "fundamentalist," "mainline," "liberal," or "other" Protestant, resulting in about 7 percent of the population being classified as evangelicals; anyone who answers a combination of questions in a way that signals conservative belief, such as questions about Jesus, the Bible, the importance of being saved, or having proselytized others, usually resulting in about 20 percent of the population being classified as evangelicals; and the variable developed by Steensland, et al., and used here, resulting in about 20 percent of the population being classified as evangelicals. The value of the Steensland approach is that it focuses on preferences for religious *organizations* that have taken stands on various theological and social issues and have a recognizable identity in American religious history; on the various approaches to defining evangelicalism, see especially Gallup and Lindsay, *Surveying the Religious Landscape*; Hunter, *American Evangelicalism* and *Evangelicalism: The Coming Generation*; and Smith, *American Evangelicalism*. Penning and Smidt, *Evangelicalism: The Next Generation*, is of particular interest because of its focus on young adults.

8. One of the advantages of combining the General Social Surveys conducted between 1972 and 1976 and those conducted between 1998 and 2002 is that the number of cases is large enough in each period to allow further analysis of the people in each religious tradition. The specific numbers for the two periods, respectively, are: evangelicals, 790, 772; mainline Protestants, 936, 535; black Protestants, 331, 286; Catholics, 1031, 1120; Jews, 89, 66; other faiths, 134, 264; and nonaffiliated, 339, 762.

9. Examination of the trend line for mainline membership as a percentage of adults 21 through 45 shows a decline of .682 (or approximately two-thirds of a percentage point per year) from 1972 through 1987, but a decline of only .495 (or half a percentage point per year) from 1987 through 2002; thus suggesting that the rate of decline was diminishing. Denominational membership figures for all adults in the six largest mainline denominations were almost constant between 1991 and 1998 (as discussed in Wuthnow and Evans, *The Quiet Hand of God*, chap. 1).

10. Several of the best contributions (which also provide reviews of the earlier literature) are Hadaway, "The Problem with Father as Proxy," Sherkat, "Preferences,

Constraints, and Choices in Religious Markets," and Smith, "Social Predictors of Retention in and Switching from the Religious Faith of Family of Origin."

11. Having served on the Board of Overseers for the General Social Survey, I can state that the GSS staff and board are fully aware of this problem, but have been stymied by the National Science Foundation in securing the additional funding needed to rectify it.

12. I consider Hispanic Catholics and Protestants again in chapter 9.

13. In the General Social Surveys, the proportion of adults age 21 through 45 nationally who lived in the South rose from 31 percent in 1972–76 to 35 percent in 1998–2002, whereas the proportion of young evangelicals living in the South declined from 58 percent to 51 percent. Nationally, the proportion of younger adults living in the Northeast declined from 24 percent to 20 percent and in the Midwest from 27 percent to 24 percent; among young evangelicals, the respective increases were from 7 percent to 10 percent and from 22 percent to 26 percent. Nationally, the percentage of younger adults living in the West rose from 18 percent to 21 percent, but among evangelicals declined from 14 percent to 13 percent.

14. Among converts to evangelicalism, 58 percent live outside of the South, whereas among life-long evangelicals, only 46 percent do.

15. In the 1972–76 surveys, 82 percent of respondents age 21 through 45 who had been raised as evangelicals were married; that figure dropped to 52 percent in the comparable 1998–2002 surveys. Among those raised in mainline denominations, the respective figures were 78 percent and 49 percent.

16. The respective figures are 42 percent and 35 percent, 1998–2002 surveys.

17. These conclusions are drawn from logistic regression analysis of the differences between evangelicals and mainline Protestants age 21 through 45 in which the resulting coefficients for 1972–76 and 1998–2002, respectively, are: any children, .761 and .637; race, .603 and .700; degree, 1.475 and 1.504; suburb, 1.267 and .949; and region, .557 and .769, controlling for marital status, age, and gender.

18. By region, the percentages of young adults raised Jewish who have converted to something else are: Northeast, 16; Midwest, 23; South, 18; West, 41; by marital status: married, 14, divorced, 27; and never married, 36; and by children: any children, 10; no children, 38.

19. See the discussion of people who are spiritual but not religious in chapter 6.

20. As shown in figure 4.4; for the general population the increase in nonaffiliation has been examined by Hout and Fischer, "Why More Americans Have No Religious Preference," who note not only the generational factor, but also the possibility that political liberalism has become more strongly associated with nonaffiliation.

CHAPTER 5
THE BIBLE TELLS ME SO (I THINK): RECENT TRENDS IN RELIGIOUS BELIEFS

1. Jack D. Shand, "The Decline of Traditional Christian Beliefs in Germany."

2. The vitality of fundamentalism in the United States and elsewhere was extensively documented and examined in the Fundamentalism Project directed by Martin E. Marty and R. Scott Appleby and sponsored by the American Academy of Sciences; see Marty and Appleby, *Fundamentalisms Observed*; Marty and Appleby,

The Glory and the Power; Marty, *Fundamentalism and Evangelicalism*; Marty and Appleby, *Fundamentalisms and Society*; Marty and Appleby, *Fundamentalisms and the State*; and Marty and Appleby, *Fundamentalisms Comprehended.*

3. On these debates, see the useful essays in Hammond, *The Sacred in a Secular Age*; see also Bruce, *Religion and Modernization.*

4. This view has become popular in evolutionary psychology and cognitive anthropology; see Boyer, *The Naturalness of Religious Ideas*; Boyer, *Religion Explained*; and Atran, *In Gods We Trust.*

5. Steve Bruce, *Religion in the Modern World*, 56–58.

6. Berger, *Sacred Canopy.*

7. Warner, "Work in Progress."

8. Hunter, *American Evangelicalism*; Hunter, *Evangelicalism: The Coming Generation.*

9. Marsden, *The Soul of the American University*; Marsden and Longfield, *The Secularization of the Academy*; see also Burtchaell, *The Dying of the Light.*

10. Smith, *American Evangelicalism.*

11. Gallup and Lindsay, *Surveying the Religious Landscape*, is an excellent source for Gallup data; Public Opinion Online, available through Lexis-Nexis, provides a keyword searchable database for the results of these and all other national polls archived at the Roper Center at the University of Connecticut.

12. Gallup, CNN, USA Today Survey conducted in December 1994 by telephone among 1,016 respondents.

13. The 1980 and 2000 figures, respectively, for men in their twenties were 94 and 93 percent; for men in their thirties, 96 and 94 percent; for men in their early forties, 98 and 96 percent; for women in their twenties, 97 and 95 percent; for women in their thirties, 98 and 99 percent; and for women in their forties, 96 and 97 percent.

14. Greeley and Hout, "Americans' Increasing Belief in Life after Death."

15. The respective figures for belief in life after death for respondents age 21 through 45 in the 1972 to 1976 and 1998 to 2002 General Social Surveys, respectively, are 91 and 88 percent for evangelicals, 83 and 87 percent for mainline Protestants, 72 and 82 percent for black Protestants, 75 and 83 percent for Catholics, 26 and 67 percent for Jews (based on relatively small numbers), 75 and 75 percent for other faiths, and 51 and 65 percent for the nonaffiliated.

16. I think it is obvious enough that comparing younger people and older people is not the same thing as comparing younger people at two different time periods; in case anyone is confused on this point, though, I mention it here.

17. The Gallup and Pew figures are from Public Opinion Online, available through Lexis-Nexis. The Gallup Polls conducted in the 1970s were part of in-home surveys using a quota sampling design, whereas the more recent studies made use of random-digit dialing and telephone interviewing.

18. The best fitting linear trend line suggests an annual decline of less than two-tenths of a percentage point.

19. Marsden, *Fundamentalism and American Culture*; in *Reforming Fundamentalism*, Marsden cites evidence of declining belief in biblical inerrancy among faculty at the more moderate evangelical Fuller Seminary; see also Hatch and Noll, *The Bible in America.*

20. For instance, see Sherkat, "Counterculture or Continuity," and Woodrum and Hoban, "Support for Prayer in School and Creationism."

21. Among respondents age 21 through 45 in the Religion and Diversity Survey, the proportions who believed that Jesus was the only divine son of God who died and rose again among those who gave each response to the Bible question, respectively, were: literal, 93 percent; inspired, 59 percent; fables, 20 percent. The gamma summarizing this relationship was .812. On other questions, the respective gammas were as follows: God's word is not revealed in any other writings besides the Bible (.459), Christianity is the only way to have a true personal relationship with God (.624), Christianity is the best way to understand God (.602), God's truth is fully revealed only in the Bible (.667), I mostly trust the Bible for spiritual guidance (.668), I consider myself a Christian (.612). In comparison, the average gamma in the General Social Surveys among respondents age 21 through 45 for each survey between 1984 and 2002 for the relationship between the Bible question and the life after death question was only .270.

22. Thirty-eight percent of the respondents in the survey fell into the "low" category, 35 percent into the "middle" category, and 28 percent into the "high" category. Because of the larger proportions who had contact with Jews, a substantive interpretation of the index is that most of those in the middle category only had contact with Jews, while those in the high category also had contact with at least one of the three non-Western religions.

23. Hunter, *American Evangelicalism*; Bartkowski, "Beyond Biblical Literalism and Inerrancy," also examines the extent to which orthodox belief is modified by hermeneutic interpretation.

24. These particular questions do not point to ways of combining orthodox and heterodox beliefs that are unique to young adults. The patterns shown in figure 5.4 also appear among older adults.

25. The slope for the linear trend among those with no college is -.513, while the slope for those with some college is .306.

26. Because larger proportions of young adult women currently attain college training than in the past, a plausible interpretation of the increase in biblical literalism among college-trained people would be that this increase is a reflection of the changing gender composition of young adults. I could find no evidence that this was the case, however. Logistic regression models for the relationship between biblical literalism and level of education for each year in which the question was asked were not significantly different when gender was controlled than when it was not controlled. When the trend between 1984 and 2002 among young adults with at least some college training was examined, there was only a slight increase in biblical literalism among women but a more substantial increase among men (r-squared of .02 and .27, respectively). If biblical literalism was increasing because the proportion of the college trained who are women was increasing, then logistic regression coefficients should have been different when gender was controlled than when it was not controlled. And if rising biblical literalism was simply a function of rising numbers of college trained women, biblical literalism should not have increased among college trained men.

27. Cherry, DeBerg, and Porterfield, *Religion on Campus*.

CHAPTER 6
SPIRITUALITY AND SPIRITUAL PRACTICES: THE ROLE OF FAITH IN PERSONAL LIFE

1. James, *Varieties of Religious Experience.*

2. These observations about spirituality are based on the extensive qualitative interviews I conducted for my books *After Heaven* and *Growing Up Religious*; some of the main themes were summarized in Wuthnow, "Morality, Spirituality, and Democracy"; see also Wolfe, *The Transformation of American Religion.*

3. Roof, *Spiritual Marketplace*, is particularly good on the nature of spiritual seeking; see also Roof, "God is in the Details," Roof, "Modernity, the Religious, and the Spiritual," Roof, "Religious Borderlands," Cimino and Lattin, *Shopping for Faith*, and Cimino, *Trusting the Spirit.* Other useful sources include Kessler, "Seeking Spirituality," Hays, Meador, Branch, and George, "The Spiritual History Scale," Davie, *Women in the Presence*, Wink and Dillon, "Spiritual Development across the Adult Life Cycle," Dillon, Wink, and Fay, "Is Spirituality Detrimental to Generativity," and Wink and Dillon, "Religiousness, Spirituality, and Psychosocial Functioning."

4. Journalistic discussions of church shopping and church hopping include Shrieves, "Miles of Aisles," Cain, "Behind the Trend of Church-Hopping," and Vogel, "Church Hopping."

5. People who had not attended religious services while growing up were less likely to have been involved in churches as adults; thus, excluding them focuses more accurately on those who were interested enough in religion to have shopped. All but 17 percent of adults age 21 through 45 had gone to religious services at least once a month while they were growing up.

6. Lenski, *Religious Factor*; see also Roof, *Community and Commitment.*

7. Berger, *Sacred Canopy.*

8. Wuthnow, *Saving America?* Gregariousness was measured by an index of self-description questions that referred to enjoying being around people; frequent church goers also say they have more friends than less frequent attenders or nonattenders do.

9. The conclusions about congregational friendships are based on a logistic regression equation in which having six or more friends in one's congregation is the dependent variable. The odds-ratio for each increment in age (21–29, 30–39, 40–45) is 1.355; for being married, 1.342; and for number of addresses lived at since age 18, .816; the coefficients for having any children and for gender were not significant.

10. The 2004 *Religion and Ethics Newsweekly* Survey was conducted between March 16 and April 4, 2004, by Greenberg Quinlan Rosner Research, Inc. to a sample drawn by random digit dialing. The sample included 900 nationally representative respondents and oversamples of 401 white evangelical respondents, 160 African American respondents, and 149 Hispanic respondents. The data were weighted by gender, age, race, and religion to ensure an accurate reflection of the population. I was an advisor to the study and the data were graciously made available to me for further analysis. For present purposes (unless otherwise indicated), I have drawn information only from the nationally representative sample, rather than including the evangelical, African American, and Hispanic oversamples. The results I report are based on weighted data. Although the study included respondents age 18 and older, I have focused here on respondents between the ages of 21 and 45. There were

388 respondents in this age range, 118 age 21 through 29, 163 age 30 through 39, and 107 age 40 through 45. Readers should note that these numbers are smaller than for most of the other surveys from which I have drawn information, meaning that sampling error is also larger (between 5 and 9 percentage points). For that reason, I have not broken down the results into smaller categories (such as by gender or race). Further details about the survey are included in the appendix.

11. Forty-nine percent of those in their twenties talked about religion with their friends weekly, 41 percent of those in their thirties did, and 35 percent of those in their early forties did.

12. Cuddihy, *The Ordeal of Civility*.

13. Ammerman, "Golden Rule Christianity."

14. Specifically, 59 percent of white evangelicals in their twenties agreed strongly that it is important to convert others (another 27 percent agreed somewhat), while the respective figures for other age groups were: 48 percent of those in their thirties, 52 percent of those in their early forties, 52 percent of those between age 46 and 64, and 69 percent of those age 65 and older. For this purpose, I have used an operational definition of white evangelical developed by University of Akron political scientist John C. Green (who served as a consultant to the *Religion and Ethics Newsweekly* project). Green's operational definition is very similar to the "Reltrad" variable I used in chapter 4. It defines evangelicals in terms of the denominations to which they belong, rather than more subjective beliefs or self-definitions. This definition gives slightly different percentages for the responses under consideration than in some draft reports provided by the organization that conducted the survey.

15. Hoffer, *The True Believer*.

16. See especially Stromberg, *Language and Self-Transformation*.

17. These questions were asked in my Arts and Religion Survey.

18. For readers who might be interested in the exact numbers, the percentages, respectively, among those age 20 to 29, 30 to 39, 40 to 45, 46 to 64, and 65 or older who had spent a lot of time trying to imagine each question was as follows: what is God like (39, 45, 42, 49, 42), what angels are like (31, 33, 35, 35, 31), what heaven is like (51, 52, 48, 54, 47), how the universe came into existence (46, 45, 40, 42, 37), if there is life on other planets (39, 36, 31, 28, 25), if there is a reality beyond the one we know (40, 35, 29, 35, 26).

19. Arts and Religion Survey.

20. Among respondents age 21 through 45, 66 percent said their thinking about religion or spirituality had been influenced by music, philosophy, science, Hinduism, Buddhism, or Islam. Among subgroups of these respondents, the percentages, respectively, were: single, 74; not single, 61; no children, 70; children, 63; parent with college degree, 74; no parent with college degree, 61; college degree, 78; some college, 66; no college, 57; travel outside the United States, 71; no travel outside the United States, 59.

21. Wuthnow, *After Heaven*; Wuthnow, *Growing Up Religious*; Wuthnow, *Creative Spirituality*.

22. Arts and Religion Survey.

23. Arts and Religion Survey.

24. Discussed in my book *Creative Spirituality*.

25. For a broader discussion, see Fuller, *Spiritual, but Not Religious*.

26. The comparable proportion who could be defined as spiritual but not religious among people over age 45 would be between a tenth and a quarter.

27. Among adults age 21 through 45 who attend religious services less than once a month, the percentages who say their interest in spirituality is increasing, respectively for each group, are: age 21 through 29, 34; age 30 through 39, 48; age 40 through 45, 40; never married, 30; married, 49; children, 45; no children, 36; male, 35, female, 50; high school education, 37; some college, 45; college graduate, 49.

CHAPTER 7
FAITH AND FAMILY: FACING THE DIFFICULT CHOICES

1. A number of book-length treatments of various aspects of the relationship between religion and family life were produced through the auspices of a research project directed by Don Browning; these include Browning, *From Culture Wars to Common Ground*, and Anderson, Browning, and Boyer, *Marriage: Just a Piece of Paper?* See also Browning and Rodriguez, *Reweaving the Social Tapestry: Toward a Public Philosophy and Policy for Families*. Journal articles dealing with the influences of religious belief and practice on such topics as cohabitation, the decision to marry, marital happiness, marital disagreements, marital fidelity, spousal abuse, sexual behavior, and parenting, or summarizing this research, include Weaver, Samford, Morgan, Larson, Koenig, and Flannelly, "A Systematic Review of Research on Religion in Six Primary Marriage and Family Journals"; Buss, "Sex, Marriage, and Religion"; Mahoney, Pargament, Murray-Swank, and Murray-Swank, "Religion and the Sanctification of Family Relationships"; Schuiling, "The Benefit and the Doubt"; Oggins, "Topics of Marital Disagreement among African-American and Euro-American Newlyweds"; King, "The Influence of Religion on Father's Relationships with Their Children"; Waite and Lehrer, "The Benefits from Marriage and Religion in the United States"; Kemkes-Grottenthaler, "More than a Leap of Faith"; Lehrer, "The Role of Religion in Union Formation"; and Dempsey and deVaus, "Who Cohabits in 2001?"

2. These figures are from the 2004 Religion and Ethics Newsweekly Survey. Evangelicals were also especially likely to say they were worried (79 percent did), compared with 62 percent of mainline Protestants, 59 percent of black Protestants, 60 percent of Catholics, and 37 percent of the religiously nonaffiliated (results for respondents age 21 through 45).

3. Logistic regression analysis of the question about marriage being outdated shows that the odds of agreeing with this statement are .555 as great among weekly church goers as among those who attend less often, taking account of marital status, age, gender, and year of the survey.

4. With marital status, age, gender, and year of survey controlled, the odds of agreeing that marriage is outdated are .715 as large among those who say God is important as among those who do not (statistically significant only at the .08 level of probability); and these odds are .676 as large among those who say they derive comfort from religion as among those who do not (significant at the .05 level).

5. Besides the possibility that young adults who attend church learn pro-marriage values, another possible interpretation of these results is that a "selection

process" occurs, such that young adults who do not value marriage choose not to attend church, while those who do value it are more likely to attend. In either interpretation, the differences between 1980 and 2000 suggest, as we saw in chapter 5, that there is a growing lifestyle gap between young adults who attend church and young adults who do not.

6. Bailey, *From Front Porch to Back Seat*, is a valuable cultural history of dating and courtship patterns in the United States.

7. These figures are from General Social Surveys; the one slight shift is that 3 percent more in recent surveys believe sex before marriage is not wrong at all. For a broader discussion of trends in attitudes toward premarital sex and other issues, see Thornton and Young-DeMarco, "Four Decades of Trends."

8. Putnam, *Bowling Alone*.

9. Among people in their thirties, the number was 117 and among those age 40 to 45, 118. These results are from my Civic Involvement Survey, conducted in 1997.

10. From logistic regression analysis, the adjusted odds-ratio for religious attendance is 1.348 (significant at the .001 level), controlling for age, gender, race, and education (age 21 through 45 only). With religious tradition variables added, the odds of marital happiness among evangelical Protestants, mainline Protestants, and Catholics were between 1.2 and 1.4 greater than the odds of marital happiness among the religiously nonaffiliated.

11. Evolutionary psychologists like to speculate that religion must somehow be good for the survival of the human species (why else would so many people be religious, they ask), but if this is true there is very little evidence that *nonreligious* people will die out simply because they devalue having children and thus will fail to reproduce themselves. Only 3 percent of the nonaffiliated say they prefer no children and only 8 percent say they would like only one child; the modal response (56 percent) is that 2 children are ideal. Of course evolutionary psychologists consider science a matter of predicting something that might happen over tens of millions of years, meaning that actual data is largely irrelevant.

12. The percentages refer to respondents who selected each childrearing value as the most important or second most important among the various values asked about.

13. The percentages who selected thinking for oneself as their most important or second most important childrearing value, respectively, were: evangelicals, 60; mainline Protestants, 78; black Protestants, 63; Catholics 71; Jews, 86; nonaffiliated, 76; corresponding figures for obedience were 37, 21, 49, 24, 14, and 18.

14. The percentages who said each was never justified in 1980 and in 2000, respectively, were: claim benefits, 75 and 60; avoid a transportation fare, 65 and 45; homosexuality, 56 and 32; prostitution, 54 and 44; abortion, 36 and 26; and euthanasia, 34 and 20.

15. Wuthnow, *Learning to Care*; Colby and Damon, *Some Do Care*.

16. The scale is described in Davis, *Empathy: A Social Psychological Approach*; further details on the General Social Survey results are presented in Smith, "Altruism in Contemporary America: A Report from the National Altruism Study."

17. The percentages scoring high on empathy, respectively, for men and for women in each age group was: age 21 to 29, 20 and 43; age 30 to 39, 19 and 39; age 40 to 45, 22 and 48; age 46 to 64, 31 and 50; and age 65 and over, 24 and 48.

18. Among married women age 21 through 45 who had children, 58 percent of frequent church attenders scored high on empathy, compared with 39 percent of infrequent attenders; among married men with children, only 16 percent of frequent church attenders scored high, compared with 23 percent of infrequent attenders.

19. Among respondents in the 1998 General Social Survey who were age 21 through 29, 54 percent said their congregation would help a great deal, as did 56 percent of those age 30 through 39, and 50 percent of those age 40 through 45. Again, it is important to remember that these results are for respondents who attended religious services at least once a year.

20. See especially Wuthnow, *Saving America?*

21. The 1991 study was the basis for my book *Sharing the Journey*. The 1999 figures are from my Forgiveness Survey, a nationally representative survey of Americans involved in Bible studies, prayer groups, and other self-help groups. The Forgiveness Survey is described in the appendix.

22. Another way of considering these attitudes is the proportion in each age group who said they would "not object"; respectively, the percentages who said this about Muslims were 58 for age 21–29, 43 for age 30–39, 42 for age 40–45, 40 for age 46–64, and 33 for age 65 and older; the comparable figures for Hindus were 51, 48, 57, 42, and 37.

23. The proportions of adults age 21 through 45 who would object to a child of theirs marrying a Muslim were 31 percent among those with college degrees or higher, 35 percent among those with some college, and 33 percent among those with no college. Thirty-four percent of those with a least one college-educated parent would object, compared with 32 percent of those without a college-educated parent. Having traveled outside the United States was also an insignificant influence. Women were slightly more likely to object than men (37 percent versus 29 percent). Similar differences were evident between those who lived in the South and those who did not (39 percent versus 30 percent) and between those who lived in small towns or rural areas and those who lived in cities and suburbs (37 percent versus 30 percent).

24. For instance, 32 percent of those who were married said they would object, compared with 24 percent of those who were not married; 32 percent of those with children said they would object, compared with 22 percent of those without children; 44 percent of those who attended religious services almost every week said they would object, while only 19 percent of the remainder did so; the percentages who said they would object within each religious tradition were: evangelicals, 44; mainline Protestants, 22, black Protestants, 36, Catholics 21, Jews, 47.

25. These and related issues are discussed in my book *America and the New Challenges of Religious Diversity.*

26. The percentages of adults age 21 through 45 who said they would be bothered a little or a lot by a large mosque being built in their community, respectively, among each subgroup were: married, 45, unmarried, 37; children, 43, no children, 37; attend religious services almost weekly, 49, attend less often, 36; evangelical, 55, mainline Protestant, 34, black Protestant, 41; Catholic, 42, Jewish, 38; South, 50, elsewhere, 36; small towns or rural areas, 49; elsewhere, 36; six or more ad-

dresses, 34, three to five addresses, 40, one or two addresses, 46; one or two parents with college degrees, 38, neither, 43.

CHAPTER 8
THE DIVIDED GENERATION: RELIGION AND PUBLIC LIFE

1. Tipton, *Getting Saved from the Sixties: Moral Meaning in Conversion and Cultural Change*; see also Glock and Bellah, *The New Religious Consciousness*.

2. Roof, *Generation of Seekers*; Roof, *Spiritual Marketplace*; Hoge, Johnson, and Luidens, *Vanishing Boundaries*.

3. Variously discussed in Weber, *From Max Weber: Essays in Sociology*; Weber, *Economy and Society*; Weber, *Sociology of Religion*.

4. This framework is most fully developed in Wuthnow, *Communities of Discourse*; and with brevity in *Meaning and Moral Order* and *Producing the Sacred*. Unsettledness is emphasized in Swidler, *Talk of Love*, and Peterson, *Production of Culture*, remains a valuable source on the topic of its title. Selection and institutionalization are emphasized especially in the literature on organizational ecology and neoinstitutional approaches to organizations; see Powell and DiMaggio, *The New Institutionalism in Organizational Analysis*; Aldrich, Auster, Staber, and Zimmer, *Population Perspectives on Organizations*; Aldrich, *Organizations and Environments*; Meyer and Scott, *Organizational Environments*; and Scott and Meyer, *Institutional Environments and Organizations*.

5. Zablocki, *Alienation and Charisma*; Zablocki and Robbins, *Misunderstanding Cults*; the decline of communes and cults is an interesting empirical disconfirmation of the thesis that "strictness" within a marketplace is sufficient for understanding why some organizations grow and other decline.

6. Wuthnow, *Restructuring*.

7. Hunter, *Culture Wars*; see also Williams, *Cultural Wars in American Politics*.

8. Martin, *With God on Our Side*; FitzGerald, *Cities on a Hill*; Luker, *Abortion and the Politics of Motherhood*.

9. Summarized in Wuthnow, *Restructuring*.

10. Excluding respondents who said "don't know," the standard deviation for the trichotomized scale rose from .662 in 1984 to .747 in 1999. The Religion and Politics Survey, conducted in 2000, largely confirmed these results, although it is not as comparable to the 1984 survey as the 1999 survey because it was conducted by telephone through a random-digit dialing procedure; it showed that among respondents age 21 through 45, 11 percent identified themselves at the most conservative point on the scale and 21 percent did at the two most conservative points; 17 percent selected the most liberal option and 30 percent chose one of the two most liberal options; 26 percent were slightly conservative, 20 percent were slightly liberal, and 4 percent refused to answer.

11. Respectively, the proportion of religious conservatives, moderates, and liberals who attended religious services every week or almost every week while growing up were 82, 79, and 68; the respective percentages who said they had no religious affiliation growing up were 1, 5, and 8.

12. Bellah, *Beyond Belief*; Bellah, *The Broken Covenant*.

13. The data discussed in this paragraph are from my 2003 Religion and Diversity Survey; further detail is presented in my book *America and the Challenges of Religious Diversity*.

14. The four statements were: the United States was founded on Christian principles, America has been strong because of its faith in God, our democratic form of government is based on Christianity, and in the twenty-first century, the United States is still basically a Christian society. The percentages who scored high on the civil religion index in each age group were: 21 to 29, 31; 30 to 39, 41; 40 to 45, 49; 46 to 64, 55; and 65 or older, 70.

15. In a logistic regression equation where scoring high on the Civil Religion Index is the dependent variable, the odds of scoring high on that index are reduced by .853 with each increase in education (using a five-point education scale that ranges from less than high school to postgraduate degree), by .493 for having majored in the social sciences or humanities, and by .923 by each parent who graduated from college.

16. The coefficient in the previously mentioned logistic regression equation for age is 1.432, compared with 1.441 when none of the education variables were included.

17. Wasby, "More on Religion in Court"; Uslaner, "Trust but Verify"; Abdel-Monem, "Posting the Ten Commandments."

18. Eight states are different, two of which (New Hampshire and South Dakota) had to few respondents in the survey to provide reliable estimates.

19. Manza and Brooks, "The Religious Factor in U.S. Presidential Elections, 1960–1992."

20. On voting among conservative Catholics, see also Bendyna, Green, Rozell, and Wilcox, "Uneasy Alliance: Conservative Catholics and the Christian Right"; and Bendyna, Green, Rozell, and Wilcox, "Catholics and the Christian Right: A View from Four States."

21. These figures are from my Religion and Politics Survey.

22. The differences are on the order of about 6 percent.

23. For religious leaders appearing on television talk shows, the specific percentages who would like to see more of this were: evangelicals, 48, mainline, 32, black Protestant, 59, Catholic, 38, and unaffiliated, 26; the comparable percentages, respectively for wanting religious leaders to form political movements were: 46, 30, 66, 35, and 28. There were too few Jews in the sample for valid comparisons.

24. These changes in attitudes toward abortion among young evangelicals and nonevangelicals are also evident statistically in the fact that the odds of evangelicals opposing abortion compared with the odds of nonevangelicals opposing abortion increased; from logistic regression equations, the odds-ratios for each variable for the 1972–76 respondents and the 1998–02 respondents, respectively, were: abortion because of birth defects, 1.131, 2.141; abortion because of wanting no more children, 1.873, 2.631; abortion because woman's health is in danger, 1.040, 1.717; abortion because the woman is poor, 1.769, 2.608; abortion because of rape, 1.529, 2.371; abortion because woman is unmarried, 1.780, 2.496.

25. Warm attitudes toward pro-life groups were expressed by 55 percent of black Protestants, 65 percent of Catholics, and 50 percent of Jews; warm attitudes toward Jerry Falwell were expressed by 40 percent, 33 percent, and 8 percent, respectively.

26. Wolfe, *Transformation of American Religion.*

27. This information is from my Religion and Politics Survey, conducted in 2000. Twelve percent of respondents age 21 through 29 had attended a political meeting or rally in the past year and 26 percent had attended a class or lecture about social or political issues.

28. For instance, 30 percent of weekly attenders had contacted an elected official in the past year, compared with 19 percent of those who attended a few times a year or never. Fifteen percent of the former and 8 percent of the latter had attended a political rally or meeting.

CHAPTER 9
EMERGING TRENDS: IMMIGRATION AND ETHNIC DIVERSITY

1. Ebaugh and Chafetz, *Religion and the New Immigrants*; Kwon, Kim, and Warner, *Korean Americans and Their Religions*; Warner and Wittner, *Gatherings in Diaspora*; Alumkal, *Asian American Evangelical Churches.*

2. These religious affiliations resemble those in Putnam's Social Capital Benchmark Survey, where 66 percent of Hispanics age 21 through 45 identified themselves as Catholics, 11 percent as Protestant, 2 percent as other, and 11 percent as having no religion. Putnam's religious affiliation question did not provide as many response categories and the survey included only a few other questions about religion, making it less desirable as a primary source. Although it does not lend itself as well for comparisons with white Anglo Catholics, valuable information on Hispanic Catholics is also available in Espinosa, Elizondo, and Miranda, *Hispanic Churches in American Public Life.*

3. In Putnam's Social Capital Benchmark Survey, 59 percent of Hispanic Catholics age 21 through 45 had family incomes below $30,000, compared with 18 percent of non-Hispanic Catholics in the same age group.

4. Among Catholics in their twenties, marital patterns among Hispanics closely resembled those of non-Hispanics, with approximately two-thirds of each saying they have never been married and slightly more than a quarter saying they are currently married. In their thirties, a majority of both Hispanics and non-Hispanics say they are married; however, 25 percent of non-Hispanics have never been married, compared with 14 percent of Hispanics; in contrast 25 percent of Hispanics are divorced or separated, compared with 10 percent of non-Hispanics. In their early forties, the two groups are again quite similar. A question about number of children in Putnam's Social Capital Benchmark Survey showed that 59 percent of Hispanic Catholics age 21 through 45 had family incomes below $30,000, compared with 18 percent of non-Hispanic Catholics in the same age group. Fifty-five percent had two or more children, compared with 39 percent of non-Hispanic Catholics.

5. In Putnam's Social Capital Benchmark Survey, 69 percent of Hispanic Catholics age 21 through 45 reported that they were not U.S. citizens.

6. Espinoza, et al., *Hispanic Churches*, estimate that 22 percent of adult Latino Catholics are "charismatic."

7. Putnam's Social Capital Benchmark Survey included 178 Hispanics age 21 through 45 who listed their religion as Protestant, making it possible to draw some

limited comparisons with Hispanic Catholics. Twenty-eight percent of these Hispanic Protestants listed their denomination as Pentecostal, 20 percent as Baptists, and 12 percent as Lutherans; most of the remainder were mainline Protestants, such as Methodists, United Church of Christ, and Presbyterian.

8. Bankston and Zhou, "The Ethnic Church, Ethnic Identification, and the Social Adjustment of Vietnamese Adolescents"; Ecklund, *The "Good" American*; Kim and Zhou, "Chinese Christians in America"; Zhou, "God in Chinatown"; Chen, "The Religious Varieties of Ethnic Presence"; Chong, "What It Means to Be Christian."

9. Warner, "Work in Progress."

10. For a more detailed analysis of adherents of non-Western religions (Buddhists, Hindus, and Muslims) in these data, see Wuthnow and Hackett, "The Social Integration of Practitioners of Non-Western Religions in the United States."

11. Putnam, *Bowling Alone*; for empirical evidence on the differences between church going that promotes bonding and church going that promotes bridging, see Wuthnow, *Saving America?* See also Wuthnow, "Religious Involvement and Status-Bridging Social Capital" and Wuthnow, "Overcoming Status Distinctions?"

12. Denominational affiliations were asked about in somewhat less detail than in other surveys on which I have drawn so it was necessary to develop a classification scheme that categorized evangelicals and mainline Protestants as accurately as possible and then selecting only white respondents in order to focus on interethnic ties. For this purpose, evangelicals included all Baptists, Christian and Missionary Alliance, Church of the Nazarene, Free Methodist, Salvation Army, Wesleyan, Independent Fundamentalist, Lutheran Church Missouri Synod, Pentecostal Assemblies of God, Pentecostal Church of God, Churches of Christ, "born again" Christian, Full Gospel, Bible, and Charismatic. Mainline Protestant included Episcopalian, United Church of Christ, Lutheran—Evangelical Lutheran Church in America, Methodist, Presbyterian, Reformed Church in America, Disciples of Christ, and Christian. Regular church goers here are defined as those who scored "high" on Putnam's faith-based social capital index (which included frequent attendance, being a member, and participating in church groups in addition to worship services). The comparisons are with those scoring low on the same scale (those in the middle category of the scale are excluded). The odds-ratios were computed from logistic regression equations, where coefficients greater than "1" mean positive relationships. Respondents were coded as having an interethnic friend if they said they had an African American, Hispanic, or Asian American friend. The details of Putnam's scale are included in the codebook for the Social Capital Benchmark Survey.

13. The scale of interethnic trust for these white respondents was created by giving each respondent one point if he or she said that African Americans could be trusted "a lot" and a similar point for questions about Hispanics and Asian Americans. The cutting point used for the scale was between respondents who received 3 points on the scale and respondents who received fewer than 3 points. The odds-ratios were again computed from logistic regression equations.

14. Those scoring high on the faith-based involvement scale among people in their twenties were 25 percentage points more likely to have volunteered to help the poor or elderly in the past year; in their thirties, 30 points more likely; and in their early forties, 27 points.

CHAPTER 10
THE VIRTUAL CHURCH: RELIGIOUS USES OF THE INTERNET

1. The questions about information technology were included in the 2000 and 2002 General Social Surveys; among respondents age 21 through 45, 2600 said they sometimes use a computer and 1935 said they sometimes use the Internet; responses to questions asked in both years are based on these numbers; responses to questions asked in only one of the surveys are based on numbers approximately half this size. See the *General Social Survey Codebook* for additional details about filtering of questions.

2. Although Internet religion has been the focus of several studies (e.g., Beaudoin, *Virtual Faith*; Brasher, *Give Me that Online Religion*), discussions have generally focused on the content of Web sites, rather than on information from surveys of users.

3. Among General Social Survey respondents 21 through 29, 15 percent had consulted a religion site in the past 30 days, 23 percent of respondents age 30 through 39 said they had done so, as had 20 percent of respondents age 40 through 45.

4. Elena Larsen, *CyberFaith: How Americans Pursue Religion Online*; available at www.pewInternet.org.

5. Women were only slightly more likely to have visited a religion Web site than men (22 percent versus 18 percent); the same difference separated people with graduate degrees from those with high school degrees, and married and single people differed by only 2 percentage points, as did people with or without children; these results pertain only to adults age 21 through 45 who used the Internet for any purpose.

6. Among these religious surfers, those in their early forties attached greater importance than those in their twenties to nearly all these religious practices; for instance, 53 percent of religious surfers age 40 to 45 said small group study or prayer was very important, compared with 49 percent of those age 30 to 39 and 39 percent of those 21 through 29; the percentages, respectively, who said going online to get religious or spiritual information was very important were 18, 12, and 9.

7. Research done at the time religious television programming was expanding suggested that it was largely an add-on, rather than a substitute for congregation-based religious practices; Wuthnow, "The Social Significance of Religious Television."

CHAPTER 11
VITAL CONGREGATIONS: YOUTHFUL AND DIVERSE

1. Bureau of Labor Statistics, www.bls.gov/opub/ted/1998.

2. This point has been made especially in Winston, *Red-Hot and Righteous*.

3. Sargeant, *Seeker Churches*.

4. The data in this section are from Mark Chaves' National Congregations study, which is described in the Appendix. See especially Chaves, *Congregations in America*.

5. A more rigorous estimate of the possible relationship between youthfulness and growth is provided by multiple regression analysis of size (number of participating adults) by youthful or nonyouthful congregation, controlling for year of founding; the standardized coefficient for youthfulness is .055, significant at the .06 level.

6. These figures refer to children age 12 or younger, as reported by the pastor or other informant; teenagers age 13 to 18 showed similar differences: 91 in youthful congregations, 62 in older congregations.

7. Sixty-nine percent of the people who go to youthful congregations go to churches located in a predominantly urban census tract, compared with 59 percent of people who go to nonyouthful congregations. The average percentage of each ethnic or racial group in youthful and nonyouthful congregations, respectively, is: white: 66.9, 77.9; African American, 18.4, 14.0; Hispanic, 9.1, 5.0; Asian American, 4.2, 2.0.

8. These figures are from my 2000 Religion and Politics Survey, church members age 21 through 45.

9. The percentages with each kind of program among congregations with fewer than 200 members, between 200 and 999 members, and 1000 or more members, respectively were: day care among evangelicals, 33, 52, 77; daycare among mainline Protestants, 38, 52, 77; daycare among black Protestants, 32, 51, 82; daycare among Catholics, 40, 48, 57; food pantry among evangelicals, 73, 83, 85; food pantry among mainline, 82, 92, 91; food pantry among black Protestants, 62, 87, 94; food pantry among Catholics, 76, 87, 94; homeless shelter among evangelicals, 35, 48, 74; homeless shelter among mainline, 47, 62, 71; homeless shelter among black Protestants, 38, 57, 78; homeless shelter among Catholics, 53, 51, 69.

10. Flory and Miller, *GenX Religion*.

11. My research on music and worship styles is found in Wuthnow, *All in Sync*.

12. Arts and Religion Survey.

13. Religion and Diversity Survey.

14. Adults age 21 through 45 were just as likely as adults over age 45 to have gone on these mission trips, even though being younger means having had fewer years in which to have taken them and perhaps less time and fewer financial resources than many older people.

15. Civic Involvement Survey.

16. The source of these conclusions is an analysis of results from my Civic Involvement Survey, based on respondents age 21 through 45 and drawn from logistic regression models.

Selected Bibliography

Abdel-Monem, T. "Posting the Ten Commandments as a Historical Document in Public Schools." *Iowa Law Review* 87, 3 (2002): 1023–57.

Alba, R. and V. Nee. "Rethinking Assimilation Theory for a New Era of Immigration." *International Migration Review* 31, 4 (1997): 826–74.

Alba, Richard D. and Victor Nee. *Remaking the American Mainstream: Assimilation and Contemporary Immigration.* Cambridge, MA: Harvard University Press, 2003.Aldrich, Howard. *Organizations and Environments.* Englewood Cliffs, NJ: Prentice-Hall, 1979.

Aldrich, Howard. *Organizations and Environments.* Englewood Cliffs, NJ: Prectice-Hall, 1979.

Aldrich, Howard, Ellen R. Auster, Udo H. Staber, and Catherine Zimmer, eds. *Population Perspectives on Organizations.* Uppsala, Stockholm, Sweden: Almqvist & Wiksell International, 1986.

Alumkal, Antony William. *Asian American Evangelical Churches: Race, Ethnicity, and Assimilation in the Second Generation.* New York: LFB Scholarly Pub., 2003.

Ammerman, Nancy T. "Golden Rule Christianity: Lived Religion in the American Mainstream." In *Lived Religion in America: Toward a History of Practice*, edited by David D. Hall, 196–216. Princeton, NJ: Princeton University Press, 1997.

Anderson, Katherine, Don S. Browning, and Brian Boyer. *Marriage: Just a Piece of Paper?* Grand Rapids, MI: Eerdmans, 2002.

Atran, Scott. *In Gods We Trust: The Evolutionary Landscape of Religion.* New York: Oxford University Press, 2002.

Baggett, Jerome P. *Habitat for Humanity: Building Private Homes, Building Public Religion.* Philadelphia, PA: Temple University Press, 2001.

Bailey, Beth L. *From Front Porch to Back Seat: Courtship in Twentieth-Century America.* Baltimore: Johns Hopkins University Press, 1988.

Bankston, C. L. and M. Zhou. "The Ethnic Church, Ethnic Identification, and the Social Adjustment of Vietnamese Adolescents." *Review of Religious Research* 38, 1 (1996): 18–37.

Barna, George. *The Invisible Generation: Baby Busters.* Glendale, CA: Barna Research Group, 1992.

———. *Baby Busters: The Disillusioned Generation.* Chicago: Northfield Publishing, 1994.

———. *Generation Next: What You Need to Know About Today's Youth.* Ventura, CA: Regal Books, 1995.

———. *Third Millennium Teens: Research on the Minds, Hearts and Souls of America's Teenagers.* Ventura, CA: Barna Research Group, 1999.

Bartkowski, J. "Beyond Biblical Literalism and Inerrancy: Conservative Protestants and the Hermeneutic Interpretation of Scripture." *Sociology of Religion* 57, 3 (1996): 259–72.

Battaini-Dragoni, Gabriella. *Recent Demographic Developments, 2002.* Paris: Council of Europe, 2002.

Beaudoin, Tom. *Virtual Faith: The Irreverent Spiritual Quest of Generation X.* San Francisco: Jossey-Bass, 1998.

Beck, Ulrich, Natan Sznaider, and Rainer Winter. *Global America? The Cultural Consequences of Globalization.* Liverpool: Liverpool University Press, 2003.

Becker, P. E. and H. Hofmeister. "Work, Family, and Religious Involvement for Men and Women." *Journal for the Scientific Study of Religion* 40, 4 (2001): 707–22.

Becker, P. E. and P. H. Dhingra. "Religious Involvement and Volunteering: Implications for Civil Society." *Sociology of Religion* 62, 3 (2001): 315–35.

Bellah, Robert Neelly. *Beyond Belief: Essays on Religion in a Post-Traditional World.* New York: Harper & Row, 1970.

Bellah, Robert N. *The Broken Covenant: American Civil Religion in Time of Trial.* New York: Seabury, 1975.

Bendyna, M., J. C. Green, M. J. Rozell, and C. Wilcox. "Catholics and the Christian Right: A View from Four States." *Journal for the Scientific Study of Religion* 39, 3 (2000): 321–32.

Bendyna, M. E., J. C. Green, M. J. Rozell, and C. Wilcox. "Uneasy Alliance: Conservative Catholics and the Christian Right." *Sociology of Religion* 62, 1 (2001): 51–64.

Beniger, James R. *The Control Revolution: Technological and Economic Origins of the Information Society.* Cambridge, MA: Harvard University Press, 1989.

Berger, Peter L. *The Sacred Canopy: Elements of a Sociological Theory of Religion.* Garden City, NY: Doubleday, 1967.

Bernhardt, Annette, Martina Morris, Mark Handcock, and Marc Scott. "Inequality and Mobility: Trends in Wage Growth for Young Adults." In *IEE Working Paper*, No. 7. New York: Columbia University, Institute on Education and the Economy, 1998.

Beyerlein, K. and M. Chaves. "The Political Activities of Religious Congregations in the United States." *Journal for the Scientific Study of Religion* 42, 2 (2003): 229–46.

Blumer, Herbert. *Symbolic Interactionism: Perspective and Method.* Englewood Cliffs, NJ: Prentice-Hall, 1969.

Bordo, Michael D., Alan M. Taylor, and Jeffrey G. Williamson. *Globalization in Historical Perspective.* Chicago: University of Chicago Press, 2003.

Boyer, Pascal. *The Naturalness of Religious Ideas: A Cognitive Theory of Religion.* Berkeley: University of California Press, 1994.

———. *Religion Explained: The Human Instincts That Fashion Gods, Spirits and Ancestors.* London: Heinemann, 2001.

Bradshaw, Tom and Bonnie Nichols. "Reading at Risk: A Survey of Literary Reading in America, Research Division Report #46." Washington, DC: National Endowment for the Arts, 2004.

Brasher, Brenda E. *Give Me That Online Religion.* San Francisco: Jossey-Bass, 2001.

Brooks, David. "The Organization Kid." *Atlantic Monthly* 287, 4, April (2001): online.

Brooks, C. "Religious Influence and the Politics of Family Decline Concern: Trends, Sources, and Us Political Behavior." *American Sociological Review* 67, 2 (2002): 191–211.

Brooks, C. and C. Bolzendahl. "The Transformation of Us Gender Role Attitudes: Cohort Replacement, Social-Structural Change, and Ideological Learning." *Social Science Research* 33, 1 (2004): 106–33.

Browning, Don S. *From Culture Wars to Common Ground: Religion and the American Family Debate.* Louisville: Westminster John Knox Press, 1997.

Browning, Don S. and Gloria G. Rodriguez. *Reweaving the Social Tapestry: Toward a Public Philosophy and Policy for Families.* New York: W. W. Norton, 2002.

Bruce, Steve. *Religion and Modernization: Sociologists and Historians Debate the Secularization Thesis.* New York: Oxford University Press, 1992.

———. *Choice and Religion: A Critique of Rational Choice Theory.* New York: Oxford University Press, 1999.

Burtchaell, James Tunstead. *The Dying of the Light: The Disengagement of Colleges and Universities from Their Christian Churches.* Grand Rapids, MI: W. B. Eerdmans Pub. Co., 1998.

Buss, D. M. "Sex, Marriage, and Religion: What Adaptive Problems Do Religious Phenomena Solve?" *Psychological Inquiry* 13, 3 (2002): 201–03.

Cain, Cindy Wojdyla. "Behind the Trend of Church-Hopping Is a New Search for Hope." *Associated Press Newswires,* February 26, 1999.

Caplovitz, David and Frederick Sherrow. *Religious Drop-Outs: Apostasy among College Graduates.* Beverly Hills: Sage, 1977.

Carroll, Jackson W. and Wade Clark Roof. *Bridging Divided Worlds: Generational Cultures in Congregations.* San Francisco: Jossey-Bass, 2002.

Chaves, Mark. "On the Rational Choice Approach to Religion." *Journal for the Scientific Study of Religion* 34 (1995): 98–104.

———. "Abiding Faith." *Contexts* 1, 2, Summer (2002): 19–26.

Chaves, Mark and Laura Stephens. "Church Attendance in the United States." In *Handbook of the Sociology of Religion,* edited by Michele Dillon, 85–95. New York: Cambridge University Press, 2003.

Chaves, Mark. *Congregations in America.* Cambridge, MA: Harvard University Press, 2004.

Chen, C. "The Religious Varieties of Ethnic Presence: A Comparison between a Taiwanese Immigrant Buddhist Temple and an Evangelical Christian Church." *Sociology of Religion* 63, 2 (2002): 215–38.

Cherry, Conrad, Betty A. DeBerg, and Amanda Porterfield. *Religion on Campus.* Chapel Hill, NC: University of North Carolina Press, 2001.

Cheung, Edward. *Baby-Boomers, Generation-X and Social Cycles.* Toronto: Longwave Press, 1995.

Chong, K. H. "What It Means to Be Christian: The Role of Religion in the Construction of Ethnic Identity and Boundary among Second-Generation Korean Americans." *Sociology of Religion* 59, 3 (1998): 259–86.

Cimino, Richard P. and Don Lattin. *Shopping for Faith: American Religion in the New Millennium.* San Francisco: Jossey-Bass, 1998.

Cimino, Richard P. *Trusting the Spirit: Renewal and Reform in American Religion.* San Francisco: Jossey-Bass, 2001.

Colby, Anne and William Damon. *Some Do Care: Contemporary Lives of Moral Commitment.* New York: Free Press, 1992.

Craig, Stephen C. and Stephen Earl Bennett. *After the Boom: The Politics of Generation X, People, Passions, and Power*. Lanham, MD: Rowman & Littlefield Publishers, 1997.

Cross, Whitney R. *The Burned-over District: The Social and Intellectual History of Enthusiastic Religion in Western New York 1800–1850*. Ithaca: Cornell University Press, 1950.

Cuddihy, John Murray. *The Ordeal of Civility: Freud, Marx, Lévi-Strauss, and the Jewish Struggle with Modernity*. New York: Basic Books, 1974.

Davie, Jody Shapiro. *Women in the Presence: Constructing Community and Seeking Spirituality in Mainline Protestantism*. Philadelphia: University of Pennsylvania Press, 1995.

Davis, Mark H. *Empathy: A Social Psychological Approach*. Boulder, CO: Westview Press, 1996.

Dempsey, K. and D. deVaus. "Who Cohabits in 2001? The Significance of Age, Gender, Religion and Ethnicity." *Journal of Sociology* 40, 2 (2004): 157–78.

Dillon, M., P. Wink, and K. Fay. "Is Spirituality Detrimental to Generativity?" *Journal for the Scientific Study of Religion* 42, 3 (2003): 427–42.

DiMaggio, P., J. Evans, and B. Bryson. "Have Americans' Social Attitudes Become More Polarized?" *American Journal of Sociology* 102, 3 (1996): 690–755.

Durkheim, Emile, Carol Cosman, and Mark Sydney Cladis. *The Elementary Forms of Religious Life*. Oxford and New York: Oxford University Press, 2001.

Ebaugh, Helen Rose and Janet Saltzman Chafetz. *Religion and the New Immigrants: Continuities and Adaptations in Immigrant Congregations*. Walnut Creek, CA: AltaMira Press, 2000.

Eck, Diana. *A New Religious America: How a 'Christian Country' Has Now Become the Most Religiously Diverse Nation on Earth*. San Francisco: Harper San Francisco, 2001.

Eckes, Alfred E. and Thomas W. Zeiler. *Globalization and the American Century*. New York: Cambridge University Press, 2003.

Ecklund, Elaine Howard. "The 'Good' American: Religion and Civic Life for Korean Americans." Cornell University, 2004.

Edgell, P. "Evangelical Identity and Gendered Family Life." *Journal of Marriage and the Family* 65, 4 (2003): 1089–90.

Ellison, C. G., J. D. Boardman, D. R. Williams, and J. S. Jackson. "Religious Involvement, Stress, and Mental Health: Findings from the 1995 Detroit Area Study." *Social Forces* 80, 1 (2001): 215–49.

Espinosa, Gaston, Virgilio Elizondo, and Jesse Miranda. "Hispanic Churches in American Public Life: Summary of Findings." Notre Dame, IN: University of Notre Dame, Institute for Latino Studies, 2003.

Evans, J. H., B. Bryson, and P. DiMaggio. "Opinion Polarization: Important Contributions, Necessary Limitations." *American Journal of Sociology* 106, 4 (2001): 944–59.

Evans, J. H. "Polarization in Abortion Attitudes in Us Religious Traditions, 1972–1998." *Sociological Forum* 17, 3 (2002): 397–422.

———. "Religion and Human Cloning: An Exploratory Analysis of the First Available Opinion Data." *Journal for the Scientific Study of Religion* 41, 4 (2002): 747–58.

FitzGerald, Frances. *Cities on a Hill: A Journey through Contemporary American Cultures.* New York: Simon & Schuster, 1986.

Flory, Richard W. and Donald E. Miller. *GenX Religion.* New York: Routledge, 2000.

Foner, Nancy. *From Ellis Island to JFK: New York's Two Great Waves of Immigration.* New Haven and New York: Yale University Press and Russell Sage Foundation, 2000.

Fuller, Robert C. *Spiritual, but Not Religious: Understanding Unchurched America.* New York: Oxford University Press, 2001.

Furstenberg Jr., Frank F., Sheela Kennedy, Vonnie C. McCloyd, Ruben G. Rumbaut, and Richard A. Settersten Jr. "Between Adolescence and Adulthood: Expectations About the Timing of Adulthood." In *Network on Transitions to Adulthood and Public Policy Working Papers.* Philadelphia: University of Pennsylvania, 2003.

Gallup, George, Jr. and D. Michael Lindsay. *Surveying the Religious Landscape: Trends in U.S. Beliefs.* Philadelphia: Morehouse, 1999.

Glock, Charles Y. and Rodney Stark. *Religion and Society in Tension.* Chicago: Rand McNally, 1965.

Glock, Charles Y. and Robert N. Bellah, eds. *The New Religious Consciousness.* Berkeley and Los Angeles: University of California Press, 1976.

Greeley, Andrew. *The Denominational Society: A Sociological Approach to Religion in America.* Glenview, IL: Scott Foresman, 1972.

Greeley, Andrew M. and Michael Hout. "Americans' Increasing Belief in Life after Death: Religious Competition and Acculturation." *American Sociological Review* 64, December (1999): 813–35.

Grimm, Matthew. "Hitch Switch." *American Demographics* 25, 9 (2003): 34–36.

Hadaway, C. K., P. L. Marler, and M. Chaves. "What the Polls Don't Show—A Closer Look at United-States Church Attendance." *American Sociological Review* 58, 6 (1993): 741–52.

Hadaway, C. K. and P. L. Marler. "The Problem with Father as Proxy: Denominational Switching and Religious Change, 1965–1988." *Journal for the Scientific Study of Religion* 35, 2 (1996): 156–64.

Hadaway, C. K., P. L. Marler, and M. Chaves. "Overreporting Church Attendance in America: Evidence That Demands the Same Verdict." *American Sociological Review* 63, 1 (1998): 122–30.

Halberstam, David. *The Fifties.* New York: Villard Books, 1993.

Hammond, Phillip E. and Benton Johnson. *American Mosaic: Social Patterns of Religion in the United States.* New York: Random House, 1970.

Hammond, Phillip E., ed. *The Sacred in a Secular Age: Toward Revision in the Scientific Study of Religion.* Berkeley: University of California Press, 1985.

Hatch, Nathan O. and Mark A. Noll, eds. *The Bible in America: Essays in Cultural History.* New York: Oxford University Press, 1982.

Hays, J. C., K. G. Meador, P. S. Branch, and L. K. George. "The Spiritual History Scale in Four Dimensions (SHS-4): Validity and Reliability." *Gerontologist* 41, 2 (2001): 239–49.

Herberg, Will. *Protestant-Catholic-Jew: An Essay in American Religious Sociology.* Garden City, NY: Doubleday, 1955.

Hinojosa, V. J. and J. Z. Park. "Religion and the Paradox of Racial Inequality Attitudes." *Journal for the Scientific Study of Religion* 43, 2 (2004): 229–38.

Hoffer, Eric. *The True Believer: Thoughts on the Nature of Mass Movements.* New York: Harper and Row, 1951.

Hoge, Dean R. and Gregory Petrillo. "Determinants of Church Participation and Attitudes among High School Youth." *Journal for the Scientific Study of Religion* 17 (1978): 359–80.

Hoge, Dean R. and David A. Roozen. "Some Sociological Conclusions About Church Trends." In *Understanding Church Growth and Decline, 1950–1978*, edited by Dean Hoge and David A. Roozen. New York: Pilgrim Press, 1979.

Hoge, Dean R., Benton Johnson, and Donald A. Luidens. *Vanishing Boundaries: The Religion of Mainline Protestant Baby Boomers.* Louisville, KY: Westminster/John Knox Press, 1994.

Hook, J. L. "Reconsidering the Division of Household Labor: Incorporating Volunteer Work and Informal Support." *Journal of Marriage and the Family* 66, 1 (2004): 101–17.

Hout, M. and A. M. Greeley. "The Center Doesn't Hold: Church Attendance in the United-States, 1940–1984." *American Sociological Review* 52, 3 (1987): 325–45.

Hout, M. and A. Greeley. "What Church Officials' Reports Don't Show: Another Look at Church Attendance Data." *American Sociological Review* 63, 1 (1998): 113–19.

Hout, Michael, Andrew Greeley, and Melissa J. Wilde. "The Demographic Imperative in Religious Change in the United States." *American Journal of Sociology* 107 (2001): 468–500.

Hout, Michael, C. S. Fischer, and Nancy Latham. "The Time Bind and God's Time." Berkeley, CA: University of California, Survey Research Center, 2001.

Hout, M. and C. S. Fischer. "Why More Americans Have No Religious Preference: Politics and Generations." *American Sociological Review* 67, 2 (2002): 165–90.

Howe, Neil and William Strauss. *Millennials Rising: The Next Great Generation.* New York: Vintage Books, 2000.

Hunter, James Davison. *American Evangelicalism: Conservative Religion and the Quandary of Modernity.* New Brunswick, NJ: Rutgers University Press, 1983.

———. *Evangelicalism: The Coming Generation.* Chicago: University of Chicago Press, 1987.

———. *Culture Wars: The Struggle to Define America.* New York: BasicBooks, 1991.

Hutchison, William R. *Religious Pluralism in America: The Contentious History of a Founding Ideal.* New Haven, CT.: Yale University Press, 2003.

Iannaccone, L. R. "Religious Markets and the Economics of Religion." *Social Compass* 39, 1 (1992): 123–31.

———. "Why Strict Churches Are Strong." *American Journal of Sociology* 99, 5 (1994): 1180–211.

James, William. *The Varieties of Religious Experience: A Study in Human Nature.* New York: Longmans, Green, 1902.

Karniol, R., E. Grosz, and I. Schorr. "Caring, Gender Role Orientation, and Volunteering." *Sex Roles* 49, 1–2 (2003): 11–19.

Kelley, Dean M. *Why Conservative Churches Are Growing: A Study in the Sociology of Religion.* New York: Harper & Row, 1972.

Kemkes-Grottenthaler, A. "More Than a Leap of Faith: The Impact of Biological and Religious Correlates on Reproductive Behavior." *Human Biology* 75, 5 (2003): 705–27.

Kessler, D. C. "Seeking Spirituality: Guidelines for a Christian Spirituality for the Twenty-First-Century." *Ecumenical Review* 53, 2 (2001): 277–78.

Kim, K., J. Sobal, and E. Wethington. "Religion and Body Weight." *International Journal of Obesity* 27, 4 (2003): 469–77.

Kim, P. H. "Conditional Morality? Attitudes of Religious Individuals toward Racial Profiling." *American Behavioral Scientist* 47, 7 (2004): 879–95.

King, V. "The Influence of Religion on Fathers' Relationships with Their Children." *Journal of Marriage and the Family* 65, 2 (2003): 382–95.

Kofman, Eleonore and Gillian Youngs. *Globalization: Theory and Practice.* London and New York: Continuum, 2003.

Kwon, Ho Youn, Kwang Chung Kim, and R. Stephen Warner, eds. *Korean Americans and Their Religions : Pilgrims and Missionaries from a Different Shore.* University Park, PA: Pennsylvania State University Press, 2001.

Larsen, Elena. "Cyberfaith: How Americans Pursue Religion Online." Washington, DC: Pew Internet and American Life Project, 2002.

Lehrer, E. L. "The Role of Religion in Union Formation: An Economic Perspective." *Population Research and Policy Review* 23, 2 (2004): 161–85.

Lenski, Gerhard. *The Religious Factor: A Sociological Study of Religion's Impact on Politics, Economics, and Family Life.* Garden City, NY: Doubleday, 1961.

Lévi-Strauss, Claude. *The Savage Mind, The Nature of Human Society Series.* Chicago: University of Chicago Press, 1966.

Luker, Kristin. *Abortion and the Politics of Motherhood.* Berkeley: University of California Press, 1984.

Mahoney, A., K. I. Pargament, A. Murray-Swank, and N. Murray-Swank. "Religion and the Sanctification of Family Relationships." *Review of Religious Research* 44 3 (2003): 220–36.

Mannheim, Karl. *Man and Society in an Age of Reconstruction: Studies in Modern Social Structure.* New York: Harcourt Brace & World, 1940.

———. *Ideology and Utopia: An Introduction to the Sociology of Knowledge.* New York: Harcourt Brace & World, 1955.

———. *Essays on the Sociology of Culture.* London: Routledge & Paul, 1956.

Mannheim, K. "Problem of Generations." *Psychoanalytic Review* 57, 3 (1970): 378–404.

Manza, J. and C. Brooks. "The Religious Factor in U.S. Presidential Elections 1960–1992." *American Journal of Sociology* 103, 1 (1997): 38–81.

Marcum, J. P. "Measuring Church Attendance: A Further Look." *Review of Religious Research* 41 (1999): 122–30.

Marsden, George M. *Fundamentalism and American Culture: The Shaping Twentieth Century Evangelicalism, 1870–1925.* New York: Oxford University Press, 1980.

———. *Reforming Fundamentalism: Fuller Seminary and the New Evangelical* Grand Rapids, MI: W. B. Eerdmans, 1987.

Marsden, George M. and Bradley J. Longfield, eds. *The Secularization* emy. New York: Oxford University Press, 1992.

Marsden, George M. *The Soul of the American University: From Protestant L ment to Established Nonbelief.* New York: Oxford University Press, 1994.

Marsden, Peter V. "Religious Americans and the Arts in the 1990s." In *Crossro. Arts and Religion in American Life*, edited by Alberta Arthurs and Glenn Wallac. New York: New Press, 2001.

Martin, William C. *With God on Our Side: The Rise of the Religious Right in America.* New York: Broadway Books, 1996.

Marty, Martin E. and R. Scott Appleby, eds. *Fundamentalisms Observed*, The Fundamentalism Project, vol. 1. Chicago: University of Chicago Press, 1991.

———. *The Glory and the Power: The Fundamentalist Challenge to the Modern World.* Boston: Beacon Press, 1992.

Marty, Martin E. *Fundamentalism and Evangelicalism.* New York: K. G. Saur, 1993.

Marty, Martin E. and R. Scott Appleby, eds. *Fundamentalisms and Society: Reclaiming the Sciences, the Family, and Education*, The Fundamentalism Project, vol. 2. Chicago: University of Chicago Press, 1993.

Marty, Martin E. and F. Scott Appleby, eds. *Fundamentalisms and the State: Remaking Polities, Economies, and Militance*, The Fundamentalism Project, vol. 3. Chicago: University of Chicago Press, 1993.

———, eds. *Accounting for Fundamentalisms: The Dynamic Character of Movements*, The Fundamentalism Project, vol. 4. Chicago: University of Chicago Press, 1994.

Marty, Martin E. and R. Scott Appleby, eds. *Fundamentalisms Comprehended*, The Fundamentalism Project, vol. 5. Chicago: University of Chicago Press, 1995.

Marty, Martin E. *The One and the Many: America's Struggle for the Common Good.* Cambridge, MA: Harvard University Press, 1997.

Marx, Karl and Friedrich Engels. *The German Ideology.* New York: International Publishers, 1967.

Mathisen, James A. "Tell Me Again: *Why* Do Churches Grow?" *Books & Culture* 10, 3, May/June (2004): 18.

Meyer, John W. and W. Richard Scott, eds. *Organizational Environments: Ritual and Rationality.* Updated ed. Newbury Park, CA: Sage Publications, 1992.

Milbank, John. *Theology and Social Theory Beyond Secular Reason.* Oxford, UK and Cambridge, MA: B. Blackwell, 1991.

Miller, A. S. and R. Stark. "Gender and Religiousness: Can Socialization Explanations Be Saved?" *American Journal of Sociology* 107, 6 (2002): 1399–423.

Myers, S. M. "Religion and Intergenerational Assistance: Distinct Differences by Adult Children's Gender and Parent's Marital Status." *Sociological Quarterly* 45, 1 (2004): 67–89.

Niebuhr, H. Richard. *The Social Sources of Denominationalism.* New York: World, 1929.

Oggins, J. "Topics of Marital Disagreement among African-American and Euro-American Newlyweds." *Psychological Reports* 92, 2 (2003): 419–25.

Ozorak, E. W. "Love of God and Neighbor: Religion and Volunteer Service among College Students." *Review of Religious Research* 44, 3 (2003): 285–99.

Penning, James M. and Corwin E. Smidt. *Evangelicalism: The Next Generation*. Grand Rapids, MI: Baker Academic, 2002.

Perl, P. and J. L. Wiggins. "Don't Call Me Ishmael: Religious Naming among Protestants and Catholics in the United States." *Journal for the Scientific Study of Religion* 43, 2 (2004): 209–28.

Peterson, Richard A. *The Production of Culture*. Beverly Hills, CA: Sage Publications, 1976.

Ploch, D. R. and D. W. Hastings. "Effects of Parental Church Attendance, Current Family Status, and Religious Salience on Church Attendance." *Review of Religious Research* 39, 4 (1998): 309–20.

Popenoe, David, Jean Bethke Elshtain, and David Blankenhorn. *Promises to Keep: Decline and Renewal of Marriage in America*. Lanham, MD: Rowman & Littlefield Publishers, 1996.

Portes, Alejandro and Rubén G. Rumbaut. *Immigrant America: A Portrait*. Berkeley: University of California Press, 1996.

———. *Legacies: The Story of the Immigrant Second Generation*. Berkeley and New York: University of California Press and Russell Sage Foundation, 2001.

Potvin, Raymond H. and Douglas M. Sloane. "Parental Control, Age, and Religious Practice." *Review of Religious Research* 27 (1985): 3–14.

Powell, Walter W. and Paul DiMaggio. *The New Institutionalism in Organizational Analysis*. Chicago: University of Chicago Press, 1991.

Presser, S. and L. Stinson. "Data Collection Mode and Social Desirability Bias in Self-Reported Religious Attendance." *American Sociological Review* 63, 1 (1998): 137–45.

Putnam, Robert D. *Bowling Alone: The Collapse and Revival of American Community*. New York: Simon & Schuster, 2000.

Putnam, Robert D., Lewis M. Feldstein, and Don Cohen. *Better Together: Restoring the American Community*. New York: Simon & Schuster, 2003.

Rheingold, Howard. *The Virtual Community: Homesteading on the Electronic Frontier*. Cambridge, MA: MIT Press, 2000.

Ritzer, George. *The Mcdonaldization of Society: An Investigation into the Changing Character of Contemporary Social Life*. Newbury Park, CA: Pine Forge Press, 1993.

Roof, Wade Clark. *Community and Commitment: Religious Plausibility in a Liberal Protestant Church*. New York: Elsevier, 1978.

Roof, Wade Clark and William McKinney. *American Mainline Religion : Its Changing Shape and Future*. New Brunswick, NJ: Rutgers University Press, 1987.

Roof, Wade Clark. A Generation of Seekers: The Spiritual Journeys of the Baby Boom Generation. San Francisco: HarperSanFrancisco, 1993.

Roof, W. C. "God Is in the Details: Reflections on Religion's Public Presence in the United States in the Mid-1990." *Sociology of Religion* 57, 2 (1996): 149–62.

———. "Modernity, the Religious, and the Spiritual." *Annals of the American Academy of Political and Social Science* 558 (1998): 211–24.

Roof, W. C. "Religious Borderlands: Challenges for Future Study." *Journal for the Scientific Study of Religion* 37, 1 (1998): 1–14.

Roof, Wade Clark. *Spiritual Marketplace: Baby Boomers and the Remaking of American Religion*. Princeton, NJ: Princeton University Press, 1999.

Rosen, Bernard Carl. *Masks and Mirrors: Generation X and the Chameleon Personality.* Westport, CT: Praeger, 2001.

Sacks, Peter. *Generation X Goes to College: An Eye-Opening Account of Teaching in Postmodern America.* Chicago: Open Court, 1996.

Sargeant, Kimon Howland. *Seeker Churches: Promoting Traditional Religion in a Nontraditional Way.* New Brunswick, NJ: Rutgers University Press, 2000.

Scheufele, D. A., M. C. Nisbet, and D. Brossard. "Pathways to Political Participation? Religion, Communication Contexts, and Mass Media." *International Journal of Public Opinion Research* 15, 3 (2003): 300–24.

Schoeni, Robert and Karen Ross. "Material Assistance Received from Families During the Transition to Adulthood." In *On the Frontier of Adulthood: Theory, Research, and Public Policy,* edited by Richard A. Settersten Jr., Frank F. Furstenberg Jr., and Ruben G. Rumbaut, chapter 12. Chicago: University of Chicago Press, 2004.

Schuiling, G. A. "The Benefit and the Doubt: Why Monogamy?" *Journal of Psychosomatic Obstetrics and Gynecology* 24, 1 (2003): 55–61.

Scott, W. Richard and John W. Meyer, eds. *Institutional Environments and Organizations: Structural Complexity and Individualism.* Thousand Oaks, CA: SAGE Publications, 1994.

Settersten Jr., Richard A., Frank F. Furstenberg, and Ruben G. Rumbaut, eds. *On the Frontier of Adulthood: Theory, Research, and Public Policy.* Chicago: University of Chicago Press, 2004.

Shand, J. D. "The Decline of Traditional Christian Beliefs in Germany." *Sociology of Religion* 59, 2 (1998): 179–84.

Sherkat, D. E. and J. Wilson. "Preferences, Constraints, and Choices in Religious Markets: An Examination of Religions Switching and Apostasy." *Social Forces* 73, 3 (1995): 993–1026.

Sherkat, D. E. "Counterculture or Continuity? Competing Influences on Baby Boomers' Religious Orientations and Participation." *Social Forces* 76, 3 (1998): 1087–114.

Shrieves, Linda. "Miles of Aisles: Americans Are Church Shopping in Increasing Numbers." *Dallas Morning News,* July 1, 1995.

Skrentny, John. *The Minority Rights Revolution.* Cambridge, MA: Belknap Press of Harvard University Press, 2002.

Smith, T. W. "A Review of Church Attendance Measures." *American Sociological Review* 63, 1 (1998): 131–36.

Smith, Christian. *American Evangelicalism: Embattled and Thriving.* Chicago: University of Chicago Press, 1998.

Smith, C., R. Faris, M. L. Denton, and M. Regnerus. "Mapping American Adolescent Subjective Religiosity and Attitudes of Alienation toward Religion: A Research Report." *Sociology of Religion* 64, 1 (2003): 111–33.

Smith, C. and D. Sikkink. "Social Predictors of Retention in and Switching from the Religious Faith of Family of Origin: Another Look Using Religious Tradition Self-Identification." *Review of Religious Research* 45, 2 (2003): 188–206.

Smith, Tom W. "Altruism in Contemporary America: A Report from the National Altruism Study, Gss Topical Report No. 34." Chicago: University of Chicago, National Opinion Research Center, 2003.

Smith, Christian and Melinda L. Denton. *Soul Searching: The Spirituality of American Youth*. New York: Oxford University Press, 2004.

Stark, Rodney. "Physiology and Faith: Addressing the 'Universal' Gender Difference in Religious Commitment." *Journal for the Scientific Study of Religion* 41, 3 (2002): 495–507.

Starr, Paul. *The Creation of the Media: Political Origins of Modern Communications*. New York: Basic Books, 2004.

Steensland, B., J. Z. Park, M. D. Regnerus, L. D. Robinson, W. B. Wilcox, and R. D. Woodberry. "The Measure of American Religion: Toward Improving the State of the Art." *Social Forces* 79, 1 (2000): 291–318.

Stromberg, Peter G. *Language and Self-Transformation: A Study of the Christian Conversion Narrative*. New York: Cambridge University Press, 1993.

Sullivan, Teresa A., Elizabeth Warren, and Jay Lawrence Westbrook. *The Fragile Middle Class: Americans in Debt*. New Haven, CT: Yale University Press, 2000.

Sullivan, Teresa A., Deborah Thorne, and Elizabeth Warren. "Young, Old, and in Between: Who Files for Bankruptcy?" *Norton Bankruptcy Law Adviser*, September (2001): 1–12.

Sutherland, J. A., M. M. Poloma, and B. F. Pendleton. "Religion, Spirituality, and Alternative Health Practices: The Baby Boomer and Cold War Cohorts." *Journal of Religion & Health* 42, 4 (2003): 315–38.

Swidler, Ann. *Talk of Love: How Culture Matters*. Chicago: University of Chicago Press, 2001.

Thau, Richard D. and Jay S. Heflin. *Generations Apart: Xers vs. Boomers vs. The Elderly*. Amherst, NY: Prometheus Books, 1997.

Thornton, A. and L. Young-DeMarco. "Four Decades of Trends in Attitudes toward Family Issues in the United States: The 1960s through the 1990s." *Journal of Marriage and the Family* 63, 4 (2001): 1009–37.

Tipton, Steven M. *Getting Saved from the Sixties: Moral Meaning in Conversion and Cultural Change*. Berkeley: University of California Press, 1982.

Uslaner, E. M. "Trust but Verify: Social Capital and Moral Behavior." *Social Science Information Sur Les Sciences Sociales* 38, 1 (1999): 29–55.

Vogel, Marta. "Church Hopping: Looking for Reverence in All the Wrong Pews." *Washington Post*, May 11, 1997.

Waite, Linda J. and Christine Bachrach. *The Ties That Bind: Perspectives on Marriage and Cohabitation, Social Institutions and Social Change*. New York: Aldine de Gruyter, 2000.

Waite, Linda J. and Maggie Gallagher. *The Case for Marriage: Why Married People Are Happier, Healthier, and Better Off Financially*. New York: Doubleday, 2000.

Waite, L. J. and E. L. Lehrer. "The Benefits from Marriage and Religion in the United States: A Comparative Analysis." *Population and Development Review* 29, 2 (2003): 255–75.

Warner, R. S. "Work in Progress toward a New Paradigm for the Sociological-Study of Religion in the United-States." *American Journal of Sociology* 98, 5 (1993): 1044–93.

Warner, R. Stephen and Judith G. Wittner, eds. *Gatherings in Diaspora: Religious Communities and the New Immigration*. Philadelphia: Temple University Press, 1998.

Warren, Elizabeth and Amelia Warren Tyagi. *The Two-Income Trap: Why Middle-Class Mothers and Fathers Are Going Broke*. New York: Basic Books, 2003.

Wasby, S. L. "More on Religion in Court: Failed Challenges to Displays of the Ten Commandments." *Justice System Journal* 18, 3 (1996): 335–36.

Waxman, Chaim Isaac. *Jewish Baby Boomers: A Communal Perspective, Suny Series in American Jewish Society in the 1990s*. Albany: State University of New York Press, 2001.

Weaver, A. J., J. A. Samford, V. J. Morgan, D. B. Larson, H. G. Koenig, and K. J. Flannelly. "A Systematic Review of Research on Religion in Six Primary Marriage and Family Journals: 1995–1999." *American Journal of Family Therapy* 30, 4 (2002): 293–309.

Weber, Max. *The Sociology of Religion*. Boston: Beacon Press, 1963 [1922].

Weber, Max, Guenther Roth, and Claus Wittich. *Economy and Society: An Outline of Interpretive Sociology*. 2 vols. Berkeley: University of California Press, 1978.

Weber, Max, Hans Heinrich Gerth, C. Wright Mills, and Bryan S. Turner. *From Max Weber: Essays in Sociology*. New York: Routledge, 1991.

Weber, Max, Talcott Parsons, Anthony Giddens, and ebrary Inc. *The Protestant Ethic and the Spirit of Capitalism*. London: Routledge, 2001.

Westerhoff, John. *Will Our Children Have Faith?* New York: Seabury, 1976.

Whyte, William H. *The Organization Man*. New York: Simon and Schuster, 1956.

Wilcox, W. Bradford. *Soft Patriarchs, New Men: How Christianity Shapes Fathers and Husbands*. Chicago: University of Chicago Press, 2004.

Williams, Rhys H., ed. *Cultural Wars in American Politics: Critical Reviews of a Popular Myth*. New York: Aldine de Gruyter, 1997.

Wilson, J. and M. Musick. "Who Cares? Toward an Integrated Theory of Volunteer Work." *American Sociological Review* 62, 5 (1997): 694–713.

Wilson, J. "Volunteering." *Annual Review of Sociology* 26 (2000): 215–40.

Wink, P. and M. Dillon. "Spiritual Development across the Adult Life Course: Findings from a Longitudinal Study." *Journal of Adult Development* 9, 1 (2002): 79–94.

———. "Religiousness, Spirituality, and Psychosocial Functioning in Late Adulthood: Findings from a Longitudinal Study." *Psychology and Aging* 18, 4 (2003): 916–24.

Winston, Diane H. *Red-Hot and Righteous: The Urban Religion of the Salvation Army*. Cambridge, MA: Harvard University Press, 1999.

Wolfe, Alan. *One Nation after All: What Americans Really Think About God, Country, Family, Racism, Welfare, Immigration, Homosexuality, Work, the Right, the Left and Each Other*. New York: Viking, 1998.

———. *The Transformation of American Religion: How We Actually Live Our Faith*. New York: Free Press, 2003.

Woodrum, E. and T. Hoban. "Support for Prayer in School and Creationism." *Sociological Analysis* 53, 3 (1992): 309–21.

Wuthnow, Robert. "Recent Patterns of Secularization: A Problem of Generations." *American Sociological Review* 41, 5 (1976): 850–67.

———. *The Consciousness Reformation*. Berkeley: University of California Press, 1976.

———. *Experimentation in American Religion: The New Mysticisms and Their Implications for the Churches*. Berkeley and Los Angeles: University of California Press, 1978.

———. *Meaning and Moral Order: Explorations in Cultural Analysis*. Berkeley: University of California Press, 1987.

———. "The Social Significance of Religious Television." *Review of Religious Research* 29, 2 (1987): 125–34.

———. *The Restructuring of American Religion: Society and Faith since World War II*. Princeton: Princeton University Press, 1988.

———. *Communities of Discourse: Ideology and Social Structure in the Reformation, the Enlightenment, and European Socialism*. Cambridge, MA: Harvard University Press, 1989.

———. *Sharing the Journey: Support Groups and America's New Quest for Community*. New York: Free Press, 1994.

———. *Producing the Sacred: An Essay on Public Religion*. Urbana: University of Illinois Press, 1994.

———. *Learning to Care: Elementary Kindness in an Age of Indifference*. New York: Oxford University Press, 1995.

———. *Loose Connections: Joining Together in America's Fragmented Communities*. Cambridge, MA: Harvard University Press, 1998.

———. *After Heaven: Spirituality in America since the 1950s*. Berkeley and Los Angeles: University of California Press, 1998.

———. "Morality, Spirituality, and Democracy." *Society* 35, 3 (1998): 37–44.

———. *Growing up Religious: Christians and Jews and Their Journeys of Faith*. Boston: Beacon, 1999.

———. *Creative Spirituality: The Way of the Artist*. Berkeley and Los Angeles: University of California Press, 2001.

Wuthnow, Robert and John H. Evans, eds. *The Quiet Hand of God: Faith-Based Activism and the Public Role of Mainline Protestantism*. Berkeley and Los Angeles: University of California Press, 2002.

Wuthnow, Robert. "Religious Involvement and Status-Bridging Social Capital." *Journal for the Scientific Study of Religion* 41, 4 (2002): 669–84.

———. "Studying Religion, Making It Sociological." In *Handbook of the Sociology of Religion*, ed. Michele Dillon, 16–30. Cambridge: Cambridge University Press, 2003.

———. "Is There a Place for 'Scientific' Studies of Religion?" *The Chronicle Review* 49 (2003): B10.

———. *All in Sync: How Music and Art Are Revitalizing American Religion*. Berkeley and Los Angeles: University of California Press, 2003.

Wuthnow, R. and C. Hackett. "The Social Integration of Practitioners of Non-Western Religions in the United States." *Journal for the Scientific Study of Religion* 42, 4 (2003): 651–67.

Wuthnow, Robert. "Overcoming Status Distinctions? Religious Involvement, Social Class, Race, and Ethnicity in Friendship Patterns." *Sociology of Religion* 64, 4 (2003): 423–42.

———. *Saving America? Faith-Based Services and the Future of Civil Society*. Princeton: Princeton University Press, 2004.

Wuthnow, Robert. "The Religious Factor Revisited." *Sociological Theory* 22, 2 (2004): 205–18.

———. *America and the New Challenges of Religious Diversity.* Princeton: Princeton University Press, 2005.

Zablocki, Benjamin David. *Alienation and Charisma: A Study of Contemporary American Communes.* New York: Free Press, 1980.

Zablocki, Benjamin David and Thomas Robbins. *Misunderstanding Cults: Searching for Objectivity in a Controversial Field.* Toronto: University of Toronto Press, 2001.

Zhou, M. "God in Chinatown: Religion and Survival in New York's Evolving Immigrant Community." *Journal for the Scientific Study of Religion* 43, 2 (2004): 284–85.

Zullo, James R. *God and Gen-X: Faith & the New Generation.* Romeoville, IL: Lewis University, 1999.

Index